The Art and Craft of International Environmental Law

The Art and Craft of International Environmental Law

DANIEL BODANSKY

Harvard University Press
Cambridge, Massachusetts London, England

First Harvard University Press paperback edition, 2011

Library of Congress Cataloging-in-Publication Data

Bodansky, Daniel.
The art and craft of international environmental law / Daniel Bodansky.
  p.   cm.

Includes bibliographical references and index.
ISBN 978-0-674-03543-0 (cloth:alk. paper)
ISBN 978-0-674-06179-8 (pbk.)
1. Environmental law, International.   I. Title.
K3585.B63 2010
344.04'6—dc22

                              2009013723

To my lovely and loving daughters, Sarah and Maria,
as a small contribution to intergenerational equity.

Contents

Preface

Although international environmental law is a comparatively new field, its rules and standards now fill books—and not short books either. A leading treatise on the principles of international environmental law runs to more than 1,000 densely packed pages, detailing rules of virtually every description on virtually every subject.[1] The volumes in a monographic series that I once co-edited now occupy almost six feet of bookshelf space.[2] And a compilation of international environmental documents included thirty volumes in its first series, with another six since then.[3] Not so long ago, international environmental law was considered a narrow specialty within the general field of international law. But today international environmental law has become a field in its own right, with subspecialties on wildlife law, marine pollution, freshwater resources, climate change, sustainable development, chemicals, and so forth.

Most people have little familiarity with the field; they have heard, perhaps, of the Kyoto Protocol but little else. However, international environmental norms are often closer to home than they realize:

- When my air conditioning system broke down a few years ago, the technician reported that the coolant had leaked out. In its place he put in a synthetic chemical called HCFC-22. If the same problem had occurred twenty years earlier, the replacement would have been a more ozone-unfriendly chemical, CFC-12. In the future, it will be an even more environmentally benign chemical that does not contain chlorine. The changes have been driven not by changes in technology or in domestic law (though technology and domestic law have both played a part) but by developments in the international treaty to protect the ozone layer.

- In the Wal-Mart near my house, fish packages now display labels saying that the fish were harvested in a sustainable manner, in compliance with standards developed by the Marine Stewardship Council. The Council is an independent non-profit organization that, according to its web site, "promote[s] sustainable fishing practices." Along similar lines, a leading home improvement store, Home Depot, has announced that it will, to the extent possible, buy wood from sustainably managed forests.
- At home, my nine-year-old daughter refuses to eat tuna fish because she believes that doing so will harm dolphins. Recently, she asked, in a worried tone, whether we have any ivory in the house. And when, to be provocative, I asked "Is Rhino horn ok?," she answered emphatically, "No, it is not!"

In countless ways, we are affected by international environmental norms, some social, others legal; some quite general, others very specific. The norms limiting the refrigerants used in air conditioners have been agreed to internationally, in legal form, and are mandated and enforced by the federal government. The sustainable fishery and forestry standards used by Wal-Mart and Home Depot were developed more informally by environmental groups and business, and are applied to producers through supply-chain contracts, without any government involvement. The reluctance to eat tuna fish or own elephant ivory reflects more general social norms, disseminated through education and culture.

How and why do these norms arise? In what ways do they affect behavior? Do they change what states and individuals actually do, and, if so, why? How effective are they in solving international environmental problems? These are the fundamental questions I examine in this book.

As the questions suggest, the book focuses on the processes by which international environmental law is developed, implemented, and enforced rather than on the substance of international environmental law itself— already the subject of several excellent treatises.[4] Process issues have received increased attention in recent years but have not yet received a book-length treatment. This work aims to fill that gap. Rather than focus on one or two aspects of the international environmental process, it examines the process as a whole, from beginning to end, synthesizing recent research on international environmental negotiations, treaty design, social norms, policy implementation, and effectiveness.

Understanding the international environmental process involves many disciplines—not only law, but also political science, economics, and, to a more limited degree, philosophy, sociology, and anthropology. So this book is multidisciplinary. The aim is to provide the reader with the analytical tools necessary to understand what international environmental law is, how it operates, and what role it can play in addressing environmental problems.

In a wonderful book entitled *Nuts and Bolts for the Social Sciences*, Jon Elster wrote that his subtitle might have been "Elementary Social Science from an Advanced Standpoint"—or perhaps, alternatively, "Advanced Social Science from an Elementary Standpoint."[5] Like Elster, I have attempted to write an elementary book from an advanced standpoint, with a stronger methodological and philosophical orientation than is typical in an introductory work. And, like Elster, "I have tried to avoid flogging dead horses or belaboring the obvious; to be honest about the inevitable simplifications; to write simply and without jargon; to respect the reader's intelligence as well as his ignorance."[6]

In addition to studying international environmental law as an academic, I have worked for many years on international environmental issues as a U.S. government negotiator, NGO adviser, and UN consultant. This experience colors my approach in this book in at least three ways.

First, the book is U.S.-centric. Although it attempts to address a wide range of issues from a broad array of perspectives, the choice of topics and examples inevitably leans on my background working in the United States.

Second, in the spectrum between what one analyst refers to as "moral outrage" and "cool analysis," the book's tone tends toward the latter.[7] Certainly, moral outrage is an understandable response to the environmental devastation wrought by modern industrialized societies. Indeed, solutions to problems such as climate change may, in the end, depend as much on moral outrage as on cool reason. But my experience as an international environmental lawyer has reinforced an inborn tendency to see the world in various shades of gray—to understand problems as involving complex trade-offs.

Finally, in the same vein, this book aims to be pragmatic. Although it is theoretical, it tries to provide a real-world perspective on how international environmental law works—and sometimes doesn't work. Students and scholars of international law fall along a spectrum, from true believers at one end to complete cynics at the other. This book seeks a middle course. It reflects a degree of skepticism—hopefully a healthy skepticism!—about some of the more visionary claims regarding the role of international environmental law. But it does not throw out the baby with the bath water. Rather, it seeks a realistic understanding of both the role and the limits, the process and the prospects, of international environmental law.

Abbreviations

AOSIS   Alliance of Small Island States
ATCM   Antarctic Treaty Consultative Meeting
BAT   best available technology
CBD   Convention on Biological Diversity (1992)
CCD   Convention to Combat Desertification (1994)
CEC   Commission on Environmental Cooperation (U.S.-Canada-Mexico)
CFC   chlorofluorocarbon
CITES   Convention on International Trade in Endangered Species (1973)
COP   conference of the parties
CSD   UN Commission on Sustainable Development
EIA   environmental impact assessment
EMEP   European Monitoring and Evaluation Programme (short for Co-operative Programme for Monitoring and Evaluation of the Long-Range Transmissions of Air Pollutants in Europe)
ENMOD   Convention on the Prohibition of Military or Any Other Hostile Use of Environmental Modification Techniques (1976)
EPA   U.S. Environmental Protection Agency
ESA   U.S. Endangered Species Act

FAO Food and Agriculture Organization

FIELD Foundation for International Environmental Law and Development

FSC Forest Stewardship Council

G-8 Group of Eight

GATT General Agreement on Tariffs and Trade

GEF Global Environment Facility

IAEA International Atomic Energy Agency

IBRD International Bank for Reconstruction and Development (World Bank)

ICJ International Court of Justice

ICRW International Convention for the Regulation of Whaling (1946)

IFAD International Fund for Agricultural Development

IJC International Joint Commission (U.S.-Canada)

ILC International Law Commission

ILM International Legal Materials

ILO International Labor Organization

IMO International Maritime Organization

IO international organization

IPCC Intergovernmental Panel on Climate Change

ISO International Organization for Standardization

ITLOS International Tribunal on the Law of the Sea

ITTO International Tropical Timber Organization

IUCN International Union for the Conservation of Nature (also known as the World Conservation Union)

IWC International Whaling Commission

LRTAP Long-Range Transboundary Air Pollution Convention (1979)

MARPOL International Convention for the Prevention of Pollution from Ships (1973/1978)

MEA multilateral environmental agreement

MOU memorandum of understanding

NAAEC North American Agreement on Environmental Cooperation (1993)

NAFTA	North American Free Trade Agreement (1993)
NAMMCO	North Atlantic Marine Mammal Commission
NCP	non-compliance procedure
NEPA	U.S. National Environmental Policy Act
NGO	non-governmental organization
NO_x	nitrous oxides
NPP	net primary productivity
ODS	ozone-depleting substance(s)
OECD	Organization for Economic Cooperation and Development
OILPOL	International Convention for the Prevention of the Pollution of the Sea by Oil (1954)
OSPAR Convention	Convention for the Protection of the Marine Environment of the North-East Atlantic (1992)
PIC	prior informed consent
POP	persistent organic pollutant
R&D	research and development
SIRS	systems of implementation review
SO_2	sulfur dioxide
SPREP	South Pacific Regional Environment Programme
TED	turtle excluder device
TOVALOP	Tanker Owner Voluntary Agreement Concerning Liability for Oil Pollution
TRAFFIC	Trade Records Analysis of Flora and Fauna in Commerce (wildlife trade monitoring network established in 1976 by IUCN and WWF)
UNCED	United Nations Conference on Environment and Development (1992) (also known as Rio Summit or Earth Summit)
UNCLOS	United Nations Convention on the Law of the Sea (1982)
UNDP	United Nations Development Programme
UNECE	United Nations Economic Commission for Europe
UNEP	United Nations Environment Programme
UNESCO	United Nations Educational, Scientific and Cultural Organization
UNFCCC	United Nations Framework Convention on Climate Change (1992)

UNICEF	United Nations International Children's Emergency Fund
UNTS	United Nations Treaty Series
VOC	volatile organic compound
WHO	World Health Organization
WMO	World Meteorological Organization
WSSD	World Summit on Sustainable Development (2002) (also known as Johannesburg Summit)
WTO	World Trade Organization
WWF	World Wide Fund for Nature

CHAPTER ONE

What Is International Environmental Law?

Too many people assume, generally without having given any
serious thought to its character or its history, that international
law is and always has been a sham. Others seem to think that it
is a force with inherent strength of its own, and that if only we
had the sense to set the lawyers to work to draft a comprehensive
code for the nations, we might live together in peace and all
would be well with the world. Whether the cynic or the sciolist is
the less helpful is hard to say, but both of them make the same
mistake. They both assume that international law is a subject on
which anyone can form his opinions intuitively, without taking
the trouble, as one has to do with other subjects, to inquire into
the relevant facts.

J. L. Brierly, *The Outlook for International Law*

A Story

One evening a few years ago, a volunteer for a well-known environmental organization rang my doorbell to solicit a contribution. I declined, saying that I disagreed with the organization's positions on various issues.
The volunteer demanded to know which ones. "Whaling," I replied—
using the first example that came to mind—". . . your organization's
campaign against the resumption of commercial whaling by Norway."
Not easily discouraged, the volunteer began to argue. "Norway's actions
threaten the whales with extinction," he said. "No," I responded, rising
to the bait, "most scientists think that the target species (minke whales)
are abundant in the Northeast Atlantic and will not be endangered by the
small number taken by Norway." After an inconclusive debate about the
current state of whale science, the volunteer, in exasperation, played his
trump card, exclaiming, "I suppose it doesn't matter to you that Norway
is violating international law!" He had pressed the wrong button. I informed him, somewhat pedantically, that I happened to be a *professor* of

international law and that, as a legal matter, Norway is free to whale, since it submitted a timely objection to the International Whaling Commission's decision prohibiting commercial whaling. The environmentalist stomped off in search of greener pastures.

I mention this story at the outset because it illustrates many of the basic issues that we will be exploring in this book. To begin with, notice how the environmental volunteer made two different types of arguments regarding Norwegian whaling: first a policy argument and then a legal one. His policy argument was that Norwegian whaling is wrong because it threatens the viability of the Northeast Atlantic minke whale stock. The argument consists of (a) an implied goal, namely, management of whale stocks to ensure their continued existence, and (b) a factual claim that Norwegian whaling endangers the Northeast Atlantic minke whale stock. Crudely speaking, our disagreement was about facts rather than values. I accepted his implicit goal but disagreed about whether Norway's whaling is inconsistent with that goal. If minke whales are abundant, then conservation requires only that whaling be limited, not completely halted.

Many environmental disputes are of this factual variety. What is the likelihood of a nuclear reactor accident? Do persistent organic pollutants pose a fundamental threat to human and animal reproduction? Will the buildup of greenhouse gases in the atmosphere cause significant global warming? And, above all, are we approaching real physical limits on further economic growth? On these and many other essentially factual questions, there are a wide variety of views. My quarrel with the environmentalist thus epitomized a much broader category of disputes concerning the real state of the world. On the one hand, neo-Malthusians[1] have argued for decades that there are limits to growth, which we are fast approaching. On the other hand, "Cornucopians"[2] respond that environmental problems tend to be exaggerated, that on the whole the environment is improving, and that human capital (in the form of human ingenuity) will continue to find ways to make up for any loss of natural capital.

The non-governmental activist could have made a different policy argument that did not depend on the status of minke stocks and therefore would have rendered our factual disagreement irrelevant: whales are intelligent (or at least sentient) beings, whose killing is wrong. If he had made this argument, then our disagreement would have been about values, not facts: should our goal be the conservation of whale stocks, or the preservation and protection of individual whales?

Often, it may not be clear whether an environmental dispute is really about facts or values. When an environmentalist argues that whale populations are too low to support whaling or that continued economic growth is unsustainable—or, conversely, when a climate skeptic argues that global warming is a myth—are these factual disputes, or are they value judgments masquerading as factual ones? Are people's views based on an objective assessment of the science or on value judgments about the appropriate balance between economic growth and environmental sustainability, the morality of current lifestyles, and the appropriate role of government?

After failing to convince me with a policy argument, the door-to-door solicitor switched to a legal argument: Norwegian whaling is wrong because it violates the International Convention for the Regulation of Whaling. This argument does not depend on whether Norwegian whaling makes sense ecologically or is morally justified. Regardless, it is illegal. In essence, he was saying to me, even if you think that minke whales may be safely whaled, *the law* imposes certain requirements, which Norway is obliged to obey. The argument turns on what those requirements are and on whether Norway has in fact met them. It turns, that is, on legal issues.

At first glance, the legal issues seem straightforward: Norway has accepted a convention regulating whaling, and therefore it must comply with the requirements of that convention. In 1982, the International Whaling Commission (IWC) adopted a decision by a vote of 25 to 7, with 5 abstentions, imposing a moratorium on commercial whaling in order to provide time for a comprehensive scientific assessment of whale stocks. Under the terms of the Convention, such decisions are legally binding. The Convention, however, provides that states may opt out of decisions with which they disagree by filing a written objection within 90 days. Norway had done so in this case—hence my conclusion that Norway is not legally bound by the moratorium decision.

Legal matters are rarely so simple, however. Even in this case, where the legal rules are clear, my interlocutor might have offered some response. In addition to treaty law, most scholars agree that international law includes both customary norms and general principles of law. Perhaps one of these types of law forbids Norwegian whaling. For example, some legal scholars have asserted that whales have an emerging right to life as a matter of customary international law;[3] if so, this customary obligation not to kill whales may bind Norway independent of the Whaling Convention. Alternatively, my interlocutor might have argued that the status of whale stocks is uncertain and that the so-called precautionary principle requires states not to act when scientific uncertainty exists. Or he might have argued that, after its initial objection, Norway implicitly accepted the IWC moratorium decision through its actions from 1987 to 1993, when it ceased whaling. These arguments, though in my view weak, illustrate the potential for disputes about the content of international environmental law.

Three Perspectives on International Environmental Law

The whaling case is, of course, only one of many international environmental problems that we will consider in this book. Global warming, depletion of the stratospheric ozone layer, loss of biological diversity, pollution of coastal waters, nuclear accidents, persistent organic pollutants, acid rain—the litany is by now familiar.[4] Consider the following:

- Atmospheric concentrations of carbon dioxide are now one-third higher than in preindustrial times and are higher than at any time in hundreds of thousands of years.[5]
- The rate of known species extinctions in the past century is roughly 50 to 500 times higher than the background extinction rate calculated from the fossil record, and possibly as much as 1,000 times higher.[6]
- Each year humans remove about 85 million metric tons of fish from the oceans, and 75 percent of the world's fisheries are fished to capacity or overfished.[7]
- Approximately 60 percent of the Earth's ecosystem services are being degraded or used unsustainably.[8] Since 1990, 6 million hectares of primary forests have been lost or modified each year.[9] A third of the world's forests and half of the wetlands have disappeared as a result of human activities.
- In the last several decades, 20 percent of the world's known coral reefs have been destroyed, and an additional 20 percent degraded.[10]
- Each year, about 5–6 billion pounds of pesticides are applied, more than 1 billion pounds in the United States alone.[11]
- Globally, 1.3 billion people live in urban areas that do not meet World Health Organization standards for particulate matter, and each year more than 2 million die prematurely as a result of air pollution.[12]
- Global water use has doubled in the past forty years. Today, humans use between 40 and 50 percent of all available freshwater runoff, and water scarcity affects roughly 1 to 2 billion people worldwide.[13]

- More than 1 billion people lack access to clean drinking water, and more than 2.5 billion lack basic sanitation, contributing to the death of 1.5 million children under the age of five from diarrhea each year.[14]

... The list could go on and on.

What are the causes of these problems? What can we do to solve them? And what role can law play in doing so? These are the fundamental questions of international environmental law. In addressing them, I will employ three perspectives—what I will refer to as the doctrinal, the policy, and the explanatory approaches to international environmental law.[15]

The Doctrinal Approach

The most common perspective for lawyers is the doctrinal approach, illustrated by the legal analysis earlier as to whether Norway violated international law by resuming commercial whaling. Lawyers ordinarily employ this approach in their day-to-day activities. They attempt to determine what the legal norms are and how those norms apply to particular situations. This book will discuss many of these issues of legal doctrine, describing what international environmental law has to say about transboundary pollution, pollution of the global commons, and conservation of natural resources.

How does one ascertain the rules of international environmental law? Anyone with even a modicum of legal training has more or less conscious knowledge of how to do so for domestic law. An important part of legal education is teaching students how to determine the relevant legal rules and apply them to particular cases—how to read cases and statutes and to reason from one case to another. This is perhaps the most important function of the first year of law school: namely, to teach students to "think like a lawyer."

The task is more difficult, however, for international law, whose basic sources are both unfamiliar and contested. Judicial decisions are few and far between and, in theory, lack the force of precedent. There is no legislature to enact statutes, and no administrative agency to adopt regulations. Thus, at the outset, it is necessary to spend some time examining the sources of international environmental norms. Only then will we have the tools to determine whether a particular norm—say, the whale's right to life—has achieved the status of international law.

The Policy Approach

The doctrinal approach focuses on what the law *is*. Often, however, we may feel that existing legal norms are unsatisfactory, either because they do not address an important topic at all or because they do so inadequately. For most of us, such feelings are particularly common in a relatively new field like international environmental law, whose norms are just emerging on important topics such as deforestation, desertification, and species loss. As a result, it is important to consider not only what the law is but what it *should* be. I will call this the policy approach to international environmental law. The policy arguments about Norwegian whaling described earlier in this chapter exemplify this perspective.

The policy approach focuses on the question: what should be the international rules regarding whaling? This issue requires us to consider both means and ends. Core variables that must be addressed, whether explicitly or implicitly, include:

- What should be the *goal* of international policy? Should we take a utilitarian standpoint, for example, attempting to maximize benefits relative to costs, or should we adopt a more ecocentric or rights-based approach? What shorter-term results do we seek to achieve, such as reductions in emissions? And what longer-term effects do we wish to further, such as a change in values?
- *Who* should promulgate or communicate the policy? What is the appropriate forum in which to proceed? Should we proceed through public or private channels—an international organization, for example, or a private group, such as the Forest Stewardship Council? Should we choose a global or a more local forum? An institution with general competence, such as the UN General Assembly, or an organization with a more limited, expert purview?
- What should be the *legal form* of the international response? A new treaty? Modification of an existing treaty? Recommendations or decisions by international organizations? Private standard-setting initiatives?
- What *policy instruments* should we use? Government-mandated controls? Market-based instruments such as taxes or tradable allowances? Technology programs? Voluntary partnerships with industry? Or some other approach?
- Finally, *to whom* should these policy instruments be directed? States? Industry? Individuals?

Ideally, in developing a policy strategy, we would identify the range of options for each variable, evaluate their desirability, and decide which represents the best mix of ambition and realism. But in practice, we must usually settle for much less, given our limited time and knowledge.

Are these policy questions legal in nature? That depends on how narrowly or broadly one conceives of law as a discipline. Certainly, the questions require us to consider issues that are not specifically legal. They require us to draw on other disciplines to determine the appropriate rules of international environmental law. For example, our ultimate choice among policy objectives—sustainable utilization of whales, absolute protection of whales against killing, and so forth—is a matter of ethics. In contrast, the question of how to achieve our goals involves issues of science, economics, and public policy. Designing a sustainable management plan, for example, is primarily an issue of biology and population dynamics. For this reason, the task of devising a new management plan for whaling has been undertaken primarily by scientists, not lawyers.

The day has passed, however, when any lawyer seriously thinks that his or her task is simply to describe the law as it is. Domestic lawyers play an important role in developing new legislation, and international environmental lawyers play a comparable role in negotiating treaties. Questions of legal design are prescriptive rather than doctrinal in character but are of central concern to international lawyers. For example, what are the appropriate participation rules in an environmental agreement? What kind of compliance regime should a treaty establish? How precisely should legal norms be defined? And at what geographic scale should regulation be undertaken?

Moreover, even when one is addressing doctrinal issues, the line between what the law *is* and what it *should be* is not always clear. Often, legal rules are ambiguous or point in different directions. In hard cases, lawyers cannot mechanically describe and apply the law as it is; they must make arguments based on policy or principle about what the appropriate legal rule should be. States arguably have a legal duty to prevent significant transboundary pollution. But what constitutes "pollution"? And when is pollution "significant"? Applying a legal rule to concrete cases requires interpretation—and that process of interpreting and applying legal rules involves policy considerations; it represents an attempt to determine the "best" rule.[16]

That said, the policy and doctrinal approaches nevertheless represent quite different orientations. It is one thing to say that countries *should* stop whaling or that they *should* reduce their emissions of greenhouse gases significantly in order to combat global warming; it is quite another to say that the law *requires* them to do so. The policy approach is that taken by legislatures in creating new laws or by states in negotiating new treaties. The doctrinal approach is the paradigmatic approach of lawyers and judges in interpreting and applying the existing law.

Often, writers blur the distinction between the doctrinal and the policy approaches to international environmental law. It is not clear whether they are attempting to describe the law as it is or whether they are engaging in wishful thinking about what the law should be. Take, for example, the claims that whales have an emerging right to life,[17] that "ecocide" is an international crime,[18] that states must take steps to protect endangered species,[19] or, more prosaically, that states have a duty to provide notice and engage in consultations concerning activities that may cause transboundary harm.[20] Many believe that these norms are desirable and *should* be part of international environmental law; but whether they have yet achieved that status is a different matter.

The Explanatory Approach

Though distinguishable, the doctrinal and the policy approaches to international environmental law are similar in one important respect: they represent the viewpoint of participants within the legal realm—states, courts, international lawyers, non-governmental groups, and so forth— who are working with, or attempting to change, the legal rules. This "insider's" perspective on international environmental law distinguishes both the doctrinal and policy approaches from a third perspective—the viewpoint characteristic of political scientists, who study international environmental law from the "outside" in order to determine its role in international society. The difference in perspective is like the difference between the perspective of a person who inhabits a culture's world of meanings, roles, and taboos, and that of an anthropologist approaching the culture as an object to be explained.

The explanatory approach to international environmental law focuses on two topics: first, the emergence (or non-emergence) of international environmental norms, and second, their effectiveness (or ineffectiveness). To what extent, for example, can the development and effects of international environmental law be explained in terms of the rational self-interest of states? What are the roles of scientific knowledge, intergovernmental organizations, and non-governmental groups? These are the kinds of questions that political scientists ask.

Political scientists have traditionally separated into different "schools," each with a different causal model to explain how international norms emerge and affect behavior, or fail to do so. *Realists* emphasize the role of power;[21] *institutionalists* the role of interests more generally;[22] *liberals* the role of domestic politics;[23] and *constructivists* the role of values and knowledge.[24] Interestingly, students of international environmental politics have tended to eschew the methodological preference of most political scientists for a single explanatory model, and have instead acknowledged the multiplicity of causal factors and pathways that help explain the emergence and effectiveness of international environmental norms.[25] My approach, too, will be eclectic: I will consider the role of power and interests and knowledge and ideology and domestic politics, as appropriate to the occasion. To my mind, the traditional schools of international relations are like the blind men and the elephant: each has something to contribute, but presents only part of the picture. State interests are important, but how a state conceives of its interests depends on its values and knowledge, as well as on its domestic political processes. Actors apply a "logic of consequences," calculating the costs and benefits of their actions. But what counts as a cost and benefit depends on many other factors. In any event, individuals (and states) not only calculate consequences; they also consider the appropriateness of different courses of action, based on their values and their self-identity—their conception of "who they are." Attempts to reduce this complex reality to a simple causal model hold the promise of scientific rigor but at too steep a price for the international environmental lawyer, who must operate in the real world—in all its messiness.

The three perspectives I have outlined—doctrinal, policy, and explanatory—are all essential parts of the international environmental lawyer's analytical toolkit. Whether one wants to defend the status quo or to change it, one must begin by attempting to determine what the current law says. This doctrinal approach, though important, is not enough, however. To be an effective lawyer, one must also be able to make policy arguments for keeping or changing the existing law, and to understand the factors that influence its development and effectiveness.

What Is International Environmental Law?

In a book about international environmental law, it is useful to examine, at the outset, the scope of our subject matter. Each term in the phrase "international environmental law" raises important issues.

Environment

Let us start with *environment*. Surprisingly few definitions of this term can be found in international agreements. It is, to borrow a phrase, "a term everyone understands and no one is able satisfactorily to define."[26] Indeed, even the *Dictionary of Environment and Development* fails to define the term![27] Among the definitions ventured are two by the European Community, which describe "environment" as "[t]he relationship of human beings with water, air, land and all biological forms,"[28] or, alternatively, as "the combination of elements whose complex interrelationships make up the settings, the surroundings and the conditions of life of the individual and of society, as they are and as they are felt."[29] But whether these definitions actually clarify the term is open to doubt.

For our purposes, two points are worth noting. First, as the definitions suggest, international environmental law focuses primarily on the interactions of humans and the natural world—the air, water, soil, fauna, and flora. It thus presupposes a separation between humans and nature. Some changes are natural and beyond the purview of international environmental law: natural climate variability, for example, volcanoes, earthquakes, and so forth. Other changes are caused by humans and are thus susceptible to social control via legal regulation. The injection of millions of tons of sulfate aerosols into the atmosphere by the eruption of Mount Pinatubo in 1991, which temporarily cooled the Earth by approximately 0.5°C, was natural and not a significant source of concern, whereas proposals to geoengineer the climate by similar means have aroused considerable alarm. The focus on human activities is manifest in the concept of "pollution," which typically is defined as the anthropogenic introduction of harmful substances or energy into the environment. It is these human-induced changes that international environmental law seeks to address.[30]

Second, people's understanding of what constitutes an *environmental* problem has evolved considerably over the last half century. If this book had been written fifty years ago, its title might have been "international conservation law," since early efforts to protect the environment (for example, the 1946 Whaling Convention) focused on the conservation of nature, particularly wildlife. By comparison, contemporary international environmental law has a much wider scope, including the protection of the air, water, and land against pollution. Conversely, if this book were to be (re)written fifty years hence, it might need to be renamed "the international law of sustainable development." For, by then, sustainable development—still more of a buzzword than a coherent concept—may have emerged out of its infancy to become the organizing paradigm for environmental protection.[31]

The boundaries of what constitutes an "environmental" issue have already become blurred. Problems such as global warming and loss of biological diversity result from a wide variety of factors, including population growth, energy use, consumption patterns, and trade. If international environmental law is to address not merely the surface manifestations but the root causes of environmental degradation, then our understanding of what constitutes an environmental issue must grow to encompass economic, social, and trade policy. Indeed, if, as some claim, everything is interconnected, then everything becomes an environmental problem. For now, however, this kind of integration is still more of an aspiration than a reality.[32] Accordingly, treating international environmental law as a discrete field of study, which focuses on the relationship of humans to their environment—rather than on the social and economic factors that drive that relationship—still makes considerable sense.

International

The term *international* raises equally challenging issues. What makes an environmental issue international? In some cases, the answer is obvious. Consider, for example, the problem of acid rain in Europe and North America. This is clearly an international problem because it involves pollutants originating in one country that cause environmental damage in another. The use of transboundary resources—migratory birds, international rivers, border lakes, and the like—is just as obviously an international problem; the only difference is that the natural resource rather than the pollution crosses the international boundary. Not surprisingly, transboundary resources and transboundary pollution were the first subjects of international environmental regulation, in boundary water and migratory bird treaties, and in cases such as *Trail Smelter*, still the lodestar of international environmental law.[33] Closely related to these transboundary environmental problems are global commons problems such as whaling, pollution of the high seas, and depletion of the stratospheric ozone layer, which involve areas beyond national jurisdiction. What ties these problems together is that they all involve physical spillovers: the resource or pollution in question spills over an international border or is found in an area beyond national jurisdiction, making international cooperation essential.

How about a problem such as conservation of the African elephant? African elephants do not typically migrate across an international border and are not in that sense an international resource. There are no immediate physical spillovers responsible for the elephant's decline. Why is elephant conservation nevertheless an international issue? Part of the answer is that elephant conservation is vulnerable to economic spillovers:[34] the primary threat to the African elephant, at least until recently,[35] has been the demand for ivory by consumers in East Asia. Deforestation in Southeast Asia has a similar dynamic; trees are cut down not primarily to satisfy local demand but to produce timber for export. As these examples remind us, the modern world is becoming increasingly interconnected economically as well as physically: one country can have a substantial effect on the environment of another country, not only through physical pollution, but also through investment and trade. The destruction of the Ecuadorian Amazon (and of indigenous habitats) resulting from oil development by American companies[36] and the Union Carbide disaster in Bhopal are further illustrations of environmental problems driven in part by international economic forces.

Even when economic as well as physical interconnections are included, however, they do not fully account for the issues on the international environmental agenda. Take the case of the giant panda, a non-migratory species found only in China, whose habitat is disappearing owing to a rapidly expanding human population. Is this an international problem? Not for either of the reasons I have described thus far. The panda is not threatened by foreign pollution and, while there is a limited international demand for panda skins, this is a relatively small part of the problem. Nonetheless, saving the panda has become an international *cause célèbre*.

What makes the panda an international issue? The obvious answer is: because the international community has taken it up as such. This argument is essentially circular, however, and simply leads to the further question: why is there international concern? The answer is that, although the causes of the panda's decline are purely internal, the effects are not. A resource like the panda is of international concern because it provides international benefits. In the panda's case, the benefits are principally psychological: people in other countries value the panda and desire its continued existence. These psychological spillovers are another manifestation of increasing global interdependence. If these psychological spillovers are included, the test of whether an environmental issue is "international" assumes a subjective rather than a strictly objective character. The answer depends on what people consider to be international, rather than on the existence of transboundary environmental or economic effects.

Although physical, economic, and psychological spillovers differ, all three by definition have an international character: they involve more than one country and therefore cannot be addressed by individual states acting on their own. This international dimension distinguishes international environmental law from what some refer to as "global environmental law,"[37] which focuses on the growing convergence of national environmental laws around the world through processes of mimicry, persuasion, and harmonization. Scholars attribute this global convergence to many factors: common functional demands, transnational expert networks, and the spread of "world culture."[38] But whatever their cause, convergent national laws, though important, are not my focus here. They are the subject of *comparative* rather than *international* environmental law.

Admittedly, the line between comparative and international environmental law is blurry. Just as there is no clean break between "national" and "international" environmental problems, no sharp line can be drawn between convergent national rules (for example, requiring environmental impact assessment) and a common international rule. Indeed, in some cases, the two can be causally interrelated. On the one hand, international agreements may impose requirements concerning national implementation that result in similar national laws throughout the world. The treaties on trade in endangered species and in hazardous wastes provide two examples. On the other hand, convergent national laws (say, on public participation) may inspire the negotiation of an international agreement.

Nevertheless, international environmental rules represent a distinctive phenomenon, and arise and influence behavior through distinctive processes. These international rules and processes are the subject of this book.

Law

For many people, *law* is the most problematic term in the phrase, "international environmental law." Many skeptics argue that law, properly so called, requires enforcement mechanisms and that, in the absence of such mechanisms, international environmental standards are simply political or moral norms. This viewpoint has a venerable history, dating back to the nineteenth-century English legal philosopher, John Austin, who once called international law "positive morality" because it lacks sanctions.

Whether or not one agrees with this view, it is no easy matter to distinguish international law from international politics on the one hand and from international morality on the other. According to the "orthodox" view, international law is defined by its sources. A norm qualifies as law if (and only if) it was created through a recognized lawmaking process— for example, by means of a treaty such as the International Whaling Convention or the UN Framework Convention on Climate Change.[39] But even with respect to treaties, which are the source of most international environmental standards, the matter is not so simple. On the one hand, environmental agreements sometimes contain "non-binding" norms, which simply recommend a course of action. For example, the UN Framework Convention on Climate Change provided that industrialized states should "aim" to return their emissions of greenhouse gases to 1990 levels.[40] On the other hand, norms that lack a legal source are sometimes treated as "binding" by states—for example, the UN General Assembly's resolution establishing a moratorium on high seas driftnet fishing.[41] According to the orthodox view, this resolution represents at most "soft law," since, under the UN Charter, the General Assembly may make only recommendations, not legally binding decisions. Nonetheless, states whose vessels engaged in high seas driftnet fishing implemented the resolution as if it were binding, by disbanding their fleets or converting them to other methods of fishing. Arguably, the resolution has had a greater impact on the actual behavior of states than many ostensibly legal norms.[42]

The very term *soft law* betrays some confusion about the definition of law. Much of what one finds discussed in law journals and legal treatises—codes of conduct, declarations, guidelines, and recommendations—falls into this legal limbo. Are they a type of law? The phrase "soft law" suggests that they bear a family resemblance to hard law such as treaties (both are species of the genus law) but fall short in an important respect, since they lack a "legal" source (that is why they are only soft rather than hard).

The difficulty of distinguishing law from politics is particularly acute in international environmental law, which often addresses issues in a pragmatic, non-legalistic way. For example, when the parties to the Montreal Protocol wished to adopt the 1990 London Amendment, they sidestepped the applicable requirements concerning the number of ratifications needed for entry into force, and instead specified a much lower entry-into-force requirement. In the climate change regime, the detailed rules for how the Kyoto Protocol will work—rules that are now serving as the basis for a tremendous amount of private-sector activity—were adopted by a simple decision of the parties, leaving their precise legal status subject to debate. Meanwhile, the new compliance committee under Kyoto has an "enforcement branch" whose decisions are not, strictly speaking, legally binding. The blurring of the line between law and politics is reflected even in the terminology of international environmental law, which often speaks of "commitments" rather than "obligations," "non-compliance" rather than "breach," and "consequences" rather than "remedies" or "sanctions."

For the purposes of this book, I consider the family resemblance among different types of international environmental norms more important than any jurisprudential scruples about the proper definition of law. Thus, my discussion will encompass not only the traditional sources of international law, such as treaties, but also newer sources of environmental norms, including declarations, codes of conduct, guidelines, action plans, and the like, together with the international institutions that help develop, implement, and enforce these norms.

The Thirty-Percent Solution

In my debate with the environmental fund-raiser about whaling, his comments suggested that the legality (or, in his view, illegality) of Norway's actions mattered. Indeed, the alleged illegality of Norwegian whaling was his trump card. Although I disagreed with his legal conclusion, his belief in the importance of international environmental law was heartwarming, particularly since many take the opposite view, namely, that international environmental law is simply rhetoric, which does not affect how states behave.[43]

Is such faith in international environmental law justified or misplaced? That issue will be a significant theme of this book. In my view, the answer lies somewhere in between. International environmental law is neither a panacea nor a sham. It can play a constructive role, but that is all. It might be called a "thirty-percent" solution.

Critics of international law often presume a coercive model of law, which seeks to transcend the decentralized international system of sovereign states. According to this view:

- The aim of international law should be to impose specific obligations on states (which states then impose domestically on their subjects).
- These obligations should be enforceable through compulsory, binding dispute resolution, both internationally and domestically.
- Violators (including both states and persons) should be subject to sanctions.

Judged by these criteria, contemporary international environmental law is, in general, a dismal failure because enforcement mechanisms are in short supply. Proponents of this approach seek to transform the law by developing rules with "teeth." For example, the former prime minister of New Zealand, Geoffrey Palmer, once argued that environmental problems such as climate change require the development of new types of international institutions:

First, there must be a legislative process which is capable of making binding rules which states must follow, even when they do not agree. Second, there must be some means of having compulsory adjudication of disputes, if not to the International Court of Justice, then perhaps to a special tribunal. . . .

Finally, there needs to be ... an institutional authority capable of monitoring what the nation states are doing, blowing the whistle on them when necessary, and acting as an effective coordinator of what action needs to be taken.[44]

The 1989 Hague Conference Declaration, which called for the development of "new institutional authority," with non-unanimous decision-making and enforcement powers, to protect the Earth's atmosphere reflects this coercive approach. Proposals to create an Environmental Protection Council within the United Nations are similar.

Whether international institutions with coercive powers would be a good idea is open to question—particularly without any theory as to what would make such power legitimate.[45] But leaving this issue aside, the coercive model faces a more pressing problem: it bears little relationship to the realities of international politics. Countries are extremely reluctant to cede authority to international institutions. And, even if they were to agree to do so, what would keep them from reneging later on?

An alternative approach to international environmental law is less ambitious but more realistic. It views international environmental law as a process to encourage and enable, rather than require, international cooperation. Instead of pushing for the development of supranational institutions, this facilitative approach accepts state sovereignty as a given. It attempts to help states achieve mutually beneficial outcomes, for example, by building scientific and normative consensus[46] and by addressing barriers to compliance, such as mistrust between states and lack of domestic capacity.[47]

This is a comparatively modest agenda. Over time, however, it can contribute to greater international cooperation, and thereby to the solution of environmental problems. To be effective, international environmental law must understand not only its role but its limits. It must focus on those aspects of a problem where it can make a difference, recognizing that it is part—but only part—of the solution.

Recommended Reading

Patricia Birnie, Alan Boyle, and Catherine Redgwell, *International Law and the Environment* (Oxford: Oxford University Press, 3rd ed. 2009).

Daniel Bodansky, Jutta Brunnée, and Ellen Hey, eds., *The Oxford Handbook of International Environmental Law* (Oxford: Oxford University Press, 2007).

Pamela S. Chasek, David L. Downie, and Janet Welsh Brown, *Global Environmental Politics* (Boulder, CO: Westview Press, 4th ed. 2006).

Peter M. Haas, Robert O. Keohane, and Marc A. Levy, eds., *Institutions for the Earth: Sources of Effective International Environmental Protection* (Cambridge, MA: MIT Press, 1993).

Peter H. Sand, *Transnational Environmental Law: Lessons in Global Change* (London: Kluwer Law International, 1999).

Philippe Sands, *Principles of International Environmental Law* (Cambridge: Cambridge University Press, 2d ed. 2003).

Christopher D. Stone, *The Gnat Is Older than Man: Global Environment and Human Agenda* (Princeton, NJ: Princeton University Press, 1992).

CHAPTER TWO

How We Got Here: A Brief History

Nothing is as powerful as an idea whose time has come.

Victor Hugo, *The History of a Crime*

INTERNATIONAL ENVIRONMENTAL LAW is still a comparatively young field. As recently as 1964, Wolfgang Friedmann, in his influential book about the changing nature of international law, did not include environmental protection or nature conservation among his "new fields of international law."[1] Even more recently, the third edition of Ian Brownlie's authoritative treatise, *Principles of Public International Law*, published in 1979, still had no entry for "environment" in its index, and discussed environmental issues only in passing in chapters on the law of the sea and "common amenities," rather than in a discrete section.[2]

The development of international environmental law has been part of a larger transformation in the subject matter of international law. Classical international law (as crystallized in the nineteenth century) concerned the coexistence of states in times of peace and war, focusing on such topics as diplomatic relations, sovereign immunities, treaty relations, and the laws of war. In the twentieth century, international law expanded in two directions to include (1) how states treat their own citizens (i.e., human rights law) and (2) how states and other international actors cooperate to achieve common ends such as economic development and social welfare.[3] The development of international environmental law has been part of this second transformation and is founded on the common interest of humankind in protecting the natural environment.[4]

Environmental degradation is not a new phenomenon.[5] Humans have affected the environment, sometimes in substantial ways, since ancient times. The classical Greeks noted the problems of deforestation and soil erosion in the hills of Attica. Elephants, rhinoceros, and giraffes disappeared from the Nile Valley by 2000 B.C. and from North Africa by the early centuries A.D. And in a particularly dramatic illustration of man's power to change the environment, the society of Easter Island collapsed in the sixteenth century, apparently as a result of overpopulation and deforestation.[6]

Only in relatively recent years, however, have pollution and depletion of natural resources been widely *perceived* as problems. The growth of international environmental law is sometimes portrayed as a simple cause-and-effect relationship between the growing scale of environmental problems and the political-legal response. But whether a particular phenomenon is considered a "problem" depends, in part, on human perceptions and values. The disappearance of the wolf from England in the 1500s, or the extinction of the dodo in 1681, did not occasion much interest, let alone concern.[7] Indeed, some presumably agreed with the English clergyman, Edmund Hickeringill, who wrote in the seventeenth century, "So noisome and offensive are some animals to humankind, that it concerns all mankind to get quit of the annoyance with as speedy a riddance and despatch as may be, by any lawful means."[8] The emergence of international environmental law required a change in human consciousness, an increased value placed on the environment and concern about its destruction, which began to emerge in the early nineteenth century through the writings of naturalists such as Gilbert White and Alexander von Humboldt[9] and romanticists such as Thoreau.[10]

In part, economic development may help explain the growth of environmental awareness. As societies grow richer, they can afford to focus not just on the provision of basic human necessities, such as food and housing, but also on "luxury goods," such as a cleaner environment.

The evolution of environmental consciousness was also the product of improved scientific understanding, going back to the work of nineteenth-century naturalists such as George Perkins Marsh, who described the despoliation of nature by man and argued that "the earth was given to him for usufruct alone, not for consumption, still less for profligate waste."[11] Most of the major developments in international environmental law have had their origin in science. The linkage drawn by Swedish researchers between sulfur emissions in England and Germany and acid rain in Scandinavia was a major impetus for the 1972 Stockholm Conference and later the 1979 Long-Range Transboundary Air Pollution Convention. The discovery of the ozone hole in the mid-1980s contributed to the successful conclusion of the Montreal Protocol on Substances that Deplete the Ozone Layer. And the growing scientific consensus about the reality, causes, and severity of global warming, reflected in the reports of

---

Box 2.1.   Milestones in the Development of International Law

---

1868   German ornithological meeting proposes development of international treaty on bird conservation.

1893   *Behring Sea Fur Seals Arbitration.*

1909   International Boundary Waters Treaty (U.S.-Canada) adopted.

1911   North Pacific Fur Seals Convention adopted.

1916   Migratory Birds Treaty (U.S.-Canada) adopted.

1941   *Trail Smelter* case articulates duty to prevent transboundary pollution.

1946   International Convention for the Regulation of Whaling adopted.

1948   International Union for the Conservation of Nature (IUCN) established (now the World Conservation Union).

1954   International Convention for the Prevention of Pollution of the Sea by Oil (OILPOL) adopted.

1962   Publication of Rachel Carson's *Silent Spring.*

1967   Torrey Canyon oil spill leads to negotiation of Intervention Convention and Civil Liability Convention.

1970   First Earth Day. *Time* magazine names the environment "issue of the year."

1972   Stockholm Conference on the Human Environment. UNEP established. World Heritage Convention and London Dumping Convention adopted.

1973   CITES and MARPOL adopted.

1976   First UNEP Regional Seas Convention adopted.

1979   Long-Range Transboundary Air Pollution Convention (LRTAP) adopted.

1987   Brundtland Commission Report *(Our Common Future).* Montreal Protocol on Substances that Deplete the Ozone Layer adopted.

1988   *Time* magazine names "endangered earth" "Planet of the Year."

1990   Global Environment Facility (GEF) established. London Amendments to Montreal Protocol adopted.

1992   UN Conference on Environment and Development (Earth Summit). Climate Change and Biodiversity Conventions adopted.

1997   Kyoto Protocol adopted.

1998   Rotterdam Convention on trade in hazardous chemicals adopted.

2001   Stockholm Convention on Persistent Organic Pollutants (POPs) adopted.

2002   Johannesburg World Summit on Sustainable Development.

---

the Intergovernmental Panel on Climate Change, have helped propel the development of the international climate change regime.

Whatever the exact causes, the growth of environmental consciousness has proceeded in fits and starts, following a pattern familiar to political scientists: a problem is discovered with alarm, often as a result of some dramatic event such as an oil spill; public interest surges, leading to a flurry of new initiatives; environmental responses diffuse to other countries through a process of mimicry; the difficulties and costs of addressing the problem slowly become apparent; people become discouraged, bored, or diverted by the emergence of a new issue; and the earlier issue moves into a more quiescent phase, continuing to be addressed in a routine, low-key manner.[12]

In the emergence of international environmental law, three such cycles or waves can be discerned: (1) a conservationist stage, focusing on the protection of wildlife, stretching from the late nineteenth century through the first half of the twentieth century; (2) a pollution-prevention stage, spanning the so-called environmental revolution of the 1960s and early 1970s, marked by the Stockholm Conference, the establishment of the United Nations Environment Program (UNEP), and the negotiation of numerous multilateral agreements, particularly in the field of marine pollution; and (3) a sustainable development phase, beginning in the mid-1980s with the work of the Brundtland Commission and continuing through the 1992 Earth Summit and the 2002 Johannesburg Summit up to today.[13] Each successive stage has not displaced its predecessors. Rather, the phases have had a cumulative quality, and, today, the international environmental landscape includes elements of all three.

The Classical Approach: Applying International Law to Environmental Disputes

International environmental law, as a distinctive enterprise, seeks to promote cooperation among states in order to achieve joint gains. Classical international law, by contrast, focused on coexistence rather than cooperation by demarcating the respective jurisdiction of states.[14] Generally, this demarcation was accomplished on a territorial basis, through rules that defined the territory over which a state exercises sovereignty. As long as states operated within their territory, they could coexist peacefully and avoid conflicts. Resources in areas beyond national jurisdiction, such as the high seas, were generally seen as inexhaustible by classical writers on international law such as Pufendorf and Vattel, and thus not a source of conflict. They could be treated as *res nullius*—that is, belonging to no one and therefore open to all.

But environmental impacts do not respect national borders, nor are resources of the commons inexhaustible. As the nineteenth century progressed and the scale of environmental impacts increased, both of these facts became apparent. Activities in one state began to have environmental effects on others. The diversion of the waters of the Rio Grande by farmers and ranchers in the United States harmed communities on the Mexican side of the border. Fumes from the Trail Smelter in Canada blew south into Washington State, causing damage to American agricultural communities. And the hunting of fur seals by Canadian vessels in the Behring Sea made it impossible for the United States (which possessed the islands where the seals bred) to protect them against depletion and eventual extinction. In these and similar cases, the demarcation of states along territorial lines no longer sufficed as a strategy to avoid conflict.

How did classical international law attempt to resolve these disputes? In general, it did so on a case-by-case basis, by adjudicating the competing sovereign claims of the states concerned.[15] In transboundary pollution cases, for example, does the polluting state have the sovereign right to do whatever it chooses within its territory, even if its actions cause damage to another state—the view put forward by U.S. Attorney General Judson Harmon in the Rio Grande dispute? Or does the injured state have a right of territorial integrity, which limits the polluting state's right to use its territory as it pleases, as the United States maintained several decades later in the *Trail Smelter* case? Similarly, do states have the right to hunt fur seals on the high seas without limit, even if those resources are exhaustible? Or may coastal states protect seals that breed in their territory, even when the seals are on the high seas? These were the types of questions addressed in early cases such as *Trail Smelter* and the 1893 *Behring Sea Fur Seals Arbitration*. The decisions aimed at determining the respective rights and responsibilities of the contestants—in the *Fur Seals Arbitration* by deciding that coastal states may not restrict the high seas freedoms of other states (even in order to save a species from extinction) and in the *Trail Smelter* case by deciding that a state's freedom to use its territory as it pleases must yield to the right of other states to be free of significant injury.

Nature Conservation in the Early Twentieth Century

Although the principles and techniques of classical international law proved useful in resolving individual disputes, international environmental problems typically require ongoing management rather than merely an adjudication of the rights and responsibilities of the parties. That is, they require cooperation rather than merely coexistence among states. International environmental law developed in the twentieth century in response to this functional need. The *Fur Seals* case provides a good illustration of this point. Ultimately, the issue was resolved not through the 1893 arbitral decision, but through the negotiation of the 1911 North

Pacific Fur Seals Convention, establishing a cooperative management regime that led to a dramatic recovery in fur seal populations.[16]

International environmental law had its origins in the conservation and nature protection movement of late nineteenth- and early twentieth-century Europe and North America. In 1872, the United States established the first national park, and soon other countries followed suit. Government agencies were created (such as the National Forest Service in the United States), and non-governmental organizations (NGOs) began to spring up—the Audubon Society and Conservation Foundation in the United States, the National Trust in England, the Swedish Society for the Protection of Nature, and the Swiss League for the Conservation of Nature, to name a few.

Why after so many years of disinterest did the protection of nature become a concern at this time? Historians have suggested several factors. In part, the conservation movement was related to a larger response to increasing urbanization and industrialization. In part, it grew out of the growth of knowledge about natural history in the nineteenth century and the increase in foreign travel. It was also a reaction to two particularly dramatic illustrations of man's power to alter nature: the decimation of the bison in North America, which dropped from 50 million to just eighty-five by the end of the nineteenth century, and the extinction of the passenger pigeon from 1890 to 1910. The last large flocks of passenger pigeons were reported in 1888, the last confirmed sighting occurred in 1900, and the last passenger pigeon died in captivity in 1914.

Although the conservation movement had a national rather than an international focus, the international dimension of conservation received some attention—in particular, the problems of migratory species (primarily birds) and commercially-exploited species found in common areas such as the oceans (fish, fur seals, and whales). Already in the nineteenth century, states had negotiated several fisheries treaties on a bilateral basis, including a treaty between France and Great Britain to conserve oysters, and treaties concerning fishing in the Rhine and the North Sea. In 1868, a German ornithological meeting proposed the development of an international treaty on bird protection. The Convention to Protect Birds Useful to Agriculture was ultimately adopted in 1902 by twelve European nations and is widely considered the first multilateral environmental treaty.[17] Like many of its successors, it was stronger on good intentions than on follow-through; it established strict obligations (including absolute protection of certain species, as well as protection of nests, eggs, and breeding places), but little implementation machinery. The 1902 Convention was followed by several bilateral treaties, including the 1916

Migratory Birds Convention between the United States and Canada (represented internationally at the time by Great Britain) and a similar agreement in 1936 between the United States and Mexico. More general regional initiatives included the 1900 African Wildlife Convention (a response to game hunting in Africa) and the 1909 North American Conservation Congress, followed later by the 1933 African Wildlife Convention and the 1940 Western Hemisphere Convention. International environmental NGOs also began to emerge during this same general period, including the Society for the Preservation of the Wild Fauna of the Empire in 1903, the International Committee for Bird Protection in 1922 (now the International Council for Bird Preservation), and the International Office for the Protection of Nature in 1928.

This initial stage in the development of international environmental law was important, but it had several limitations:

First, its focus of interest was narrow. Although some conservationists advocated nature preservation as an end in itself, early conservation efforts did not reflect a generalized concern about environmental protection or pollution. Instead, the conservation movement's dominant strain was utilitarian and anthropocentric, emphasizing the rational use of natural resources by humans. For example, early efforts at bird conservation, including the 1902 Birds Convention, attempted to distinguish between birds useful to agriculture, particularly as aids in the control of pests, from those that were "noxious."[18] Marine conservation treaties similarly focused on the regulation of fishing to ensure the continued viability of the fishing industry. The stated objective of the 1946 International Convention for the Regulation of Whaling, namely, to "make possible the orderly development of the whaling industry," provides a good illustration of the prevailing ethos of its time.

Second, in conserving nature, the early conservation movement tended to focus on direct threats—in particular, the hunting of wildlife by humans—rather than indirect threats such as habitat loss, pollution, and the introduction of non-native species. There was, of course, some effort to protect habitats through the creation of national parks and nature reserves. The regional conservation conventions for Africa and the Western Hemisphere included obligations to create such reserves. But the emphasis of most wildlife treaties—including the migratory bird treaties between the United States, Canada, and Mexico, the 1911 Fur Seals Convention, and the 1946 Whaling Convention—was on the regulation of hunting.[19]

Third, states adopted conventions in a piecemeal, ad hoc manner, and there was little development of institutions. An attempt in 1913 to establish an intergovernmental Consultative Committee for the International

Protection of Nature was still-born, as a result of the outbreak of World War I. Following the war, attempts to revive the organization proved unsuccessful. Even as late as 1940, the Western Hemisphere Convention failed to provide for regular meetings of the parties or any other institutional follow-up. As a result, it became a "sleeping beauty"[20]—its excellent substantive provisions virtually devoid of influence. The situation did not begin to change until after World War II, with the adoption of treaties such as the 1946 Whaling Convention, which established the International Whaling Commission. At a more general level, in 1948, a UNESCO-sponsored conference established the International Union for the Protection of Nature (or IUCN for short), a highly unusual organization that includes both government agencies and non-governmental organizations.

What were the effects of the early twentieth-century conservation movement? In terms of actual effectiveness, one commentator concludes that "[w]ith the exception of the North Pacific Fur Seal Convention, a plausible case could be made that, had none of the international conservation agreements negotiated prior to 1970 been consummated, the state of fisheries and world wildlife generally would not have been significantly different."[21] But the new agreements and conventions put environmental issues onto the international agenda and, at least in that respect, contributed to the evolution of environmental consciousness.

Although the scope of international environmental law has grown dramatically since the 1950s, nature conservation has remained an important strand. Indeed, the emphasis of the conservation movement on the economics of resource use has made a comeback in recent years, after a period in the 1970s when economic factors were discounted. But today, many people see nature conservation as an end in itself rather than as simply useful to humans. This change in perspective is reflected in the 1950 International Convention for the Protection of Birds, which in contrast to its 1902 predecessor, was aimed at protecting all birds, not simply those useful to agriculture. Modern-day descendants of the early twentieth-century conservation movement include the 1971 Ramsar Convention on Wetlands of International Importance Especially as Waterfowl Habitat (the first treaty aimed at protecting a particular ecosystem), the 1972 Convention on the Protection of the World Cultural and Natural Heritage, the 1973 Convention on International Trade in Endangered Species (CITES), the 1979 Bonn Convention on the Conservation of Migratory Species of Wild Animals, and the numerous fisheries treaties addressing high seas fisheries and stocks found in waters under the jurisdiction of more than one country.[22]

The Emergence of Pollution Issues: 1962–1975

Despite the achievements of the conservation movement, the environment remained quite marginal in international affairs as late as 1945, the year the United Nations was established. Significantly, the UN Charter made no reference whatsoever to environmental protection or nature conservation and instead concentrated on the protection of human rights, which the Charter identified as a central purpose of the new organization. Nor did states establish a UN specialized agency focused on the environment. International environmental issues did not come into their own until the late 1960s, as part of a more general upsurge of interest in the environment often referred to as the "environmental revolution."

The revolution began with the 1962 publication of Rachel Carson's *Silent Spring*, which sold more than a half million copies and remained on the *New York Times* best-seller list for thirty-one weeks.[23] From 1965 to 1970, the number of people in the United States who identified the environment as a major policy problem increased by a factor of four.[24] Membership in environmental organizations grew dramatically. Hundreds of thousands of people (by some estimates, millions) participated in the first Earth Day on April 22, 1970. The Council of Europe declared 1970 as "European Conservation Year" and *Time* magazine named the environment "issue of the year."[25]

The environmental movement of the 1960s differed from its predecessors in several respects. First, in contrast to the conservation movement, which had been "the creation of a few enthusiasts,"[26] environmentalism in the 1960s was a mass movement. Second, it focused on broader issues of pollution, technology, population, and economic growth, rather than just on the conservation of nature. Finally, it moved from the earlier focus on economics and science—on the rational utilization of natural resources—to a more zealous, antiestablishment orientation, part of the new politics of the 1960s.

Like the conservation movement of the early twentieth century, the environmental revolution of the late 1960s and early 1970s was primarily a Western phenomenon and focused more on national than on international issues. During this period, the United States and many Western European nations established environmental agencies and enacted basic laws protecting the air and water and requiring environmental impact assessments. In a span of just three years, from 1969 to 1972, the United States adopted the National Environmental Policy Act (NEPA), established the Environmental Protection Agency (EPA), and passed the Clean Air and Clean Water Acts. The European Union (then the European

Community) followed a similar time frame, adopting its first environmental directive in 1967 (addressing the classification, packaging, and
labeling of dangerous substances) and its first environmental action plan
in 1973.

Prior to the 1960s, most pollution problems still seemed relatively localized. Occasionally, pollution had transboundary effects leading to
an international response—most notably the *Trail Smelter* arbitration,
which first enunciated the principle that states have a responsibility to
prevent significant transboundary pollution. *Trail Smelter* was an isolated case, however, and did not achieve its landmark status until much
later, after transboundary pollution had emerged as a more general concern. In the first half of the twentieth century, pollution of boundary
waters was the only environmental issue to receive any regular attention,
generally on a bilateral basis, as in the treaties the United States negotiated with Canada and Mexico.

The first multilateral pollution problem to receive international attention was oil pollution from tankers. In 1954, a conference organized by
the International Maritime Organization adopted the International Convention for the Prevention of Pollution of the Sea by Oil (OILPOL),
which established coastal zones within which tankers could not discharge
oil except in very limited amounts. Four years later, the 1958 Convention
on the High Seas committed states more generally to prevent oil pollution and the dumping of radioactive wastes. Following the *Torrey Canyon* oil spill off the English coast in 1967—the first major accident involving the new generation of supertankers—maritime and coastal states
quickly adopted two conventions to address accidental discharges of oil:
one recognized the right of coastal states to intervene, and the other established a liability regime. A series of further tanker accidents helped
spur the adoption of a more general convention in 1973 (and its subsequent revision in 1978) that addresses not only oil pollution, but also
other types of vessel-source pollution, including sewage and garbage.[27]
In addition, states adopted two conventions in 1972 limiting the dumping of wastes at sea, one regional (focusing on the North Sea) and the other
global.

The dangers of nuclear weapons and nuclear energy also received significant international attention at an early date. The 1963 Nuclear Test
Ban Treaty and the 1968 Nuclear Non-Proliferation Treaty were not primarily motivated by environmental factors, but they indirectly helped
protect the environment against the dangers of nuclear radiation and are
often included in lists of international environmental agreements. More
clearly environmental in character were several conventions on nuclear

energy, including an International Labour Organization (ILO) Convention Concerning the Protection of Workers against Ionizing Radiation, an Organisation for Economic Cooperation and Development (OECD) Convention on Third Party Liability in the Field of Nuclear Energy, and the 1963 Vienna Convention on Civil Liability for Nuclear Damage.

By comparison to marine and nuclear issues, transboundary air pollution problems received much less attention initially, despite the *Trail Smelter* ruling of 1941, which had focused on this subject. The first international resolution addressing air pollution was not adopted until 1966 by the Council of Europe.

Yet it was the Nordic countries' concern about transboundary air pollution, in particular acid rain, that led them to propose an international conference on the environment. The conference was held in Stockholm in 1972 and served as a major catalyst—perhaps *the* major catalyst—in the emergence of international environment law. Stockholm was not the first international conference focusing on the environment. It was preceded by the 1949 Conference on the Conservation and Utilization of Resources and the 1968 Biosphere Conference. But in contrast to these earlier, primarily scientific, gatherings, Stockholm received high-level political attention and aroused tremendous popular interest. Everything about it was big: it was attended by 6,000 persons, 114 countries, 400 non-governmental groups, and 1,500 journalists; it generated 100,000 pages of preparatory documents and 40 tons of conference documents.[28] In addition to the official conference, activist groups organized separate events—an Earth Forum and an even more radical Peoples Forum—popularly dubbed "Woodstockholm."[29]

Stockholm was the first major United Nations "theme conference"[30] and served as the prototype for subsequent conferences on population, desertification, women's rights, human settlements, and social development. Although UN mega-conferences can, in some cases, be little more than consciousness-raising exercises,[31] the Stockholm process had several tangible results.

Perhaps least significant were the two direct outputs of the conference: the Stockholm Declaration and the Action Plan. The Stockholm Declaration set forth sixteen principles for the preservation and enhancement of the human environment.[32] Most of these principles are seldom cited; the exception is Principle 21, which echoed *Trail Smelter* by articulating the responsibility of states to ensure that activities under their jurisdiction and control do not adversely affect other states or areas of the global commons. Principle 21 is now widely regarded as part of international law, a view endorsed by the International Court of Justice.[33] Apart from Principle 21, however, it is hard to disagree with the conclusion of one diplomat that the Stockholm Declaration has "little concrete bite" and "its concrete effect has been very limited."[34] And if the Stockholm Declaration has for the most part had little influence, the Stockholm Action Plan has had even less. Like other action plans adopted by UN conferences, it operates at a high level of generality and was forgotten almost before the ink dried.

A more important consequence of Stockholm was the UN General Assembly's decision in December 1972 to establish the United Nations Environment Program (UNEP), located in Nairobi, Kenya. Owing in part to opposition by the existing UN specialized agencies, the General Assembly did not give UNEP any management responsibilities. Instead, UNEP was intended to play a coordinating and catalytic role. Although it never succeeded in fulfilling its coordinating function, due to its lack of leverage over other UN agencies, UNEP has played a significant role in helping to stimulate the development of international environmental law, particularly during the late 1970s and 1980s. Important UNEP initiatives have included its regional seas program, which protects the Mediterranean and Caribbean seas among others, as well as its sponsorship of treaty negotiations to protect the stratospheric ozone layer and to regulate international trade in hazardous wastes.

The Stockholm process also led, more indirectly, to the negotiation of several important treaties. Among these treaties were the London Dumping Convention (regulating the dumping of hazardous wastes at sea), the World Heritage Convention, and the Convention on International Trade in Endangered Species. None of these conventions was adopted at Stockholm, and all might have emerged even had Stockholm not occurred. But the intense interest in the environment generated by the run-up to Stockholm served as a catalyst in producing this unusual surge in treaty-making activity.

Stockholm spurred national developments as well. It was part of a larger process by which environmental protection has become part of the definition of what it means to be a modern nation-state.[35] In 1972, for example, only 11 states had national environmental agencies; in 1980, this number had grown to 102.[36] The decade after Stockholm saw a similarly sharp increase in the prevalence of national environmental assessment laws. The emergence of environmental protection as a widely shared value also helped to "mainstream" environmental issues at the international level, for example, through the development of environmental procedures for the World Bank, the OECD and other international organizations.

Finally, the global scale of the Stockholm Conference brought developing countries into the debate. Previously, environmental issues had been largely the preserve of industrialized countries, with developing countries displaying little interest. During the course of the Stockholm process, however, developing countries emerged as a forceful voice, insisting, among other things, that UNEP be located in a developing country and that environmental issues be considered in conjunction with development.

In evaluating the role of the Stockholm Conference, it is difficult to determine the extent to which Stockholm itself contributed to the emergence of environmental awareness, or was merely a symptom of other causal factors. Stockholm was part of a broader movement, which had already produced significant changes prior to the conference and would undoubtedly have prompted further developments in national and international environmental law even if Stockholm had not occurred. Nevertheless, the Stockholm Conference contributed to these developments by focusing public and political attention, producing significant institutional development, and illustrating in dramatic terms that the environment had become a matter of international concern.

Sustainable Development, 1987 to the Present

The late 1970s and early 1980s saw the negotiation of several important treaty regimes, including the 1976 Barcelona Convention for the Protection of the Mediterranean Sea (the first of the UNEP regional seas agreements) and the 1979 Long-Range Transboundary Air Pollution Convention (LRTAP), which addressed the problem of acid rain in Europe. Generally, however, this period marked a downturn, at least compared to what came before and after. UNEP encountered resistance from other UN agencies and got off to a relatively slow start, and some of the reforms initiated as a result of Stockholm, such as the mainstreaming of environmental practices in the World Bank, failed to take hold. In 1982, for the tenth anniversary of Stockholm, the UN General Assembly merely adopted a new resolution, the World Charter for Nature, rather than convening a major follow-up conference (as it would ten years later at the Rio Summit). The shift was particularly apparent in the United States, where membership in environmental organizations declined, and the Reagan Administration resisted Canada's efforts to address the acid rain issue and attempted to turn back the clock on domestic laws.

Interest in environmental issues began to revive again only in the mid-1980s, as a result of the discovery of the Antarctic ozone hole in 1985 and the beginning of concern about global warming. The year 1987, in particular, witnessed two seminal events: (1) the adoption of the Montreal Ozone Protocol, which has cut the use of ozone-depleting substances dramatically and is widely considered to be the most successful environmental agreement to date; and (2) the publication of *Our Common Future*[37] by the World Commission on Environment and Development, led by former Norwegian Prime Minister Gro Brundtland (and referred to as the Brundtland Commission), which became a best seller and popularized the concept of sustainable development. By 1988, environmental issues had become so prominent that *Time* magazine again named the environment "Newsmaker of the Year." The next several years saw a flurry of activity, including the adoption of the Basel Convention on the Transboundary Movements of Hazardous Wastes in 1989, the London Amendment to the Montreal Protocol in 1990, and agreements between the United States and Canada and among European countries to address the problem of acid rain. The process culminated in the 1992 UN Conference on Environment and Development in Rio de Janeiro (popularly known as the Earth Summit)—one of the largest assemblages of world leaders ever—and the negotiation of the climate change and biological diversity conventions.

In many respects, these efforts represented a continuation of the pollution prevention paradigm of the 1970s, albeit in a new, more sophisticated version. Just as MARPOL and the London Convention had regulated various sources of marine pollution and LRTAP had addressed transboundary air pollution, the Montreal Protocol and its subsequent amendments aimed at eliminating pollution by ozone-depleting substances.

But the more recent phase in international environmental law differs in important ways from the environmental movement of the 1970s. First, it involves much more complex environmental problems such as climate change and biological diversity, whose solutions may require fundamental economic and social changes rather than a relatively simple pollution-prevention fix. Climate change, for example, implicates virtually every aspect of countries' economies. It is not simply an environmental problem, but a problem of energy policy, transportation policy, agricultural policy, and even land-use policy to address the potential impacts of sea-level rise on coastal communities. This means that many more actors have a stake in the outcome and may seek to influence the decision-making process. It also means that international measures represent a much greater potential intrusion on national decision making and thus on national sovereignty.

Second, international environmental issues have assumed a more pronounced North-South dimension. The problems of the 1960s and 1970s, such as vessel-source pollution, ocean dumping, and acid rain, primarily involved industrialized countries. Although developing countries participated actively in the Stockholm Conference, they played a more peripheral role in the treaty-making process. Neither MARPOL nor the 1972 London Dumping Convention—the two main pollution-prevention treaties of the 1970s—had large numbers of developing country participants. But problems such as climate change and biological diversity cannot be solved by developed countries alone; they require action by developing countries as well. Accordingly, developing countries have played a much more central role in establishing these treaty regimes.

The shift in emphasis is evident in the evolution of the Montreal Protocol. During the 1987 Montreal Protocol negotiations, the primary split was between the United States and the European Community, with only limited involvement by developing countries. As a result, the Montreal Protocol included only weak provisions on financial and technical assistance. By 1990, however, when the London Amendments to Montreal were negotiated, developing countries had become much more assertive and demanded the establishment of a financial mechanism as a condition of joining the Protocol.

The increased influence of developing countries in international environmental law also can be seen in the greater focus on issues of equity and capacity building. Developing countries argue that, in addressing problems such as climate change and ozone depletion, it is unfair to expect them to shoulder the same burden as industrialized countries. For one thing they are less responsible for causing the problems, and for another they have less capacity to act. In response, treaties such as the Montreal Protocol and the Kyoto Protocol establish less stringent obligations for developing countries than for developed countries. Multilateral environmental agreements have also begun to tackle environmental problems of primary interest to the South, beginning with the 1989 Basel Convention on the Transboundary Movements of Hazardous Wastes (which responds to concerns of developing countries that they will become the dumping ground for rich countries' wastes) and continuing with the 1994 Convention to Combat Desertification.

Third, the current generation of environmental problems, such as climate change and loss of biodiversity, involve a high degree of scientific uncertainty. With respect to some issues, such as the dangers posed by genetically modified organisms, it is not clear whether a threat exists at all. As a result, techniques to address uncertainty have gained increasing prominence; of particular importance is the so-called precautionary principle, which urges action against environmental threats even in the face of scientific uncertainties. The shift in emphasis toward precaution is reflected in the transformation of the international regime on ocean dumping in the 1990s from a negative-listing approach, which allowed wastes to be dumped unless a waste was prohibited, to a positive-listing approach, which prohibits dumping unless a substance can be shown to be safe.

The organizing principle of this third phase in the development of international environmental law has been sustainable development. The concept is not new. It has been expressed, in various ways, since the birth of environmentalism, and it featured significantly in the Stockholm process. The publication of the Brundtland Commission report in 1987, however, helped to popularize sustainable development, which the report defined as "development that meets the needs of the present without compromising the ability of future generations to meet their own needs."[38]

Initially, developing countries resisted the concept, fearing that it focused on them rather than on industrialized countries, whose excessive (and unsustainable) consumption was responsible, they argued, for global environmental problems such as climate change and ozone depletion. Before they were willing to accept the concept, developing countries required reassurance that sustainable development addressed the developmental process of all countries and could be used as a basis to criticize the consumption patterns of industrialized countries as unsustainable. The shift in view is apparent in the titles chosen for the 1992 Rio Summit and the 2002 Johannesburg Summit. In 1990, when the UN General Assembly decided to convene a conference to commemorate the twentieth anniversary of Stockholm, developing countries insisted that it be called the UN Conference on Environment *and* Development (UNCED)—a name that reflected the separation they still made between environmental protection (which they viewed as the concern of industrialized countries, not themselves) and economic development. By 2002 they agreed to call the Johannesburg Summit the World Summit on Sustainable Development.

Sustainable development has been defined in countless ways and still has no generally accepted meaning.[39] It reflects two general themes: integration and long-term planning. First, environmental issues should not be seen as stand-alone items—adding a catalytic converter here or a scrubber there—but as important aspects of economic and social decision making more generally. As such, they should be the concern not only of environmental agencies but of all government departments. This idea of integration has a long history. It was one of the goals of the environmental impact assessment (EIA) requirements adopted in the 1970s and of the requirements set forth in various environmental agreements for integrated planning and management.[40] Despite these requirements, however, the environmental agenda of the 1970s tended to focus on pollution control: restricting ocean dumping of hazardous wastes, limiting oil pollution from ships, reducing emissions of sulfur dioxide, and so forth. Sustainable development, in contrast, gives greater prominence to an alternative agenda that includes energy policy, trade policy, debt relief, and poverty alleviation.[41]

Second, sustainable development focuses attention on the issue of intergenerational equity. It requires thinking in a long-term manner about how to manage resources sustainably, so that the resources will be available to future generations. Again, this idea has a long history and is reflected in many environmental instruments, including the 1946 Whaling Convention, the 1972 World Heritage Convention, and Principle 1 of the Stockholm Declaration, which affirms that humans bears "a solemn responsibility to protect and improve the environment for present and future generations." The concept of sustainable development builds on these instruments by putting intergenerational equity front and center.

If the Stockholm Conference was the focal point of the second phase of international environmental law, the Rio Summit filled that role for the third. In many respects, Rio was Stockholm redux; indeed, it even had the same secretary-general, Maurice Strong of Canada. Like Stockholm, Rio was huge—13,000 participants from 176 states and 1,400 nongovernmental groups, including 103 heads of state. Like Stockholm, its outputs included a declaration of environmental principles (the Rio Declaration) and a detailed action plan (Agenda 21).[42] Also like Stockholm, it declined to undertake a fundamental institutional reorganization. Instead it created a new institution with only limited authority, the UN Commission on Sustainable Development. And, like Stockholm, its most significant results were not the conference outputs themselves, but the two treaties negotiated in parallel: the UN Framework Convention on Climate Change and the Biological Diversity Convention.[43]

Despite the failure to achieve a breakthrough at Rio—politically, legally, or institutionally—the momentum that led to Rio carried forward through much of the 1990s, leading to a flurry of further treaty-making. Agreements were negotiated addressing a wide variety of topics, including desertification, pesticides, persistent organic pollutants, Antarctica, fisheries, and genetically modified organisms. Perhaps the most ambitious of these agreements, and certainly the most politically important, was the Kyoto Protocol, which requires significant reductions in emissions of greenhouse gases by industrialized countries and establishes a number of innovative mechanisms for achieving these reductions, including emissions trading. Meanwhile, states have continued to elaborate the earlier generations of environmental agreements, addressing such topics as transboundary air pollution, vessel-source pollution, trade in endangered species, and ocean dumping—in some cases through the negotiation of additional agreements, in others by elaborating existing ones. As we will survey in Chapter 5, the result has been a tremendous growth in both the scope and density of international environmental regulation.

Contemporary International Environmental Law

The first years of the twenty-first century have been a period of retrenchment and consolidation for international environmental law. The proliferation of treaty regimes has led to concerns that participation in the international environmental process is becoming a burden, particularly for developing countries: there are too many meetings to attend, too many secretariats to finance, and too many reports to file. In this view, the problem is not too little environmental law but too much. This problem of "treaty congestion," as it has been called, also creates the potential for duplication of effort, lack of coordination, and even conflict between different environmental regimes.

At the same time, some commentators question whether the accumulating mass of international environmental law has done very much to improve the environment—whether the game is worth the candle, so to speak. The growing concern about effectiveness reflects the perception that, despite the proliferation of international environmental instruments, environmental threats such as climate change continue to worsen. It also reflects the more general revival of interest in the issue of effectiveness, which has resulted from the increasing interaction between international lawyers and political scientists, as well as the turn toward empiricism in many areas of legal scholarship.[44]

In a sense, both trends reflect the maturation of international environmental law. In the early years of any new legal field, attention tends to focus on the development of rules to fill the legal void. Only after a significant body of norms has developed do people begin to ask: Are all of the different norms coherent? To what extent are they actually doing any good?

Experience teaches that the first steps in any endeavor—whether it be business, environmental policy, or diplomacy—are the easiest. As the simplest gains are achieved, progress becomes more difficult. International environmental law emerged quite rapidly over the past half century. Now, it is undergoing the complex transition from youth to middle age.

Recommended Reading

Richard Elliot Benedick, *Ozone Diplomacy: New Directions in Safeguarding the Planet* (Cambridge, MA: Harvard University Press, 1998).

Robert Boardman, *International Organization and the Conservation of Nature* (Bloomington: Indiana University Press, 1981).

Tony Brenton, *The Greening of Machiavelli: The Evolution of International Environmental Politics* (London: Earthscan, 1994).

Lynton Keith Caldwell, *International Environmental Policy: Emergence and Dimensions* (Durham, NC: Duke University Press, 2d ed. 1990).

Tuomas Kuokkanen, *International Law and the Environment: Variations on a Theme* (New York: Kluwer Law International, 2002).

John McCormick, *Reclaiming Paradise: The Global Environmental Movement* (Bloomington: Indiana University Press, 1989).

Clive Ponting, *A New Green History of the World: The Environment and the Collapse of Great Civilizations* (New York: Penguin Books, 2007).

Philip Shabecoff, *A New Name for Peace: International Environmentalism, Sustainable Development, and Democracy* (Hanover, NH: University Press of New England, 1996).

Mostafa K. Tolba, *Global Environmental Diplomacy: Negotiating Environmental Agreements for the World, 1973–1992* (Cambridge, MA: MIT Press, 1998).

Donald Worster, *The Wealth of Nature: Environmental History and the Ecological Imagination* (New York: Oxford University Press, 1993).

CHAPTER THREE

Diagnosing the Causes of Environmental Problems

> The progress of civilization [can be charted] in terms of the
> internalization of costs formerly viewed as external.
>
> Harold M. Hubbard, "The Real Cost of Energy," *Scientific American* (April 1991)

FOR THE INTERNATIONAL environmental lawyer, law is a set of tools to help solve problems. Just as a doctor seeks to diagnose a disease in order to know what cure to prescribe, understanding the causes of an environmental problem can help to identify the most appropriate policy responses.[1]

Of course, environmental problems, like diseases, can be the product of many different causes, operating at many different levels. So there are many potential solutions. Consider malaria, for example. If we ask, what causes malaria, our immediate response might be, a mosquito bite. And this, of course, is true, insofar as it goes. But malaria is also caused by the swamps and other areas where mosquitoes breed. And, in terms of the etiology of the disease itself, the cause of malaria is not the mosquito bite itself, but rather the parasite transmitted in the mosquito's saliva and its reproduction within the human body. This complex chain of causation means that to combat malaria we can intervene in many different ways, at many different stages along the causal chain: we can drain swamps; we can use insecticides such as DDT to kill mosquitoes; we can wear protective clothing to avoid mosquito bites; or we can take drugs such as chloroquine that kill the malarial parasite in the bloodstream.

International environmental problems typically involve even more complex chains of causation. Global warming provides a good illustration. At one level, global warming is caused by emissions of carbon dioxide and other greenhouse gases, which trap heat in the atmosphere. Thus, many proposals to address climate change focus on cutting emissions. But emissions do not directly cause global warming; they do so only to the extent that they accumulate in the atmosphere, causing concentrations of greenhouse gases to increase. So another possible response would be to remove carbon dioxide from the atmosphere, for example, by planting trees or increasing the activities of other so-called carbon sinks. Or, proceeding further down the causal chain, we could try to break the causal link between increased concentrations of greenhouse gases and temperature change. For example, we could inject dust into the atmosphere to screen out incoming sunlight and thereby counterbalance the warming effect of greenhouse gases.

Moreover, even if we focus our attention on emissions, these have many causes and therefore many possible responses. Greenhouse gas emissions are produced primarily from the burning of fossil fuels—coal and, to a lesser extent, oil and natural gas. So we could try to reduce emissions by developing alternative fuel sources such as nuclear power, solar energy, and hydrogen fuel cells. Or we could tackle the demand side of the equation. For example, we could try to improve the efficiency of appliances that consume electricity, or build mass transit to reduce reliance on automobiles, or reconfigure cities so people wouldn't need to drive as much. Or we could try to achieve some of these same results indirectly through the market by raising the price of gasoline or electricity, so that people would have a financial incentive to consume less. We could even try to change people's ethos, so that they would desire a simpler, less consumption-oriented lifestyle. The answer to global warming could thus take many forms. It might involve technology, forestry, urban design, economics, or even ethics.

Not only do environmental problems typically involve long, complex chains of causation, they often result from independently operating causes. So it is important to determine which factors contribute most significantly to a problem.

Consider, for example, the problem of species extinctions. Until recently, hunting appeared to pose the principal threat to biological resources—for example, killing whales for their oil, or seals for their fur, or elephants for their ivory. Accordingly, international environmental law initially focused on regulating direct human uses of wildlife. Migratory bird treaties defined open and closed seasons; the North Pacific Fur Seals Convention prohibited pelagic sealing; and the Convention on International Trade in Endangered Species (CITES) regulated trade in animal parts such as elephant ivory and rhino horn.

Today, scientists believe that habitat loss and the introduction of nonnative ("exotic") species account for significantly more extinctions than overexploitation by humans.[2] So a strategy focusing primarily on direct human uses will do little to halt the loss of biodiversity. CITES, for example, could successfully eliminate all trade in elephant ivory, but as long as human settlements continue to advance, resulting in the conversion of grassland to farmland, elephants will still face a serious threat.

Disentangling the various factors that contribute to an international environmental problem thus constitutes an important first step in determining the range of possible responses. It can show the different options for intervening in the long causal chains that end in environmental degradation, as well as the limitations of policies that focus on secondary (or tertiary) causes.

Before beginning our causal investigation, a preliminary caution is in order. Although investigating the causes of environmental problems is, in itself, a neutral, empirical inquiry, it is fraught with political overtones because of the association between causation and responsibility. Is deforestation in the developing world the result of local corruption or economic globalization? The answer may be both. But depending on which cause we choose to emphasize, the policy implications will be quite different. As with any subject, how we conceptualize an international environmental problem conditions how we understand the potential solutions.

The IPAT Model

If we trace back the chain of causation, some environmentalists contend that we can reduce environmental problems to just three factors: population, affluence, and technology. According to this approach, the impact of humans on the environment (I) is a function of the number of people on Earth (Population), the rate of consumption per person (Affluence), and the rate of pollution per unit of consumption (Technology)—or, to put it symbolically, I=PAT.[3]

Ever since Thomas Malthus, many demographers have emphasized population as a driver of environmental harms. By now, the exponential character of population growth is familiar.[4] Since 1798, when Malthus wrote, the world's population has increased by a factor of six, from 1 to 6 billion people. In just the last 150 years, population has quadrupled; and in the last fifty years alone, it has doubled, meaning that the world's population grew as much in those fifty years as in all of human history before.[5] Although demographers debate how many people the world can accommodate—and hence whether we face a problem of *over*population[6]—population growth has clearly been a significant cause of environmental degradation, at least at the local level, since time immemorial.[7] Today, population growth continues to contribute to a variety of environmental problems. In Africa, for example, it drives the cutting of trees for fuelwood, as well as the conversion of elephant habitat to cropland.

If the number of people has skyrocketed in the past two centuries, the amount they consume has risen even faster—and, in contrast to population growth, the end is nowhere in sight. Whereas population has grown fourfold since 1900, global per capita income has increased by a factor of five.[8] Over the past twenty years alone, global energy use has increased by 40 percent, global meat consumption by 70 percent, global auto production by 45 percent, and global paper use by 90 percent.[9] As Bill McKibbin writes, the effect of this increased consumption has been transformative:

> In hunter-gatherer times, [the amount of energy human beings use each day] was about 2,500 calories, all of it food. That is the daily energy intake of a common dolphin. A modern human being uses 31,000 calories a day, most of it in the form of fossil fuel. That is the intake of a pilot whale. And the average American uses six times that—as much as a sperm whale. We have become, in other words, different from the people we used to be.... We've ... gotten bigger. We appear to be the same species, with stomachs of the same size, but we aren't.[10]

In the years to come, we are likely to get bigger still. Despite the huge growth in consumption over the past century, many people around the world remain desperately poor. As Gus Speth notes, "Close to half the world's people live on less than two dollars per day. They both need and deserve something better."[11] Providing them with an adequate standard of living will require even higher global levels of consumption. In 1987, the Brundtland Commission estimated that bringing people living in the Third World up to First World standards would require a sevenfold increase in manufacturing and a fivefold increase in energy use.[12] At current rates of pollution, this would have enormous environmental consequences. If China were to increase its energy use per capita to American levels, then, all other things being equal, this alone would more than double global emissions of carbon dioxide.[13] As one commentator graphically puts it, "if the Chinese try to eat as much meat and eggs and drive as many cars (per capita) as the Americans now do, the biosphere will fry."[14]

Finally, as technology's capabilities have grown, its potential for environmental destruction has increased. Consider, for example, depletion of the stratospheric ozone layer, a problem that originated in 1928 with the invention of chlorofluorocarbons (CFCs). When they first appeared,

CFCs were viewed as wonder chemicals. They are stable, non-flammable, and non-toxic, with an astonishing range of uses as refrigerants, foams, solvents, and propellants. However, as scientists belatedly realized in the 1970s, their stability is not only a strength but a danger. Because CFCs are so stable, they persist in the atmosphere, eventually migrating to the stratosphere where they break down ozone in a catalytic reaction. When the ozone depletion problem catapulted into public prominence in the 1980s, it demonstrated, for the first time, that human technology has the capacity to bring about global change, not just localized impacts.

The role of technology in causing the ozone depletion problem is not an isolated example. Industrialization has led to the development of many technologies with the potential to inflict widespread, long-term and, in some cases, irreversible harm. The persistent organic pollutants (POPs) problem, for example, is essentially technological in origin, resulting from the development of new chemicals such as DDT and dioxin. These chemicals bioaccumulate in the food chain, causing cancer, reproductive disorders, and disruption of the immune system. Global warming is also, in part, a technological problem, resulting from the fossil fuel technologies that produce greenhouse gas emissions—in particular, coal-fired power plants to generate electricity and the internal combustion engine to power cars.[15] Similarly, the acid rain problem resulted from the building of taller factory smokestacks in the first part of the twentieth century to alleviate local air pollution by spreading pollutants over a much wider area.

Indeed, technological developments have even contributed significantly to problems that are not usually seen as technological in nature, such as the overhunting of whales. At the beginning of the twentieth century, the whaling industry appeared to be dying, owing to the decimation of slower-moving whale species that could be hunted from rowboats.[16] What revived the industry were technological improvements such as the development of steam-powered boats (which allowed whalers to hunt faster species of whales), compressed air pumps (which allowed whalers to fill whale carcasses with air to prevent them from sinking), and factory ships (which could process whales more efficiently and operate further from shore).

What are the implications of the IPAT model? Depending on which variable in the equation we focus on, it has significantly different implications for environmental policy, especially for the issue of who bears responsibility for addressing environmental problems. If we see environmental problems as the result of "overpopulation," this focuses attention on the developing world, where most population growth is occurring. If we see the problem as one of increasing consumption, then this implicates rapidly growing economies such as China and India. But if we see environmental problems as resulting, not from growing consumption, but instead from "overconsumption"—that is, consumption beyond what is required to satisfy our basic human needs—then this shifts attention to Western industrialized countries, whose rates of consumption per capita dwarf those of developing countries.

Some proponents of the IPAT model extrapolate from current trends and foresee a looming environmental catastrophe. According to a recent estimate, humans already appropriate almost a quarter of the world's net primary productivity (NPP)—that is, the growth in biomass through photosynthesis.[17] If the world's economy quadruples again in size in the next half century, as it did in the last, then we may finally reach or even exceed the world's limits.[18]

Past trends do not necessarily indicate future directions, however. In recent years, rates of population growth have begun to ease. Since the 1960s, birth rates have been cut in half and, in industrialized countries, have fallen below replacement rates. Demographers now predict that global population will peak later this century at about 9 billion people and will then begin to decrease.[19]

Even if population and consumption were to continue to increase, leading to an increase in the overall scale of human activities, environmental degradation would not necessarily increase as well. The IPAT formula implies that increased population and consumption will cause more pollution only if we hold the other variable in the equation—technology—constant. This may not be a valid assumption, however. Technology may allow us to produce more with less. Ever since Malthus wrote about the population problem back in the early 1800s, environmental Cassandras have been prophesying disaster—most prominently in the 1970s, with the publication of *Limits to Growth* and the *Global 2000 Report*. But despite the tremendous growth in population and consumption since then, the world's environment has not collapsed—at least, not yet.[20] Indeed, according to some observers, the overall trends have been positive.[21] Although famines still occur, they are generally attributable to political rather than environmental failures.[22] Global grain production, for example, has tripled during the last fifty years, outpacing the rate of population growth and confounding those who predicted widespread famine. Similarly, resources have not run out. Although commodity prices have risen sharply since 2001, they are still lower, as of 2007, than they were a century ago.[23] So it not clear that the world's population is too high or that we are consuming too much.[24]

The stratospheric ozone problem is perhaps the poster child for the Promethean view that technology has the potential to solve many, if not most, environmental problems. Just as the ozone problem had a technological origin, it has also had a technological solution through the development of substitute chemicals and replacement technologies.[25] In principle, the same could be true of global warming—it could have a technological solution as well. Possibilities include the development of new nuclear power designs, cheap solar energy, hydrogen fuel cell cars to replace internal combustion engines, capture and sequestration of the carbon dioxide emitted from power plants, and perhaps even fertilization of the oceans with iron filings, which could increase the removal of carbon dioxide from the atmosphere by phytoplankton.

Moreover, even if a complete technological "fix" to global warming does not prove possible, technology could make a significant contribution. For example, nuclear power could replace coal- and gas-fired power plants, and more efficient cars and appliances could replace current models. If every country in the world produced the same fraction of its electricity from nuclear power as France does, then this alone would cut carbon dioxide emissions by almost a fifth.

Will technology necessarily provide an answer to environmental problems? Will improvements in agricultural productivity, for example, continue to outpace population growth? No one knows for sure.[26] Just as past population growth no longer serves as a good predictor of future growth, past increases in agricultural productivity may not be a reliable predictor either, since the factors that accounted for the past increases—improvements in crop strains, fertilizers, and irrigation—may not be sustainable in the future. As environmentalists are fond of noting, although the world's environment has not yet collapsed, the same is true of a pond half covered by lilies that double in extent every day. "It would be very easy to look at the pond . . . and conclude there is plenty of clear water," writes John Dryzek.[27] But, in fact, the pond is on the brink of collapse. The very next day, the lilies will fully cover it and the pond will begin to die. Or, to use a more graphic metaphor, "The driver of an accelerating car about to hit a brick wall might well say, 'so far, so good'—but that does not mean the wall is not there."[28]

Because the IPAT model merely sets forth a logical relationship, without exploring the positive or negative feedbacks between its three variables, it does not predict how a change in any one variable will affect the environment. Greater affluence might be associated with more destructive technologies, resulting in greater environmental deterioration. Or it might result in less environmental harm, if it leads to lower birth rates, greater environmental awareness, and technological progress. According to the Environmental Kuznets Curve, the first relationship predominates in the early stages of industrialization—increasing affluence is associated with increasing pollution—but is then counterbalanced in later stages of development, when a society becomes wealthy enough to invest in pollution abatement.[29] This principle has led some (including the Brundtland Commission) to claim that poverty, not affluence, is a major cause of environmental degradation.[30]

In short, the IPAT model provides only limited policy guidance. It does not give priority to any of its three causal variables, indicate which is most susceptible to human influence, or predict future trends. Hence, it does not provide a basis for choosing among competing policy approaches. One of its originators, Paul Ehrlich, is famous for stressing the necessity of population control and the existence of physical limits to Earth's carrying capacity, which cannot be overcome by technology.[31] In the past, some environmentalists have even advocated mandatory controls on population, like those adopted by China in the 1970s, as necessary to save the planet.[32] The IPAT model is also consistent with the diametrically opposite view of so-called Cornucopians, who stress the potential for technological improvements, arguing that human ingenuity is the "ultimate resource" that makes possible limitless growth.[33] The IPAT model can also embrace the perspective of radical ecologists, who argue that the problem is overconsumption and that we must undergo a quasi-religious conversion to a simpler lifestyle.[34]

The IPAT model is valuable, not so much for its specific policy guidance, but rather as a reminder that environmental problems are influenced not only by micropolicies—government subsidies for renewable energy, for example—but also by macrotrends in population, consumption, and technology. Even small changes in these variables can have significant long-term effects. In identifying scenarios of how greenhouse gas emissions might grow over the next century, the Intergovernmental Panel on Climate Change (IPCC) found that the variance between different "families" of emission scenarios—with different assumptions about population, consumption, and technology—was significantly greater than the variance attributable to specific climate change policies such as a carbon tax or energy efficiency standards.[35] In the long run, reducing the rate of population or consumption growth even a little might prove a bigger boon to the environment than adopting specific policies to reduce pollution, which usually receive the most attention.

Behavioral Approaches

The IPAT model sees population, consumption, and technology as the driving forces of environmental change. A quite different way of conceptualizing environmental problems is in behavioral terms. In this view, population, consumption, and technology become outcomes of behavioral factors rather than root causes. Why do people have children above the replacement rate, for example, causing population to increase? Why do they consume more and more? Why do they use certain technologies rather than others? These are the types of questions a behavioral approach seeks to answer.

Behavioral accounts are a useful supplement to scientific explanations of environmental problems. Scientists have done much to illuminate the mechanisms of environmental degradation—how sulfur dioxide emissions cause acid rain, for example, or how habitat loss causes species to become extinct. "They can pinpoint with amazing detail the sources of the carbon in the tailpipes and smokestacks of the industrialized, automobilized societies. But," as Donald Worster observes,

> having done all that, the scientists still cannot tell us *why* we have those societies, or where they came from, or what the moral forces are that made them. They cannot explain why cattle ranchers are cutting down and burning the Brazilian rain forest, or why the Brazilian government has been ineffective in stopping them. They cannot explain why we humans will push tens of millions of species toward extinction over the next twenty years, or why that prospect of ecological holocaust still seems irrelevant to most of the world's leaders.[36]

These questions require an understanding not of science, but of fields such as economics, psychology, political science, and ethics.

Consider, again, the problem of global warming. At one level, global warming is a technological problem, but, at another, it is behavioral. Energy production is driven by demand for heating, lighting, and refrigeration, together with all of the consumer goods produced using electricity. Transportation emissions result from reliance on cars rather than other means of transportation and, in the United States, from consumers' preference (until recently) for gas-guzzling models such as SUVs. These patterns of behavior are not immutable; they have causes, which we can try to influence. In different parts of the world, rates of energy use vary dramatically, as do the number of miles driven per person.[37] Even among Western industrialized countries, with roughly the same level of wealth, per capita emissions of carbon dioxide vary by a factor of more than two.

Thus, although from a technological standpoint, the solution to the climate change problem may appear relatively straightforward, the matter is not so simple. Technologies currently exist that could go a long way toward reducing greenhouse gas emissions—high-efficiency appliances and construction designs, nuclear power, and so forth. If people simply adopted these technologies, global warming could be solved. But people do not automatically adopt the "best" available technologies, even though, in some cases, this might actually save them money, given the projected efficiency gains. If we hope to influence behavior more effectively, we need to understand the barriers to change, including factors such as inertia, consumer tastes, and market failures.

Economic Perspectives

Most environmental damage does not result from an affirmative intent to cause harm.[38] Rather, it is the product of ordinary, everyday activities such as driving cars, using electricity, heating homes, and manufacturing and disposing of consumer products.

How might we try to influence this behavior? Economics gives us one possible answer: by changing people's incentives. According to economic theory, humans are rational utility maximizers; they seek to maximize the satisfaction of their preferences. If we wish to change people's behavior, we need to change their incentive structure by giving them an interest in engaging in environmentally sound behavior.

Consider the climate change problem again. In the absence of governmental regulation, neither producers nor consumers bear any cost for emitting greenhouse gases, so they have no incentive to reduce their emissions by switching to cleaner fuels, consuming less, or using more efficient products. From the economic standpoint, the solution is to increase the price of emitting activities (for example, through a tax on gasoline and on electricity generated from coal-fired power plants) so that the prices of gasoline and electricity reflect the full environmental, economic, and health costs of climate change. This would not only reduce consumption; it would also help drive the development of new technologies (such as hydrogen fuel cells) as well as the diffusion and adoption of existing ones.

We ordinarily rely on competitive markets to set prices and to allocate resources to their most efficient uses. Producers have an incentive to conserve their resources and so will use resources only to the extent that the marginal benefit exceeds the marginal cost. The invisible hand of the market guides individuals, each pursuing his or her own self-interest, to produce the maximum benefit for all; that is perhaps the central insight of classical economics.

From this perspective, the diagnosis of environmental problems is plain: the existence of an environmental problem implies a market failure of one kind or another, a failure to include environmental costs in prices.[39] The task of environmental policy is therefore to identify these market failures and to find possible solutions.

Consider a simple example—an island inhabited by a single person, Roberta Crusoe. In this setting, environmental problems should not arise. The island castaway, rationally pursuing her self-interest, should undertake the optimal level of environmental protection, weighing all of the costs and benefits. Just as animals do not foul their own nest, Crusoe should not, metaphorically speaking, foul her own island.

In saying that environmental problems should not develop on Crusoe's island, an initial caveat is in order: we are considering the matter solely from Crusoe's perspectives; we are accepting her valuation of the costs and benefits of different courses of action, her view as to whether, say, killing a rare species or destroying a coral reef is problematic. Pollution and even litter may occur. But as long as Crusoe considers that the costs of reducing the pollution would outweigh the benefits, then, from an economic perspective, the pollution or litter does not represent an environmental problem. There is nothing further that she should do.[40]

In this simplified setting, how might environmental problems arise? One possibility is that Crusoe lacks important information about the effects of her actions and therefore cannot accurately assess their pros and cons. She may use CFCs as a coolant without knowing that they tend to deplete the ozone layer; or she may use DDT as a pesticide without knowing that it can harm wildlife. As we shall see in Chapter 4, a variety of environmental measures aim to provide actors with information, so that they can rationally weigh the costs and benefits of their actions.

Crusoe also may not be fully rational (Who among us is?). She may succumb to temptation and eat pineapples or coconuts, for example, at an unsustainable rate. An economist might simply say that she is revealing a high discount rate with respect to the future; she prefers present pleasures to future ones.[41] But then the hypothesis of rationality becomes essentially tautological. A person who smokes cigarettes and gets cancer at an early age, or who engages in binge eating, is simply revealing his or her preferences, not behaving irrationally.[42]

Although lack of knowledge and irrational behavior can be important, economists argue that environmental problems are primarily the result of "externalities"—that is, costs that an actor does not bear herself but instead fall on others, which are conveyed outside the market and hence do not have a price. If garbage that Roberta Crusoe throws into the water is carried by an ocean current to a neighboring island, occupied by the Robinsons, Crusoe might be inclined to choose this method of waste disposal because, from her perspective, it is free. The environmental costs are borne by others and do not factor into her cost-benefit calculus. Because her private costs do not reflect the social costs of disposal, she has no economic incentive to reduce her production of wastes or to consider other methods of disposal that might produce less environmental harm.

Many environmental problems can be understood as externalities, including emitting sulfur dioxide from power plants, dumping hazardous wastes into the ocean, and discharging pollutants into rivers. In all of these cases, what one person—or state—does affects others. Unless these effects are priced, actors have no incentive to take them into account and the market cannot ensure that resources are used efficiently. In upstream–downstream situations, such as Crusoe's pollution of the Robinsons' island, the externality flows in one direction and affects only a small number of actors; it is "unidirectional" and "private." In contrast, emissions of greenhouse gases, which affect the global climate, are an example of a "public externality."

Environmental externalities result from the interconnectedness of life. Historically, externalities were produced primarily by physical interconnections, as in the Crusoe example, where ocean currents physically transport garbage from one island to another. Transboundary externalities between neighboring states stimulated some of the earliest developments in international environmental law, including the *Trail Smelter* arbitration, which concerned air pollution from a Canadian smelter that blew into the State of Washington, causing damage there.[43]

Today, the problem of transboundary externalities can have a much wider geographic scope, owing in part to more powerful technologies that disperse pollutants more widely and in part to improved scientific understanding of the extent of physical transport. In the 1960s, Swedish scientists began to recognize that sulfur dioxide emissions in other parts of Europe were causing the acidification of lakes in Scandinavia. This problem is now addressed by the 1979 Long-Range Transboundary Air Pollution Convention and its many protocols. More recent evidence suggests that air pollution originating in East Asia reaches the United States and, hence, that transboundary externalities can occur at the global scale, not just the local or regional level.[44]

As globalization progresses and the economies of different countries become more intertwined, these economic interconnections can also produce what, in a broad sense, might be considered externalities. Weak environmental standards in one country, for example, may put pressure on other countries to lower their labor standards in order to compete, resulting in a race to the bottom. Trade can also produce externalities more directly, as the spread of invasive species in ballast water and cargo containers illustrates. Again, because the potential harms are felt elsewhere, shippers lack adequate incentives to take action on their own against invasive species; they will do so only to the extent that the importing state is able to impose effective regulations.

The threat to wildlife posed by international trade illustrates another consequence of economic integration. In this case, demand for wildlife products by importing states produces an environmental harm in the range states, where species may become endangered or even extinct as a result of overhunting or overharvesting. Just as a country may not be able to protect its environment against physical threats from other countries—it may not be able to protect its lakes, for example, from becoming acidified owing to air pollution originating outside its borders—it may not be able to protect its resources against economic threats arising elsewhere.

Globalization has shrunk the world not only from an economic standpoint, but from a psychological one as well. As we saw in Chapter 1, what happens in one country is increasingly of interest to people in other countries, even when they suffer no physical or economic effects. The mere existence of a resource provides people elsewhere with what economists call non-use values. That is why the Taliban's destruction of the giant Buddhas at Bamiyan provoked intense international concern. Similarly, the extinction of a butterfly species on Crusoe's island—even if of no value to her—might be of concern to other people. At least in part, international concern about the destruction of the Amazonian rain forest and the possible extinction of the African elephant reflect these "psychological" externalities.[45] Cutting the rain forest or killing species imposes costs on others by diminishing their non-use values, which do not enter into the cost-benefit calculus of those engaged in the destructive activity.

The existence of externalities may suggest the need for government regulation because actors have no incentive to minimize the costs of their behavior unless they bear those costs themselves—that is, unless the costs are internalized. As the economist Ronald Coase demonstrated, however, government regulation is not the only way to overcome the problem of externalities.[46] If bargaining is possible, the market may be able to do so on its own.

Consider, again, the garbage that Crusoe dumps into the ocean, whose environmental effects are felt downstream on the neighboring island inhabited by the Robinsons. Although Crusoe has no incentive to stop dumping, the Robinsons have an incentive to pay Crusoe to stop doing so. This means that a negotiated solution may be possible. For example, if the garbage causes $10 of damage per ton, but could be cleaned up by Crusoe for $5 per ton, then the Robinsons should be willing to pay Crusoe between $5 and $10 per ton not to dump her garbage. A result requiring Robinson to pay Crusoe to stop polluting may not seem fair. But it leaves everyone better off and hence, from an economic standpoint, is what economists call Pareto superior.[47] So externalities do not in themselves preclude the possibility that the market will achieve an efficient solution. Efficient outcomes can still be achieved through negotiations among the parties. This is one result of the Coase Theorem, for which Coase is justly celebrated.[48]

According to Coase, market failures derive not from externalities themselves, but from the barriers to negotiated solutions that economists refer to as transaction costs. If it is expensive for the Robinsons to discover the source of the garbage washing up on their shore, or to establish communications with Crusoe, then successful bargaining will not be possible. The market would fail to protect the environment because high transaction costs keep the parties from reaching agreement on a collectively rational outcome to reduce pollution.

What types of factors raise transaction costs and thereby preclude successful negotiations? For one, the greater the distance between an action and its effects, the higher the "search costs" to locate a negotiating partner. Similarly, the more difficult it is for the Robinsons to monitor whether Crusoe is upholding her end of the bargain, the higher the policing and enforcement costs.

Most importantly, the greater the number of parties involved, the higher the bargaining costs and the greater the potential for strategic behavior and free riding. When externalities involve just two actors, such as Crusoe and Robinson, bargaining costs typically are low and strategic behavior is easier to address. But as the number of actors involved increases, this complicates the negotiations and makes free riding more difficult to deter. That is why public externalities, such as pollution of the high seas or global warming, tend to be more difficult to solve than private externalities, such as pollution in border areas.[49]

The Crusoe example is comparatively simple because the environmental resources are, in essence, privately owned. Crusoe and the Robinsons each have an interest in managing their own island so as to maximize its value. Assuming that the resources on their islands are scarce, they have an incentive to use those resources wisely because the resources are, in essence, theirs: if they misuse or waste a resource, they will bear the consequences. Crusoe will reduce her pollution as long as the benefits from reduction (including any side payments the Robinsons make to Crusoe) outweigh the costs. And the Robinsons should be willing to pay Crusoe to stop polluting their island as long as the environmental benefits outweigh the costs.

These incentives to use resources wisely tend to disappear if property is not privately owned. In a famous essay, Garrett Hardin described what he called the tragedy of the commons:

> Picture a pasture open to all. It is to be expected that each herdsman will try to keep as many cattle as possible on the commons. . . . As a rational being, each herdsman seeks to maximize his gain. Explicitly or implicitly, more or less consciously, he asks, "What is the utility *to me* of adding one more animal to my herd?" This utility has one negative and one positive component.
>
> 1) The positive component is a function of the increment of one animal. Since the herdsman receives all the proceeds from the sale of the additional animal, the positive utility is nearly +1.
>
> 2) The negative component is a function of the additional overgrazing created by one more animal. Since, however, the effects of overgrazing are shared by all the herdsmen, the negative utility for any particular decision-making herdsman is only a fraction of –1.
>
> Adding together the component partial utilities, the rational herdsman concludes that the only sensible course for him to pursue is to add another animal to his herd. And another; and another. . . . But this is the conclusion reached by each and every rational herdsman sharing a commons. Therein is the tragedy. Each man is locked into a system that compels him to increase his herd without limit—in a world that is limited. Ruin is the destination toward which all men rush, each pursuing his own best interest in a society that believes in the freedom of the commons. Freedom in a commons brings ruin to all.[50]

In the tragedy of the commons, individually rational behavior—adding another cow to the commons—produces a collectively irrational result. The reason is simple: because the commons is owned by none and open to all, externalities are endemic. Herdsmen keep putting more cows on the commons because they receive all of the benefit from the additional cows but bear only a fraction of the costs.

As historical description, the tragedy of the commons has been widely criticized. What leads to the tragedy in Hardin's story is not simply that the land is held in common, but that it is subject to an open access regime in which each individual herdsman is free to add as many cows as he or she chooses. In practice, however, in the kind of small, close-knit communities described in Hardin's parable, the users of commons have tended to develop informal regulatory regimes that limit uses, thereby preventing the tragedy from unfolding.[51]

But even if historically inaccurate, the tragedy of the commons provides an accurate diagnosis of many current global environmental problems, which, unlike traditional pastures, involve open-access resources. High seas fisheries are a classic example. Under the law of the sea, fishing is considered a high seas freedom, which customarily was subject to few constraints, other than the general duty to have due regard to the interests of other states.[52] Since each individual user receives all of the benefits from the fish it catches, but shares the costs with other users (including lower rates of reproduction and fewer fish), it has an incentive to take as many fish as possible. From the perspective of the individual fisherman, taking fewer fish does not make any sense, as long as other fishermen continue to fish without restriction. The result is that fish stocks decline, fishermen need to expend greater and greater effort to catch fewer and fewer fish, and eventually the fishery is exhausted altogether.[53]

Problems such as stratospheric ozone depletion and global warming can also be understood as tragedies of the commons, except, unlike fisheries, they involve putting bad things into the commons (CFCs and carbon dioxide) rather than taking good things out. Each individual country gets the benefits of the activities that release CFCs and carbon dioxide into the atmosphere (generating electricity, insulating buildings, and so forth) but bears only a small fraction of the costs to the global environment. So, from an individual perspective, states have no incentive to limit their use of the atmosphere, the oceans, or other global commons, even when the total costs of their actions outweigh the total benefits—that is, even when their behavior is collectively irrational.

What can be done to address the tragedy of the commons? In some cases, a commons can be privatized, as the enclosure movement in England in the seventeenth century demonstrated. The 1982 Law of the Sea Convention takes a somewhat analogous approach for coastal fisheries. It recognizes the right of coastal states to create an exclusive economic zone out to 200 miles from shore, within which they have exclusive jurisdiction over natural resources, including fisheries. By recognizing this right, which includes the power to exclude others, the Law of the Sea Convention gives coastal states an incentive to manage their fisheries effectively, so as to maximize the value of the fisheries over time.

Not all commons problems can be addressed through privatization, however. Some resources are incapable of subdivision. Consider, for example, the atmosphere. In certain respects, the atmosphere can be subdivided and "privatized": for example, the air space above each country can be considered part of its territory for the purpose of air travel. And geostationary orbits above Earth can be assigned to particular users for the purposes of launching satellites. In other respects, however, the atmosphere resists subdivision because it is affected by substances that mix on a global scale, such as CFCs and carbon dioxide.

These indivisible features of the atmosphere are examples of what economists refer to as public goods. "The defining characteristic of a public good," explain Robert and Nancy Dorfman, "is that no member of the community who wants its services can be excluded from them if they are available to any other member."[54] National defense is the classic example of a public good; it protects everyone in a country, whether or not they have contributed to its production. Other examples of public goods include lighthouses and public signs. Because producers of public goods cannot exclude others, they cannot charge users for the benefits derived from the public good. As a result, public goods tend to be undersupplied by the market. Even though they produce a social gain, private actors lack an incentive to supply them, since most of their benefits go to others.

In essence, public goods involve "positive" externalities: benefits transferred to others without any market price. As with any such transfer, the market does not operate to produce an efficient result. Because actors receive the benefits of public goods whether or not they contribute, they have an incentive to free ride on the efforts of others. As Todd Sandler asks, "Why pay for something that you are going to receive anyway?"[55]

Overcoming this tendency to free ride ordinarily requires some form of governmental compulsion—for example, mandatory taxation to ensure that everyone contributes to the provision of public goods. Free riding thus poses a particular problem at the international level, where regulation generally depends on consent rather than coercion, an issue to which we will return in Chapter 7.

Cultural and Ethical Perspectives

The economic perspective takes peoples' preferences as a given—the desire for sport utility vehicles, bigger homes, air conditioning, and all of the other accouterments of modern consumer society. Economics seeks to modify behavior, not by changing people's preferences, but rather by changing the incentive structure within which they operate, primarily through the manipulation of prices.[56] This approach of treating preferences as a given reflects a common tendency to accept without question the value of unending growth and ever greater consumption. For many, these values are so deeply ingrained that they seem part of the natural order and thus not a matter of choice. As the Once-ler put it in Dr. Seuss's environmental parable, *The Lorax,* "I meant no harm. I most truly did not. But I had to grow bigger. . . . So bigger I got."

Personal preferences are not necessarily fixed, however. They may have social and cultural causes that we can seek to influence. Nor does the desire for ever greater consumption necessarily reflect a fundamental feature of human nature, as some economists seem to believe.[57] Rather, it is partly a social construction that ethics and education might seek to change.

Our consumer habits, for example, are influenced by the efforts of producers to cultivate a culture of consumption.[58] As one retailing expert proclaimed, shortly after World War II:

> Our enormously productive economy demands that we make consumption our way of life, that we convert the buying and use of goods into rituals. . . . We need things consumed, burned up, worn out, replaced, and discarded at an ever increasing rate.[59]

Preferences about consumption and the environment may also have deeper cultural roots. Ever since the Romantics, critics of modern society have contrasted its materialist, technological orientation with a halcyon past in which humans lived in harmony with nature. In a controversial but influential essay, the historian Lynn White Jr. attributed the present ecological crisis to the Judeo-Christian worldview, which exalts science and technology over nature. "By destroying pagan animism," he wrote, "Christianity made it possible to exploit nature in a mood of indifference to the feelings of natural objects."[60]

The contrast between a rapacious West (as exemplified by the United States) and ecologically minded traditionalism is an oversimplification. On the one hand, recent historical evidence has cast doubt on the sustainability of indigenous cultures.[61] On the other, modern society has produced not only ozone depletion, acid rain, and species extinctions, but also Green parties, animal welfare groups, and environmental reforms.

But although the importance of culture relative to other factors is debatable, it would be difficult to dispute the fact that culture affects the way we live and the things we value. Taking it off the table, as economists typically do, by treating it as a given, means that we give up one of the potentially most powerful levers to effectuate environmental change.

Consider, for example, the role of advertising. In the process of shaping consumer preferences, advertising plays a key part. That, at least, is what companies presumably believe, given their expenditures of more than $350 billion on advertising in 2004.[62] So we could try to limit advertising for environmentally destructive products, much as we have already done for cigarettes.

Some believe that a solution to our environmental problems will ultimately require a fundamental change in values. Gus Speth, for example, argues that global environmental problems result from "pernicious habits of thought"—most importantly, the "undisputed primacy" given to economic growth (described by one historian as "easily the most important idea of the twentieth century").[63] In Speth's view, saving the Earth will require a "revolution in attitudes and values."[64] Similarly, Lynn White believes that the "the roots of our trouble are . . . largely religious" and that "the remedy must also be essentially religious, whether we call it that or not. We must rethink and refeel our nature and destiny."[65]

A religious conversion of the sort that White envisions is probably beyond the ken of international environmental law. But just as law played a role during the civil rights movement in delegitimizing racism, through decisions such as *Brown v. Board of Education,* law may have a role in changing people's environmental ethos through education and moral suasion, so that they choose more efficient appliances and cars, or rely more on bicycles and mass transit for transportation, or discover the virtues of a simpler, less consumption-oriented lifestyle.

A Placeholder for Politics

Thus far, we have been exploring environmental issues as technological, economic, or cultural and ethical problems. For our purposes, however, environmental issues are, above all, political problems. As we will explore in the next chapter, an issue such as climate change has many potential solutions: we could invest in new technologies, impose a tax on emissions of carbon dioxide, or require cars to be more fuel-efficient. The problem is to get these policies adopted and implemented, and this is primarily a political task.

At this stage, I simply wish to flag politics as an additional way of thinking about the causes of environmental problems. We will return to it in Chapters 6 and 7, after considering the potential policy responses to international environmental problems and the nature and role of environmental norms.

Recommended Reading

John S. Dryzek, *The Politics of the Earth: Environmental Discourses* (Oxford: Oxford University Press, 2d ed. 2005).

Paul Harrison, *The Third Revolution: Population, Environment and a Sustainable World* (London: Penguin, 1992).

A. J. McMichael, *Planetary Overload: Global Environmental Change and the Health of the Human Species* (Cambridge: Cambridge University Press, 1993).

Kevin T. Pickering and Lewis A. Owen, *An Introduction to Global Environmental Issues* (London: Routledge, 2d ed. 1997).

William L. Thomas Jr., ed., *Man's Role in Changing the Face of the Earth* (Chicago: University of Chicago Press, 1956).

World Commission on Environment and Development, *Our Common Future* (Oxford: Oxford University Press, 1987).

CHAPTER FOUR

Prescribing the Cure: Environmental Policy 101

> In effect, to follow, not to force the public inclination; to give a
> direction, a form, a technical dress, and a specific sanction, to the
> general sense of the community, is the true end of legislation.
>
> Edmund Burke, "Letter to the Sheriffs of Bristol"

ASSUME THAT YOU HAVE just been installed as the head of a
newly established International Environmental Organization
(IEO), with broad authority to address the world's environmental problems. How should you proceed?

In essence, the policy problem boils down to two issues:

- First, what are the ends of environmental policy? Which problems
  deserve our attention, and what should be our goals in addressing
  them?
- Second, what means should we use to achieve those ends? What
  are the best policy instruments—government-mandated controls,
  market-based instruments such as taxes or tradable allowances,
  technology programs, voluntary partnerships with industry, or
  some other approach?

The analytic tools described in this chapter could be applied to any
environmental problem, whether international or domestic. International
environmental problems are a subset of environmental problems more
generally. In examining the policy process, I will begin by taking the perspective of a rational decision maker—the head of the IEO—seeking to
develop the optimal environmental policy.[1] If one were in charge, what
should one do? In later chapters, I will consider how multiple actors,
each with his or her own interests and perspectives, complicate the situation. That is to say, I will introduce politics into the equation. Before

resigning ourselves to the art of the possible, however, it will be useful to consider the ideal, if only to provide a benchmark against which to evaluate our options. We begin, then, by examining environmental problems in *policy* rather than *political* terms.

What Are the Goals of Environmental Policy?

What is the goal of international environmental law? This apparently simple question is harder than it looks. Should environmental policy seek to protect the environment for its own sake or for the benefit of humans? Should it aim to prevent any damage from occurring (indeed, is this even possible?) or only significant damage—and if the latter, how should it define what damages are significant? Put another way, should it protect the environment at all costs or only to the extent that the environmental benefits exceed the economic costs? How should it value future harms and benefits as compared to present ones? And how should it value uncertain risks versus more definite ones?

Our answers to these questions have important implications for every facet of environmental policy. Consider the most basic issue: what environmental changes constitute *problems?* Would the disappearance, say, of the malaria mosquito be cause for celebration or sorrow? Opinions differ, depending on the value one places on biological diversity. Some see the extinction of any species as a loss, even those dangerous to humans. Others would welcome the elimination of the malaria mosquito, which is a leading cause of infant mortality worldwide and, according to one estimate, costs Africa more than $12 billion a year in lost growth.[2] Indeed, some have even suggested that if "specicide" were to become feasible (for example, through genetic engineering), the malaria mosquito would be the ideal candidate.[3] This perspective may perhaps show that we have not completely given up the view expressed by Reverend Hickeringill in the eighteenth century, that our goal should be to get rid of "noisome and offensive" animals "with as speedy a riddance and despatch" as possible.[4]

The relative priority we give to different issues also raises issues of environmental values. Global warming, for example, may cause long-term, irreversible damage for coastal communities, agriculture, human health, and biological diversity. But lack of access to safe drinking water kills more than a million people per year right now. How should we assess the relative importance of these problems? Given limited resources, which deserves our attention? That depends on our views about the larger objectives of international environmental law.

Finally, once an environmental problem has been identified and put on the policy agenda, what should be our goal in addressing it? What should be the objective, say, of international climate change policy? Should it seek to prevent global warming altogether, or only warming above some "dangerous" limit? If we could prevent climate change by injecting dust into the upper atmosphere to block incoming sunlight, or by putting mirrors into space to reflect it away, would these represent "solutions"? Or would it be unethical, in some way, to purposefully remake nature? What we consider a solution to an environmental problem depends on how we define the problem, which in turn depends on our values.

The role of values in environmental decision making is nicely illustrated by a cartoon I once saw showing a logger with a chainsaw looking at a tree labeled "the very last tree," while thinking "the very last chair." The contrasting characterizations reflect the difference between valuing nature as an end in itself and as useful for humankind. The person who sees trees as wilderness finds the destruction of old-growth forest problematic; the person who sees them only as proto-chairs does not, as long as sufficient trees remain.

Running through much of the debate about international environmental policy are two different conceptions of the aims that we should pursue—what Daniel Farber facetiously calls the "tree hugger" and the "bean counter" approaches.[5] Tree huggers define the goal of environmental policies in absolutist terms: preventing pollution, preserving species, and so forth. Bean counters see the world in terms of trade-offs and seek to balance costs and benefits to achieve the optimal outcome. Tree huggers tend to reflect "moral outrage," bean counters "cool analysis."[6]

Absolutist Approaches

From an absolutist perspective, the goal of environmental policy should be to prevent environmental harm. Consider, for example, the acid rain problem. Acid rain emerged as an international issue in the 1970s, first in Europe and then in North America. It is caused by emissions of sulfur dioxide (SO_2) and nitrous oxides (NO_x) from a wide variety of sources, including power plants, automobiles, and industrial facilities such as smelters. These emissions constitute "pollution" in the strict sense of the term—that is, substances introduced by humans into the environment with harmful effects, in particular for forests and lakes.[7]

From a tree hugger perspective, our goal in addressing acid rain should be to reduce emissions of SO_2 and NO_x to the level at which no harm is caused—if such a threshold exists—or, if not, to eliminate emissions altogether.[8] The 1994 Sulfur Protocol to the Long-Range Transboundary Air Pollution Convention (LRTAP) moved in this direction through its adoption of a "critical loads" approach, which seeks to determine the maximum levels of acid deposition that will not cause significant environmental damage and then to reduce emissions so as not to exceed these critical loads.[9]

Of course, trying to eliminate pollution altogether comes at a very high cost, potentially. The emissions of SO_2 and NO_x that result in acid rain are produced by a host of activities central to modern industrial society, such as electricity generation, transportation, and industrial production. Until viable substitutes are developed, eliminating emissions (or even reducing them drastically) could have dire economic effects. In recognition of this fact, the 1994 Sulfur Protocol did not try to close the gap entirely between current emissions and the lower levels necessary not to exceed critical loads; instead, it set a goal of achieving gap closure of only 80 percent.[10]

These same economic considerations apply to other environmental problems as well. Stopping anthropogenic climate change, conserving biological diversity, eliminating marine pollution, and phasing out the use of dangerous pesticides and chemicals would all involve significant costs, particularly since the marginal costs of abatement typically escalate as pollution is progressively reduced. To what extent are we willing to incur these costs in order to solve a particular environmental problem?

A dyed-in-the-wool tree hugger might respond by saying, in essence, "damn the expenses, full speed ahead." This was the approach initially taken by the U.S. Endangered Species Act (ESA). In *Tennessee Valley Authority v. Hill,* the Supreme Court ruled that the ESA required that the federal government take action to prevent the extinction of species regardless of the cost.[11] Similarly, the Clean Water Act attempted to eliminate all water pollution by 1985, and the Delaney Clause continues to require the prohibition of any food additive that has been shown to cause cancer, regardless of the cost of doing so and no matter how remote the cancer risk. Polling since the early 1980s indicates that a majority of Americans consistently claim to support the view that "protecting the environment is so important that requirements and standards cannot be too high, and continuing environmental improvements must be made regardless of cost."[12]

This absolutist attitude can be justified in various ways. One rationale is to frame the environmental debate in terms of rights.[13] If one sees environmental protection as a right and not simply as a policy preference—a right, for example, to a clean environment—then this implies that people (or nature itself, if the rights in question are ecological rather than human rights) should be able to vindicate these rights regardless of the costs. In 1968, Senator Gaylord Nelson even proposed a constitutional amendment guaranteeing the "inalienable right to a decent environment."[14] Although this provision was never adopted, several states and countries have adopted similar provisions,[15] and a number of human rights cases have found that environmental damage can violate an individual's human rights.[16]

The rights-based approach reflects an attempt to privilege environmental goals—to take them out of the normal hurly-burly of politics and give them a higher status. The more one venerates nature and casts environmental protection as an ethical imperative, the more appropriate this attitude may seem. If one takes the view expressed by Aldo Leopold, that a "thing is right when it tends to preserve the integrity, stability, and beauty of the biotic community [and] . . . wrong when it tends otherwise,"[17] then this might seem to suggest that a consideration of economic costs—or anything else for that matter, other than what is good for the environment—is not just inappropriate but almost immoral.[18]

Uncertainty provides a second basic rationale for an absolutist approach. To the extent that environmental risks are uncertain, we cannot weigh their costs and benefits with any confidence, nor can we be certain that any particular level of activity is "safe." To ensure safety, we must ban risky activities altogether. In essence, this is the rationale for the moratorium on commercial whaling, described in Chapter 1: since we cannot be certain that any level is safe, we must stop commercial whaling completely.

The implications of this precautionary perspective go further than the rights-based approach because it does not simply aim to eliminate environmental harms, but environmental risks. Consider, for example, the critical loads approach in the 1994 Sulfur Protocol and its analogue in water pollution policy, assimilative capacity. These standards require a great deal of information about the thresholds below which emissions or discharges are safe. Given the uncertainties in our scientific understanding, however, information of this kind may not be reliable. On this basis, those who stress the problem of uncertainty argue that we should shift away from an assimilative capacity approach to a "best available technology" standard. International environmental law addresses this problem of uncertainty through the precautionary principle, which, in its strongest form, says, "if in doubt, don't."[19]

The problem with both the rights-based and the precautionary versions of absolutism is that public policy inevitably involves trade-offs.

Reducing environmental harm is important, but it is not the only factor in the equation; we must also consider the economic and social costs of doing so. Similarly, "[c]aution should be high on everyone's agenda," as Christopher Stone notes,[20] but this does not mean it should be the only objective. Nor, in any event, is it achievable, since reducing one risk often increases another. Setting environmental goals in absolutist terms prevents one from even considering these trade-offs, much less addressing them in a systematic way.

Trade-offs exist not only between environmental protection and economic well-being, but between the environment and other values such as human health. On the one hand, malaria infects an estimated 300 to 500 million people per year worldwide and kills an estimated 2 million people, mostly children. On the other hand, the most effective pesticide against the malaria mosquito, DDT (which helped Northern countries eliminate malaria in the 1950s) is now known to be a persistent organic pollutant that harms birds and fish. Since the publication of Rachel Carson's *Silent Spring* in 1962, DDT has become the symbol in the West of an insidious chemical killer. Should environmental policy ban DDT, even if this means more malaria? Or should it allow the limited use of DDT in order to save children's lives? However we come down on this question, we face a difficult trade-off.[21]

Balancing Approaches

Rather than viewing environmental policy in moral terms, economists—bean counters *par excellence*—take a consequentialist approach, arguing that the objective of environmental policy should be to maximize social welfare as a whole. This requires considering, in a systematic way, the costs as well as the benefits of environmental actions, including the compliance costs for the private sector, the administrative costs for government, and the indirect economic costs resulting from general equilibrium effects. In order to maximize social welfare in addressing acid rain, for example, we should reduce emissions of SO_2 and NO_x only insofar as the marginal benefits of a reduction (the environmental and health benefits resulting from less acid rain) exceed its marginal costs—that is, only insofar as the reductions are "efficient." This is how an economist would define the objective of environmental policy. Further reductions beyond this "optimal" level of pollution would not make sense, even if they provided environmental benefits, because their costs would exceed their benefits.[22]

Cost-benefit analysis requires us to be able to compare the costs and benefits of environmental policies systematically. We need a metric, for

---

Box 4.1. Costs and Benefits of Environmental Regulation

Costs

- *Direct compliance costs*—Environmental regulation typically imposes direct costs on the regulatory target. For example, a regulation might require companies to install new equipment or to hire additional personnel.
- *Opportunity costs*—By requiring resources to be used for one purpose, environmental policies preclude those resources from being used for other purposes. Establishing a protected area for elephants, for example, prevents land from being used for agricultural purposes.
- *Administrative costs*—Environmental policies may entail substantial monitoring and enforcement costs for government.
- *Indirect economic costs*—Changes in prices in one sector have effects on the rest of the economy, referred to by economists as "general equilibrium effects." If markets are operating efficiently, policy-induced price changes introduce inefficiencies that may cost more than the direct compliance costs of environmental regulation.

Benefits

- *Health benefits*—Better air or water quality may result in reduced medical expenses and fewer days of illness.
- *Direct economic benefits*—Protection of commercially exploited resources, such as trees or fisheries, provide economic benefits to those using the resources.
- *Ecosystem services*—Protection of resources such as wetlands provide indirect benefits in the form of ecosystem services—for example, water purification, flood control, protection against coastline erosion, and so forth. One study estimated the global value of seventeen ecosystem services at $16–54 trillion per year. (Robert Costanza et al., "The Value of the World's Ecosystem Services and the Natural Capital," *Nature* 387 (1997), pp. 253–260, at 259.)
- *Existence (non-use) value*—Regardless of whether a species or other resource provides any direct or indirect economic benefit, some people may value its continued existence.

example, to compare the economic costs of installing a scrubber or switching to cleaner coal with the environmental benefits of healthier forests or cleaner lakes. The standard economic tool for making such comparisons is prices. The prices people are willing to pay are assumed to reveal their preferences about how much they value different things. The problem, of course, is that many environmental resources, including clean air, clean water, and biological diversity, are not traded in the market and thus do not have a market price.[23]

A considerable amount of environmental economics is devoted to the problem of how to put a price on non-market goods. Economists have devised several tools to answer this question. "Contingent valuation" relies on surveys about what people say they would be willing to pay for environmental goods (or how much they would be willing to accept in return for agreeing to allow a resource to be degraded).[24] In contrast, "hedonic property pricing" attempts to examine empirically how changes in environmental factors (say, clean air or proximity to a hazardous waste site) affect property prices.[25]

Cost-benefit analysis has many weaknesses, which critics are fond of noting. To begin with, environmentalists argue that cost-benefit analysis is skewed against environmental regulation. On the one hand, it tends to downplay environmental benefits such as ecosystem services and aesthetic values, which may be omitted from cost-benefit analyses because they are difficult to value. On the other hand, it tends to overemphasize the costs of satisfying regulations, both because of its (over?) reliance on industry estimates and because many economists are professionally skeptical about the potential for efficiency gains that both improve the environment and reduce costs.[26]

A second objection to cost-benefit analysis relates to the problem of valuing the future. Cost-benefit analysis requires valuation not only of non-market goods, but also of future costs and benefits; it requires a methodology to compare costs and benefits across time. Most people would prefer to have a dollar now to a dollar ten years in the future, even leaving aside the effects of inflation. They would prefer to "get it while [they] can," as Janis Joplin cogently put it. The degree to which people value the present more than the future is measured by what economists refer to as the "discount rate."[27] If the discount rate is, say, 5 percent per year, then the "present value" of having a dollar a year from now is only 95 cents. As we look further into the future, the present value of future benefits declines steeply as the discount rate increases. With a 5 percent discount rate, the present value of a dollar ten years from now is only 61 cents; but if one discounts the future more steeply, say at 10 percent, then the present value of that same future dollar drops to only 39 cents.

Because most international environmental regulation involves incurring costs now to gain environmental benefits in the future, discounting plays a huge role in cost-benefit analyses. Depending on whether we apply a 5 or 10 percent discount rate, the amount we should be willing to spend today to gain a dollar's worth of environmental benefit in ten years' time varies from 61 to 39 cents. The further into the future we look, the bigger the effect of discount rates. At a 5 percent discount rate, a dollar's worth of environmental benefit received seventy-five years hence is worth only 3 cents now, but at a 10 percent discount rate, the present value of that same dollar of environmental benefit plummets to a tenth of a penny. Thus, for very long-term problems such as climate change, which have a century-plus time horizon, cost-benefit analysis is extremely sensitive to the choice of discount rate. Which discount rate we use—10 percent or 5 percent or 2 percent—is crucial in determining how much we should spend now to avert climate change damages far off in the future.[28]

The effective discount rate of private parties is revealed by examining the minimum rate of return they expect in their investment and spending decisions.[29] This "private discount rate" varies from place to place and from time to time, depending on the level of uncertainty about the future. In the United States and other Western industrialized countries, which enjoy considerable stability and where people, as a result, have a high degree of confidence about the future, the private discount rate is comparatively low—about 4 to 6 percent. In developing countries, which are less stable, much higher discount rates apply, in the range of 10 to 25 percent.[30]

Although private discount rates can be determined in a relatively objective manner, public discount rates are much more controversial. Should public policies discount the future, and, if so, to what degree? What is the appropriate "social" discount rate? Is the continued existence of whales 100 years from now really less valuable than their existence today, as discounting analysis would suggest? Is their continued existence 400 years from now significantly less valuable than 300 years from now? Are future generations not entitled to equal consideration as our own? If so, how is this consistent with discounting? Ultimately, the answers to these questions are ethical rather than economic in nature.

On a more fundamental level, some critics of cost-benefit analysis challenge the view that people's self-interested preferences as consumers are equivalent to their views as citizens about public policy.[31] An individual, as a consumer, might not be willing to pay 50 cents more per gallon of gasoline to improve air quality; but the same individual, in her capacity as a publicly minded citizen, might support government regulations with similar costs. Indeed, some argue that the entire exercise of cost-benefit analysis is misguided because it considers only human preferences, rather than the value of the environment as an end in itself, and attempts to put a price on resources that are, in some sense, priceless.[32]

Although these objections to cost-benefit analysis require careful consideration, none to my mind is decisive. Most relate to the way that cost-benefit analysis is practiced, rather than to the approach itself, which can be more flexible than its critics contend. Valuation techniques, for example, can factor in people's views as citizens rather than consumers, as well as their views about the existence value of a resource (that is, the value they place simply on its existence), not just its instrumental value (that is, its value because of the benefit it provides to humans).[33] Moreover, if private discount rates seem too high, we can apply a lower social discount rate for environmental protection.

The bigger problem with cost-benefit analysis is practical—namely, that, in many cases, estimates of how people value non-market goods are simply not reliable. This can cut both ways, of course; it can lead to over- as well as undervaluation of environmental resources. It is easy to say, in a survey, that one would be willing to pay $1,000 to protect a species, but whether one would do so in practice, with a limited budget, is a different question.

Moreover, with respect to long-term problems such as climate change, we face tremendous scientific and economic uncertainties. How much global warming will occur over the next 50 to 100 years, and what will be its impacts? How much will technology improve over the same time horizon? What will be the cost of solar power 100 years hence, or carbon sequestration, or some other technology that we have not yet even discovered? Given these uncertainties—not to mention the sensitivity of long-term cost estimates to the choice of a social discount rate—quantitative cost-benefit assessments seem of only limited use in deciding what we should do now to address a long-term problem such as climate change. In such cases, cost-benefit analysis is likely to give a false sense of precision and objectivity.[34] Niels Bohr once reputedly observed, "Never express yourself more clearly than you are able to think."[35] A similar thing might be said of cost-benefit analysis: never calculate more clearly than you know.

But even though, in practice, quantitative cost-benefit analysis may rarely be feasible, this does not relieve us of the need to think about both costs and benefits; it just means that we should do so in a more qualitative manner. As Benjamin Franklin wrote in a letter to Joseph Priestly, explaining his process of decision making:

[T]ho' the Weight of Reasons [pro and con] cannot be taken with the Precision of Algebraic Quantities, yet when each is thus considered separately and comparatively, and the whole lies before me, I think I can judge better, and am less likely to make a rash Step; and in fact I have found great Advantage from this kind of Equation, in what might be called *Moral* or *Prudential Algebra*.[36]

Whether we like it or not, environmental policies almost always involve both pros and cons. The only question is whether we consider these trade-offs explicitly—as Franklin suggested—or keep them hidden, allowing very different approaches to be taken in different regulatory contexts.[37]

So the bottom line is this: attempts to balance costs and benefits may be imperfect and imprecise. Ultimately, the choice of regulatory goals is not fully determined by objective, "cool" analysis; it involves value choices. However, decisions about whether something is an environmental problem and, if so, what to do about it, should be informed by a systematic examination of the costs and benefits of inaction versus action. This "prudential algebra" introduces a useful discipline to policy analysis. Without it, we are more likely to have a regulatory mishmash, difficult to defend on any rational basis, involving large expenditures of time and effort on relatively minor problems and smaller expenditures on more significant ones.

Other Policy Desiderata

Assume that we have agreed on an environmental goal for a given issue area, whether on the basis of a careful cost-benefit analysis or, as is more common, of some political compromise. Say, for example, we have decided to reduce consumption of ozone-depleting substances by 50 percent in order to protect the stratospheric ozone layer or to reduce emissions of carbon dioxide by 20 percent to combat climate change. The next task is to choose the means that we will use to achieve this end. In evaluating the various options, at least three policy desiderata are relevant: environmental effectiveness, cost-effectiveness, and equity.

Environmental Effectiveness

The starting point of any assessment of policy options is to consider how well a particular approach achieves its environmental goal. This much goes without saying, but answering this question is complicated. An environmental measure—say, an oil discharge standard for tankers aimed at limiting coastal oil pollution—might, on its face, appear sufficient to achieve its goal. However, what is the likelihood that tankers will actually comply with this requirement? This may depend, in part, on how easy it is to monitor and enforce the discharge standard. And will the requirement merely displace pollution from one place to another? Will it have "leakage"?

In some cases an environmental measure might have other environmental benefits (or harms) that should be taken into account in considering its environmental effectiveness. A renewable portfolio standard (requiring utilities to produce a certain amount of electricity from renewable sources) might be chosen to address the problem of acid rain, for example. But unlike other possible regulatory approaches, such as a requirement to install scrubbers, the renewable standard would have the added benefit of helping to address the climate change problem.

Different approaches might also differ in the degree to which they help induce technological advances or change public attitudes and awareness. A policy instrument that tends to lock in a particular technology may be less environmentally effective, in the long run, than an instrument that provides incentives for ongoing technological innovation, such as an emissions trading system. In assessing the issue of environmental effectiveness, we must therefore consider not only the immediate requirements of a proposed policy measure, but also issues of implementation, leakage, co-benefits, technological change, and public awareness.

Cost-Effectiveness

However we go about establishing our environmental goals—whether on the basis of cost-benefit analysis or exclusively environmental considerations—most people would agree that we should seek to achieve those goals at the lowest cost possible. We want to get the most bang for our buck, so to speak. In general, a policy is cost-effective if it equalizes the marginal cost of compliance across time and place. Whenever pollution could be reduced more cheaply in the future than now, or by one country rather than another, then the same level of environmental result could be achieved at a lower cost by shifting some of the pollution reductions into the future or to the other country with the lower abatement costs.

Because the terms are similar, it is easy to confuse cost-benefit and cost-effectiveness analysis. The difference is that cost-benefit analysis encompasses the goals of environmental policy, whereas cost-effectiveness analysis considers only the means. In essence, cost-effectiveness is a subpart of cost-benefit analysis. Environmentalists generally find cost-effectiveness less objectionable than cost-benefit analysis because it does not require comparing economic costs and environmental benefits; it simply requires comparing the economic and administrative costs of one policy option versus another.

Equity

Another important consideration in evaluating environmental policies is whether they entail a fair distribution of costs and benefits. This issue is important for both normative and practical reasons. From a normative standpoint, equity is a policy desideratum in its own right. In addition, from a practical standpoint, if a policy is not perceived as equitable, then it is less likely to be accepted and followed.

Cost-benefit analysis itself does not address the equity issue; it seeks simply to maximize aggregate economic value. If one group of people (or countries) bears the costs of a policy and another receives the benefits, the policy is still efficient as long as, in the aggregate, the benefits exceed the costs. Some economists argue that, in designing environmental policies, we should focus only on cost-effectiveness, not equity. In their view, if a policy has unfair distributional effects, we should not shift to a less efficient but more equitable policy, which reduces a society's aggregate welfare. Rather, we should tackle the equity issue directly, through redistributive mechanisms such as taxes (or, in the international arena, through financial and technical assistance). But this reasoning, though logical, is unrealistic at best and disingenuous at worst. The political reality is that significant redistributive policies are unlikely to be adopted internationally. So if equity is not addressed in the design of environmental standards, it may not be addressed at all.

In addressing environmental or resource problems, what would constitute an equitable response? One possibility is that people have equal entitlements to commons resources. In international environmental law, this principle underlies arguments by developing countries such as India that states have an equal entitlement to the atmosphere and that climate change policy should therefore aim to equalize per capita levels of emissions among countries.

In contrast, unidirectional externalities suggest a different principle of equity, based on the idea of responsibility. Why does it seem unfair to require the victim to pay the polluter to stop? The answer is that we generally feel that the actor who causes damage should be held responsible[38] and that the polluter should pay. This equation of causation with responsibility is at the heart of tort law.

Ability to pay represents a third distributional principle. If the polluting state is rich and the victim state poor, then a "victim pays" solution seems even more inequitable.[39] In the context of climate change, for example, poor developing countries would be among the principal beneficiaries of an effective agreement because they are most vulnerable to the adverse effects of global warming. However, no one in the negotiations expects them to pay rich industrialized countries to reduce their greenhouse gas emissions. Quite the contrary. The widely shared assumption, by rich and poor countries alike, is that rich industrialized countries should pay not only for their own abatement costs, but also for some of the abatement and adaptation costs of poor developing countries that will be adversely affected by climate change.

Whom Should We Regulate?

Another preliminary consideration in environmental policy is to determine the appropriate target of a regulatory instrument. At the domestic level, environmental regulations typically set standards for private conduct—for example, emissions standards for electric utilities, or vehicle standards for car manufacturers or owners. Governmental conduct is the target of environmental regulation only infrequently; for example, the National Environmental Policy Act (NEPA) requires that the federal government perform environmental impact assessments before making major federal decisions.

At the international level, the situation is reversed: legal requirements almost always apply to states rather than to private actors, even though, as in domestic environmental law, private action is usually the real concern. The Kyoto Protocol, for example, is ultimately aimed at reducing greenhouse gas emissions by private actors such as electric utilities, manufacturers, and individuals, but its emissions targets apply to states.

One of the few exceptions to this general rule is found in the international agreement addressing oil pollution from ships (MARPOL), which sets forth detailed specifications for the construction and design of oil tankers, as well as rules limiting discharges of oil, garbage, and other dangerous materials by operators of private vessels.[40] Even MARPOL, however, does not attempt to make these rules applicable to private actors directly; instead, its requirements apply to flag states, which are required to make MARPOL's rules applicable, as a matter of national law, to ships flying their flag.[41]

Could international environmental law, in the future, apply directly to private actors? The development of international criminal law demonstrates that, in theory, the answer is yes. The statute of the International Criminal Court defines rules of conduct for individuals, which if violated constitute international criminal offenses. Although, at present, international law imposes obligations on private actors only with respect to war crimes and crimes against humanity, not the environment, there is nothing to prevent international environmental law from moving in that direction. Even if it were to do so, however, it would still need to rely on national governments for implementation and enforcement, given the absence of international institutions with strong administrative powers. Indeed, even the Statute of the International Criminal Court, which establishes an international prosecutor and court, still depends on national governments to arrest and turn over suspects.

Policy Toolkit

With these initial considerations in mind, let us consider the environmental policy toolkit. What is the range of policy instruments for addressing environmental problems such as acid rain, global warming, or habitat loss?[42]

Further Research

When uncertainty is high, one easy option is to pursue further study, either to understand the problem better (through basic scientific research) or to develop better responses (through technology R&D). This was the preferred approach of the Reagan Administration to the acid rain problem in the 1980s and of the second Bush Administration to climate change.

Does a research-oriented strategy make sense, or is it simply a cop-out, a way to avoid doing anything now? Like so much else, it depends. In some cases, a problem might turn out to be overblown, or much cheaper solutions might be developed, so a policy focusing on research might result in significant savings. That has been the argument of climate change skeptics, who point to other "crises" that never materialized. In other cases, however, delay causes the problem to become entrenched and necessitates more drastic response measures later, resulting in higher long-term costs.

Informational Measures

Measures aimed at providing information represent another, comparatively unintrusive type of policy response.[43] They do not regulate environmentally destructive behavior directly. Instead, they seek to affect behavior in other ways.

First, informational measures can help actors make choices that they themselves regard as better. As we discussed earlier, according to economic theory, people are rational actors, but they can behave rationally only if they have sufficient information. If Roberta Crusoe does not know that disposal of garbage on her island will poison her water supply, for example, then she will have no reason to stop doing so. Ignorance can thus be one source of market failure. By informing people (and governments) about the environmental consequences of their behavior, informational measures allow them to make a rational decision as to whether they wish to change how they act.[44]

Several specific types of measures seek to give actors the information they need to make better informed choices:

Product information and labeling.   Product information and labeling programs aim to promote consumer choice. The theory is that, if people know how much pollution a car causes, or how much electricity a refrigerator or computer uses, or whether tuna was caught in a manner that harmed dolphins, this knowledge might influence their buying decisions. Even in the absence of government requirements, third-party assessors (or the sellers themselves) could provide such information in response to consumer demand, but governmental labeling programs help ensure that information is provided in a consistent, trustworthy manner. Examples of consumer labeling policies include the European Community's eco-labeling program, which awards eco-labels to products that have low environmental impacts over their entire life cycle, and the U.S. Energy Star program, which awards labels to energy-efficient products.

Environmental impact assessment (EIA).   Just as labeling measures promote better-informed consumer choice, environmental impact assessments promote better informed government decision making by requiring governments to consider in advance the environmental impacts of their actions. EIA requirements originated at the national level (initially, in the United States in the National Environmental Policy Act of 1969) but have now migrated to the international level, where they have been incorporated into a number of environmental treaties, most notably, the 1991 Espoo Convention on Environmental Impact Assessment in a Transboundary Context, a regional treaty that applies principally in Europe.[45] The World Bank and other international financial institutions also now include EIAs as part of their project approval process.

Prior informed consent (PIC).   In contrast to labeling and EIA requirements, PIC requirements allow governments to make informed choices, not about their own activities, but about whether to allow potentially hazardous activities by private actors. They safeguard the sovereign decision-making authority of national governments by requiring companies to provide information to the government in advance and to proceed only if they receive the government's prior informed consent. PIC requirements are a central element of international regimes regulating trade in hazardous substances, such as the Basel Convention on the Transboundary Movements of Hazardous Wastes and the Rotterdam Convention on trade in hazardous chemicals and pesticides.

Hazard warnings.   Without knowledge of a potential or an actual danger, actors cannot respond appropriately. Warnings can be provided in advance—for example, labeling requirements for containers that need special handling because they contain hazardous substances.[46] Or warnings can be provided after the fact—for example, emergency notifications of oil spills or nuclear accidents, which are often critical in enabling other states to minimize their damages.[47]

Thus far we have been considering measures intended to enable actors to make better decisions by providing them with information. In some cases, however, simply providing actors with information may not be enough to change their behavior. Information is useful when environmental harms occur out of ignorance. But when actors are able to externalize the consequences of their behavior, then engaging in environmentally destructive behavior may be fully rational. In such cases, informational measures must play a different role if they are to be effective. They must promote accountability and deterrence by providing information, not to those causing the environmental damage, but to others who are able to exert pressure over the polluter—states, NGOs, international organizations, and the general public.

Sometimes, sunlight itself may be enough to induce a change in behavior; it may be, as Louis Brandeis once wrote, the "best of disinfectants."[48] People (and governments) tend to behave differently when they must do so openly rather than in secret. If a company is discovered to be dumping toxic chemicals or employing child labor, for example, then its reputation is likely to suffer, possibly affecting consumer behavior and ultimately the company's bottom line. Even when an actor is impervious to diffuse social pressure, information can play an important role in enabling others to exert more specific forms of pressure. This can be done either informally (for example, through non-governmental boycotts of fish sold by whaling countries) or formally (through intergovernmental procedures for dispute settlement).

Information measures that serve an accountability/deterrent function include:

Advance notification requirements.   A number of international instruments require states to notify one another about activities likely to have a significant adverse transboundary impact.[49] These requirements afford potential victims the opportunity to weigh in before any damage has been done, in order to persuade the other state to mend its ways and to prevent disputes from arising.

Disclosure requirements.   Informational requirements can also be designed to allow the public at large to influence environmental decision making more effectively.[50] Principle 10 of the Rio Declaration states that governments shall provide individuals with appropriate access to information concerning the environment. This requirement has been further spelled out in the 1998 Aarhus Convention, a regional agreement applying in Europe.[51] In parallel, information measures can require disclosure by industry of potentially dangerous activities such as toxic releases.[52] The underlying rationale of these disclosure requirements is that information is empowering and that citizens, if informed, will be able to exert influence more effectively.

Reporting requirements.   Finally, information measures can require states to report to international bodies on their environmental performance— for example, their emissions of greenhouse gases, the number of prosecutions brought to enforce MARPOL's vessel-source pollution standards, or the permits issued pursuant to the Convention on International Trade in Endangered Species (CITES). As discussed further in Chapter 11, international bodies (and other countries) can use this information both to assess compliance by a country with its existing international obligations and to evaluate overall progress in addressing a problem, in order to determine whether additional measures are needed.

Although our discussion has distinguished between information measures aimed at helping actors make better informed choices about their own behavior and those intended to allow one actor to influence the behavior of another, often no clear line exists between the two. Reporting requirements, for example, can serve both functions. Not only do they allow others to evaluate a country's performance, but the process of preparing the report may force a country to take a hard look at itself, possibly catalyzing internal changes.

On the whole, informational requirements are the least intrusive form of environmental regulation. They empower rather than limit actors by helping them to decide what products to buy, what projects to undertake, and what activities by others to protest. Informational measures thus pose the least opportunity for "government failure," in which government imposes policies that promote special interests rather than the public interest. At the same time, reliance on voluntary changes in behavior and on informal pressure rather than legal compulsion may render informational measures less environmentally effective than other types of environmental regulation.

Command-and-Control Regulation

In contrast to informational measures, which leave decision-making authority in the hands of individual actors, command-and-control regulation centralizes decision making. Instead of allowing individuals to choose the fuel economy of their car, the government might mandate corporate average fuel economy (CAFE) standards. Or, at the international level, rather than allowing each individual country to decide on its level of carbon emissions, states might collectively negotiate emission limitations, as they did in the Kyoto Protocol.

Command-and-control regulation can intervene at various points along the causal chain from individual activities to environmental effects. The further along this causal chain that regulation impinges, the more flexibility individuals have in deciding how they will comply. Consider, for example, different regulatory approaches to limiting smog caused by auto emissions of carbon monoxide, volatile organic compounds (VOCs), and nitrogen oxides:

- A requirement that all cars have catalytic converters applies to the polluting activity itself and would leave auto manufacturers and consumers with little if any discretion about what they must do to comply.
- A requirement that cars not emit more than a certain amount of pollution per mile driven would give car manufacturers flexibility about what technologies to use.
- A requirement that automobiles not emit more than a certain amount over the course of a year would leave car owners with even more flexibility (for example, they might simply drive less in order to comply).
- A requirement that urban areas take measures to reduce smog below specified levels would give the regulatory target (in this case, local governments) tremendous flexibility about how to comply.

International environmental lawyers commonly refer to requirements to do particular things as *obligations of conduct,* and obligations to achieve particular results as *obligations of result.* An obligation to impose a national carbon tax would be an obligation of conduct, whereas a national emissions target (say to reduce emissions by 30 percent) would be an obligation of result.

SPECIFICATION STANDARDS

Specification standards anchor one end of the regulatory spectrum; they represent the most directive type of command-and-control regulation. A requirement that power plants use scrubbers to remove sulfur dioxide from their emissions is an example of a technology-based specification standard; packaging requirements for shipments of hazardous chemicals are another.

At the international level, specification standards are rare. One of the few agreements that sets specification standards is MARPOL, which establishes construction, design, and equipment standards to limit pollution from ships. These standards include requirements that oil tankers have double hulls, segregated ballast tanks, and oil discharge monitoring equipment. The limitations adopted by the International Whaling Commission on the types of harpoons that may be used to kill whales are further examples of what amount to technology standards.

Specification standards have several significant drawbacks.[53] Government does not have a good track record in picking particular technologies, so the standards chosen may not reflect the most effective or cheapest ways to reduce pollution. Moreover, once a particular technology is selected, companies have no incentive to engage in further innovation in order to discover better ways to reduce pollution. Specification standards are also typically uniform; they treat all pollution sources and regions the same, even though pollution sources and regions often differ in important respects.[54] The costs of installing a technology may vary significantly from one plant to another, and particular regions may not all be equally vulnerable to a particular type of pollution. Some ecosystems, for example, have a high buffering capacity, making them less sensitive to particular types of pollution, whereas others are highly vulnerable. So a one-size-fits-all solution (say, requiring all power plants to use scrubbers or all cars to have catalytic converters) means high costs for some companies and low costs for others, overregulation in less vulnerable areas, and underregulation in more vulnerable ones.

At the same time, specification standards can provide two benefits that are particularly important internationally. First, these standards are comparatively easy to implement, monitor, and enforce.[55] It is easy to inspect a car to see if it has a catalytic converter, or an oil tanker to see if it has a double hull and segregated ballast tanks. Moreover, since the design and equipment of a ship are enduring characteristics, they allow enforcement measures to be taken against the vessel at any point in time, wherever it may go. According to one study, MARPOL's effectiveness in reducing oil pollution is attributable largely to its use of such standards.[56]

Second, if a technology creates what economists refer to as network externalities, then once a sufficient number of actors have adopted the technology, others will have an incentive to do so as well. The technology standard becomes self-enforcing and thus avoids the enforcement issues that otherwise plague international environmental law.[57] California's automobile pollution standards provide an illustration. California is a sufficiently big market that, once it adopts an automobile standard (such as a requirement to use catalytic converters) automobile manufacturers may find it easier to manufacture a single car that meets the California standard rather than different cars for different markets. Similar "tipping effects" may, in part, account for the success of MARPOL's construction and design standards for oil tankers. Since any state may take action against a vessel while in port, shipbuilders are unwilling to build, and financial institutions unwilling to finance and insure, vessels that fail to comply. As Scott Barrett explains, "The value of a particular tanker increases with the number of ports to which it has access. So, as more coastal states participated in [MARPOL], barring other kinds of oil tankers from entering their ports, the greater became the incentive for yet other states to participate."[58]

PERFORMANCE STANDARDS

In contrast to specification standards, performance standards look further down the causal chain at indicators of performance rather than at the specific technologies used to achieve those results. Performance standards come in many varieties. Some apply to particular products, such as fuel efficiency for cars and energy efficiency standards for appliances. Others apply to the production process, such as the effluent discharge standards in the U.S. Clean Water Act and the emissions standards in the U.S. Clean Air Act. Some are based on best available technologies (BATs), and others on cost-benefit balancing or the achievement of environmental objectives. An important issue in establishing performance standards is the choice of regulatory target. Does a performance standard seek to regulate the performance of individual facilities, companies as a whole, or larger governmental units?

In international environmental law, an early example of a performance standard was the oil discharge requirement set forth in the 1954 agreement on oil pollution (OILPOL), which limited discharges from oil tankers to no more than 100 parts per million of oil.[59] This discharge standard has been progressively strengthened and is now included in the MARPOL Convention.

In contrast, international air pollution regimes use a quite different type of performance standard, applicable not to the performance of individuals products or producers, but to the performance of a country as a whole. The European acid rain regime, for example, imposes limits on overall national emissions of pollutants such as sulfur dioxide, NO_x, and volatile organic compounds. Similarly, the ozone regime limits national consumption and production of ozone-depleting substances, and the Kyoto Protocol limits national emissions of a basket of six greenhouse gases, including carbon dioxide.

As with specification standards, uniform performance standards, which set the same requirements for all actors everywhere in the world, may be inefficient because of differences in the marginal cost of abatement for different polluters, the vulnerability of different regions to environmental damage, or both. To avoid these problems, performance standards can be differentiated more easily than specification standards. For example, MARPOL imposes stricter discharge limits when a vessel is close to shore or in an area that has been designated as specially vulnerable than when the vessel is on the high seas. Similarly, Kyoto's emissions targets are differentiated for each participating country.

Otherwise, the pros and cons of performance standards tend to be the mirror image of specification standards. On the positive side, performance standards give the regulatory target flexibility as to how it will achieve its obligations. This makes them more cost-effective than technology standards by enabling the regulatory target to choose the cheapest way to improve its performance. Under OILPOL, for example, oil tankers were free to limit discharges by installing segregated ballast tanks or a clean oil-washing system or by instituting more careful operational procedures. Similarly, states can achieve their Kyoto emissions targets by adopting a domestic technology standard, a performance standard for private emitters, or one of the market-based mechanisms that we will explore below, such as a pollution tax or "cap-and-trade" system.

The more comprehensive the performance standard, the greater is its flexibility and cost-effectiveness. The Kyoto Protocol's emissions reduction targets apply to a basket of six greenhouse gases. As a result, when implementing their targets, states have flexibility in their choice of which gases to reduce. If one state can reduce its emissions of methane more cheaply than carbon dioxide, and another the reverse, then each is free to make whatever reductions are cheapest.[60]

On the negative side, discharge standards are more difficult to implement and enforce than technology-based specification standards. It is easy to determine under MARPOL whether an oil tanker has segregated ballast tanks, but much harder to determine its discharges of oil at sea. For this reason, regulation of vessel-source pollution has moved from a focus on performance standards in OILPOL to a focus on construction, design, and equipment standards in MARPOL.

ENVIRONMENTAL QUALITY STANDARDS

Environmental quality standards apply even further down the causal chain that runs from technologies to performance to environmental effects. They go directly to the bottom line of environmental policy—namely, ensuring a satisfactory level of environmental quality. Examples in U.S. law include the Clean Air Act's ambient air quality standards and the Clean Water Act's goal of making lakes and rivers "swimmable and drinkable."[61] Environmental quality standards form the basis of the 1978 Great Lakes Water Quality Agreement between the United States and Canada and are also used in some European Union directives.

Environmental quality standards give the regulated actor maximum flexibility in developing pollution control requirements tailored to the ultimate objective of environmental quality. Rather than having to meet a uniform emissions standard, the regulated actor can establish a less stringent emissions standard if it has lower vulnerability to pollution damage, for example, because of greater absorptive capacity.

This flexibility brings with it two downsides, however. First, environmental quality standards are information intensive. To set pollution control requirements, we need information about what level of pollution loadings are safe for each locale—information that may prove incorrect, owing to uncertainty. Second, environmental quality standards impose relatively little control over the actors that they aim to regulate. Given informational uncertainties, states have significant discretion in deciding what levels of emissions reductions are compatible with an environmental quality standard. For these twin reasons, the North Sea pollution regime, which began as one of the few international regimes to employ environmental quality standards, eventually moved in the direction of uniform emissions standards.[62]

Today, environmental quality objectives are often employed in international agreements to provide guidance in setting more specific international performance or specification standards, rather than in place of them.[63] For example, the 1994 Sulfur Protocol to LRTAP employs a "critical loads" approach, an environmental quality standard based on the maximum levels of acid deposition that will not cause significant harm to the most vulnerable ecosystem in a given geographic area. Similarly, the UN Climate Change Convention defines its objective in environmental quality terms, namely, to stabilize greenhouse gas concentrations at a level that will avoid dangerous climate change.[64] In both cases, the environmental quality objectives do not serve as obligations on states. Rather, they are intended to guide the development of more specific regulatory requirements.

Market-Based Approaches

Market-based instruments, which aim to ensure that environmental externalities are properly priced, represent a final type of regulatory approach. The principal advantage of market-based approaches is cost-effectiveness: by allowing the market to determine how pollution can be reduced most cheaply, potentially large cost savings are possible. Studies of actual and proposed emissions trading programs in the United States estimate cost savings of between 20 and 90 percent.[65] The emissions trading program under the 1990 Clean Air Act, for example, allowed utilities and consumers to reduce sulfur dioxide emissions for about one-quarter of the original cost estimates. In addition, market-based instruments give polluters a continuing incentive to reduce pollution to the efficient level (where the marginal cost of abatement equals the marginal benefit) in the most cost-effective manner possible.

POLLUTION TAXES OR CHARGES

Pollution taxes (often referred to as "Pigovian taxes" after the British economist, Albert Pigou, who initially proposed them) put a price on pollution, thereby internalizing the pollution's externalities. This gives actors an incentive in the marketplace to reduce their pollution. If a pollution tax is set at a level that corresponds to the environmental externality, then actors will reduce their pollution to the economically efficient level. They will reduce their pollution as long as doing so is less costly than paying the tax. The United States implemented its obligations under the Montreal Protocol, in part, by imposing an excise tax on ozone-depleting substances. Similarly, Denmark has used a carbon tax to cut its greenhouse gas emissions. One problem with imposing taxes at the international

level is determining how the revenues will be spent. This problem may help explain why, thus far, no international regime has imposed taxes on pollution.

SUBSIDIES

Subsidies for measures that reduce pollution are the mirror image of taxes. Rather than raising the cost of inaction, subsidies lower the cost of action. Because it is usually easier, politically, for governments to provide individuals with a benefit than to impose a burden (to lower taxes, for example, rather than to raise them), subsidies are a popular environmental policy instrument.

Subsidies can take many forms: investments in R & D, tax credits, lower interest rates on loans, and direct payments, to name a few. In the United States, the federal government provides tax breaks for hybrid and other low-emission cars. Similarly, Japan subsidizes homeowners' installation of solar panels on roofs; and Germany and Denmark subsidize wind power through support for research and development, cheaper loan rates, and electricity rate regulation. As these examples suggest, subsidies tend to be technology specific and therefore raise some of the same problems that we considered earlier in connection with specification standards. In contrast, a tax on emissions of carbon dioxide is technology neutral. A polluter could lower its tax burden through any pollution reduction strategy: wind, solar, energy conservation, and so forth.

A variety of international environmental regimes involve financial transfers to developing countries, which are a type of subsidy. For example, the Global Environment Facility provides assistance to developing countries for their "incremental costs" of producing global public goods, including by reducing their greenhouse gas emissions and their consumption of ozone-depleting substances. We will explore these financial transfers further in Chapter 11.

LIABILITY RULES

At first glance, imposition of liability for pollution damages (as wa done in the *Trail Smelter* case, for example) might not seem to constitu a market instrument. Like other market instruments, however, liabil rules have the effect of raising the cost of pollution and thereby pro ing a price incentive to polluters to clean up their act. One common cism of liability rules is that environmental policy should aim to pr pollution, rather than simply provide a remedy to victims. This arg is ill-founded inasmuch as liability rules have a deterrent as w

compensatory effect. The only real difference between a liability regime and a pollution tax is that a pollution tax is calculated *ex ante,* based on an estimate of the expected pollution damage, and does not require proof of the causal relationship between the taxed activity and particular environmental damages. In contrast, a liability regime operates, *ex post,* after the pollution damage has occurred, and requires proof of damages and causation. Thus, where evidence of causation is limited, the likelihood that a liability system will result in payments of damages may be low and the price signal correspondingly weak.[66]

Internationally, states have shown little inclination to develop a general liability regime for environmental damage and only mixed support, at best, for issue-specific regimes imposing civil liability on private actors. To the extent liability rules are used at all, they typically serve not as the primary policy instrument, but rather as a backstop to provide compensation when damage occurs despite a regime's preventive rules—for example, when the construction and design standards in MARPOL fail to prevent an oil spill. The earliest liability regimes were developed in freestanding instruments, which addressed high-risk activities such as the transport of oil by sea and nuclear activities.[67] More recent liability regimes have been add-ons to existing multilateral environmental agreements, such as the Antarctic Environment Protocol and the Basel Convention on the Transboundary Movements of Hazardous Wastes.[68]

TRADABLE ALLOWANCES

A tradable allowance—or "cap-and-trade"—system combines a performance standard with a market-based approach. As with a performance standard, emissions are capped at a defined level and each polluter receives allowances for their permitted level of emissions. In contrast to a pure performance standard, however, each polluter need not achieve its emissions target by reducing its own emissions. Instead, if reducing its own emissions is expensive, a polluter can buy allowances from other actors who are able to reduce their emissions more cheaply. Through these trades of emissions allowances, the market directs emissions reductions to those actors who can reduce their emissions most cost-effectively. The allowance market gives them an incentive to reduce their emissions by more than the required amount and then sell their excess emissions allowances to other polluters with higher abatement costs. Tradable allowances were first used in a significant way at the national level in the 1990 U.S. Clean Air Act Amendments for sulfur emissions from power plants and are widely seen as having significantly reduced compliance costs. The Kyoto Protocol established the first tradable allowance system at the international level.

PRICE- VS. QUANTITY-BASED INSTRUMENTS

Pollution taxes, subsidies, and liability rules are all examples of what economists refer to as *price-based instruments*. They seek to influence behavior either by raising the costs of pollution or by lowering the costs of abatement. How much pollution will actually decrease as a result of this price signal is uncertain and will depend on the responsiveness of behavior to changes in price (which economists measure using the concept of price elasticity). In contrast, a cap-and-trade system is a *quantity-based instrument*. It starts by setting an overall level of pollution reduction (determined through the number of emissions allowances that are created) and then uses the market to achieve that permissible level of emissions in the most cost-effective manner.

If there were perfect information about the responsiveness of behavior to prices, then price- and quantity-based instruments would produce exactly the same result. To the extent there is uncertainty, then they differ. Price-based instruments provide certainty about prices—that is, the costs of abatement—and place the risk of uncertainty on the amount of pollution abatement that will result. A given tax rate may reduce pollution by more than the intended amount or less. In contrast, quantity-based instruments provide certainty about the level of pollution reduction (to the extent, of course, that there is perfect compliance) but uncertainty about the cost. Achieving the required level of emissions reduction might be cheaper than expected or more expensive. In some cases, this uncertainty about costs can prove to be a major political problem, as the Kyoto Protocol illustrates. Critics argued that the costs of complying with Kyoto would be economically ruinous, an argument that contributed to the Bush Administration's decision to reject Kyoto.

To address concerns about the potentially high costs of complying with quantity-based instruments, some economists have proposed combining features of a quantity- and a price-based approach, through what has become known as a safety valve device.[69] Under this approach, emissions are capped, and tradable emissions allowances are issued. However, if the market price for allowances rises above a predetermined, safety-valve level—in other words, if the costs of compliance go too high—then the target is relaxed through the issuance of additional emissions allowances at the safety-valve price.

By ensuring that compliance costs cannot rise above a predetermined level, a safety valve removes one of the principal obstacles to the negotiation and acceptance of emissions reduction targets. As with a pollution tax, however, this economic predictability comes at the expense of environmental predictability: if mitigation costs prove high and the safety valve kicks in, then the level of actual emissions reductions achieved will be less than that under a fixed target.

So there are risks either way. Just as we have no assurance as to the levels of reductions a given price will achieve, we have no assurance about how much a particular emissions reduction will cost. The difference is that the economic risks of excessive costs are near-term, while the environmental risks of insufficient reductions in emissions are longer-term and may be correctable through stronger measures later. Moreover, with a guaranteed ceiling on costs, countries might be willing to accept more ambitious commitments, leading to greater environmental benefits if costs prove low and the safety valve does not kick in.

Conclusions

From a policy perspective, there is no shortage of regulatory instruments to address environmental problems. Informational approaches are the least intrusive and hence pose the least danger of "government failure," but they may result in less environmental change. Command-and-control regulations are blunt instruments that often create inefficiencies but can be effective in providing environmental benefits (at least in states with strong administrative capacities). Market-based mechanisms are the most cost-effective but are appropriate primarily for global problems such as climate change, where the location of the emissions reductions does not matter. Each has its strengths and weaknesses, but together they represent a sophisticated toolkit for international environmental lawyers.

The problem in international environmental law lies less in formulating desirable policy options than in getting these policies adopted and implemented. In other words, the challenge is less one of policy than of politics. Even in domestic political systems, with established institutions and procedures to make and enforce the law, environmental policy faces daunting political challenges. This is even truer in a decentralized international system, with more than 190 states, which depends, in large part, on mutual agreement to make the law and on self-compliance to implement it.

Recommended Reading

Alan Boyle and Michael Anderson, eds., *Human Rights Approaches to Environmental Protection* (Oxford: Clarendon Press, 1996).

Andrew Dobson and Paul Lucardie, eds., *The Politics of Nature: Explorations in Green Political Theory* (London: Routledge, 1993).

Paul R. Portney and Robert N. Stavins, eds., *Public Policies for Environmental Protection* (Washington, DC: Resources for the Future, 2d ed. 2000).

Kenneth R. Richards, "Framing Environmental Policy Instrument Choice," *Duke Environmental Law and Policy Forum* 10 (2000), pp. 221–285.

Mark Sagoff, *The Economy of the Earth: Philosophy, Law, and the Environment* (Cambridge: Cambridge University Press, 2d ed. 2008).

Richard B. Stewart, "Instrument Choice," in Daniel Bodansky, Jutta Brunnée, and Ellen Hey, eds., *The Oxford Handbook of International Environmental Law* (Oxford: Oxford University Press, 2007).

Robert N. Stavins, ed., *Economics of the Environment: Selected Readings* (New York: W. W. Norton, 4th ed. 2000).

Edith Stokey and Richard Zeckhauser, *A Primer for Policy Analysis* (New York: W. W. Norton, 1978).

Norman J. Vig and Michael E. Kraft, eds., *Environmental Policy: New Directions for the 21st Century* (Washington, DC: CQ Press, 7th ed. 2009).

Jonathan Baert Wiener, "Global Environmental Regulation: Instrument Choice in Legal Context," *Yale Law Journal* 108 (1999), pp. 677–800.

CHAPTER FIVE

Varieties of Environmental Norms

The [pirate's] code is more what you'd call "guidelines" than actual rules. Welcome aboard the Black Pearl, Miss Turner.

Captain Barbossa, *Pirates of the Caribbean*

DO NOT KILL WHALES for commercial purposes. Use only sustainably produced timber. Reduce emissions of greenhouse gases. Export hazardous wastes only to those countries that have given their prior informed consent. Do not use scientific uncertainty as an excuse not to take action against serious, irreversible, environmental threats. All of these are examples of international environmental norms.

Because international environmental law is a system of norms, it is useful, initially, to examine the nature of these norms more closely. What are their central features, and how might norms influence behavior? How do we determine which ones are "legal" in character? In the absence of judicial enforcement of international law, or sanctions for violations, does the legal status of a norm even matter? In what sense can we say that a non-enforceable norm is "binding"?

The answers to these questions are not self-evident. Most people unconsciously transpose their understanding of domestic law to the international sphere and assume, in a common-sense way, that, if an agreement is legal in character, then its provisions are "legally binding" and the penalties for violation are also binding. The Kyoto Protocol negotiations indicate otherwise. The negotiating mandate for the Protocol was to develop a "protocol or another legal instrument"[1] containing quantified limits on emissions of carbon dioxide and other greenhouse gases. For the first year of the negotiations, however, a central issue was whether these limitations should be "legally binding," suggesting that, at the international level, a legal instrument can contain provisions that are not themselves binding. Then, after states agreed to negotiate legally binding emission targets,[2] they adopted a provision on compliance that left open the "binding" character of the consequences imposed against countries that violated the Protocol.[3] It is no wonder that confusion is widespread.

In working on the Kyoto Protocol negotiations, I often encountered the view that, if the Protocol's compliance committee cannot impose "binding" consequences on states that violate the Protocol, then this means that the Protocol itself is not legally binding. Such a view is certainly understandable. How can a norm be legally binding if the legal consequences for its violation are not also binding? Isn't this like saying that stealing is illegal, but the jail sentences imposed against violators are optional?[4]

To try to make sense of these puzzles, this chapter begins by exploring the nature of norms, together with the relation of norms and behavior. It then turns to the issue of what it means to characterize a norm as "legal" or "binding." It concludes by examining a number of other important dimensions along which international environmental norms vary.

What Is a Norm?

As many have noted, the term *norm* has a double meaning, one descriptive and the other prescriptive.[5] As a descriptive matter, a "norm" refers to a behavioral regularity; as a prescriptive matter, it refers to an evaluative standard. Although the two meanings are conceptually distinct, it is no coincidence that the same word is used in both ways. As custom illustrates, we tend to see what is normal as good and what is abnormal as bad. As a result, over time a behavioral regularity can become a prescriptive standard. In turn, the causal arrow can run in the opposite direction: the prescriptive standard can tend to reinforce the behavioral regularity.

In speaking of international environmental "norms," we are using the term in its prescriptive rather than its descriptive sense. A norm of international environmental law is a community standard that aims to guide or influence behavior—traditionally, the behavior of states, but also, more recently, the behavior of institutions and private actors. The International Whaling Convention aims to limit the activities of whalers; the rules of the International Convention for the Prevention of Pollution from Ships (MARPOL) seek to influence how oil tankers will be built and operated; and the World Bank's Operational Guidelines focus on how the Bank will conduct its lending operations.

Norms guide behavior by providing a model of appropriate action (or non-action), what the Danish legal philosopher Alf Ross called an action-idea[6]—do not whale, provide compensation for environmental damage, install segregated ballast tanks in oil tankers, and so forth.[7] These models or ideals do not simply influence action; they provide reasons for action.[8] The fact that there is a law requiring drivers to stop at red lights is a *reason* to stop at red lights. Similarly, the fact that the UN General Assembly adopts a resolution against high seas driftnet fishing is a reason to stop using driftnets.

As a means of guiding behavior, norms function as a type of directive.[9] In his writings on speech acts, John Searle defines a directive as an attempt "by the speaker to get the hearer to do something."[10] Verbs that express directives include "direct, request, ask, urge, tell, require, demand, command, order, forbid, prohibit, enjoin, permit, suggest, insist, warn, advise, recommend, beg, supplicate, entreat, beseech, implore, and pray."[11] As Searle notes, directives "may be very modest 'attempts' as when I invite you to do [something] or suggest that you do it, or they may be very fierce attempts as when I insist that you do it."[12] Directive norms include prohibitions ("a state may not engage in commercial whaling"), requirements ("states must provide notifications of actions that might cause transboundary harm"), and permissions ("a state may claim jurisdiction over its continental shelf").[13]

Prohibitions, requirements, and permissions are all examples of regulatory norms: they attempt to guide or regulate conduct by defining which actions are forbidden, which are required, and which are permitted. Although people often think of regulations as the paradigmatic type of norm, not all norms are regulatory in character; instead, some are constitutive. Like regulatory norms, constitutive norms provide a model of action that can be used to evaluate (justify and criticize) behavior. But they do not merely "regulate antecedently or independently existing forms of behavior ...," they create or define new forms of behavior."[14] As Searle notes, "the rules of football or chess, for example, do not merely regulate playing football or chess, ... they create the very possibility of playing such games. The activities of playing football or chess are constituted by acting in accordance with (at least a large subset of) the appropriate rules."[15]

The distinction between regulatory and constitutive norms is similar to the distinction drawn by the English legal philosopher H. L. A. Hart between primary and secondary rules. As Hart explains, primary rules require people "to do or abstain from certain actions"—they regulate behavior. In contrast, secondary rules of recognition, change, and adjudication "confer powers, public or private."[16] In the international arena, constitutive norms are common. Examples include the provisions of the UN Charter that create and define the functions and powers of the Security Council, General Assembly, and International Court of Justice; the rules relating to the adoption, interpretation, modification, and termination of treaties (originally found in customary international law and now codified in the Vienna Convention on the Law of Treaties); and the instrument creating the Global Environment Facility (GEF).[17]

Norms and Behavior

Although norms provide reasons for action, there is no necessary link between norms and behavior. Instead, it is an empirical question whether, and to what degree, actors are guided by those reasons, thereby making norms causally effective.

In theory, how might a norm influence behavior? As legal philosophers have long recognized, there are two general possibilities, which for simplicity I will refer to as the normative and the instrumental approaches.

First, an actor might have what H. L. A. Hart called an internal point of view with respect to a norm: an actor might accept the norm as providing a standard of appropriate conduct and might therefore be guided by the norm in its decision making.[18] A state might accept, for example, that it has a duty to prevent transboundary pollution and accordingly take steps to reduce its pollution. Note that in this context acceptance is not equivalent to consent. An observant Jew might never have consented to the kosher rules, yet still might accept them as providing a reason for action. Acceptance simply means that an actor treats the norm *as a norm,* that is, as a guide to action.[19]

Why might an actor accept a norm as a standard of conduct? There are many possible answers:

- First, an actor might believe in the "ideals and values embodied in . . . norms."[20] It might believe, for example, that it is wrong to harm another, and therefore accept that it has a duty to prevent transboundary environmental harms.
- Second, an actor might accept a norm as providing a reason for action because it believes that the norm serves its interest. The norm might solve a coordination problem, for example, such as whether to drive on the right or the left side of the road. Many of the harmonized standards developed in organizations such as the International Organization for Standardization (ISO) have this character. With respect to these norms, actors have no incentive to

defect, so there is no need for sanctions; the norms are self-enforcing. Or an actor might believe that a norm serves its long-term interests (for example, by solving a collective action problem) and thus might be reluctant to violate the norm for fear that the norm would collapse, even though violation would provide immediate benefits. It might accept, for example, a norm limiting the use of ozone-depleting substances because it believes that the norm is necessary to preserve the stratospheric ozone layer. Or it might believe that it has a systemic interest in supporting the authority of rules generally, in order to promote order and predictability.

- Third, an actor might accept a norm because it was adopted in a manner that the actor accepts as legitimate—for example, through treaty-making or majority decision making. In this case, the reason for accepting the rule is independent of the rule's content; it depends not on the substance of the rule but on its source or pedigree. For positivists, legal norms have this content-independent basis.

- Finally, an actor's acceptance of a norm might be explained by psychological or social factors such as mimicry or the desire for esteem.

Regardless of why an actor treats a norm as a reason for action (and because the explanations are not mutually exclusive, more than one might apply), what matters is simply that the actor does so, rather than looking behind the norm to its underlying rationale.[21] The prohibition on the use or threat of force in Article 2(4) of the UN Charter, for example, has as its rationale "to save succeeding generations from the scourge of war."[22] But to say that a state accepts Article 2(4) of the UN Charter as a norm means that it views Article 2(4) as a reason not to threaten the use of force, even when it believes, in a particular instance, that such a threat might advance the underlying purposes of the United Nations. The norm provides a reason for action in and of itself, separate from the reasons that justify the norm. That is why the environmentalist whom I described in Chapter 1, in our discussion about Norwegian whaling, used the IWC moratorium on commercial whaling as his trump card. In his view, it provided an effective argument against Norwegian whaling, whether or not Norwegian whaling in fact poses environmental risks.

This feature of law is nicely expressed in a poster I have in my office showing Isaac Newton sitting beneath the apple tree, with an apple just beginning to fall. The poster proclaims, "Gravity: It's not just a good idea. It's the law!" Of course, with gravity, its status as "law" adds nothing to its force—that is the joke. But the joke depends on our understanding the term *law* not merely in terms of physical regularities, but in a second, legal sense, as providing a reason for action in and of itself, because of its status as "law." Like the law of gravity, an international norm may be adopted by states because they consider it a good idea. Once adopted, however, its legal force does not depend on states continuing to accept the rule as a good idea; its status as law constitutes an independent reason for action.[23]

Often, actors experience norms as constraints or pressures, like the ropes that bound Ulysses to prevent him from following the Sirens' song.[24] In the absence of the norm against transboundary pollution, for example, a state might prefer to pollute. Because it accepts the norm as a guide to conduct, however, it takes steps to limits its pollution. When the feeling of constraint or pressure is strong—when the norm's guiding function has significant weight—then we refer to the norm as an "obligation."[25]

Norms can also influence behavior more subtly by changing an actor's preferences or values.[26] As a result of norms regarding animal welfare, for example, people might have no desire to wear furs or might find the thought of eating whale meat distasteful. When a norm has become fully internalized, it assumes a "taken-for-granted" quality, and an actor may no longer have any sense of being guided by a norm at all.[27] That it accepts the norm as a standard of conduct can be inferred only from its critical reaction to deviations from the norm by others, who continue to wear furs or eat whale meat.[28]

This first account of the relation of norms and behavior, which relies on an actor's "internal point of view," can be described as the "normative" view of behavior because it takes norms seriously *as norms*—that is, as reasons for action. Actors with this internal point of view follow what March and Olson have called "a logic of appropriateness."[29]

Even when an actor lacks an internal point of view and does not treat a norm as a guide to conduct—as a standard of appropriate behavior—it might still follow the norm for instrumental reasons, to the extent that violations are sanctioned or compliance is rewarded. It might follow the norm based purely on a "logic of consequences." A corporation such as Wal-Mart or Home Depot might accept a code of conduct, for example, to gain a safe harbor from government regulation or to avoid an NGO-organized boycott. Or a country might comply with the International Whaling Commission's moratorium on commercial whaling because, otherwise, the United States will impose trade sanctions. Or a country might honor its treaty obligations in order to avoid harm to its reputation.

In such cases, the norm's status *as a norm* has no effect on the actor's behavior. Instead, the norm operates simply as a pricing mechanism, changing the actor's external environment by raising the costs of non-compliance or lowering the costs of compliance. *Ab initio,* following the norm is not in the actor's self-interest; compliance becomes in the actor's interest only because of the incentives that are offered for following the norm or because of the sanctions that are imposed for violating it.

Perhaps the most famous proponent of this purely instrumental view of norms was Oliver Wendell Holmes, who argued that we need to look at law from the perspective of the "bad man, who cares only for the material consequences [of violating the law]," not from the perspective of the "good one, who finds his reasons for conduct, whether inside the law or outside of it, in the vaguer sanctions of conscience."[30] Because this instrumental view of norms shapes how many people think law works, a central focus of international lawyers has been to identify—in the absence of hierarchical enforcement—alternative (horizontal) sanctioning mechanisms among states, such as loss of reputation, which would give even the "bad state" a reason to comply with international law.[31]

Although instrumental accounts of behavior are sometimes seen as reducing norms to an epiphenomenal status, with no causal role,[32] this perspective is plainly false. Even when an actor lacks an internal point of view and responds only to the threat of sanctions or the promise of rewards, norms still make a difference, as even Holmes's "bad man"—who adhered only to a logic of consequences—recognized.[33]

More fundamentally, instrumental accounts of behavior are not incompatible with actors having an internal point of view and being guided by norms *qua* norms. Indeed, some of the explanations we identified earlier for why an actor might follow a norm were themselves instrumental in nature. The internal point of view does not presuppose that actors have pure transcendental wills, obeying a norm simply because that is the right thing to do, without regard to the consequences. In other words, the internal point of view does not presuppose a purely non-instrumental account of behavior. Nor, conversely, does an instrumental account of behavior presuppose that actors view norms only from an external point of view, as Holmes's bad man does. Instead, as rational choice theorists have done, it is possible to combine the two approaches by constructing an instrumental account of norms *qua* norms, which shows how accepting a norm as a guide to behavior can sometimes be in an actor's long-term interest.[34]

Do states, in fact, have an internal point of view? Do they view norms as reasons for action, and hence have a propensity—all other things being equal—to follow them, independent of any immediate consequences? Not all scholars agree. Some dismiss the internal point of view on methodological grounds as vague and lacking predictive value,[35] or deny as a factual matter that norms play any role whatsoever in explaining state behavior.[36] However, there is no reason to believe, *a priori,* that norms influence behavior in only a single way. Indeed, empirical studies suggest the opposite, namely, that both the normative and instrumental accounts are necessary to explain behavior.[37]

To my mind, the view that actors sometimes implement their obligations because they believe that they ought to do so seems self-evident and is an important factor in explaining behavior.[38] Consider a simple example from everyday life: I promise my daughter that I will take her to the zoo on a particular day—a day that unbeknownst to me is Super Bowl Sunday. If I had known about the game, I would not have made the promise; whatever reasons resulted in the promise would not have been determinative. But I believe that I should keep my promises, if possible. So having made the promise, I take her to the zoo. In what sense does my normative belief in the importance of keeping promises have no explanatory value? To be sure, it does not explain why I sometimes break my promises. Nor does it exclude the possibility that instrumental factors may also play a role—for example, my desire to "look good" to my daughter and others. So it does not offer a full account of my behavior with respect to promises. This is not the same thing, however, as saying it lacks explanatory value.

Two final points are worth noting about these different accounts of the relation between norms and behavior:

First, they are a useful way to think about the behavior of actors at all levels: private individuals, states, government decision makers, negotiators, and judges. A judge, for example, may be guided by a norm in reaching a decision because she thinks the norm derives from a valid source; but in some cases, judges may be guided by moral norms or act out of self-interest.

Second, both accounts represent ideal types. In any society, different actors are likely to follow norms for different sorts of reasons at different times. Sometimes, self-interest may play a greater role; other times, external sanctions are determinative; and still other times, a sense of obligation may be more important. Even H. L. A. Hart, who in the *Concept of Law* stressed the importance of the internal point of view toward the law, did not believe that all actors within a society have an internal point of view.[39] He acknowledged that many, like Oliver Wendell Holmes's bad man, instead experience law as an external constraint.

As Hart recognized, however, even in such cases, the internal point of view plays a vital role, not in explaining the behavior of the bad person, who cares only about consequences, but in explaining the behavior of the "good" person, who treats the norm as an obligation and imposes sanctions out of a sense of "righteousness"—for example, an NGO that engages in a mobilization of shame to pressure a country to observe human rights, or organizes consumer boycotts of countries that engage in whaling. The two accounts of behavior are not mutually exclusive, but rather complementary.

Identifying the Norms of International Environmental Law

Assume that you have been given the task of identifying the norms of international environmental law. Where should you look? Relevant materials might include:

Intergovernmental agreements. Treaties are, of course, a principal source of international environmental norms. Whaling, for example, is addressed by the International Convention for the Regulation of Whaling. Similarly, the rules regulating the chemicals that can be used in home air conditioners derive from the Montreal Protocol on Substances that Deplete the Ozone Layer. Other agreements limit emissions of the pollutants that cause acid rain and global warming; regulate the dumping of hazardous wastes at sea; require large oil tankers to have double hulls; limit the use of persistent organic pollutants such as dioxins and DDT; encourage states to conserve wetlands; and regulate trade in endangered species.

Decisions of treaty bodies. As discussed further in Chapter 8, treaties not only articulate norms directly, they also do so indirectly by establishing institutions that supplement, elaborate, and interpret the norms in the treaty itself. In many treaty regimes, the vast majority of the substantive rules are articulated not in the main body of the agreement, but in decisions of the treaty parties. The Ramsar Convention on Wetlands, for example, requires that states promote the "wise use" of wetlands within their territory; but the detailed guidelines spelling out what "wise use" means were adopted by the Convention's meeting of the parties. Similarly, the Kyoto Protocol authorizes parties to engage in emissions trading of greenhouse gas allowances, but left it up to the conference of the parties to develop the rules for how emissions trading will work.

Decisions of international organizations. Every year the General Assembly and the UN Environmental Programme (UNEP) adopt long lists of environmental resolutions. Most are routine, but a few articulate important rules—for example, the 1991 UN General Assembly resolution that called for a global moratorium on large-scale high seas driftnet fishing, a practice that critics argue kills large numbers of non-targeted species. In some cases, international organizations adopt decisions that establish complex procedures, along the lines of a treaty, though non-legal in nature. For example, in 1989, the UNEP Governing Council established a system of prior informed consent (PIC) for exports of hazardous chemicals.[40] That same year, the Food and Agriculture Organization (FAO) adopted a similar PIC procedure for exports of pesticides,[41] which together with the UNEP procedure became the basis for the Rotterdam Convention, adopted a decade later.

Conference resolutions and declarations.   Resolutions and declarations adopted by international conferences are another source of environmental norms. Undoubtedly, the most prominent example is Principle 21 of the 1972 Stockholm Declaration, which provides that states have the duty to ensure that activities within their jurisdiction or control do not cause transboundary harm. There are many other examples, such as the detailed rules on land-based sources of marine pollution contained in the declarations of the five North Sea Conferences held since 1984.

Claims by states.   In their interactions with one another, as well as in international forums, states often justify their own actions, and criticize those of other states, in terms of more general normative claims about what actions are required, forbidden, and permitted. In 1896, for example, in a dispute concerning the flow of the Rio Grande River into Mexico, the U.S. attorney general, Judson Harmon, proposed what became known as the Harmon Doctrine, the now discredited principle that states have absolute territorial sovereignty and can use their territory as they wish, even if this causes harm to a neighbor. Conversely, throughout the 1980s, Canada argued for the opposite rule, namely, that states have a duty to prevent transboundary pollution. On this basis, Canada contended that the United States was obliged to reduce its emissions of sulfur dioxide, which Canada claimed were causing acid rain in its territory.

Judicial and arbitral decisions.   Although adjudication is comparatively rare in international environmental law, judicial decisions have articulated several important environmental norms.[42] The duty to prevent transboundary pollution, for example, was first clearly expressed in the *Trail Smelter* case. Similarly, the duty to consult and to negotiate in good faith with neighboring states about possible transboundary pollution is usually traced back to the *Lac Lanoux* arbitration between France and Spain.[43] National courts also occasionally get in on the act—for example, by articulating the principles of intergenerational equity, precaution, and sustainable development.[44]

Business codes of conduct.   Increasingly, business groups, sometimes in conjunction with environmental organizations, have attempted to self-regulate by developing codes of conduct. In some cases, they have been motivated by a wish to forestall intergovernmental regulation, in others to improve their public image, and sometimes, perhaps, out of a genuine desire to improve the environment. The Marine Stewardship Council rules on sustainable fisheries, which Wal-Mart has pledged to honor, are one example; the rules on Antarctic tourism developed by the International Association of Antarctic Tour Operators are another.

Legal scholars and experts.   Finally, legal experts have contributed to the development of international environmental norms through their individual writings, as well as through collective projects to identify and elaborate general principles of international environmental law.[45]

What Does It Mean to Say that a Norm Is Legally Binding?

How are we to think about this wide array of international environmental norms? Traditionally, the starting point for international lawyers has been to distinguish those norms that are "legal" in nature from those that are not. From a doctrinal perspective, this makes perfect sense, since determining the content of international environmental law requires that we identify which norms count as "law."

The question, "what is law?" has long been a staple of jurisprudence. How do we distinguish legal norms from other varieties of social norms, such as political commitments, custom, morality, or etiquette? Is there a separate domain of "law"? Or is law impossible to differentiate rigorously from politics and morality?

Although these questions preoccupy philosophers, they rarely disturb domestic lawyers, who inhabit a world of "legal" phenomena—courts, legislatures, police, lawsuits, judgments—and in general take for granted the existence and importance of law. International lawyers, in contrast, cannot afford this luxury. The peripheral role of legal institutions and legal enforcement makes the relation of law and "non-law" more immediate and pressing. Given the scarcity of courts to find the law and of mechanisms to sanction violations, how does one draw a distinction between "legal" and "non-legal" norms? Is the distinction a sharp one, or are there degrees of greater and lesser "lawness," as the category of "soft law" would seem to suggest? And, from a practical standpoint, is the distinction between law and non-law significant? In what ways does it matter whether an international norm is legally binding or is "only" a political or a moral obligation?[46]

International lawyers have answered these questions in various ways, but the most common answer defines international law in terms of the social processes by which it was created—that is, in terms of its *formal source* or pedigree. Some sources are recognized as having law-creating effect; others not. In developed legal systems, the formal sources of law are expressly stated in rules—what H. L. A. Hart termed "secondary rules," as we discussed earlier (in contrast to the primary rules that govern everyday behavior). In the United States, for example, the Constitution specifies the process by which legislation is enacted: passage by a majority of both houses of Congress followed by signature by the president (or, if the president vetoes the bill, an override of the president's veto by a two-thirds vote of each house of Congress). In contrast, the formal sources of law in traditional cultures may be implicit rather than explicit. For example, a norm prohibiting casting a shadow on the king might be viewed as valid because "that's the way it's always been." Here custom would be the source of the norm.

Although it is easy to confuse the concept of formal source with that of cause, the two are very different.[47] Almost any norm is the product of a wide variety of causes. For example, the rules relating to liability for oil spills found in the 1969 Civil Liability Convention drew on national law and were adopted in reaction to the 1967 *Torrey Canyon* oil spill, which devastated the southeast coast of England. The 1989 Basel Convention on the Transboundary Movements of Hazardous Wastes resulted in part from the individual efforts of Mostafa Tolba, then the executive director of the UN Environment Program. And the Kyoto Protocol on climate change reflects the domestic politics of the participating states. In recent years, so-called constructivists in political science have attempted to develop a general causal account of the evolution of norms, focusing on norm entrepreneurs, tipping points, norm cascades, and internalization.[48]

The concept of a formal source, in contrast, refers to those social processes or practices that have a law-creating effect. For example, the formal source of the norms contained in the Civil Liability Convention and in the Basel Hazardous Waste Convention was the treaty-making process. This was the process that constituted these norms as law. The *Torrey Canyon* spill and Mostafa Tolba's efforts may have been essential, from an explanatory point of view, to the adoption of these norms, but they are not essential to an account of how the norms came into existence as legal norms. In this sense, the concept of source seems closer in meaning to "origin" or even "basis" than to "cause." It refers to those social processes or mechanisms that generate or constitute a legal norm *as such*.

The formal sources of international law also differ from the various types of *evidence* of international law that we examined in the previous section. In some cases, of course, the sources and evidence of international law overlap: a treaty both creates new legal norms and is evidence of those norms. But some materials that provide evidence of international law are not themselves formal sources of new law. Expert initiatives, for example, provide evidence of existing law, but they are not usually seen as creating new law.[49] They are no different from law review articles, which can help us determine what the law is (for example, when we do not have time to do our own primary research on the legislative history of a statute) but cannot directly create new legal norms.

According to orthodox accounts of international law, judicial opinions fall into the same category. Because international decisions must be made on the basis of existing law, they cannot serve as a formal source of new international environmental norms. Given the centrality of decisions such as *Trail Smelter*, however, this cramped view of judicial decision making has an air of unreality.

The canonical statement of the formal sources of international law— Article 38 of the Statute of the International Court of Justice—identifies three sources: treaties, custom, and general principles.

- *Treaties* are explicit agreements in writing.
- *Custom* is a more amorphous legal source than treaties. Customary norms are, in theory, generated through the regular practice of states, engaged in out of a sense of legal obligation. The rules of diplomatic immunity, for example, evolved over centuries through the repeated interaction of states.
- Finally, *general principles* are norms that reflect fundamental propositions of law, shared by legal systems around the world.

We will examine treaties in greater detail in Chapter 8 and custom and general principles in Chapter 9. At this stage, it is useful to note the central difference between treaties on the one hand and custom and general principles on the other: treaties are the product of a purposive process of negotiation, whereas customary norms and general principles emerge through more diffuse processes. How about the distinction between custom and general principles? To some degree, custom focuses on the actual behavior of states, whereas general principles find their basis in logic and reason. In practice, however, the distinction between customary norms and general principles is often blurred.[50] It is not clear, for example, whether the fundamental rule stated by the arbitral panel in the *Trail Smelter* case—namely, that "no State has the right to use or permit the use of its territory in such a manner as to cause injury by fumes in or to the territory of another or the properties or persons therein, when the case is of serious consequence and the injury is established by clear and convincing evidence"[51]—is a rule of customary law, reflecting the actual practice of states, or a general principle of law.

Although treaties are very different, as a source of law, from customary norms and general principles, all three sources are typically classified as "hard law," in contrast to a wide variety of norms that do not qualify as "legal" in character, including resolutions of international organizations, conference declarations, and business codes of conduct. The General Assembly, for example, lacks legislative authority, so its resolutions have the status of recommendations. For the same reason, neither the Stockholm Declaration nor the Rio Declaration on Environment and Development is itself legal in nature; both would achieve that status only if they were incorporated into a treaty or were deemed to constitute norms of customary international law. And business codes of conduct are developed by nonstate actors, without any lawmaking authority.

If conference resolutions, business codes of conduct, and the like are not legal norms, what are they? Do they have any status at all? A common answer is to categorize them as "soft law."[52] Like hard law, they are normative: they are intended to guide or influence behavior by providing *reasons* for action. The fact that the UN General Assembly, for example, adopted a resolution calling for a moratorium on high seas driftnet fishing is a *reason* to stop using driftnets. The resolution provides a standard of evaluation. Compliance serves as a justification for one's own actions, and violation is a ground for criticism of others. Moreover, like hard law, these non-legal instruments are a social creation; they are the product of identifiable processes of norm-making. From this perspective, soft law does not simply represent the absence of law; it represents a kind of legal purgatory.

International environmental lawyers have traditionally devoted considerable effort to debating whether a particular norm has the status of hard law or is "only" soft law. Are the decisions of the Kyoto Protocol's meeting of the parties (for example, adopting the rules for emissions trading) legal in nature?[53] How about measures adopted by the Antarctic

Treaty parties?[54] Has the precautionary principle achieved the status of customary international law? A great deal of ink has been spilt on these and similar questions.

The premise underlying all of these questions is that the legal status of a norm matters, that legal norms are somehow superior or preferable to non-legal norms, presumably because they are more effective. Consider, for example, the reactions to the Paris AIDS Declaration,[55] adopted on December 1, 1994, by forty-two states at a World Health Organization (WHO)-sponsored conference. The Declaration set forth the legal and social rights of people with AIDS. In paying tribute to the participants, the director-general of WHO, Dr. Hiroshi Nakajima, commented that the Paris Declaration implies both accountability and responsibility. Nonetheless, some NGOs criticized the Declaration as "non-binding" and "not enforceable"—as a political commitment rather than international law.[56]

Is this assumption correct that hard law is somehow superior to soft law? Does it really make a difference whether an environmental norm—the precautionary principle, for example, or Stockholm Principle 21—has the status of international law? Would a forest convention be superior to a statement of forest principles? Superior enough to justify the negotiating effort? And, if so, in what way does soft law fall short of hard law? Only recently have these questions begun to attract serious attention.

In the domestic context, the legal status of a norm matters because legal violations can be sanctioned. People care that the payment of taxes is legally required, rather than simply a recommendation, because, if one fails to pay, one can be fined and even imprisoned. The criticism of the Paris AIDS Declaration that, because it did not have the status of law, it was unenforceable, transfers this way of thinking to the international level. It assumes that, had the Paris AIDS Declaration been adopted as a treaty rather than a declaration, it would have been enforceable.

This assumption is, to say the least, misleading. International law lacks any general enforcement mechanisms to sanction violations (except where a violation of international law threatens international peace and security, in which case the Security Council can take action). In this respect, there is no difference between soft law instruments such as the Stockholm Declaration or the Paris AIDS Declaration and hard law instruments such as the Ramsar Convention on wetlands. Although some environmental treaties establish compliance procedures that can impose weak forms of sanctions (for example, publication of violations, removal of benefits, and so forth), these tend to be quasi-political and don't make bright line distinctions between violations of hard and soft provisions.[57] Similarly, a U.S. law that provides for the discretionary imposition of trade sanctions against countries that "diminish[] the effectiveness" of an international conservation agreement, such as the Whaling Convention, looks at the actual effects of a country's actions, without regard to whether those actions are illegal under international law.[58]

At the domestic level, a rule's legal status also matters because legal rules can generally be applied by courts, whereas soft law cannot.[59] If judicial application of the precautionary principle turned on whether it constitutes hard or soft law, then this would indeed be an important difference.[60] But the link between legal status and judicial application is also comparatively weak. At the international level, there is no general system of legalized dispute settlement, which can adjudicate violations of legal norms. In most cases, dispute settlement is not available, regardless of whether a norm is legal in nature. Moreover, even when a judicial forum is available, courts do not invariably apply a norm when it represents hard law. U.S. domestic courts, for example, refuse to give judicial effect to treaty norms—the paradigmatic example of hard law—unless the treaty is deemed "self-executing."

These long-standing critiques of international law have led some to deny that any norms of international law should be considered "hard" or that international law really deserves the appellation of "law" at all. For example, the nineteenth-century legal philosopher, John Austin, who made sanctions central to his theory of law, characterized international law as "positive morality." A similar philosophy underlies the common belief that, if the Kyoto Protocol lacks binding enforcement measures, this somehow means that its requirements fall short of "law."

These are important criticisms, but they do not negate the significance of the distinction between "hard" and "soft" norms—or perhaps, more precisely, between law and non-law. Ultimately, what makes a norm "hard" is not that violations can be sanctioned, at least in the way that we ordinarily mean, or that the norm can be applied by courts. Instead, what matters is the state of mind of the actors that comprise the relevant community— what we referred to earlier as the actor's internal point of view—a sense that the norm represents an obligation and that compliance is therefore required rather than optional. The rules contained in the Montreal Protocol or in MARPOL are "hard" because states and individuals view treaty commitments more seriously than non-binding instruments, both in guiding their own actions and in evaluating the actions of others. Presumably that is why, in many countries, special domestic procedures must be fulfilled in order to enter into a treaty—procedures that would seem unnecessary if international law were, in fact, a fiction.

In any particular case, an actor's internal sense of obligation to comply with legally binding norms may be weak or may be outweighed by other considerations. So the fact that compliance with legal norms is mandatory rather than optional does not mean that states will always comply. A sense of legal obligation does, however, contribute to a norm's influence on behavior. Hence, all other things being equal, states are more likely to comply with legal than with non-legal norms. That is why the legal status of a norm matters.

A Typology of International Environmental Norms[61]

In the real world, of course, all other things are rarely equal. Although the legal versus non-legal quality of a norm is important, norms differ along many other dimensions that may be relevant to their effectiveness and that we therefore need to consider, including:

- Whether they are the product of a purposeful, reflexive process, such as a negotiation, or whether they arise in a more organic, decentralized way.
- Whether they depend for their authority on state consent.
- Whether they are expressed in mandatory or hortatory language—that is, in the language of "shall" versus "should."
- Whether they are precise or vague—that is, whether they are *rules* or *standards*.
- Whether they are self-administering by states or involve some delegation of implementation to others.[62]

Together, these variables define a multidimensional normative space within which we can locate any particular norm. Categorizing norms in this more rigorous fashion allows us to assess the relative importance of particular features of norms, such as whether they are negotiated or non-negotiated, precise or vague, legal or non-legal. Are some types of norms more effective than others? Why do states choose one type versus another? And how do their choices about the different dimensions interrelate?

Purposiveness

One important dimension of norms—because it helps determine all the others—is whether they are the product of a purposive process of norm creation (for example, a negotiation among states), or whether they emerge in a more organic, decentralized way. As with other variables, this dimension cuts across the divide between legal and non-legal norms. On the one hand, conference resolutions and business codes of conduct, though non-binding, are all developed through a self-conscious process of norm creation, leading to their adoption at a particular point in time. On the other hand, customary norms, though in theory binding, emerge in a more decentralized way through the uncoordinated behavior of different actors. This distinction between purposive, negotiated norms and more organic, non-negotiated norms is the basis for the division between Chapters 8 and 9.

Consent

A second, related dimension of a norm is whether it is consensual in nature. A defining feature of treaties, as a source of law, is that they bind only those states that have given their explicit consent through ratification or accession. In contrast, UN Security Council decisions apply to all UN member states, whether or not they agree;[63] consent is required only of the five permanent members of the Council, who can veto decisions that they dislike.

Interestingly, consent is an important factor for non-legal as well as for legal norms. Although the 1992 Rio Declaration on Environment and Development, for example, is non-binding, the United States and France nevertheless entered interpretive statements to certain provisions in order to qualify the substance of their consent.[64]

Consent is often seen as important because it provides a basis for the legitimacy of international norms and increases the likelihood of compliance. At the same time, the requirement of consent makes it more difficult for international environmental regimes to address the problem of free riding or respond quickly to new developments.[65] Think how difficult it would be to adopt national laws if they required unanimous consent rather than a simple majority.

To allow greater flexibility in the development of international environmental law, many multilateral environmental agreements establish an implied or tacit consent procedure, under which amendments to regulatory annexes can be adopted by a qualified majority vote, which bind all parties except those that expressly opt out.[66] The Montreal Ozone Protocol eliminates the requirement of consent altogether by allowing the stringency of regulatory measures to be "adjusted" by a qualified majority vote.[67]

Mandatory Quality

A norm can attempt to guide the behavior of those to whom it is directed in a stronger or weaker fashion.[68] At one pole, a directive can request, recommend, ask, suggest, or advise; at the other, it can direct, require, command, order, or forbid. I use the term *mandatory* rather than *binding* to refer to this dimension of norms because the term *binding* is ambiguous. Sometimes it is used to describe a norm's formal source: treaties are binding, for example, whereas UN General Assembly resolutions are only recommendations. On other occasions, the term is used to refer to what I am calling *mandatory*. This is apparent when writers characterize a treaty-norm as non-binding. Since a treaty provision clearly has the formal status of law, what they mean is that the provision is non-mandatory. The confusion leads some writers to add the qualification "legally" to the term *binding*, suggesting that a norm can be binding in non-legal ways and that a legal norm may not be binding. Our separation between the dimensions of legal status and mandatory intention makes this distinction apparent.

International environmental norms span the spectrum of control intentions. Many are stated in mandatory terms. They use verbs such as shall, must, require, and may not. The use of these terms in legal instruments such as treaties is, of course, unsurprising. More interesting is the use of mandatory language in instruments that are not considered legal in nature. For example, the UN General Assembly Resolution on driftnet fishing, to which I referred earlier, called upon states to "ensure that a global moratorium . . . is fully implemented" by a particular date, and reaffirmed the importance it attached to "compliance" with this provision.[69]

Conversely, some treaty norms are stated in hortatory or programmatic terms, using verbs such as should, may, and recommend, which signal a low level of control intention. For example, the Technical Annex to the 1988 Nitrous Oxides (NO_x) Protocol to the Long-Range Transboundary Air Pollution Convention (LRTAP) has an explicitly "recommendatory" character.[70] As the Annex notes, "its aim is to provide guidance to Parties in identifying best available technologies which are economically feasible."[71] Similarly, Article 4.2 of the UN Framework Convention on Climate Change recognized the desirability of industrialized states returning their emissions to 1990 levels by the year 2000 but did not actually require that they do so.

Precision

A fourth dimension of norms is their precision.[72] International environmental norms vary widely in this regard. At one extreme, Article 2(1) of the 1985 Vienna Convention for the Protection of the Ozone Layer requires simply that states take "appropriate measures" to protect against ozone depletion. Similarly, Article 3 of the Ramsar Convention on Wetlands of International Importance requires parties "to promote . . . as far as possible the wise use of wetlands in their territory," without elaborating what uses of wetlands are "wise" or "unwise." At the other end of the spectrum, Annex I of MARPOL prohibits oil tankers from discharging more than 60 liters of oil per nautical mile and requires new oil tankers weighing 70,000 deadweight tons or more to have segregated ballast tanks;[73] the Montreal Protocol sets precise limits on the consumption and production of ozone-depleting substances; and the Kyoto Protocol establishes quantitative targets to reduce greenhouse gas emissions.

In analyses of domestic law, the term *rules* is typically used to refer to precise norms, like the Kyoto emissions targets, and *standards* to less precise ones.[74] Although this terminology may not be familiar, the distinction between these two types of norms is commonplace. Consider, for example, how a speed limit might be articulated. On the one hand, we could define a specific maximum speed—say, 55 miles per hour. On the other hand, we could simply require people to drive at a "safe speed." The former is an example of a rule, and the latter, a standard. The distinction between rules and standards is, in essence, that between *ex ante* and *ex post* decision making.[75] Rules define in advance what conduct is permissible and impermissible. Standards, in contrast, set forth more open-ended tests, whose application depends on the exercise of judgment or discretion—for example, to determine what represents a safe driving speed in a specific context, or what represent "appropriate measures" to combat ozone depletion.

The distinction between rules and standards cuts across other important aspects of environmental norms. Examples of both rules and standards, for example, can be found in both non-legal and legal instruments. The UN General Assembly resolution on driftnet fishing established a very specific schedule for the phaseout of driftnet fishing, calling for a 50 percent reduction in fishing effort during the first six months of 1992 and a global moratorium by the end of 1992. Other examples of non-legal instruments that establish specific rules include the ISO 14000 series, which sets forth detailed rules on environmental management for business, and the International Maritime Dangerous Goods Code. Conversely, as the Vienna Ozone Convention and the Ramsar Convention illustrate, treaties can contain very imprecise standards requiring states to take "appropriate" measures or to "wisely" use their wetlands.[76]

The question of whether a norm represents a rule or a standard is also separate from the question of its stringency. Very precise rules can be extremely lax. This was true of the whaling quotas adopted by the International Whaling Commission in the 1960s, during the so-called Whaling

Olympics, when catch limits were set very high, allowing tens of thousands of whales to be killed. Conversely, a standard, though imprecise, can be quite stringent—for example, a standard requiring the adoption of best available technology.

What might influence the choice between rules and standards? By putting off much of the decision making until later, standards provide a number of benefits: they do not require as much information, they preserve flexibility, and they are easier to negotiate. Rules, by contrast, can be useful in addressing collective action problems, which depend on reciprocity, by defining the precise contribution each state is required to make. In doing so, rules also make compliance more likely by making violations more clear-cut, with higher reputational costs.[77]

Implementation Mechanisms

A final dimension along which norms vary is in their mode of implementation. Does a norm have associated with it any international mechanism to address issues of implementation and compliance—for example, relating to monitoring and review? Are any sanctions available in cases of violation?

As with other variables, there is no necessary connection between the legal status of a norm and the availability of implementation mechanisms. The 1975 Helsinki Accord on human rights, for example, was, by its terms, not legally binding. However, it established an elaborate follow-up process, involving high-level review conferences, which arguably gave the Helsinki Accord more influence over the human rights situation in Eastern Europe in the late 1970s and 1980s than any international human rights treaty.[78] Conversely, many legal agreements lack any implementation mechanisms. We will return to the subject of implementation mechanisms in Chapter 11.

Conclusion

Although the issue of hard versus soft law has been much discussed in the literature, this is only one of many dimensions along which international norms vary. Arguably, too, it is not the most important dimension, given the lack of enforcement mechanisms or judicial decision making, which ordinarily make the distinction between law and non-law so important.

This is not to say that the legal status of a norm makes no difference. Despite the infrequency of enforcement or judicial application, a norm's status as law still matters because relevant actors think it does. Sometimes, they violate their legal obligations, but, in general, they view compliance as more obligatory—and violations as more blameworthy—with respect to legal than non-legal norms. In other words, they take legal obligations more seriously than non-legal ones. Hence, their greater reticence to enter into them.

It is important to remember, however, that international lawyers have many other variables to play with in designing environmental norms. They can make a norm more or less precise, more or less mandatory, and more or less subject to international review and implementation. They can even pursue norm-making activities outside the intergovernmental process altogether, through private-standard setting. As a result, the question "what is law?," though still a favorite, has lost its preeminence.

Recommended Reading

Martha Finnemore and Kathryn Sikkink, "International Norm Dynamics and Political Change," *International Organization* 52 (1998), pp. 887–917.

Judith L. Goldstein, Miles Kahler, Robert O. Keohane, and Anne-Marie Slaughter, eds., *Legalization and World Politics* (Cambridge, MA: MIT Press, 2001).

H. L. A. Hart, *The Concept of Law* (Oxford: Oxford University Press, 2d ed. 1994).

Laurence R. Helfer, "Nonconsensual International Lawmaking," *University of Illinois Law Review* (2008), pp. 71–125.

Kal Raustiala, "Form and Substance in International Agreements," *American Journal of International Law* 99 (2005), pp. 581–614.

Frederick Schauer, *Playing by the Rules: A Philosophical Examination of Rule-Based Decision-Making in Law and in Life* (Oxford: Clarendon Press, 1991).

Dinah Shelton, ed., *Commitment and Compliance: The Role of Non-Binding Norms in the International Legal System* (Oxford: Oxford University Press, 2000).

CHAPTER SIX

Who's Who in the Legal Process

The 2007 Conference of the Parties of the UN Framework Convention on Climate Change had more than 10,000 participants.[1] I say "participants" advisedly because when I served on the U.S. negotiating team in the late 1990s, we used to joke that, out of the many thousands of people attending climate change conferences, only about a hundred actually did anything. And by the phrase, "did anything," we meant, "participated actively in the negotiations." All of the rest of the people at the meetings were, in our view, merely hangers-on; what they did while there—if anything—was a bit of a mystery.

Our sense of self-importance, however, reflected a narrow view of the international legal process—that intergovernmental negotiations are at the center of the conference universe and that we, as government negotiators, were masters of that domain. Both assumptions are, of course, wrong:

- International conferences (much less the international environmental process more generally) are multi-ring circuses. They are trade shows, public relations and educational arenas, and quasi-academic conferences. Intergovernmental negotiations occupy only a single ring.
- Moreover, even within that ring, government negotiators do not operate freely. They are subject to a tight set of constraints, emanating from a wide array of actors.

This chapter introduces the basic cast of characters in international environmental law—its *dramatis personae,* so to speak. Who are they?

What role do they play? What influences their behavior and, in turn, how do they themselves exercise influence? Subsequent chapters will put these actors into motion and examine how they develop and implement international environmental law.

States

As the term *inter-national* suggests, international environmental law operates largely as a system of law between states rather than regulating conduct more broadly.[2] Although it aims ultimately to change the private behavior that is responsible for most environmental problems, its rules apply primarily to states, and few of these rules create rights or duties for companies, individuals, or other non-state actors.[3]

From the doctrinal perspective, the state-centric character of international environmental law has at least three dimensions. First, when a government enters into an international obligation—the Montreal Protocol, say, or the Kyoto Protocol—the obligations bind the state as an abstract, persisting entity, including successor governments that had nothing to do with joining the treaty (and may have even opposed it). The Panama Canal Treaty negotiated by President Carter in the late 1970s, for example, did not represent Carter's personal commitment, but rather a commitment by the United States, which continued to apply even after he was succeeded as president by Ronald Reagan (who had campaigned against the treaty). By the same token, if the United States were to become a party to the Kyoto Protocol, the treaty would continue to bind future administrations.

As a corollary, a breach of international environmental law generally gives rise to state rather than individual responsibility. In the 1930s, when the Trail Smelter in Canada emitted toxic fumes that traveled downwind and caused damage in the State of Washington, Canada, not the smelter's private owner, was held responsible. Similarly, if the United States failed to meet its obligations under the Montreal Protocol on ozone depletion, it would be the United States that would be responsible rather than the president or the Environmental Protection Agency (EPA) administrator. In this respect, international environmental law differs from international criminal law, which holds individuals responsible for crimes such as genocide, torture, grave breaches of the laws of war, and, more recently, certain terrorist acts.

Finally, international environmental obligations are owed, in general, to other states, not individuals, so that claims for violation must be asserted by states. The damage caused by Trail Smelter primarily affected private property in Washington State. Nevertheless, the United States was the party that had to assert the claim that Canada had failed to meet its duty under international law to prevent significant transboundary harm. International environmental law treats pollution caused by a private actor in one state that harms a private actor in another state as a dispute between the two states concerned, and not as a dispute between two private parties—just like, in the recent trade dispute concerning imports of genetically modified organisms into the European Union, American biotechnology companies were the real parties at interest, but a legal claim for violation of international trade law had to be submitted by the United States.

States remain the key actors not only from a doctrinal perspective but from an explanatory perspective as well. To be sure, non-state actors increasingly contribute to treaty regimes such as the Montreal Protocol and the UN Framework Convention on Climate Change. But these agreements are still primarily the product of interstate negotiations and rely on states for implementation. Moreover, states influence the international policy process in less direct ways, by funding scientific research, influencing public opinion, exerting pressure on other states, and undertaking environmental projects.[4] Despite occasional claims about the diminishing importance of states in international affairs—what some refer to as the "de-centering" of the state—states continue to have the greatest power, both hard and soft, of any international actor. They play the dominant causal role in the development, implementation, and enforcement of international environmental law.

As anyone who has worked in government would tell you, understanding state behavior is complex. A useful (even if unrealistic) starting point is to think of states—like individuals—as rational actors, each seeking to advance their own self-interest. This instrumental account of state behavior unites two of the principal approaches to international relations: realism and liberal institutionalism.[5] Both theories understand international relations in terms of states rationally pursuing their national interests, although they differ in how they think states define their interests.

So-called realists argue that states seek to maximize their power relative to other states, resulting in a competitive world in which cooperation is difficult to achieve and sustain.[6] This minimizes the prospect that states will cooperate to protect the environment; indeed, realists tend to deny that much meaningful environmental cooperation takes place. What passes for cooperation, they argue, really reflects the interests of more powerful states or is merely epiphenomenal, requiring no change in state behavior.[7]

Liberal institutionalists, in contrast, contend that states wish to increase their economic and social welfare, and can mutually benefit from international cooperation by increasing the overall size of the pie. For example, according to the widely accepted theory of comparative advantage, free trade is a positive rather than a zero-sum game: it results in an overall expansion in economic wealth, leaving both sides better off.[8] Similarly, the development of international environmental regimes can produce gains for all sides and thereby result in what economists refer to as Pareto improvements.[9]

Explanations of the emergence and effectiveness of international environmental law rely heavily on state-centric, instrumentalist models of international relations, which analyze different strategies (reduce pollution, continue business-as-usual, etc.) in terms of the costs and benefits for each state involved.[10] States are assumed to have stable interests, which can be identified in advance.[11] For example:

- In transboundary pollution cases, downstream states favor strong action to limit transboundary pollution because they are the ones suffering the ill effects. Conversely, upstream states have an interest in continuing to pollute because they do not bear the costs of their pollution—the environmental damage is an externality. Hence, downstream states are typically the leaders, and upstream states the laggards, in international environmental regimes.[12]
- With respect to global pollution problems such as ozone depletion, which involve a tragedy of the commons, states generally have an interest in undertaking collective action. But each individual state has an interest in free riding, as long as it can do so without penalty (and without causing the entire international ozone regime, from which it benefits, to break down).
- Coastal states have an interest in international measures to control marine pollution, whereas states with large fleets have an interest in norms that protect freedom of navigation.
- States with a whaling industry (such as Norway and Japan) support continued whaling, whereas those states that do not (such as the United States) push for a cessation of whaling.

In all of these cases, one can analyze international environmental problems in terms of the differing national interests of the states involved. For simplicity, most instrumentalist analyses focus on a state's economic and environmental interests,[13] but other, longer-term interests could be included, such as a state's interest in maintaining good relations with its neighbors or in enhancing its reputation internationally. According to a rational actor model, states agree to international norms when the expected benefits exceed the costs, and not otherwise. Similarly, they will implement their international obligations when they have an interest in doing so, and not out of any sense of legal duty.

No doubt, the assumption that states are unitary entities, with identifiable, stable interests that they rationally pursue, can be a useful simplification. However, analyzing international environmental problems in state-centric, instrumental terms takes us only so far, for two independent reasons:

First, a more realistic account of state behavior recognizes the possibility that states, at least sometimes, are motivated by normative considerations about what is right or proper to do. That is, they respond to a *logic of appropriateness* as well as a *logic of consequences*.[14] This requires that we investigate the content of states' normative beliefs, as well as how these beliefs develop and change.

Second, states are not unitary actors; they are complex entities, with many constituent parts, often with very different interests and beliefs of their own. They are, as Robert Putnam puts it, "not a singular 'it' but a plural 'they.' "[15] As a result, we cannot assume that national interests are simply a given. In reality, interests are often contested and contingent, the outcome of domestic political processes involving complex interactions between different substate actors. In order to understand how states define their interests at any particular point in time and how those definitions of self-interest change, we must therefore look inside the state.

Consider, for example, the climate change issue. Can we understand the positions of different states in terms of stable national interests? To some degree, yes.[16] Despite considerable shifts in national politics, the positions of the main negotiating blocs have remained remarkably stable since the climate change issue first emerged twenty years ago. Small island developing states have consistently pushed for strong international action to combat climate change, reflecting their special vulnerability to sea-level rise. Big developing countries such as China and India have rejected proposals that they accept emission targets, which might limit their economic growth. Oil-producing states have tried to block progress more generally in the climate negotiations, reflecting their interest in maintaining global demand for oil, which would be reduced by measures to cut carbon dioxide emissions. And the United States has generally been more reluctant than Europe to accept stringent emission reductions, reflecting the fact that it has large coal reserves and relies heavily on cars.

But a single-minded focus on national interests leaves many questions unanswered. It fails to account for the European Union's consistent support for strong emissions targets, which continued even after the United States rejected Kyoto in 2001, despite the fact that achieving those targets could entail significant economic costs. It fails to account for the support for Kyoto by countries (such as Canada) that appear unlikely to fulfill their obligations, at a considerable cost to their international reputation. And it fails to account for shifts in national positions, such as the the Bush Administration's decision to walk away from the Kyoto Protocol, which the Clinton Administration had invested considerable effort in negotiating. To understand why states take the positions they do in international negotiations, why they ratify (or fail to ratify) different agreements, and why they implement (or fail to implement) their international obligations, we need a more fine-grained analysis, which disaggregates the state along at least four dimensions.

First, in referring to the U.S. position on climate change, what is usually meant is the position of the executive branch because in general it is the president who speaks for the United States in foreign policy. Even within the executive branch, however, different agencies and different officials within a particular agency may have divergent positions.[17] During the negotiation of the 1992 UN Framework Convention on Climate Change, for example, the EPA often seemed more closely aligned with European environmental ministries than with the U.S. Department of Energy. Conversely, during the post-Kyoto climate change negotiations, it often appeared that European finance and energy ministries secretly hoped that the United States would succeed in its efforts to restrain European environmental ministries, which typically headed their national delegations. When I worked on marine pollution issues as a civil servant in the State Department during the Reagan Administration, many working-level bureaucrats like me hoped that our issues would remain "below the radar screen," meaning outside of the attention of political appointees within the Administration.[18] In doing so, our goal was not to subvert administration policy, but rather to exercise discretion at the margin in articulating the "U.S. position" in ways that we thought made sense. Even in an administration that tries to exercise tight control over the government bureaucracy, resources are limited, and not every issue can be reviewed.

In addition, in states with a separation of powers between the executive, legislative, and judicial branches, a state's behavior does not always reflect the views of a single branch. During the negotiation of the Kyoto Protocol, for example, the Clinton Administration supported an international agreement with binding emission targets only for industrialized countries. The Senate decided to adopt a different position, calling for commitments by developing countries as well.[19] Which represented the "position" or "national interest" of the United States at the time? The question has no clear answer. The U.S. delegation supported the outcome at Kyoto, and President Clinton subsequently signed the Protocol. But he never submitted it to the Senate for advice and consent to ratification, knowing that it would be rejected.

An even more extreme example is provided by the 1982 UN Law of the Sea Convention (UNCLOS), which the United States has still not ratified, even after other countries revised UNCLOS in line with U.S. demands. The United States' failure to ratify UNCLOS cannot be explained in terms of a unitary national interest, given that ratification has been supported by the executive branch, a large majority of the Senate, and the business community. Instead, it results from the vagaries of the Senate process for treaty approval, which allows a minority to block a treaty's adoption.

In federal systems like the United States, we also need to disaggregate -the state along a third dimension, that of the central government vis-à-vis subnational units. During the Bush Administration, for example, the climate change positions of many states and cities grew increasingly distinct from that of the federal government. The Bush Administration opposed mandatory regulation of carbon dioxide emissions. In reaction, states such as California and cities such as Seattle decided to proceed on their own and adopt emissions reduction goals and policies. As a result, in the United States there was less of a split on the climate change issue between different branches of the federal government than between different levels of government.

Finally, in understanding national behavior on an issue such as climate change, we need to consider the interests and views not only of government actors, but also of various private actors: electric utilities, oil companies, solar energy producers, farmers, automakers, environmental groups, and so forth. Some of these private actors would potentially benefit from action to combat climate change—for example, manufacturers of photovoltaic cells and hybrid cars, farmers who produce corn for ethanol, and environmental groups. Others stand to lose from climate change measures, most importantly, carbon-intensive industries. The general public may win or lose, depending on whether they live in areas vulnerable to sea-level rise and extreme weather events (such as hurricanes) and, more generally, on whether the environmental benefits of emissions reduction measures outweigh the potentially higher costs of electricity and gasoline.

Further complicating the matter, not only are there significant differences between non-governmental organizations (NGOs) and business, but each group itself is heterogeneous. Electric utilities differ, depending on the extent to which they rely on coal, natural gas, or renewable sources. Environmental groups can be activist or expert in character, national or international, grass-roots or insider. Oil companies can support aggressive emissions reduction programs or oppose them, for reasons that are not always apparent, but that may depend in part on the personal values of a company's top management.[20]

A state's position on an issue such as climate change emerges from the complex interactions of these substate actors—environmental groups raising public concern and creating a demand for public regulation (sometimes assisted by dramatic events such as a hurricane or drought); businesses lobbying officials in the different branches and levels of government; and government actors themselves interacting in a game of bureaucratic politics.[21] The position that emerges may variously reflect enduring national interests, the interests of a particular group that has successfully lobbied for it, or bargaining among different governmental actors. Indeed, in some cases, a country's position on a particular issue may be like the Panda's thumb in evolution, a by-product of other factors.[22] George Bush's victory over Al Gore for president in 2000 arguably had little to do with the climate change issue, and yet the results of that election had significant implications for U.S. climate policy. In the end, decisions are made not by abstract entities, but by individuals who are motivated by a multitude of factors: promoting what they believe to be in the national interest, promoting their own interests, doing what they believe is right, doing what they believe the law requires, and so forth.

Given the multiplicity of actors, positions, and interests, identifying a stable, objective national interest may prove impossible. And even when there appears to be a clear national interest, a state's behavior internationally may not reflect it. Consider, for example, the issue of free trade. Most economists believe that free trade furthers state interests; the theory of comparative advantage teaches that free trade increases a country's overall welfare. However, this doesn't mean that all groups within a state benefit from free trade. There are losers as well as winners. And if the losers prevail in the political process, then a state may take protectionist measures that limit trade; that is, it may act in ways that go against its own national interests.

The role of domestic politics in determining foreign policy is particularly important in liberal democracies, but identifying the national interests of non-democratic states can entail difficulties as well. During the post-Kyoto climate change negotiations, Russia's position varied depending on which agency headed the delegation. At one meeting, it even appeared that Russia had two delegations, with very different views from one another. As a result, identifying the "Russian position" on any particular issue was a constant source of speculation. In the case of developing country representatives, many seemingly operate without any official instructions at all, espousing positions that reflect their own personal ideology rather than any objective national interest.

This complex process of interaction among different actors, both governmental and non-governmental, characterizes not only the negotiation of international regimes, but also their implementation and enforcement. In politics, few things are ever settled, at least not for good. Not surprisingly, then, the struggles concerning the creation of new norms carry over into the implementation and enforcement process. Implementation of an international rule requiring, say, the phaseout of ozone-depleting substances or the protection of a world heritage site may be resisted by businesses or local communities that stand to lose from the new rule, by local officials who had no part in developing it,[23] or by government officials who had opposed its adoption in the first place. Even in dictatorships, the state cannot simply order compliance; implementation depends on the willingness of a variety of governmental and private actors to act in particular ways. Although we tend to think of dictatorships as having greater powers of social control than democracies (didn't Mussolini make the trains run on time, after all?), this may not be the case. In the long run, the legitimacy conferred by democratic decision-making processes may prove more effective than coercion in influencing behavior because it requires fewer resources.

The assumption that states are unitary entities, with stable, identifiable interests, is not the only premise of the traditional, state-centric view of international law in need of modification. According to the traditional view, states are:

- Territorially defined units, with sovereignty over activities within their borders.
- Sovereign equals, with the same legal status.

Increasingly, however, neither of these postulates reflects reality.

First, pollution in one country can travel downriver or downwind and cause damage in another country. As a result, the downstream country is not fully sovereign within its territory; it is significantly affected by decisions of the source country about whether or not to regulate pollution—hence, the need for international environmental law.

Second, states are not equal, in either law or fact. Legally, international regimes often create different obligations for different categories of states; for example, there are more stringent ones for industrialized countries and less stringent ones for developing countries. In terms of their actual influence, some countries are clearly more equal than others, both in the creation of international environmental problems and in the development (or non-development) of policy responses. The United States, for example, contributes almost a quarter of global greenhouse gas emissions, much more than the next biggest emitter. And it has a disproportionate influence on the development of the international climate change regime, both positive and negative, pushing a novel approach such as emissions trading in the late 1990s, but then opposing, during most of the Bush Administration, discussions of how to proceed next, after the Kyoto Protocol's first commitment period ends in 2012.[24]

In short, although the state remains at the center of international environmental law, we need to understand it in more complex ways. First, we need to look inside the state, in order to understand the domestic determinants of international environmental decisions. Second, we need to understand the increasingly porous quality of states. Finally, we need to understand the differences among states in political influence, environmental impacts, and legal obligations.

International Institutions

International environmental law has no international institution with general governance functions—it has no World Environmental Organization to match the World Trade Organization.[25] Instead, a patchwork of international institutions address environmental issues, leading to concerns about overlap, duplication of effort, lack of coordination, and even conflict. Some institutions are global, others regional or bilateral. Some relate to a particular issue area such as whaling or forestry, others have a broader environmental mandate, and still others, a mandate encompassing non-environmental as well as environmental issues. Some are scientific in orientation, others focus on capacity building or have a more policy-oriented role.[26]

The concept of an international "institution" encompasses international organizations but is broader. In international law, an international organization has a formal basis (usually a treaty) and a permanent, tangible quality (a headquarters building, staff, and so forth).[27] In contrast, international institutions include more informal structures such as the Group of 8 (G-8), made up of the eight leading industrial countries of the world, with no treaty basis or permanent secretariat.

Although the United Nations Charter does not establish any international institution with a specifically environmental mission, the UN General

Assembly has played a significant role in promoting environmental issues, pursuant to its broad authority to discuss economic, social, and health matters. It has convened conferences such as Stockholm, Rio, and Johannesburg; initiated intergovernmental negotiations on climate change and desertification; adopted resolutions such as the 1982 World Charter for Nature; and created institutions such as the UN Environmental Programme (UNEP) and the Commission on Sustainable Development. In addition, a number of UN specialized agencies, though not created as environmental institutions, now address particular environmental problems as part of their more general mandate. The Food and Agriculture Organization, for example, addresses fisheries and forestry issues; the International Maritime Organization (IMO) focuses on marine pollution issues; and the World Bank provides financing for environmentally oriented projects. According to one count, more than thirty UN agencies "now have a stake in environmental management."[28]

The international institution with the broadest competence over environmental issues is UNEP, established in the wake of the 1972 Stockholm Conference.[29] In contrast to the UN specialized agencies, UNEP does not

---

Box 6.1.   An Alphabet Soup of International Environmental Institutions

ATCM	Antarctic Treaty Consultative Meetings
CEC	Commission on Environmental Cooperation (U.S.-Canada-Mexico)
CSD	UN Commission on Sustainable Development
FAO	Food and Agriculture Organization
G-8	Group of Eight
GEF	Global Environment Facility
IAEA	International Atomic Energy Agency
IBRD	International Bank for Reconstruction and Development (World Bank)
IJC	International Joint Commission (U.S.-Canada)
IMO	International Maritime Organization
IPCC	Intergovernmental Panel on Climate Change
ITTO	International Tropical Timber Organization
IWC	International Whaling Commission
OECD	Organization for Economic Cooperation and Development
UNDP	UN Development Programme
UNEP	UN Environment Programme
UNESCO	UN Educational Scientific and Cultural Organization
WMO	World Meteorological Organization

have a separate treaty basis. Instead, like the UN Development Programme and the Commission on Sustainable Development, it derives its authority from the UN General Assembly, which created it (and which, in turn, derives its authority from the UN Charter). UNEP is small, with only a few hundred professional staff and a budget of under $150 million per year, and it lacks significant decision-making authority. Instead, it has played a largely informational and catalytic role, helping to spur the negotiation of treaties such as the regional seas agreements in the 1970s and 1980s, the 1987 Montreal Protocol on ozone depletion, the 1989 Basel Convention on hazardous wastes, and the 1992 Biodiversity Convention, as well as the development of various soft law instruments.

Perhaps the most distinctive types of international environmental institutions are those established by individual multilateral environmental agreements (MEAs).[30] Virtually every MEA now establishes a conference of the parties (COP), which meets on a regular basis (usually annually), is open to all treaty parties,[31] and serves as the supreme decision-making body for its constitutive agreement. These meetings go by different names in different treaty regimes. In the whaling regime, for example, the annual meeting of the parties is styled the International Whaling Commission (IWC), and the state representatives are referred to as "commissioners." In contrast, the meeting of the parties to the Long-Range Transboundary Air Pollution Convention is called the Executive Body, even though it is open to all of the treaty parties.

The decision-making authority and procedures of COPs vary from agreement to agreement. Some have limited authority (usually by a two-thirds or three-fourths majority vote) to adopt new environmental rules that bind all of the treaty parties, except those that file a specific objection. Other powers may include establishing subsidiary bodies, reviewing implementation, and monitoring compliance. In addition to COPs, multilateral environmental agreements also typically provide for a permanent secretariat; in some cases, these agreements designate an existing organization such as UNEP,[32] and in others, they create a new one.[33]

Why do states create international environmental institutions such as these? To what extent are these institutions merely creatures of the states that created them, as opposed to actors in their own right? How influential and effective are they in addressing environmental problems? These are the central questions for us to consider.[34]

According to functionalist theories of international organizations, states establish international institutions to perform functions that states have difficulty performing individually. Among these functions are collecting information, monitoring compliance, and, in general, addressing collective action problems and providing public goods.[35] The most basic rationale for international institutions is efficiency: international governance can be provided more easily and efficiently through a permanent institution than on a purely *ad hoc,* decentralized basis. Imagine the difficulties of addressing ozone depletion if every time states wanted to do something collectively, they had to organize a diplomatic conference—choosing a time and place, designating a secretariat, deciding on rules of procedure, agreeing on relevant sources of information, and so forth and so on. International institutions, like business firms, reduce transaction costs by eliminating the need to define procedures and roles on a constantly recurring basis, and by allowing decisions to be made in a centralized, coordinated manner.[36] This not only promotes efficiency, but also creates greater predictability and makes commitments by states to address a particular problem through international cooperation more credible.

According to this functionalist, statist approach to international organizations, international organizations are essentially agents of states, who exercise delegated authority. As agency theory teaches, however, agents have their own interests and do not necessarily act exactly as their principals might have wished. The same is true of international environmental institutions. Although they are created by states, they are usually not merely vessels for the transmission of state preferences. Rather, they are actors in their own right, with their own functions, decision-making rules, and organizational cultures, and often their own personnel (who serve as international civil servants rather than as state representatives).

In analyzing international institutions, we can array them along a spectrum, based on their degree of autonomy from states. At one extreme, an international institution such as the G-8 or the Antarctic Treaty Consultative Meeting serves merely as an intergovernmental forum; at the other, the European Court of Human Rights operates as an autonomous actor in deciding cases under the European Convention on Human Rights, with a stable budget and independent judges. International law uses the concept of "legal personality" to denote the point along this spectrum at which an international institution is considered sufficiently autonomous to have a separate legal existence and to be able to act in its own right for certain legal purposes—asserting claims, entering into treaties, and exercising other implied powers that are necessary for it to fulfill its functions.

Most international institutions lie somewhere in between the two extremes of intergovernmental creature and autonomous actor. They have a dual or hybrid character, usually with different components reflecting their intergovernmental as opposed to their more autonomous/independent elements. The United Nations, for example, consists of the General Assembly and Security Council on the one hand, comprised of states, and the secretariat on the other, comprised of international officials. Similarly, the World Bank consists of a Board of Governors, representing the member states, as well as a permanent staff headed by a president and Board of Directors. In referring to the UN or the World Bank, it is important to be clear which component one means. When commentators criticize the UN for failing to stop the genocide in Darfur, for example, do they mean the secretariat, or the member states, or some combination of the two? Or when analysts write that the World Bank has the authority to develop operational policies relating to the environment, do they mean that the Board of Directors and permanent staff can do so on their own, or with the approval of the Board of Governors?

Most international environmental institutions lie toward the intergovernmental rather than the supranational end of the spectrum. Generally, the conference of the parties has the primary policy-making role. Its powers may include negotiating and adopting new protocols or annexes, amending existing agreements, and making decisions to elaborate or interpret the existing treaty rules. Meanwhile, international environmental secretariats, though important, are comparatively weak. None has the independence and authority of financial institutions such as the World Bank or the International Monetary Fund. Instead, they have largely administrative functions, such as organizing meetings, gathering and transmitting information, and administering training and capacity-building programs.

Although the effectiveness of international environmental institutions has not received systematic study,[37] several impressionistic observations are warranted. To begin with, even if meetings of the parties are only forums for states to meet and interact, they play a crucial role in keeping attention focused on an issue. The annual meetings of the International Whaling Commission, for example, help ensure that whaling remains on the international policy agenda, just as meetings of the parties to the Convention on International Trade in Endangered Species (CITES) provide a focal point for efforts to limit trade in elephant ivory, rhino horn, or sturgeon. In contrast, the 1940 Western Hemisphere Convention, which failed to provide for any institutional follow-up, became a "sleeping beauty,"[38] largely forgotten, with little if any effect on state behavior, despite strong substantive provisions. So important are regular meetings that the parties to the Ramsar Wetlands Convention, which initially failed to provide for such meetings, went to elaborate lengths to amend the convention in order to correct this omission.[39]

Although regular meetings of the parties lie at the intergovernmental end of the institutional spectrum, they tend to develop an identity and dynamic of their own, which serve to limit state sovereignty, at least marginally. For example, the Bush Administration might have preferred that the climate change issue simply go away internationally; but it was forced to address the issue each year at the annual conference of the UN Framework Convention on Climate Change. Regular meetings serve to enmesh states in an international process that takes on a life of its own. Attendance at regular meetings helps to socialize state representatives; they begin to develop a collective culture that tends to make them act differently, as a group, than they would act individually as agents of their states. In this manner, a COP can develop into something more than simply a vehicle for the transmission of state preferences and lead to different results than if states acted on their own.

To the extent that international institutions allow voting (rather than simply unanimous or consensus decision making) or include only a subset of the treaty parties, they assume an even more clearly corporate character. By participating in an institution that allows decisions to be made by a qualified majority vote, or that establishes bodies with limited membership (such as the UNEP Governing Council, the Global Environmental Facility (GEF) Council, or the CITES Standing Committee), a state accepts a process that can result in decisions that it opposes. To be sure, most multilateral environmental agreements give objecting states the right to opt out of decisions with which they disagree. But exercising this right can be difficult, particularly for weaker states, which fear alienating other treaty parties. As a result, states may end up acquiescing to decisions that they dislike. For example, southern African countries such as Botswana and South Africa ultimately accepted the ban on trade in elephant ivory adopted by CITES in 1990, even though they had argued strongly that the ban should not apply to them because they had successfully controlled poaching.

In addition to a regular meeting of the parties, most international environmental regimes have recognized the utility of a permanent secretariat. Even the Antarctic Treaty system, which for years had declined to establish a secretariat,[40] recently decided to do so. Treaty secretariats serve a variety of functions, ranging from the provision of administrative support for intergovernmental meetings to more substantive roles such as commissioning studies, setting agendas, compiling and analyzing data, providing technical expertise, mediating between states, making compromise proposals, monitoring compliance, and providing financial and technical assistance.[41]

Although environmental secretariats operate under the guidance of the parties and generally do not have a policymaking role, parties cannot decide every issue collectively. As a result, secretariat officials must inevitably make many decisions on their own. In doing so, they inevitably have some effect on an organization's behavior; they represent autonomous actors that "create and disseminate knowledge, shape powerful discourses and narratives on how problems are to be structured and understood, influence negotiations through ideas and expertise, and implement the standards that have been agreed."[42] The secretariat of the GEF, for example, which administers the financial mechanisms for a number of multilateral environmental agreements, has a significant influence on funding decisions through its role in screening and evaluating project proposals, even though the ultimate decisions about funding are made by intergovernmental institutions such as the GEF Council and the Executive Board of the Montreal Protocol's Multilateral Fund. Similarly, CITES gives its secretariat authority to seek information about compliance and to recommend measures addressing persistent violations by particular parties.[43]

Some fear that the autonomy of international institutions can create pathologies—perhaps most importantly, lack of accountability.[44] This concern, though valid, needs to be kept in perspective. As with any organization, international institutions can produce agency costs. At the same time, even the strongest environmental institutions are still comparatively weak. They lack an army (the fears of ultranationalist U.S. groups about UN "black helicopters" notwithstanding). They lack independent resources and are dependent on states for funding. They even lack general authority to adopt binding rules or decisions. In short, international institutions do not replace anarchy with hierarchy but, rather, with looser forms of governance. They depend for their influence not on material power, but on their perceived neutrality, expertise, and ability to provide benefits to states, all of which contribute to a belief, more generally, in the legitimacy of multilateral governance.[45]

Non-Governmental Organizations

Non-governmental organizations are not a new phenomenon; they "have a long history, dating back to the [medieval] guilds."[46] In the past thirty years, NGOs have proliferated. Today, more than 2,500 NGOs have consultative status with the United Nations, and thousands more operate primarily at the national level.[47] Although difficulties of classification preclude an exact count of the number of environmentally oriented

NGOs, a rough measure is provided by the 1,378 NGOs accredited to the 1992 Earth Summit, the 737 new NGOs accredited to the 2002 World Summit on Sustainable Development, and the more than 800 that participate in the International Union for the Conservation of Nature (IUCN).

Environmental NGOs vary along many dimensions. The majority have a national focus, working to promote, say, energy conservation or habitat protection within a particular country. Other NGOs have an international orientation, either by virtue of their participation in international meetings or networks, or their presence in multiple countries. Some are large membership organizations, such as the Audubon Society or the Sierra Club, with hundreds of thousands of members; others are "inside" players, operating primarily in international centers such as Washington, New York, or Geneva. Some have a broad environmental mandate; others focus on a particular issue such as deforestation, pesticides, or whaling. Some, like Greenpeace, are activist or grass-roots in nature; others like the World Resources Institute and the Tata Energy Research Institute are think tanks;[48] and still others such as the Nature Conservancy and Conservation International have an operational dimension, undertaking environmental projects directly.

The Role of Non-Governmental Actors

For a variety of reasons, non-governmental actors play an unusually active role in international environmental politics:

- The physical nature of international environmental problems means that scientists figure more prominently in international environmental law than in other branches of international law.
- The fact that international environmental problems are caused primarily by private rather than governmental conduct means that the private sector is the ultimate regulatory target of most international environmental norms and thus has an unusually high stake in the content of these norms.
- The fact that international environmental problems affect so many different segments of the public, and so many different aspects of domestic policy (each with its own set of interest groups), means that non-governmental groups have been particularly active in this area.

The influence of non-governmental actors varies greatly from issue to issue and can be viewed as positive or negative, depending on one's perspective. In contrast to states, which have a wide array of non-environmental interests, environmental NGOs are more single-minded and thus more willing to devote attention to environmental issues. NGO influence is typically strongest in the issue-framing and agenda-setting phase, as scientific advances identify problems and environmental groups push issues and help mobilize public concern. Conversely, non-governmental actors are less influential in the standard-setting phase, which states try to jealously guard. Nonetheless, lobbying efforts by NGOs and business help shape government positions, and NGOs have been increasingly successful in establishing norms through private standard-setting initiatives, such as the Marine and Forest Stewardship Councils. Finally, the importance of non-governmental actors in implementation, though often assumed to be high, was found by one recent study to be mixed.[49]

Sources of Influence

How do non-governmental organizations affect the international environmental process? What are their sources of influence? The answers to these questions vary depending on the NGO. In some cases, influence is based on *ad hoc* factors, such as personal ties between an NGO and government officials, resulting from the revolving door between governmental and non-governmental positions.[50] Usually, however, non-governmental actors exercise influence either by persuading government decision makers or changing their calculus of costs and benefits.

Expertise.   Often, NGO influence is epistemic in nature. NGOs exercise influence by providing information, policy analysis, and scientific and technical expertise. IUCN's Red List of Threatened Animals, for example, is a major source of scientific information about which animal species are threatened with extinction. Much of the information about illegal whaling operations and hazardous waste trade has come from Greenpeace, while TRAFFIC—an NGO monitoring network—is a leading source of information about illegal trade in endangered species. Environmental think tanks such as Resources for the Future and policy-oriented NGOs such as the Environmental Defense Fund analyze alternative policy options and often make policy proposals of their own. And in the climate change negotiations, the Foundation for International Environmental Law and Development (FIELD) has provided negotiating and legal expertise to the Alliance of Small Island States (AOSIS), sometimes serving directly as island state negotiators. In all of these cases, the influence of NGOs depends on their ability to inform and to persuade.

Public interest.   Environmental NGOs also seek to exert influence by claiming to represent the "public" interest, rather than private interests. At times, these claims may be dubious. For example, critics charge that

Greenpeace's campaign against Shell's sinking of the Brent Spar oil platform in the North Sea was a disingenuous ploy to generate publicity for fund-raising purposes.[51] Similar charges have been made about the NGO campaign to prohibit trade in elephant ivory.[52] Even so, a significant segment of the population accepts the image of NGOs as disinterested defenders of the environment, providing the NGOs with legitimacy. For many, the World Wide Fund for Nature (WWF) panda symbol serves as an environmental seal of approval for a product. This belief that NGOs speak for the environment helps enable them to mobilize public opinion—for example, in support of campaigns to ban the use of persistent organic pollutants or the purchase of unsustainably produced timber.

Representation. Large membership organizations, in espousing their positions, also sometimes make a related but more specific claim, namely, that they represent their members.[53] To the extent that an organization's policy positions are decided by its leadership rather than its members, this claim may not always hold true. People joining the Sierra Club or the Audubon Society may not be knowledgeable about the organization's specific positions on an issue such as climate change. And most NGOs have relatively weak accountability mechanisms to keep their leadership under control.[54] Nevertheless, there is undoubtedly some truth to the argument made by one defender of NGOs, namely, that "a citizen who cares very deeply about ending whaling, for instance, almost certainly will find his or her views better represented in international fora by the World Wide Fund for Nature than by his or her own government, which has many goals it must simultaneously pursue."[55] And, regardless, the fact that organizations like the Sierra Club, the Audubon Society, and WWF have hundreds of thousands of members makes them more difficult to ignore politically than smaller organizations.

Financial resources. Although most environmental groups do not have large budgets, a few large NGOs have considerable resources at their disposal. The Nature Conservancy, for example, has assets of more than $5 billion and annual operating revenues of more than $1 billion, Greenpeace has almost $200 million in annual funding, and WWF International about $225 million. Even these are relatively small sums compared to those of governmental agencies or business, but they allow NGOs to undertake or financially support a significant number of projects. In the 1980s and early 1990s, for example, WWF-U.S. contributed more than $60 million to over 2,000 projects worldwide.[56]

Pathways of Influence

NGOs can exert influence as insiders or outsiders. As insiders, their basic medium of influence is persuasion; as outsiders, pressure. The NGOs with the greatest clout as insiders tend to be repeat players, who develop close working (and sometimes personal) relationships with governmental or business decision makers. The NGOs with the greatest power as outsiders tend to be those with the greatest ability to mobilize public opinion, for example, through blaming and shaming campaigns.

NGOs seek to exercise their influence through a variety of causal pathways, focusing on different actors.[57]

National governments.   Most commonly, NGOs and businesses exert influence over international environmental policy through national governments. They lobby their own state to support a policy internationally or to implement its international obligations domestically. Or, increasingly, they work in alliance with NGOs in other countries to influence foreign states (often, through transnational coalitions such as the Climate Action Network). When I worked in the Clinton Administration on the post-Kyoto climate change negotiations in the late 1990s, environmental and business groups constantly lobbied us to adopt their positions—for example, regarding the rules for trading emissions allowances or for crediting the removal of carbon from the atmosphere by forestry activities. Similarly, throughout the 1970s and 1980s, anti-whaling groups pushed the United States to oppose commercial whaling.

NGO influence on national policy varies widely from country to country, depending on a country's domestic political process. It is much greater, for example, in representative democracies than in other types of political systems.

The effectiveness of NGOs in shaping national policy also depends on whether significant economic interests oppose them. NGOs have been able to play a very significant role in shaping U.S. whaling policy in part because the United States no longer has any whaling industry. Similarly, environmental groups successfully lobbied the United States to support the 1989 trade ban on elephant ivory because the United States lacks an economic interest in continued trade. By contrast, NGOs have been less successful in influencing the content of U.S. climate policy.

Often, NGOs attempt to exert pressure directly on the executive branch. If that doesn't work, NGOs and business actors may seek the support of Congress or the courts.[58] In the early 1980s, for example, anti-whaling groups such as the American Cetacean Society filed suit in federal court in an unsuccessful attempt to force the president to impose sanctions against Japan for its failure to accept the moratorium on commercial whaling.[59] More recently, turtle protection groups used the courts to attempt to force the federal government to impose restrictions against countries that fail to require their shrimp fishermen to use so-called turtle excluder devices (TEDs), which help prevent turtles from becoming trapped in fishing nets.[60]

Increasingly, international environmental law has sought to promote public participation in the national decision-making process because public participation is seen both as providing a source of legitimacy and as producing better decisions.[61] Principle 10 of the Rio Declaration recommends that states encourage public participation and provide effective access to judicial and administrative proceedings, a principle that has been further elaborated at the regional level by the 1998 Aarhus Convention.[62]

NGOs seek to influence their national governments not only at home, through the domestic political process, but in international forums as well. Most major environmental negotiations are now attended by numerous NGOs, who monitor their government's positions and statements to guard against potential backsliding. At the Hague climate conference in 2000, for example, a crowd of NGO participants stood in the corridors chanting at European Union negotiators to stand firm against what they saw as U.S. efforts to weaken the final outcome. Ultimately, the European Union negotiators (in most cases, environment ministry officials with close ties to the NGOs) reneged on a tentative deal reached with the United States (although whether or not this was due to NGO pressure is difficult to say).

In some issue areas such as whaling, where NGO influence is high, a state may invite a few of its NGOs to participate on its national delegation as observers. This can sometimes make for strange bedfellows. When I served on the U.S. delegation to the International Whaling Commission in the late 1980s, we weren't sure whether the NGO representatives who were our delegation colleagues one week might be our litigation adversaries the following one.

NGOs also work closely with sympathetic delegations from other countries. In 1991, the Center for International Environmental Law (now renamed the Foundation for International Environmental Law and Development or FIELD) helped establish the Alliance of Small Island Developing States (AOSIS) and represented a number of island states throughout the 1990s in the climate change negotiations. Conversely, during much of the same period, the Global Climate Coalition, a U.S.-based NGO with close ties to energy companies, worked with sympathetic delegations from oil-producing states to oppose strong climate measures.

International institutions.   Although international law does not establish general rights of NGO participation in international institutions,[63] many regimes allow some NGO participation. The Almaty Guidelines, which were adopted in 2005 by the parties to the Aarhus Convention (a regional agreement creating rights to participate in national decision making), seek to promote public participation in international forums.[64] In rare cases, NGOs have a quasi-official status internationally. IUCN, a *sui generis* organization composed of both government agencies and non-governmental groups, is the most prominent example. It initiated the negotiation of CITES, prepared the first draft of the agreement, continues to be a key source of information about the species that should be protected, and now serves as host of the Ramsar wetlands convention secretariat. States have accepted its "insider" status, in part because they see it as a neutral expert rather than an advocacy organization and in part because its membership includes government agencies as well as NGOs. Another NGO with a quasi-official status, again due to its expertise, is TRAFFIC—a joint venture of IUCN and WWF—which monitors illegal trade in wildlife under the CITES regime.[65]

More typically, however, NGOs take part in international institutions as observers rather than as full participants. Most international agreements allow NGOs to attend the annual conferences of the parties as observers,[66] a status that gives them access to the public meetings, but not the closed sessions where many of the most difficult issues are hammered out. Some international regimes go further, allowing NGOs not simply to observe, but to provide information, make statements, comment on working documents, and even, in some cases, submit formal complaints concerning an organization's activities (most notably, in the case of the World Bank Inspection Panel).[67] In addition, treaty secretariats may enlist the services of NGOs in preparing technical reports and studies, and in offering training programs to local officials, thereby providing NGOs another point of entry to international regimes.

Business.   Working through national governments or an international institution is a circuitous means of influencing the business sector, which is often the ultimate target of NGO activities. NGOs must persuade their government, and ultimately an international institution, to adopt rules that national governments then apply to industry. A simpler approach is to try to influence business directly, through publicity and consumer pressure. A dramatic example was the Greenpeace campaign against the sinking of the Brent Spar oil platform by Shell, which relied on public confrontation.

Increasingly, NGOs have focused their efforts not simply on protests against particular actions, but on working proactively with industry to develop voluntary codes of conduct. A leading sectoral example is the Forest Stewardship Council (FSC), which NGOs initiated in response to the failure at the 1992 Rio Conference to adopt a binding forest agreement. Through the FSC, environmental NGOs, indigenous groups, timber producers, and retailers have developed standards for sustainable forestry, which are implemented through a privately organized forest product certification scheme.[68] Similar ventures include the Marine Stewardship Council and the World Commission on Dams.[69]

Business

If environmental NGOs are highly heterogeneous, businesses are perhaps even more so.[70] They can be green or brown, large or small, national or multinational. Even within the same sector, businesses may take a variety of views on environmental issues, in part owing to differences in their business culture.[71] The widely divergent positions of British Petroleum (BP) and ExxonMobil on climate change are a case in point. Moreover, businesses, like states, have many constituent parts, which may themselves have different values and interests and hence different positions. There may be a gap, for example, between the environmental views of top and mid-level managers, who must actually implement an environmental policy in the field.[72]

Businesses contribute significantly both to the creation and to the solution of environmental problems. Consider, for example, an automobile company such as Toyota. It contributes to pollution directly through its own manufacturing activities, as well as indirectly through the pollution from its cars.[73] Yet it can also contribute to the solution of environmental problems by cleaning up its own production processes and by developing new, less polluting vehicles such as the Prius.

Industry's pivotal role in many environmental problems has two important implications. First, business is often the object of international environmental regulation—not directly, since international environmental law generally operates as a system of restraints on states, but indirectly, as the ultimate regulatory target. MARPOL, for example, establishes very specific requirements regarding the construction, design, equipment, and operation of oil tankers. Although these standards do not apply directly to private actors (like virtually all international agreements, MARPOL imposes requirements only on states), they functionally govern how shipbuilders and operators must behave, through their domestic application by parties.

Second, businesses act as subjects in the international environmental process. Given their stake in the regulatory process, they actively seek to shape the development and implementation of international environmental law.

Business as the Object of Environmental Regulation

In general, international environmental law applies to states, not to private actors directly.[74] Although victims of environmental wrongs have tried to sue corporations for violations of international environmental law, attempts to hold corporations directly accountable have not proved successful thus far.[75]

Instead, international environmental law applies to companies indirectly, through the intermediation of national law. This raises the question: which states can (or must) apply which international environmental standards to which actors or activities?

To the extent that companies operate within a single country, then no question arises about which state should regulate their behavior. Regulation of transnational corporations poses a choice, however. On the one hand, the states where a corporation operates (often referred to as host countries) could regulate the corporation's activities within their territory. France, for example, could regulate carbon dioxide emissions by ExxonMobil in France. Alternatively, states could regulate the activities of "their" corporations anywhere in the world. As ExxonMobil's "home" country (that is, country of nationality), the United States could regulate ExxonMobil's activities globally. Or both the host and home states could exercise concurrent jurisdiction, potentially subjecting transnational companies to conflicting requirements.

Typically, international environmental regimes presume territorial jurisdiction. International environmental norms apply to activities within a state's territory: emissions of greenhouse gases, consumption of ozone-depleting substances, protection of wetlands, and so forth. Thus, under the Kyoto Protocol, France is responsible for ExxonMobil's emissions in French territory, Germany for emissions in German territory, and Saudi Arabia for emissions in Saudi Arabian territory. The principal exception in the climate change regime concerns emissions from aircraft and ships, which are difficult to localize and therefore require a different basis of jurisdiction.

For activities that take place outside the territory of any state, international law typically relies on nationality jurisdiction. For example, under the Antarctic Treaty, states are responsible for regulating the activities of their nationals in Antarctica. Similarly, MARPOL relies primarily on flag states to apply its standards to their vessels, both because much marine pollution takes place on the high seas, outside the territory of any state, and because of a concern that strong coastal state regulation could infringe on freedom of navigation.

Business as an Actor in the International Environmental Process

Business is not simply an idle bystander in the international environmental process, waiting to be regulated. It also plays an active role—sometimes negative and sometimes positive—in shaping the development and implementation of international environmental law. To the extent that environmental regulations impose costs on business, it is clear why business actors might oppose them. But why might business play a more supportive role in the international environmental process?

In some cases, an environmental requirement might be in a company's interest. Environmental regulations rarely impose costs uniformly on all business actors: they create winners as well as losers. Limits on carbon dioxide emissions disadvantage coal relative to natural gas and disadvantage both relative to renewable energy sources such as solar and wind. Not surprisingly, then, providers of renewable energy strongly support greenhouse gas limitations.

Sometimes companies adopt environmental measures proactively, even before government regulations are adopted. For example, a number of major companies, including British Petroleum, General Electric, and Du-Pont, have adopted their own, voluntary greenhouse gas emissions targets. Some apparently do so because they believe that a green image will help them in the marketplace; they think consumers will reward them through their purchasing decisions. Others may believe that regulation is inevitable and that beginning to adjust now will lower their costs over the long run, or that their actions might help shape the governmental regulations that eventually ensue. And some may reflect the environmental values of the company's leadership. The environmental initiatives of Wal-Mart, for example, seem to be attributable in part to a desire to counteract criticisms of the company's labor practices, thereby improving its image in the marketplace, and in part to the environmental values of the Walton family.[76]

In general, business relies on the same general factors as NGOs to influence the international environmental process. Like NGOs, business influence often has an epistemic basis. Business experts, for example, serve as key players on the Montreal Protocol's Technical Expert Assessment Panels, providing information on the technical feasibility of policy options. In contrast, business has a more difficult time claiming, like NGOs, to represent the public interest. Even so, claims by business that its private interests reflect the public interest—that "what's good for General Motors is good for America" (or, conversely, that business-unfriendly policies are bad for the economy and hence for the general public)—often find a receptive audience.

Businesses also have resources at their disposal that NGOs lack, which give them considerable clout. A corporation such as Wal-Mart has tremendous market power. If it chooses to adopt environmental standards, it can impose these standards on a large number of other actors through supply-chain contracts.[77] Businesses also wield significant financial resources (in some cases, more than governments), which they can use to influence the political process. Finally, because a cooperative attitude by business makes implementation of environmental norms easier, governments are often solicitous of business in designing new rules.

Like NGOs, business actors often act indirectly through their national governments, either domestically or in international forums. This may require little active effort on their part, since governments tend to promote their country's economic interests in negotiations anyway.[78] Often, however, other industry groups or environmentalists push countervailing positions, so business actors must lobby for their positions. If a company's own government is not sympathetic, it may decide to work closely with other, more like-minded governments. The close ties between U.S. industry lobbyists and Saudi Arabia during the climate change negotiations—both of whom opposed strong requirements—provide a good illustration.

At intergovernmental meetings, business groups have the status of an NGO and participate on the same basis. Perhaps more importantly, business groups also act outside of intergovernmental processes as independent actors in their own right. In some cases, for example, they have tried to preempt international regulation by devising their own private codes of conduct in an effort to show that they are addressing a problem effectively and that international regulation is unnecessary. The oil shipping industry used this approach in the early 1970s in developing the "load-on-top" procedure as an alternative to segregated ballast tanks. Even if self-regulation by industry proves insufficient to forestall public regulation, the industry standards may serve as a model or focal point, helping to shape the public regulatory approach that emerges. The Tanker Owners Voluntary Agreement concerning Liability for Oil Pollution (TOVALOP) approach to oil pollution liability, for example, provided the basis for the 1969 Civil Liability Convention, while the load-on-top system for preventing pollution from ballast water discharge provided the basis for some of MARPOL's oil pollution regulations. In forums such as the International Organization for Standardization (ISO), which sets technical standards on a wide variety of subjects, business groups participate directly in the standard-setting process and provide crucial technical expertise. Other examples of private standard-setting initiatives include the Equator Principles, which more than sixty banks have adopted as a framework for addressing environmental and social risks in project financing,[79] and the International Chamber of Commerce Business Charter for Sustainable Development.[80]

Finally, industry often plays a key role in the implementation process; indeed, one might say that it has *the* key role. Businesses can cooperate by changing their own behavior in response to environmental regulation. Or they can resist new initiatives, either in Congress, administrative agencies, or the courts, as the automobile industry did by bringing a legal challenge against California's efforts to limit carbon dioxide emissions from automobiles. As a result, efforts to involve the business community and get them to buy into a regulatory scheme can be crucial to successful implementation.

Conclusion

International law has traditionally been state-centric, and states continue to play a major role in the development and implementation of international environmental law. But this statement comes with two caveats.

First, in order to understand how states behave, we need to consider the numerous actors that comprise a state and influence its policies: the various branches and levels of government, companies, non-governmental groups, and individuals. International environmental politics are an extension of domestic environmental politics and are subject to the same struggles among domestic groups.

Second, although states remain central, many other actors play important roles. Conferences of the parties represent a new form of international institution that is somewhere between an intergovernmental conference and an international organization. NGOs and companies not only influence their own governments, they participate at international meetings, establish their own institutions, and take action directly.

The result is a blurring of the lines between public and private, international and domestic. The private sector sometimes engages in the quintessential public task of setting standards—for example, through the International Organization for Standardization and the Forest Stewardship Council. And they implement and enforce these standards through certification processes and supply-chain contracts. We have come a long way from the world of traditional international law, which took cognizance only of states. In years to come, we are likely to go further still in developing alternative forms of international governance.

Recommended Reading

Michelle M. Betsill and Elisabeth Corell, eds., *NGO Diplomacy: The Influence of Nongovernmental Organizations in International Environmental Negotiations* (Cambridge, MA: MIT Press, 2008).

Pamela S. Chasek, David L. Downie, and Janet Welsh Brown, *Global Environmental Politics* (Boulder, CO: Westview Press, 4th ed. 2006).

Robin R. Churchill and Geir Ulfstein, "Autonomous Institutional Arrangements in Multilateral Environmental Agreements: A Little-Noticed Phenomenon in International Law," *American Journal of International Law* 94 (2000), pp. 623–659.

Neil Gunningham, Robert A. Kagan, and Dorothy Thornton, *Shades of Green: Business, Regulation, and Environment* (Stanford, CA: Stanford University Press, 2003).

Peter M. Haas, ed., *Knowledge, Power, and International Policy Coordination* (Columbia: University of South Carolina Press, 1997).

Andrew Hurrell and Benedict Kingsbury, eds., *The International Politics of the Environment: Actors, Interests, and Institutions* (Oxford: Oxford University Press, 1992).

Margaret E. Keck and Kathryn Sikkink, *Activists beyond Borders: Advocacy Networks in International Politics* (Ithaca, NY: Cornell University Press, 1998).

Thomas Princen and Matthias Finger, *Environmental NGOs in World Politics: Linking the Local and the Global* (London: Routledge, 1994).

Stephen R. Ratner, "Business," in Daniel Bodansky, Jutta Brunnée, and Ellen Hey, eds., *The Oxford Handbook of International Environmental Law* (Oxford: Oxford University Press, 2007), pp. 807–828.

Kal Raustiala, "States, NGOs, and International Environmental Institutions," *International Studies Quarterly* 41 (1997), pp. 719–740.

Jacob Werksman, ed., *Greening International Institutions* (London: Earthscan, 1996).

CHAPTER SEVEN

Overcoming Obstacles to International Cooperation

> Government and cooperation are in all things . . . the laws of life.
> Anarchy and competition . . . the laws of death.
>
> John Ruskin, *Modern Painters*

THE PROLIFERATION of international environmental norms is all the more remarkable given the infirmities of the international legal process. International law lacks a legislature to make the law, a judiciary to interpret and apply the law, and an executive to enforce the law. Despite their hackneyed quality, these observations reflect important realities. How, then, have international environmental norms emerged? What are the obstacles to cooperation, and how has international environmental law addressed them? To what extent do international environmental norms affect behavior and why? What are the means by which they are implemented and enforced? These are the fundamental challenges of the international legal process.

Having examined the relevant actors in the last chapter, we are now in a position to pick up where we left off in Chapter 3 and to explore the obstacles to international cooperation and the functions of international environmental law. In thinking about the international process, it is useful to divide it into three stages: agenda-setting, norm-making, and implementation. Of course, these stages do not follow in a simple progression, but overlap and loop back on one another. Even as one norm is adopted or implemented, other issues and norms are emerging onto the international agenda.

In trying to explain this process, the multitude of causal factors and processes that play a role make general claims perilous. Various factors can make an issue more likely to emerge, a norm more likely to develop, or a treaty more likely to be implemented and enforced: dramatic events that produce a sense of crisis, leading to a surge in public concern; strong science; support by powerful states; the absence of entrenched opponents. How these factors play out varies from issue to issue and from country to country. Thus, different treaties have different explanations, and different states may agree to the same treaty for different types of reasons. In some cases science plays a key role; in others it does not. In some cases support by powerful states seems important; but sometimes even very small states can successfully push a norm. Rather than attempt to articulate a general theory of how environmental norms emerge and affect behavior, middle-level generalizations that trace the various causal processes at work are more useful. Or, to put it differently, history is a more fruitful methodology than social scientific theory.

This chapter begins our study of the international legal process by examining how issues come onto the agenda and norms emerge. Then, Chapters 8 and 9 focus on the three main sources of international environmental norms—treaties, custom, and general principles. Chapters 10–12 conclude by examining the processes of implementation and enforcement.

Agenda-Setting

How does an issue such as acid rain, ozone depletion, or persistent organic pollutants move onto the international environmental agenda? What causes states to focus on some problems and not others?

Typically, science plays a prominent role, at least in initially identifying and framing problems. Acid rain became an international issue in the 1960s, thanks to the work of scientists such as Svante Oden, a Swedish chemist, who linked the deterioration of lakes and forests in Scandinavia with emissions of sulfur dioxide in England and Germany. Chlorofluorocarbons, which for many years were regarded as benign, were recognized as a problem only in the mid-1970s, when two atmospheric chemists, Mario Molina and Sherwood Rowland, published an article in *Nature*, hypothesizing that chlorofluorocarbons (CFCs) would slowly migrate to the upper atmosphere and catalytically react with ozone, thereby breaking down the stratospheric ozone layer.[1] Similarly, global warming emerged as an issue in the 1960s and 1970s as a result of scientific work documenting the buildup of carbon dioxide in the atmosphere.

Although science is important, two caveats are in order. First, the scientific basis of some environmental issues is weak. In Europe, for example, genetically modified food products (sometimes referred to as Frankenfoods) have become a huge concern, despite the lack of strong scientific evidence that they pose a risk to either human health or the environment. The so-called precautionary principle, which provides that action against environmental threats need not await scientific certainty, helps legitimize this focus.

Second and conversely, the emergence of a problem as a scientific issue does not automatically lead to its becoming a political issue. The organizers of the first World Climate Conference discovered this in 1979, when they tried unsuccessfully to persuade policymakers to attend.[2] So science, though an important factor, is neither a necessary nor a sufficient condition for agenda-setting.

What additional factors help explain why some issues develop as political priorities? Often, chance events play a key role. A series of dramatic oil spills in the 1960s and 1970s—most notably, the *Torrey Canyon* and *Argo Merchant* disasters—led to the negotiation of multilateral treaties addressing the problem of oil pollution from tankers.[3] The discovery of the "ozone hole" (actually, a thinning of the stratospheric ozone layer rather than an actual hole) spurred public concern about climate change, even though the two problems, though linked in the public mind, involve different causes and physical processes, and thus have relatively little to do with one another as a matter of science and policy.[4] The dramatic heat wave and drought in the summer of 1988 helped catapult global warming onto the national agenda in the United States, leading George H. W. Bush to declare, during the 1988 presidential race, that, if he were elected president, he would meet the greenhouse effect with the "White House" effect. Almost two decades later, however, science is still unable to definitively link particular weather events like the 1988 heat wave to climate change.

William Reilly, the U.S. Environmental Protection Agency administrator under the first President Bush, once likened the agenda-setting process to a game of Space Invaders. "In that game, whenever you see an enemy ship on the screen, you blast at it with both barrels—typically missing the target as often as you hit it." As he recalled his days at EPA, "[e]very time we saw a blip on the radar screen, we unleashed an arsenal of control measures to eliminate it."[5] Although he was speaking of the domestic policy process, international agenda-setting can also have this reactive, "risk-of-the-month"[6] character.

The work of policy entrepreneurs—scientists, environmentalists, and in some cases government leaders—can also be important in translating science into terms that are understandable to the public and in framing issues more generally. In the mid-1970s, a group of scientific knowledge brokers actively promoted the climate change issue through a series of international workshops and congressional hearings, helping to bring the issue to the attention of policymakers and the public. They included scientists, environmentalists, international officials, and legislators. More recently, Al Gore, through his movie and book, *An Inconvenient Truth,* has played a similar role.

Yet policy entrepreneurs need fertile soil in which to sow their seeds, and it is here that public perceptions and fears become critical. As social psychologists have shown, people do not assess potential risks in a comprehensive and comparative manner. Instead, they fear some types of risks more than others. They react more strongly to dramatic events such as a drought or a stranded whale, for example, than to routine problems such as unsafe drinking water. They tend to fear the unfamiliar more than the familiar, and visible, tangible problems more than latent, long-term ones. That is why lists of the most important environmental problems prepared by the public and by experts vary so widely.[7]

Finally, in determining the international environmental agenda, it makes a difference whether the country pushing an issue is big or small, powerful or weak. Iraq moved to the top of the international policy agenda in 2002 because the world's only remaining superpower pushed the issue relentlessly. Similarly, oil pollution became the first environmental problem to be addressed internationally (through the 1954 OILPOL Convention) because it was pushed by two powerful countries, each with long coastlines— first the United Kingdom in the 1950s and later the United States in the 1970s.

Although size matters, the factors that contribute to the emergence of an issue are complex, and sometimes even weak countries are able to get an issue onto the international agenda. Remarkably, two small Pacific island states, Nauru and Tuvalu, through persistent and skillful advocacy by an American lawyer and marine scientist, made ocean dumping of low-level radioactive wastes into a significant issue in the 1970s and early 1980s. The result was a moratorium decision in 1983 by the London Dumping Convention parties.

Obstacles to International Cooperation

The emergence of an issue onto the international policy agenda is only the first step in developing an international response. In many cases, states disagree about the significance of a problem, whether an international response is warranted at all, and, if so, what that response should be. Indeed, even with respect to global warming, which the British government's then chief scientist, Sir David King, once characterized as a graver threat to humankind than terrorism,[8] getting the second Bush Administration simply to acknowledge the problem was a struggle. What accounts for these disagreements? And what can be done to overcome them?

Often, as we saw in Chapter 1, environmental disputes are framed in factual terms. Are fertility rates going down, and, if so, are persistent organic pollutants (such as DDT) to blame? Is acid rain causing forests to die? Is pollution responsible for declining numbers of frogs and songbirds? Those who oppose taking action on problems such as these usually do so on the basis that the science is weak and not because the environment is unimportant or does not deserve protection.[9]

Consider, for example, the problem of global warming. Carbon dioxide and other greenhouse gases are clearly building up in the atmosphere. That much has been conclusively established through actual sampling of the atmosphere in remote locations such as Antarctica and Mauna Loa. With regard to many other factual issues, however, skeptics have raised doubts.

Is Earth warming, for example? Surface observations indicate yes. For many years, however, skeptics contended that satellite observations pointed the other way, suggesting that our surface observations are perhaps an artifact of the way we take measurements (primarily in urban areas) rather than of actual changes in the environment.[10]

Even if we grant the fact of global warming, what is the cause of this change? Is it due to anthropogenic (that is, human) emissions of carbon dioxide and other greenhouse gases, or does it merely reflect the natural variability of the climate system (of the sort that, over the ages, has caused ice ages to come and go)? The first report of the Intergovernmental Panel on Climate Change (IPCC) in 1991 declined to answer this question. Since then, evidence that humans are responsible for global warming has grown stronger, and the most recent IPCC report concluded that "[m]ost of the observed increase in global average temperatures since the mid-20th century is *very likely* due to the observed increase in anthropogenic greenhouse gas concentrations."[11] Nonetheless, a significant part of the U.S. public continues to question that conclusion.[12] Even true believers are often unwilling to take the next step and attribute particular weather events, such as Hurricane Katrina, to global warming. The most they will say is that these types of extreme weather events will become more likely as a result of climate change.

Moreover, the real concern is less about what is happening today than about what will occur in the future. Here the uncertainties compound:

- What will be the future rate of carbon dioxide emissions? This depends on highly variable factors such as rates of population growth, economic growth, and technological development.[13]
- How much will temperature go up as a result of the buildup of greenhouse gases? Estimates are based on complex computer

models of the atmosphere, whose reliability is questioned by climate skeptics.
- And, if these uncertainties were not enough, they pale next to the uncertainties regarding the environmental and health effects of global warming.

These multiple uncertainties remind one of Yogi Berra's adage, "Prediction is difficult, especially about the future." As skeptics are fond of noting, 200 years ago, the rise in population and the increasing use of animals for transportation and energy might have led one to worry that, by today, we would all be knee high in manure. So we should, perhaps, be humble now in our predictions about environmental problems hundreds of years hence.

I raise these controversies about global warming not to legitimize them or to suggest that nothing should be done—in my view, the case for action on climate change is very clear—but merely to illustrate the kinds of factual issues that often underlie environmental disputes. Throughout the 1980s, for example, the United States accepted that it had a duty not to cause transboundary harm but argued that the effects of acid rain on Canada were too uncertain to warrant additional measures and called for more research.[14] Today, disputes concerning genetically modified organisms are largely factual in nature. And my disagreement with the NGO volunteer, described in Chapter 1, began as a dispute over the facts. The problem of uncertainty is especially pronounced in the case of global warming. But it is pervasive in international environmental policy.

Some skeptics claim that they share the same goals as environmentalists and that their battles simply concern the facts.[15] Writing in 1990, the opinion writer, David Broder, agreed. Environmental disputes, he argued, no longer concern values. "On this score, the environmentalists have won: people now agree about the importance of protecting the environment."[16]

As is true of declarations about the end of ideology or of history,[17] however, claims of consensus about the goals of environmental policy seem premature. Environmental disputes rarely concern only facts; usually, they reflect differences in values as well, of the kind we considered in Chapter 4.

These value differences sometimes concern priorities. Traditionally, developing countries have argued that they cannot devote significant resources to environmental problems, given the multitude of other problems that they face—poverty, infant mortality, and starvation, to name a few. Development, they argue, must take priority over the environment. As the Algerian president reportedly put it in the 1970s, "[I]f improving the environment means less bread for Algerians then I am against it."[18] Developing country views have evolved considerably since then, but they still focus more on economic development than on environmental protection (as indeed do developed countries).

Differences over values can also reflect attitudes about uncertainty and risk. Two people might agree completely about the facts of climate change and yet come to different conclusions about the severity of the climate change problem, owing to their differences on risk aversion. The UN Framework Convention on Climate Change defines its ultimate objective as that of stabilizing greenhouse gas concentrations at levels that would prevent "dangerous anthropogenic interference with the climate system."[19] However, defining what is dangerous is a matter not only of facts but of values.

Future problems raise a different kind of question: How should we value the future as compared to the present? If a problem is sufficiently far off, is it really something we need to worry about? If the dangers of climate change, for example, won't manifest themselves for fifty or a hundred years, or longer, wouldn't it make sense to focus on more immediate problems instead? After all, as John Maynard Keynes once remarked, in the long run, we'll all be dead anyway.

Finally, as the whaling dispute illustrates, some environmental issues reflect more basic differences about which aspects of the environment we value—for example, between animal rights activists, who care passionately about the treatment of individual animals, and conservationists, who seek merely to perpetuate the species as a whole.

Although differences of fact and of value are important, differences of interest represent perhaps the most significant obstacle to international environmental cooperation. Of course, an actor's perception of its interests is itself the product of its beliefs and values. When the acid rain issue was first debated, Germany saw its interests very differently from those of, say, Sweden, in part because Germany remained skeptical that acid rain was damaging its forests.[20] Similarly, if a state does not value biodiversity, then it will not see species loss as a problem.

Even states with similar scientific and normative views, however, can see their interests very differently based on different national circumstances. States with significant coal or oil resources have different interests with respect to climate change than low-lying island states, which are vulnerable to sea-level rise. Upstream states have different interests from downstream states.[21] States with large areas of tropical forest such as Brazil have different interests from states without forests.

These cases all involve the kinds of incentives problems that we explored in Chapter 3. Like individuals, states have no incentive to stop polluting or to protect natural resources, to the extent that the costs and benefits affect other states—that is, to the extent that these costs and benefits represent externalities. The polluting state has different interests from those of the victim state, and states with valuable natural resources have different interests from those of the global community. That is why, in international negotiations, victim states tend to be "pushers," polluting states "draggers," and states that are both polluters and victims, "intermediaries."[22]

Global issues such as climate change raise an additional problem: even when states have symmetric interests, cooperation can prove difficult because states' individual interests differ from their collective interest.[23] Collectively, states have an interest in stopping pollution to the extent that the global benefits exceed the costs. As the tragedy of the commons teaches us, however, each individual state nevertheless has an interest in continuing to pollute, if most of the damages from its pollution are externalized.

Differences of interests do not preclude cooperation. Often, actors with different interests can reach mutually beneficial outcomes through negotiations—outcomes that leave both sides better off. This is the basic rationale of contracts and treaties. And as we will explore in Chapter 8, states have negotiated many agreements to address international environmental problems.

For a variety of reasons, however, reaching agreement can prove difficult. We have already examined one of the barriers: factual uncertainties can prevent states from calculating their interests with any confidence. Other obstacles to cooperation include distributional issues, strategic factors, and domestic politics.

In some cases, a state may reject an agreement that is in its interest because the agreement seems unfair. Although agreement would provide a collective gain, it founders over how to distribute that gain. In upstream–downstream situations, for example, agreement might require the victim to pay the polluter to stop polluting. This outcome would leave both sides better off, as long as the victim received a bigger benefit from the reduced pollution than the payment needed to get the polluter to stop. Nevertheless, the victim might still reject such a deal, arguing that, as the injured party, it should not be the one that ends up paying, since that would be unfair.

"Fair division" games illustrate the importance of distributional issues in negotiations. In these games, one person divides up a resource—say, a cake—and the other person chooses whether or not to accept the division. If the second player accepts the division, each player gets its share of the cake. But if it rejects the division, neither player gets anything. Based on a logic of consequences, one would expect the second player to accept the first's division, no matter how little it gets, since something is better than nothing—a small piece of cake, as compared to no cake at all. In fact, however, people who play "fair division" games generally prefer getting nothing to accepting a highly unequal division of the spoils; that is, they follow a logic of appropriateness rather than a logic of consequences.[24]

Fair division games suggest one possible principle of equity, namely, equal entitlements to a resource. As discussed in chapter 4, other equity principles include historical responsibility and ability to pay. The importance of equity, broadly conceived, was brought home to me when I worked in the Clinton Administration on the climate change issue. To make the Kyoto Protocol more acceptable domestically, the Clinton Administration made a major effort to persuade middle-income developing countries to accept emissions targets, so that Kyoto would have a wider scope. Our pitch to developing countries was that, through the emissions trading system, developing countries would actually come out ahead because they would be able to sell their emissions reduction allowances at a profit. Developing countries consistently rejected our arguments, perhaps in part because of an instrumental concern that, over the longer term, emissions targets would prove costly, not profitable. But my sense was that their rejection also reflected their sense of equity: since they were not responsible for creating the climate change problem and had less capacity to respond, they felt they should not be expected to assume any target.

Environmental problems involving large numbers of participants raise yet another kind of problem: the greater the number of actors involved, the more difficult it becomes to organize and sustain cooperation.[25] In smaller groups, social norms can emerge informally, which allocate use of commons resources and limit externalities.[26] Moreover, in a local community, where everyone knows one another, violations are likely to be detected and result in significant reputational costs. That is why, in traditional communities, the tragedy of the commons was not an endemic problem.

In larger groups (what political scientists refer to as "large-n" games), community-based norms tend to be weaker and violations more difficult to detect. States have less of an incentive to invest resources in negotiating an agreement because the benefits of environmental cooperation are diffuse public goods, shared by all alike. Moreover, even when they succeed in negotiating an effective agreement, states may have difficulty imposing effective sanctions against free riders and violators. If the benefits of the regime are public goods—a slowing of global warming, for example—they cannot punish a violator by excluding it from these benefits. To do so would require suspending the entire regime to punish a single state, a drastic result. Unless some other sanction can be found, states have an incentive to free ride, inasmuch as they can get the benefits of the agreement regardless of whether they participate or comply.[27]

Domestic politics can pose a final obstacle to agreement. Even when an agreement serves a state's national interests, the state may reject it because of opposition by politically powerful groups. Environmentalists argue that this, in essence, explains the Bush Administration's rejection of Kyoto. In their view, Kyoto failed not because it was contrary to U.S. interests, but rather because it imposed high costs on a few politically powerful utilities and energy companies.[28]

Public choice theory predicts that such results should be common in environmental law. In the political marketplace, policies tend to lose out when their costs are concentrated and their benefits diffuse.[29] The relatively small number of actors who face high costs have a strong incentive to organize against a policy, whereas the people who benefit, though more numerous, each gain too little to have a strong incentive to act. For environmental problems such as climate change, the obstacles are magnified, because the benefits of cooperation are not only diffuse public goods, but also uncertain and long term, whereas the costs of cooperation are immediate and concentrated. Thus failure to reach agreement should not be surprising.

Explaining the Emergence of International Environmental Law

Together, these obstacles to international cooperation present a picture that is so daunting that it is hard to conceive how international environmental cooperation has ever emerged. But emerge it has! As we saw in Chapter 5, environmental norms are all around us. So we need to explore how and why international environmental law can develop, despite apparently overwhelming odds.

To some degree, analyzing domestic environmental policy presents the same quandary. Public choice theory suggests that environmental legislation should never be adopted because it imposes concentrated costs on polluters while providing more diffuse benefits to the general public.[30] The reality is quite different, however. In fact, countries have adopted a wide variety of environmental legislation on water and air pollution, hazardous chemicals and wastes, and environmental decision making.

How can we reconcile this apparent conflict between theory and fact? One response, whenever facts clash with theory, is to question the facts.

Some public choice theorists, for example, have argued that environmental legislation does not really reflect a public environmental purpose, but instead serves the private "rent-seeking" of special interest groups.[31] Yet, even this cynical approach cannot account for international environmental agreements because the "voluntary assent" rule that lies at the heart of treaty law limits the ability of some actors to impose costs on others, as they can do in domestic systems through majority voting.[32] A related argument is that international environmental regimes have not had a significant effect in promoting environmental cooperation, so there is nothing that needs explaining.[33]

To my mind, however, a more plausible explanation of the divergence between theory and fact is that the fact of environmental cooperation is true and the theory predicting its impossibility is wrong, or at least incomplete. If so, this suggests that other causal factors must account for the emergence of environmental policies, both domestically and internationally. Some scholars, for example, explain domestic environmental legislation in terms of civic republicanism, which views politics not simply as rent-seeking by special interests groups, pursuing their own private interests, but rather as engagement by public-minded citizens to further the common good.[34] Similarly, the development of international environmental law suggests that the obstacles to cooperation we identified earlier—though real—do not represent the entire story.

The emergence of international environmental law raises two related but distinct questions. First, why do norms emerge? To the extent that they develop through a purposive process (rather than in a decentralized, spontaneous manner), who is responsible for formulating and pushing them? Why do these actors do so? What makes an actor more or less successful in influencing others? And what causes other actors to go along? These are causal questions that require us to consider a broad menu of explanatory factors, including interests, values, knowledge, power, habit, and the desire for esteem.[35] Second, what are the legal processes by which norms are adopted and changed? These are legal questions, focusing on what we earlier called the "formal sources" of international law. I will introduce the causal question in this chapter and return to it in Chapters 8 and 9, when examining the two main standard-setting processes: negotiations and custom.

The pathway by which international environmental norms emerge often begins with the formulation and advocacy of a norm by an environmental group, expert community, or other "norm entrepreneur," who persuades some government (usually its own) to push the norm internationally. In the case of successful norms, this action eventually leads to acceptance by other states. Along the way, actors may support the norm because it serves their interests or reflects an idea or value that they support. Or they might accept it to gain social approval or to avoid sanctions. The first factor is instrumental in nature, the second normative, the third cultural or social, and the last realist.

NGOs often serve as the entrepreneurs who initially advocate a norm. For example, early proposals to establish emissions targets for carbon dioxide originated at non-governmental conferences held in Villach and Toronto in the mid- to late 1980s, rather than through intergovernmental negotiations. Similarly, bird protection groups in England were among the first to advocate international regulation of discharges from oil tankers in the 1950s.

So-called epistemic communities can also play a significant role.[36] The idea of emissions trading, for example, was first developed and pushed by economists. They succeeded in getting it adopted into United States law via the 1990 Clean Air Act Amendments, and then into the Kyoto Protocol with the strong support of the United States and its negotiating allies.

NGO and expert support for a norm is most easily explained in terms of ideas and values rather than interests, but the reasons a state might accept a norm are more diverse. Sometimes, government leaders might accept a norm for the same epistemic, ideological, or ethical reasons as NGOs or expert groups. National interests also play an important role, leading coastal states to support stronger regulation of oil tankers, and small island states to advocate stronger action on global warming. In democracies, public opinion is a significant factor. Moreover, if a norm is supported by a powerful state, then it may bring pressure on other states to go along. Finally, once a norm begins to pick up support, social factors also come into play, influencing others to accept the norm as well.

These factors play out in widely varying ways. Each regime is the product of a complex set of factors and has its own interesting story to tell. In the case of pollution from oil tankers, for example, NGOs had an early role in pushing the issue in the United Kingdom and the United States. Both of these countries are democratic states with long coastlines and with significant populations who are concerned about oil pollution damage, for either environmental or economic reasons. In response to domestic political pressures (heightened by dramatic oil spills), the United Kingdom and the United States pushed the issue internationally, sometimes through the threat of unilateral action. In response, industry itself began to develop standards in order to preclude or at least influence the regulatory process. Eventually, even shipping states accepted an international approach in preference to a patchwork quilt of national regulations, which would have made international shipping more difficult.[37]

In the ozone case, non-governmental groups also played a key role in pushing the issue domestically. In 1977, the U.S. Congress amended the Clean Air Act to regulate ozone-depleting substances, and in the mid-1980s, environmental groups brought lawsuits in U.S. courts to compel additional domestic regulation. This domestic regulation gave the United States and U.S. industry an interest in international regulation in order to level the playing field. Thus, an alliance of "Baptists and bootleggers"—environmentalists and industry—emerged within the United States in favor of international regulation.[38]

Although each case is different, a few general observations are nevertheless possible:

First, ideas as well as interests matter. It is impossible to account for the positions of environmental groups, expert communities, and governments simply in terms of their interests. "[E]mpathy, altruism and ideational commitment" also play important roles, either directly or by shaping how an actor defines its interests.[39]

Second, domestic politics usually is critical in determining national positions.[40] Americans displayed greater concern than Europeans about the ozone issue in the 1980s but have shown less worry about global warming. Hence, it is not surprising that the United States supported stronger regulation than Europe on the ozone issue and weaker action on climate change. Similarly, Australia's decision to support a ban on the exploitation of Antarctic minerals was made in the context of growing domestic concern in the late 1980s about environmental issues more generally, resulting from the discovery of the ozone hole and the *Exxon Valdez* oil spill.[41] The real question is not whether domestic politics influences international politics, but why environmental issues often play out so differently in different countries.

Third, individuals and states can provide leadership by articulating shared values and interests, demonstrating potential solutions, and identifying potential compromises.[42]

Finally, once a critical mass of states and advocacy groups begin to support a norm, social factors become important, influencing others to join the norm in order to gain esteem or avoid criticism, or simply through a process of mimicry. At a certain point, a self-reinforcing cycle can take hold, leading to what some have called a norm cascade.[43]

The Functions of International Environmental Law

The factors we have been exploring thus far help explain the development of international environmental law. But international environmental law is not merely the outcome of external causal processes; it can itself promote greater international cooperation and lead to further standard-setting. Scholars have identified three general types of functions that international environmental law can serve.[44] First, it can help increase the demand for cooperation—or, to put it differently, the political will among states to establish effective regimes. Second, it can help increase the supply of agreements that effectively exploit whatever level of demand or political will exists. Finally, it can enhance the capacity of states to respond.

Building Political Will

Ultimately, success in addressing environmental problems depends on the "political will" of states. How much are states willing to do to reduce greenhouse gas emissions or to protect species? What is their receptivity, for example, to quantitative limitations on their greenhouse gas emissions? The concept of political will is a complex (not a unit) idea and can serve as a means of avoiding more serious analysis. Nonetheless, it is a useful shorthand to sum up the various causal factors that we identified earlier, which determine a state's demand for (or at least receptivity to) environmental cooperation.

As we have seen, many of the factors that influence a state's political will involve developments external (or "exogenous") to international environmental law:

- For example, technological developments may lower the costs of pollution abatement and hence make cooperation easier. DuPont's development of alternatives to CFCs, the principal ozone-depleting substances, in the mid-1980s is often cited as a critical factor leading to U.S. support for the Montreal Protocol.
- Dramatic shocks can raise public concern—for example, oil spills or, in the context of climate change, an extreme weather event such as a hurricane or heat wave.
- Elections may bring to power leaders with an environmental bent. The election of a new prime minister in Australia, for example, led to a switch in Australia's position on the Kyoto Protocol.

But although causal factors such as these are often crucial, international environmental law itself can enhance the willingness of states to cooperate. The means by which it does so depend on the nature of the obstacle to cooperation:

Building cognitive consensus. To the extent that significant disagreements about the facts exist, international institutions can help produce greater consensus about the nature of the problem and potential solutions, through scientific research, monitoring, and assessment.[45] For example, in the 1960s, after states failed to adopt effective limitations on whaling under the International Whaling Convention, they agreed to establish a Committee of Three—three (later four) eminent scientists who assessed the status of whale stocks. Although this did not immediately produce stricter regulations, it prompted public concern about the decimation of whale populations and contributed to the revitalization of the IWC in the 1980s. Similarly, in 1979, when European states adopted the Long-Range Transboundary Air Pollution Convention, they could not agree on substantive emissions limits, in part because of uncertainties about whether acid rain really caused significant harm and, if so, who was causing what harm to whom. The scientific research spurred by LRTAP helped resolve both of these uncertainties. By the mid-1980s, Germany's perception of its own interests had changed, owing to its recognition of its own environmental vulnerability to acid rain. As a result, it became a supporter rather than an opponent of emissions controls.[46] In addition, the monitoring program conducted under the auspices of LRTAP produced better understanding of how pollutants are transported from one place to another, thereby allowing the calculation of "source-receptor" relationships, which became the basis for the 1994 Sulfur Protocol.

Creation and diffusion of norms.   International regimes can also assist in the development and promulgation of environmental values. The Stockholm Conference, for example, helped spread environmental norms globally and thus, over the long term, contributed to greater demand for environmental regimes. A more specific illustration can be seen in the climate change regime, where some argue that setting a long-term target for greenhouse gas concentrations could serve as a catalyst for greater political action, much as John F. Kennedy's pledge to go to the moon in the 1960s galvanized public opinion and spurred the development of the U.S. space program.

Mobilizing and empowering supporters, both domestically and internationally.   International environmental regimes can change the political dynamic within a state by creating new constituencies for an international policy (including the bureaucracies responsible for implementing them) and by mobilizing and empowering supporters.[47] The existence of an international obligation, for example, gives domestic actors both within and outside government a "hook" for their arguments. Similarly, the preparation and submission of national reports provide domestic actors with additional opportunities to gain publicity and interject themselves into the policy process. Indeed, one of the primary rationales for the framework convention/protocol approach is to generate political will by focusing the public's attention on a problem.

Issue linkage.   Finally, an international regime can attempt to link an issue such as climate change to other issues that have greater political salience, such as energy security or economic development. The acid rain negotiations provide an illustration of such a linkage. In the late 1970s, they were used as a means of promoting East-West detente. To this end, the negotiations were conducted under the auspices of the Economic Commission for Europe (ECE), which embraces both Western and Eastern Europe.

Facilitating Agreement

In addition to increasing the demand for international cooperation, international agreements can help promote cooperative solutions:

Changing the calculus of costs and benefits.   In general, international environmental regimes promote agreement by lowering the costs of cooperation or raising the costs of non-cooperation, thereby changing the nature of the strategic game.[48] The Montreal Protocol, for example, uses both techniques. On the one hand, it lowers the costs for developing countries of participating, by establishing the Multilateral Fund (which provides them with assistance for implementation costs), and by giving them a ten-year grace period within which to comply. On the other hand, it raises the costs of non-cooperation by prohibiting trade of ozone-depleting substances (and products containing such substances) with non-parties and by establishing a non-compliance process to identify violators.[49]

Adding and subtracting parties and issues.   Negotiations can also expand the potential zone of agreement by adding or subtracting participants or issues, in an effort to find a configuration of countries and issues with respect to which collective gains are possible through agreement.[50]

Reducing transaction costs.   By establishing ongoing systems of governance, international environmental regimes can build trust among states and reduce transaction costs, thereby making it easier for states to reach agreement. This is one of the main rationales for regular conferences of the parties and for international institutions more generally.

Policing reciprocity.   When cooperation depends on reciprocity, a major obstacle to agreement is concern that the other side might cheat. Although international environmental regimes rarely provide strong sanctions, monitoring and verification mechanisms at least provide an assurance that, if other countries fail to cooperate, their violations will be detected—a topic that we will examine further in Chapter 11.

Building normative consensus about potential solutions.   Finally, international regimes can help build normative consensus not only about basic goals and values but about possible outcomes. The climate change regime, for example, encouraged a process of social learning about the role of market instruments, such as emissions trading, in addressing climate change. Although the theory of emissions trading dates back at least to 1968,[51] it was still a relatively novel concept in 1991, when Norway introduced it into the climate change negotiations. Only a year before, the United States had established the first significant emissions trading program under the 1990 Clean Air Act Amendments. For much of the next decade, many participants in the climate change negotiations resisted the idea, seeing it as a means by which rich states could buy their way out of reducing their emissions. Through a series of workshops and dialogues, however, particularly during the post-Kyoto negotiations in the late 1990s, most states have now come to accept the legitimacy of market mechanisms, and they form a key element of the Protocol's architecture.

Enhancing the Capacity of States to Respond

Finally, international environmental regimes can help countries respond to environmental problems by strengthening national institutions, providing financial assistance, and facilitating the transfer of technology. We will explore this function of international environmental law in much greater detail in Chapter 11.

Conclusion

Despite the skepticism voiced by some commentators about the value of international environmental regimes, they can help promote cooperation in a variety of ways. From a constructivist perspective, they can change a state's perception of its own interests through a process of social learning. From a liberal perspective, they can influence the domestic political process. And from an instrumentalist perspective, they can change the payoffs for cooperation versus non-cooperation.

Will international environmental law be successful in every case? Almost certainly not. For a problem such as climate change, with respect to which the costs of cooperation are potentially huge and the incentives to free ride are correspondingly great, cooperation presents an enormous challenge. Many other factors will likely be needed to solve the problem: for example, technological developments that lower the costs of alternatives to fossil fuels; sudden shocks that galvanize the public; perhaps even an evangelical awakening that broadens the popular base for rapid action. Just as we should not deride the role of international environmental law, we should not try to oversell it. Rather, we should try to gain a better, more realistic understanding of the contribution it can make in a given situation.

Recommended Reading

Scott Barrett, *Environment and Statecraft: The Strategy of Environmental Treaty-Making* (Oxford: Oxford University Press, 2003).

Abram Chayes and Antonia Handler Chayes, *The New Sovereignty: Compliance with International Regulatory Agreements* (Cambridge, MA: Harvard University Press, 1995).

Peter M. Haas, Robert O. Keohane, and Marc A. Levy, eds., *Institutions for the Earth: Sources of Effective International Environmental Protection* (Cambridge, MA: MIT Press, 1993).

Peter H. Sand, *Lessons Learned in Global Environmental Governance* (Washington, DC: World Resources Institute, 1990).

Jonathan Baert Wiener, "On the Political Economy of Global Environmental Regulation," *Georgetown Law Journal* 87 (1999), pp. 749–794.

CHAPTER EIGHT

Negotiating Agreements

The future of international law belongs to conventional
and not to customary law.

Lassa Oppenheim, "The Science of International Law"

F ROM THE INCEPTION of international environmental law, treaties and other forms of negotiated agreements have been the
predominant means of achieving international cooperation. According to one recent compilation, states have negotiated more than 990
multilateral environmental agreements and 1,500 bilateral instruments on
a wide variety of subjects: protection of the stratospheric ozone layer,
prevention of dangerous anthropogenic climate change, mitigation of acid
rain, control of hazardous waste exports, regulation of trade in wildlife,
protection of wetlands, prevention of oil pollution, and many others.[1] Indeed, in the mid-1990s, environmental treaties were proliferating so rapidly that some worried about "treaty congestion."[2]

Negotiated agreements offer several advantages over more informal
mechanisms of international cooperation:

- They enable states to address issues in a purposive, rational
  manner.
- They promote reciprocity by allowing states to delineate precisely
  what each party is expected to do.
- Because they have a canonical form, they provide greater certainty
  about the applicable norms than non-treaty sources of international law.
- Finally, they allow states to tailor a regime's institutional arrangements and mechanisms to fit the particular problem.

Traditionally, treaties were comparatively static arrangements, memo-
rializing the rights and duties of the parties as agreed at a particular point

in time. Today, environmental agreements are usually dynamic arrangements, establishing ongoing regulatory processes.[3] The result is that, in most environmental regimes, the treaty text itself represents just the tip of the normative iceberg. The majority of the norms are adopted through more flexible techniques, which allow international environmental law to respond more quickly to the emergence of new problems and new knowledge.

This chapter explores negotiated instruments as a means of addressing international environmental problems. Although it focuses on legally binding agreements between states—that is, treaties—it touches on other types of negotiated instruments such as declarations and codes of conduct, which may be non-binding or involve non-state actors. The first section of the chapter introduces the basic types of international agreements: legal and non-legal; interstate, private, and public-private; contractual and legislative; constitutive and regulatory. Then, the second section analyzes why states commit to negotiated norms, and the third describes the process of developing negotiated instruments, from the inception of negotiations to the adoption and entry into force of the resulting instrument. Finally, the fourth section explores various design issues in developing international environmental agreements.

Categorizing International Agreements: Some Initial Distinctions

Negotiated agreements vary along many dimensions. Some address a wide subject area such as the law of the sea; others are very specific, focusing on a particular problem such as persistent organic pollutants, polar bears, or wetlands. Some are global, and others regional or bilateral. Some are written, others unwritten.

In classifying international agreements, four distinctions are of particular importance: (1) whether a negotiated instrument is legal or non-legal in form; (2) whether it is between states or involves other actors, such as companies or non-governmental organizations; (3) whether it is essentially contractual or legislative in nature; and (4) whether it is constitutive or regulatory in function.

Legal Form: Legal vs. Non-Legal Instruments

We ordinarily think of negotiations as leading to the adoption of legally binding agreements. However, negotiations can also produce instruments that do not have a legal status: declarations, resolutions, codes of conduct, guidelines, recommendations, and the like. Prominent examples of non-legal outcomes include the 1972 Stockholm Declaration on the Human Environment, the 1992 Rio Declaration on Environment and Development, and Agenda 21.

Although environmentalists (not to mention international lawyers) often see the greater strength of legal agreements as an unqualified good, non-binding agreements do not necessarily represent a second-best outcome.[4] As we shall see, they have several advantages over treaties: They can be adopted and changed more quickly and flexibly than treaties because they do not require ratification. They are easier to negotiate because they represent a weaker level of commitment. In addition, they give states a way to test an approach without fully committing—a feature that is particularly attractive when uncertainties are high.[5] In essence, a non-binding approach represents a type of risk management strategy, reducing the risk to states of being bound by norms that ultimately prove undesirable.

Generally, legally binding instruments between states are referred to as treaties, but sometimes they are called protocols, conventions, charters, agreements, or accords. What matters is not an agreement's title, but whether states intend to create legal rights and obligations. Occasionally, parties include an express statement about the legal character of an instrument, generally when they do not intend to create legal obligations and they want to prevent any inference to the contrary.[6] But in most cases the parties' intent is clear from the agreement's context and language. For example, treaties typically use mandatory language, whereas non-legal agreements use more hortatory terms.[7] Similarly, treaties include "final clauses" relating to ratification, entry into force, and other legal formalities, whereas non-legal agreements do not.

An extensive body of rules governs legal agreements among states, addressing the formation, application, interpretation, modification, termination, and validity of treaties. Originally, these rules developed through the customary practice of states, but now they are codified in the 1969 Vienna Convention on the Law of Treaties, or as it is commonly known, the "treaty on treaties." In contrast, no well-defined body of rules governs non-legal agreements such as declarations or codes of conduct. An international organization that adopts a non-legal instrument may have internal rules governing how decisions are adopted and modified. However, many of the issues addressed by the law of treaties do not have a counterpart for non-legal agreements—for example, issues relating to entry into force and invalidity. Other issues are simply not addressed at all, such as the rules of interpretation for non-legal instruments.

Together with the principle of *pacta sunt servanda* (which says that agreements must be kept), the most fundamental rule of treaty law is that treaties depend on state consent.[8] This is perhaps one reason treaty norms are often characterized as "commitments" rather than "obligations"—to emphasize the self-binding quality of treaty law. Treaty norms are not obligations imposed on states; rather, they are commitments that a state voluntarily undertakes. Detailed rules of treaty law address how states manifest their consent, who has authority to give consent, and so forth. In some cases, consent may be more formal than real; as we shall see, powerful states sometimes pressure others to go along.[9] Nevertheless, consent provides a useful starting point of analysis. In contrast, non-binding instruments do not have any clear consensual limitation; they neither bind those states that support them nor exempt those that do not.

Parties: State and Non-State Actors

Although negotiated instruments at the international level have traditionally been between states, a growing number involve non-governmental actors. These reflect virtually every conceivable configuration of parties: international organization (IO)-government, IO-IO, government-industry; NGO-industry; and intra-industry. The spread of market-based thinking has spawned an interest in public-private partnerships in particular, which was a highlight of the 2002 Johannesburg World Summit on Sustainable Development. In response to NGO pressure, industry has also worked with NGOs to develop non-binding codes of conduct, such as the principles and criteria for responsible forest management developed by the Forest Stewardship Council.[10] Typically, these instruments are not legal in nature, and even when they do take a legally binding form, they are governed by municipal rather than international law because international treaty law does not extend to agreements involving non-state actors.

Contractual vs. Legislative Instruments

Traditionally, treaties have been understood essentially as contracts between states.[11] Although treaty and contract law differ in non-trivial respects,[12] they are alike in many ways: both treaties and contracts depend on consent; both define reciprocal obligations between the parties; both establish a fundamental obligation to comply, and both have similar grounds for invalidity (fraud, duress, impossibility, and so forth). Certainly, with respect to bilateral treaties, conceptualizing them as creating private, contractual obligations between the parties seems appropriate.

Treaties can also have a legislative dimension. Even bilateral treaties often establish general rules of an ongoing nature rather than provide for a single exchange between the parties.[13] The contractual model breaks down even more for multilateral agreements that address public goods problems, such as depletion of the ozone layer or global warming. These agreements do not create obligations owed on a reciprocal basis between particular states. Instead, they create obligations owed to the community of states as a whole—what international law terms *obligations erga omnes*—and typically provide for greater collective decision making and control.[14] In these respects, they are "legislative" rather than contractual in nature, although they are perhaps best understood as hybrids because unlike most legislative processes, they typically do not establish majoritarian decision-making processes, but rather rely, like contracts, on individual consent by each participating state.

Constitutive vs. Regulatory Instruments

International environmental agreements can serve two quite different functions. First, they can play a regulatory function, setting forth primary rules of conduct—for example, rules about how oil tankers are designed, how much oil they can discharge, how much chlorofluorocarbons (CFCs) a state may produce and consume, how much carbon dioxide it may emit, or what actions it must take to control the import and export of endangered species and hazardous wastes. Second, treaties can play a constitutive role, establishing a system of governance to address a particular subject matter or issue area. Prominent examples of constitutive treaties are those establishing institutions such as the United Nations, the World Trade Organization, and the International Maritime Organization. Kratochwil nicely captures the difference by contrasting agreements that establish "a framework for continuous negotiation" with those that are "historic[al]" documents that "freeze[] the 'meeting of the wills' of the parties at a given time."[15]

Although international environmental agreements often have regulatory elements, most have a fundamentally constitutive character. They establish what are, in essence, ongoing systems of governance for a given issue area, by creating institutions; defining their powers and decision-making rules; establishing procedures to adopt and amend substantive regulatory rules; and providing methods for resolving disputes. The results are dynamic arrangements that evolve considerably over time.

The Convention on International Trade in Endangered Species (CITES) provides an illustration. On the basis of relatively modest language on compliance in CITES itself, the CITES parties have elaborated a complex set of non-compliance procedures, which in some cases have resulted in trade suspensions against states with persistent compliance problems. In order to understand the regime, one therefore needs to consult not merely

CITES itself, but rather the *CITES Handbook*—a thick book that compiles the various decisions by the CITES parties on the listing process, reporting, and compliance, among other subjects.

Why Do States Negotiate and Accept International Agreements?

Treaties represent self-limitations by states; they depend on their consent. Why do states accept these limitations on their sovereignty? Why do they make commitments?

A common way to think about this issue is in terms of costs and benefits. A state will enter into an agreement when it thinks that the benefits of doing so exceed the costs, and not otherwise. In the memorable (though exaggerated) phrase of the German writer, Johannes Haller: "No state has ever entered into a treaty for any other reason than self-interest. A statesman who has any other motive would deserve to be hung."[16] Assuming statesmen everywhere wish to avoid the noose, then we would expect international agreements to be possible only when they leave all of the participating states better off—that is, when they provide what economists call a Pareto improvement.[17]

This instrumental answer to the question, "why commit?" raises a host of other questions. What are the costs and benefits of joining an international environmental agreement? Costs and benefits for whom, as determined by whom? Haller's dictum suggests that states have interests that can be objectively identified. As we explored in Chapter 6, however, states are abstractions whose policies are the product of a variety of governmental and non-governmental actors—the executive branch officials who negotiate an agreement, the legislators who ratify it, environmental groups, industry, and the public at large, to whom the government (at least in democracies) is ultimately accountable. To understand why states commit to international agreements, we need to understand how these various actors perceive the costs and benefits involved, as well as whether they are influenced by factors other than self-interest.

Costs and Benefits of Treaty Participation

To illustrate the instrumentalist approach, consider a simple case involving a pollution externality. Two states each produce fumes that cross the international border into the other. Each has an environmental interest in getting the other to stop and an economic interest in continuing its own polluting behavior. Assuming the economic interest outweighs the environmental, each should be willing to incur costly measures to reduce its own pollution, in exchange for the benefit it would receive from reciprocal action by the other side. Each side would come out ahead, making an agreement possible.[18]

Both the costs and benefits of the agreement are a function of the stringency of its commitments. All other things being equal, the more stringent the commitment—the more (and faster) it requires a state to deviate from what it would have done otherwise—the bigger the economic cost of compliance for each participant, but also the bigger the corresponding environmental benefit provided by the other state's compliance. Assuming that the marginal costs of compliance increase as a commitment becomes more stringent, and the marginal environmental benefits decline, at some point the curves representing the collective costs and benefits of the two parties cross, and more stringent commitments are not cost-effective. This is the level of stringency that produces the biggest joint gain for the two sides. Reaching agreement on this level is the object of what economists refer to as integrative bargaining; agreeing on how to distribute that gain is the outcome of distributive bargaining.[19]

Not every environmental agreement must involve an exchange of environmental commitments. Consider a slightly different case, involving a unidirectional rather than a bidirectional externality. Industria produces fumes that cross the international border into its neighbor Arcadia. In this case, the interests of the two states are asymmetric: Arcadia has an environmental interest in getting Industria to stop; Industria has an economic interest in continuing to pollute.

Nevertheless, the logic of the case is still the same. As in the first illustration, agreement should be possible if the agreement produces an aggregate gain and distributes that gain in a manner that leaves both sides better off.[20] If Arcadia's environmental interests are stronger than Industria's economic interests, then an agreement providing that Arcadia pay Industria to stop polluting would leave each side better off: Arcadia because the environmental benefits of the agreement outweigh the costs of paying Industria; Industria because the payment it receives from Arcadia is greater than the costs of stopping its pollution.[21]

This is not the end of the analysis, however. Since agreements between states have an ongoing character, they involve a second type of cost and benefit. By committing to an ongoing course of conduct—reducing its pollution, for example, or making a payment—each state incurs a cost to its own sovereignty and provides a corresponding benefit to the other participating states, to whom the commitment is owed.

Consider, first, the sovereignty cost to the country assuming a commitment. In the externality examples described above, each state's decision whether to adopt the environmental agreement was determined by its *ex ante* calculation of costs and benefits. But what if subsequent events show that a state's calculation was wrong? For example, what if a state joined the Kyoto Protocol thinking that compliance would be easy, but the agreement proves to be a millstone? Or what if domestic support for the treaty evaporates or the treaty develops in a way that the state does not like (as has happened with the Whaling Convention for Japan). Absent its international commitment, a state would be free to change its mind, should it later decide that the costs of a policy exceed the benefits. By committing to an international agreement, a state limits its freedom of action to some degree. For this reason, in considering whether to join a treaty, it must weigh not only the expected costs and benefits, but also the risk of error. As we shall see, a wide variety of design elements affect the strength of a treaty's commitments and hence the level of this risk.

What is a cost to one state may be a benefit to the other. There is a *quid pro quo* not just between economic costs and environmental benefits, but between the costs and benefits of committing. The 1990 U.S.-Canada Air Quality Agreement provides an illustration. Under this instrument, Canada agreed to reduce its emissions of sulfur dioxide and nitrous oxides, the precursors of acid rain, in exchange for a commitment by the United States to do what it had already decided to do on its own, when it enacted the Clean Air Act Amendments earlier in the year. What did Canada gain, if the United States had already decided to take the required actions? Presumably, the benefit for Canada was that, by making an international commitment, the United States limited its freedom of action. The treaty helped lock in the U.S. emissions reductions by converting them from a domestic legislative decision into an international commitment.[22]

How big are the costs and benefits of committing? The answer depends on what I will call the *strength* of the commitment—the degree to which it limits a state's sovereignty. Together, the strength and the stringency of an agreement's commitments determine its *depth*. In a later section of this chapter, I will explore the various design elements that affect the stringency and strength of commitments, and thereby affect the cost-benefit calculation of states in deciding whether to enter into an agreement—for example, whether commitments are legal or non-legal in form, precise or vague, and subject to international supervision.

Thus far we have been viewing a state's support for a treaty primarily as a function of its economic and environmental interests. States with high environmental vulnerability and low abatement costs should readily agree to a treaty; those with lower ecological vulnerability and higher abatement costs should be reluctant, absent side payments from the victim state.[23]

Decisions about whether to participate in an international environmental agreement implicate other interests as well. For example, international environmental agreements can affect a state's competitiveness. In a global market, states care about not only their absolute gains and losses (whether the treaty makes them better or worse off) but also their position relative to others. If a treaty imposes higher compliance costs on one state than another, then it gives the state with the lower compliance costs a competitive advantage. This possibility gives rise to cynical fears that ostensibly environmental agreements may really serve economic interests. Conservatives in the United States, for example, have criticized the Kyoto Protocol in these terms, as an attempt by Europe to impose a burden on U.S. industry and thereby improve its own competitive position.

In addition, international environmental agreements can further a state's foreign policy and security interests. For example, participation in an environmental agreement may:

- Help promote friendly relations with a state's neighbors by resolving environmental disputes.
- Enhance a state's reputation internationally as a good global citizen.
- Promote stability and prevent conflict by reducing environmental stresses in other countries.

These putative national interests are, of course, debatable. But in explaining why states might join an international agreement, the important point is not whether states actually have these interests, but rather whether influential domestic actors believe this to be the case.

The Problem of Free Riders

In thinking about the costs and benefits of treaty-making, it is common to think of the choice as binary and to compare the costs and benefits of the treaty and no-treaty cases. Are states better off with a climate treaty or without? With a treaty on biodiversity or without? In the simple bilateral example above, this perspective makes sense because the participation of both states is necessary for the treaty to take effect.

Multilateral treaties, however, do not require universal participation to enter into force. As a result, states often have a third option: not joining an existing treaty. In their cost-benefit calculations, they must consider not only whether they are better off with or without the treaty, but whether they are better off with party or non-party status. Simple economics suggests that when a treaty provides benefits to parties and non-parties alike, this undermines a state's incentive to join. As long as enough other states participate for the treaty to enter into force,[24] a state can get the benefits of the treaty even as a non-participant; it can free ride on the efforts of others. Conversely, when a treaty imposes costs on non-parties as well as parties, this has the opposite effect: it reduces a state's incentive to stay out.

Although most writers focus on the free rider problem, the second dynamic can also be important.[25] The Kyoto Protocol's emissions targets, for example, impose costs on oil-producing states, whether or not they join, by lowering demand for oil. For this reason, although oil-producing states might have preferred not to have had any climate change agreement at all, they have an incentive to participate in Kyoto, since doing so gives them a seat at the table and allows them to influence the treaty's development.

More commonly, however, environmental agreements have positive rather than negative externalities: they confer benefits on non-parties rather than impose costs. Treaties addressing global problems such as climate change or stratospheric ozone depletion provide public goods, which a state receives even if it refuses to participate. This gives states a significant incentive to free ride. In doing so, they not only reap the environmental benefits of the agreement, but gain a competitive advantage over participants by avoiding the costs of taking action themselves. For this reason, multilateral agreements have a third task: in addition to producing aggregate gains and distributing those gains so as to leave each participant better off, they must also seek to deter free riding by making non-participation more costly than participation.[26]

How big a problem is free riding? Thus far, it has not been a huge problem. Most environmental agreements have in practice managed to attract participation well above the minimum numbers required for entry into force. However, as international environmental agreements become more demanding and the incentives to free ride increase, free ridership poses a potentially serious challenge to participation.

Several factors help to limit free ridership and may explain why it has not caused bigger problems to date. First, over the long term, states—particularly big ones—may not have the option to free ride because their failure to participate in a treaty regime may eventually cause the treaty to collapse. Although the Kyoto Protocol, for example, went forward even after the United States withdrew, it has little chance of continuing indefinitely if the United States (and other big emitters such as China) continue to stay out.[27] Thus, in the long run, the major players may not be able to sit on the sidelines and continue to receive benefits. They may be forced to choose between the treaty and no-treaty options.

Second, doing what the agreement requires may provide national as well as global environmental benefits, which justify participation regardless of what others do. According to EPA estimates, this was true of U.S. action under the Montreal Protocol.[28] Moreover, even if the environmental benefits provided by an agreement are public goods, other benefits may be "club" goods that depend on participation—for example, the reputational benefits of joining a treaty. Through various elements of treaty design, which we will explore further below, states can enhance these benefits of participation, or impose costs on non-participants, in order to deter free riding.

Normative Factors

Although instrumental explanations go far in explaining how states behave, they do not fully account for state behavior. Normative and domestic political factors also shape how states behave, influencing them to join agreements even when they might seem better off staying out.

For example, government decision makers might believe that their state has a moral responsibility to its neighbors to conserve shared resources or to future generations to prevent the loss of biodiversity. On the basis of these beliefs, they might conclude that joining a treaty addressing transboundary resources or biodiversity is the "right" thing to do. Whether or not the treaty produces environmental benefits, joining it serves an expressive function, showing a state's support for environmental values. The decision to participate reflects a logic of appropriateness rather than a logic of consequences.

Consider, for example, the decision by the newly elected prime minister of Australia, Kevin Rudd, in December 2007, to join the Kyoto Protocol as his first official act. The decision provided no immediate benefit to Australia because the Protocol was already in effect and Australia (as a free rider) was getting whatever environmental improvement Kyoto provides. Instead, the decision to ratify the Kyoto Protocol was apparently based, at least in part, on the new government's belief about what was right.

Similarly, in the effort to reduce sulfur emissions in Europe in the 1980s, states engaged in what one commentator has described as "toteboard diplomacy." Just as office charities use tote boards to record contributions, in order to encourage other fair-minded people to give as well, some states made unilateral pledges to reduce their sulfur emissions to encourage others to do the "right" thing.[29]

As we saw in Chapter 7, a logic of appropriateness also has implications for the resolution of unidirectional externalities, as shown earlier in the example involving Industria and Arcadia. The instrumental model predicts that, in such cases, victims will ordinarily pay polluters to stop because that outcome leaves both sides better off. In fact, however, agreements addressing transboundary water pollution typically allocate the burden of abatement based on the relative wealth of the two countries. They impose the costs on whichever state has the higher per capita income, the polluting or the victim state.[30] What might explain this result? One plausible answer is that it reflects the role of non-instrumental norms in treaty-making—in this case, a social norm that the burden of preventing pollution should be borne by the state with the greater capacity to respond. This norm forms the backdrop for negotiations between the two states and suggests the unfairness of requiring a poor victim to pay a rich polluter to stop polluting.

Domestic Politics

Our discussion thus far has treated the state as a unitary actor, evaluating the costs and benefits of an agreement for the country as a whole and applying a single set of normative principles. States, however, consist of many different governmental and private actors, who often view a treaty very differently. Some groups may have strong environmental values and firmly support a treaty; others may not. Similarly, an environmental treaty may mean a gain for some but a loss for others. An agreement to reduce emissions of carbon dioxide, for example, would impose costs on oil and coal companies but provide benefits to solar energy producers. An agreement to address acid rain would benefit those parts of a country with sensitive ecosystems but impose costs on coal-producing regions. So some groups within a country are likely to support an international environmental agreement and others to oppose it.

A country's position in international negotiations generally reflects these domestic factors.[31] Indeed, in the end, a country's decision to join an international agreement may hinge as much (if not more) on the distribution of costs and benefits domestically as on general calculations of "national interest." If the winners have more influence in the national political system than the losers, then a state is likely to join, and vice versa.[32] This may be one reason European states had an easier time joining the Kyoto Protocol than the United States: the European tradition of coalition governments has given green parties considerable leverage. By contrast, the United States' two-party system has created less space for environmental groups to wield influence.[33]

Interestingly, for those groups within a country that benefit from an international agreement, the limits on sovereignty imposed by the treaty represent a benefit rather than a cost. An international commitment helps these groups lock in their gains by limiting the ability of states to backslide even if their influence should wane.[34] This desire for domestic lock-in may, in part, explain why states make unilateral commitments. Why would a state agree internationally to do something when it gets nothing in return? For example, why would it list a wetland under the Ramsar Convention? If protecting the wetland made domestic sense, a state could do so on its own, without assuming an international commitment. Why would a state wish to limit its freedom of action? The question is difficult to answer if we think of the state as a unitary actor. But if we view the state's action through the lens of domestic politics, then the rationale behind its decision to list a wetland internationally becomes clear. For domestic organizations that wish to protect the wetland, the treaty's limits on the state's freedom of action are not negatives, but instead are precisely why they want to list the wetland in the first place. In essence, the international agreement allows one group to bind others, or one generation or government to bind its successors.[35]

Power

Finally, in some cases government actors may accept a treaty (or treaty decisions) in response to pressure from other (typically more powerful) states. Although we do not think of international environmental politics as a significant arena for the exercise of power, states have sometimes used power to induce other states to agree. For example, U.S. threats in the 1970s to adopt oil tanker standards unilaterally helped spur other states to agree to international standards in the International Convention for the Prevention of Pollution from Ships (MARPOL). Similarly, U.S. pressure in the late 1970s and early 1980s to impose a moratorium on commercial whaling led first to the adoption of the moratorium decision and then to acceptance of that decision by Japan and most other whaling countries.

Steps in the Treaty-Making Process

Thus far we have been considering why states commit to treaties. It is also important to understand the process by which international agree-

---

Box 8.1.   Stages in the Treaty-Making Process

Prenegotiation	• Framing of issue
	• Formulation of national positions
Initiation of negotiations	• Choice of negotiating forum
	• Adoption of negotiating mandate
Negotiations	• Structural issues: committees, coalitions
	• Procedures: decision-making rules, transparency, access
	• Formulation of initial draft
Adoption and entry into force	• Adoption
	• National consent: signature and ratification, or accession
	Entry into force

---

ments are developed. How does the treaty-making process unfold? What are the stages, from beginning to end?[36]

Prenegotiation Phase

Even after an issue enters the international agenda, a significant period may elapse before formal negotiations actually begin. Climate change, for example, emerged as a significant intergovernmental issue in the period 1985–1988, but states did not begin the formal negotiations that led to the Framework Convention on Climate Change (UNFCCC) until late 1990. During the intervening period, states began to organize themselves domestically, stake out their positions internationally, develop coalitions with like-minded countries, and attempt to frame the issue by defining its parameters and goals.

Initiation of Negotiations

The first step in the treaty-making process is the decision to initiate negotiations. This involves two primary issues: first, the choice of negotiating forum, and second, the adoption of a negotiating mandate. The choice of negotiating forum, though often the product of happenstance rather than conscious deliberation, can be extremely consequential. Assume, for example, that a group of states wishes to negotiate a new forestry convention.[37] Should they proceed under the auspices of the existing UN Forum

on Forestry, the Food and Agriculture Organization (FAO) (the UN specialized agency with a mandate to consider forestry issues), the UN Environmental Programme (UNEP), the UN Conference on Trade and Development (the sponsoring organization for the existing International
Tropical Timber Agreement), or some other international organization?
Or should they establish an ad hoc negotiating group on their own? The
choice may influence which domestic agencies have the lead in the negotiations, who represents each country, the general orientation of the
agreement, and even which countries may take part in the negotiations, if
an organization is not universal in membership. The decision to conduct
the climate change negotiations under the auspices of the UN General
Assembly, for example, meant that the negotiations were open to every
UN member state and were conducted by countries' UN missions, which
in the case of smaller developing states often operate as independent entities, with little control from their capitals. If the climate negotiations had
proceeded within the World Meteorological Organization, as was originally considered, they might have had a more scientific, less political
orientation. Or if Western industrialized states, which originally put the
climate change issue on the international agenda, had decided to proceed
within the Organisation for Economic Cooperation and Development
(OECD), the negotiations initially would have included only developed
states. Possible choices of a negotiating forum include not only existing
organizations, such as UNEP or the International Maritime Organization
(IMO) or the OECD, but also ad hoc negotiating groups or even non-
governmental groups such as the World Conservation Union, which
sponsored the negotiations of the Ramsar Wetlands Convention and
CITES.

The decision to authorize a negotiation may give a more or less specific
mandate to the negotiators, addressing issues such as the scope of the
negotiations, the legal status of the intended outcome, the types of provisions to include, the target completion date, and the rules regarding decision making and participation. (For example, do decisions require consensus? Are meetings held in public or private? And what role, if any,
may NGOs play?) Because the mandate shapes the ultimate agreement, it
often involves hard-fought negotiations. In the drafting of the mandate
for the Kyoto Protocol negotiations, for example, developing countries
succeeded in including a provision that expressly excluded them from
any new commitments, thus effectively settling a central issue in the negotiations.[38] By contrast, developed countries proved more successful in
negotiating the mandate for the post-Kyoto climate change negotiations.
The so-called Bali Action Plan adopted in December 2007 established an

open-ended process that expressly includes the possibility of additional actions by developing countries, while excluding nothing.[39]

Negotiations

Although every negotiation has its own dynamic, they often follow a similar pattern. At first, little progress is apparent, as countries debate procedural issues and endlessly repeat their initial positions rather than seeking compromise formulations. Though frustrating to those hoping for rapid progress, this sparring process allows countries to voice their views and concerns, to learn about and gauge the strength of other states' views, and to send up trial balloons. Real negotiations, however, begin only in the final months (or even hours) before the negotiations are scheduled to conclude, when governments realize that they need to compromise if they wish to avoid failure.

With almost 200 states now comprising the international community, international lawmaking has become increasingly complex and unwieldy. To simplify the negotiating task, the closing stages of a negotiation typically involve only a small number of key delegations. In addition, states often negotiate as part of a larger group rather than individually.[40] Sometimes coalitions of like-minded states, built on common interests and positions, emerge. Examples are states with large shipping industries in negotiations on vessel-source pollution standards; oil-producing states in the climate negotiations; conservation-minded countries in the CITES negotiations; and so forth. Coalitions are particularly useful for small countries, which have greater influence collectively than individually and hence may continue to participate in coalitions even when their interests diverge from one another.[41] Even a superpower like the United States usually finds it useful to participate in such coalitions of like-minded states. For example, in the climate negotiations, it has operated as part of the "Umbrella Group," a loose coalition of states that has served as a counterweight to the European Union.

When a negotiation proceeds under the auspices of an existing international organization, the organization's secretariat often prepares the initial negotiating draft, either internally or with the assistance of outside experts. In some cases, such as the Ramsar Wetlands Convention, NGOs may contribute. But when an issue is politically sensitive, states usually seek to retain control and insist that the treaty text emerge through a more bottom-up, inductive process, starting with proposals by states of possible provisions, which are eventually combined (often by the negotiating chair) into a composite text.

Although the rules of procedure of most negotiating groups provide for voting if agreement is not possible, in practice consensus decision making prevails. This was not always the case. In the 1970s, when a much smaller community of states negotiated MARPOL, they resolved many difficult issues through voting. Today, with many more states participating in international negotiations, the trust necessary for voting to work is less common, and hence there is a strong preference for consensus.[42] In this context, consensus does not necessarily mean unanimity, but rather the absence of formal objection. In contrast to voting, where there are winners and losers, the objective is to address objections and find common ground. That is why the outcomes of consensus decision making often represent a least common denominator, or why they paper over differences through formulations that preserve the positions of all sides, are deliberately ambiguous, or defer issues to a future date.[43]

Treaties typically have significant practical consequences, but much of the actual negotiating process is linguistic in nature, with words debated as much for their symbolic and political significance as for their practical implications. Sometimes, particular formulations take on an almost talismanic quality, only distantly related to their common meaning. Why do states often seem to focus as much on words as on substance? In part, this concern with language may reflect a lack of trust prevalent in many negotiations, which leads states to fear that even seemingly innocuous words may carry some hidden meaning.[44] In some cases, linguistic debates serve as a proxy for more substantive conflicts, allowing success or failure to be measured not just by the substantive outcomes, but by the inclusion or exclusion of particular terms. Finally, the focus on words reflects the iterative, continuing nature of multilateral environmental negotiations, where words establish markers for future rounds in the process.

International environmental law places a good deal of emphasis on participation and transparency,[45] but the actual practice of negotiations has moved in the opposite direction. Back in the 1950s and 1960s, verbatim records were often kept of negotiating sessions and votes recorded. As international conferences grew larger and more public, however, the real business of negotiations tended to move behind closed doors. In the Rio process, the opening of the negotiating committees to non-governmental groups led to the creation of so-called informals, which only state representatives could attend, and then, when these meetings were in turn opened up, "informal-informals" emerged. Today, most of the business of negotiations takes place, not in public sessions, but in contact groups or meetings of the "friends of the chair," which are off the record. Official reports say little more than that a meeting was held. As a result, accounts by participants or observers have become a key source of information about what transpired: who proposed what provisions, for what reasons, and with what results.

Adoption, Signature, Ratification, and Entry into Force

At the end of a negotiation, a treaty must be adopted, signed, and, in most cases, ratified, before it can enter into force. In the case of bilateral agreements, particularly those dealing with more technical issues that do not require legislative approval, the signature of an agreement by the two sides may both conclude the negotiations and bring the treaty into effect. Usually, however, the conclusion of treaty negotiations is a multistep process. First, the negotiating body adopts the treaty, generally by a consensus decision, thereby finalizing the treaty text and ending the negotiations. Next, the treaty is opened for signature, a step signifying a state's preliminary support for the agreement. For states that wish to become bound—a decision that may require legislative approval—consent to a treaty is given by means of ratification (if a treaty has previously signed the treaty) or accession (if it has not). Finally, after a sufficient number of states have given their consent, the treaty enters into force and they become parties.

A common mistake, even among supposedly authoritative sources such as the U.S. Supreme Court or the *New York Times,* is to equate the terms *signatory* and *party.* In most cases, however, the two are not equivalent. Signature is neither a necessary nor a sufficient condition for party status. States may accede to treaties that they have not signed, and they may decide not to ratify treaties that they have signed. (The United States, for example, is a signatory to both the Kyoto Protocol and the Convention on Biological Diversity but is not a party to either agreement.) Signature is merely a waystation on the road to party status and creates only a limited duty "to refrain from acts which would defeat the object and purpose of [the] treaty"[46]—a phrase with no agreed meaning.

Often, the period of time between a treaty's adoption and its entry into force can be substantial. For example, the Montreal Protocol took two years to enter into force, the Basel Convention three years, and the Kyoto Protocol more than seven years. Indeed, in perhaps the most extreme example, fourteen years elapsed between the adoption of the UN Convention on the Law of the Sea in 1982 and its entry into force in 1996. In order not to let this time go to waste, states may agree to provisionally implement a treaty before its entry into force.[47] States may also continue to meet during this interim period in order to elaborate and develop the agreement so that it can get off to a prompt start when it eventually enters into force. In the case of the Kyoto Protocol, states were, in practice, unwilling to ratify until the detailed rules on how the agreement would work had been developed. So the adoption of the Protocol did not signify the end of negotiations. Instead, additional negotiating rounds were necessary before the agreement was complete. In the case of Kyoto, these rounds lasted four years, two more than for negotiation of the Protocol text itself.

Design Issues

The development of an international agreement raises numerous design issues. Some are familiar, such as:

- What commitments should an agreement contain? The answer, of course, depends on the nature of the problem. CITES uses a permitting system to control trade in endangered species; the International Convention for the Prevention of Pollution from Ships (MARPOL) establishes requirements for the construction and design of oil tankers; the Montreal Protocol limits the consumption and production of ozone-depleting substances; and the Kyoto Protocol imposes binding targets on national emissions relative to historic, baseline levels. We examined some of the design issues relating to the choice of policy instruments in Chapter 4.
- What institutions should the treaty establish, and what features should these institutions have? As we saw in Chapter 6, some of the most common treaty institutions include a conference of the parties (COP), secretariat, financial mechanism, and scientific body.
- How should the treaty promote implementation and effectiveness? What mechanisms should it establish to generate information about treaty compliance and effectiveness—for example, reporting requirements, monitoring programs, or review processes? And how should it respond to cases of non-compliance. We will return to these issues in Chapter 11.

This section examines several critical, but less familiar, aspects of treaty design, which have begun to receive greater attention in recent years:

- First, the breadth or scope of a treaty, both in terms of membership and subject matter.

- Second, the depth of a treaty—the degree to which it requires states to depart from business as usual.
- Third, the treaty's ability to respond flexibly to new information and changed circumstances.

We will consider these design elements from several perspectives. First, what is the range of design choices? This is essentially a doctrinal/descriptive question. Second, what are the pros and cons of these options and the potential trade-offs? These are policy issues. Finally, why do states choose to include certain design elements in a particular treaty, and, more generally, what explains the distribution of design elements across treaties? Here, we move into the realm of explanation.

Breadth[48]

WHO MAY PARTICIPATE IN A TREATY REGIME?

Who should be allowed (or entitled) to participate in an international agreement on, say, climate change, whaling, or Antarctica? Treaties answer this question in many ways.[49] Some are open to any state, making them potentially global in scope; examples are the Montreal Ozone Protocol, the UN Framework Convention on Climate Change, and the International Whaling Convention. Others set geographic limits on participation— for example, regional agreements such as the 1983 Cartagena Convention for the Protection of the Marine Environment of the Wider Caribbean Region.[50] And others define their membership along functional grounds. For example, the Antarctic Treaty limits full membership to states that engage in Antarctic research.[51]

The issue of participation raises both normative and pragmatic issues. As a normative matter, who is entitled to participate in decision making about a particular subject? The Whaling Convention allows any state to join. But why should the entire international community—including even landlocked states such as Mongolia—be entitled to have a voice? Given that one purpose of the Whaling Convention is to "make possible the orderly development of the whaling industry,"[52] why shouldn't the handful of states actually engaged in whaling be entitled to make the rules that will govern their behavior?[53]

One approach to the issue of membership is to say that anyone affected by a decision should be entitled to participate in the decision-making process. On this basis, treaties should be open to any state with a causal nexus to the problem—or, to put it differently, the scope of a treaty should be defined by the scope of the externality that it aims to control. Bilateral externalities such as pollution across the U.S.-Canadian border call for bilateral treaties; regional externalities such as acid rain in Europe call for regional treaties; and global externalities such as climate change call for global treaties.[54]

Defining the scope of environmental externalities may not be easy, however. When acid rain was first addressed in the early 1980s, it was seen as a regional problem. Today scientists recognize that air pollution in China can cause environmental effects in California. If everything is inter-connected—if the flapping of a butterfly's wings in the Amazon can cause a hurricane on the other side of the globe, as chaos theory suggests—then every environmental agreement should be open to any state.

In addition, what counts as an externality can be controversial. The 1995 UN Fish Stocks Agreement, for example, provides that regional fisheries treaties should be open to any state with a "real interest" in the fisheries concerned.[55] But what constitutes a "real interest"? Many view Antarctica as part of the global commons and therefore of concern to all states. The Antarctic Treaty, however, requires a state to "demonstrate its interest" in Antarctica through substantial research activity, in order to fully participate in the regime.[56] Efforts in the 1980s by some developing countries, led by Malaysia, to widen participation by putting Antarctica under the aegis of the UN General Assembly ultimately proved unsuccessful. In contrast, the Whaling Convention recognizes the "interest of the nations of the world in safeguarding for future generations the great natural resources represented by the whale stocks."[57] This reflects a much broader view, which recognizes the interest of the international community as a whole in the "existence value" of whales.

The pragmatic issues regarding the scope of participation are also closely balanced. On the one hand, broad participation brings important environmental and economic benefits. *Ceteris paribus*, it reduces leakage of pollution from participating to non-participating states, reduces competitiveness effects, and brings greater environmental effectiveness. Broader participation comes at a price, however: the greater the number of countries involved, the more difficult it is to negotiate and sustain cooperation.

Thus, limiting membership to a smaller club, with shared values and interests, may sometimes allow greater progress than broad membership. The Antarctic Treaty regime, for example, has proven successful in large part because of its limited membership. This has enabled the participating states to develop a high degree of cohesiveness and has helped ensure that they have both expertise and a stake in Antarctic issues. Arguably, the climate change regime would also benefit from a more limited membership. Achieving consensus among the more than 180 participating states, some with very different interests, is exceptionally difficult. A regime with fewer members might simplify the negotiating process. And since just twelve states are responsible for more than 80 percent of global greenhouse gas emissions, broad participation is not essential to solve the climate change problem. A smaller regime, with relatively few members, still has the potential to address the problem effectively.

WHAT ARE THE MINIMUM PARTICIPATION REQUIREMENTS?

Thus far we have been examining who should be allowed to participate in a treaty—that is, the maximum potential scope of the treaty. A quite different issue concerns the states that *must* participate in a treaty for it to take effect. These minimum participation requirements are defined by a treaty's entry-into-force provision.

In the case of regulatory treaties, minimum participation requirements serve to ensure a sufficient level of reciprocity. This does not require that all states participate in a treaty, but enough so that the participating states are better off cooperating with each other than not.

Consider a simple example: a regional pollution problem involving thirty states. Assume that the treaty imposes an environmental requirement that would cost each participating state $10 million but provide an environmental benefit to the thirty states collectively of $30 million ($1 million per state). Although, collectively, the treaty requirement provides a significant net benefit, individual states lack an incentive to act because doing so would cost them $10 million and provide an individual benefit of only $1 million. If a state's action in joining the agreement were reciprocated by just ten other states, however, then each participating state would come out ahead because now its $10 million investment would, in effect, buy $11 million in benefits—the $1 million provided by its own action, combined with the $1 million provided by the action of each of the other ten participating states. So, if the entry-into-force requirement is set at eleven states, ratification becomes essentially risk-free. It could make a state better off, but not worse off. If ten other states ratify and the treaty enters into force, each is better off than without the treaty. And if ten other states do not ratify, the treaty never enters into force and no one is the worse. Of course, in this scenario, the nineteen states that do not join the agreement would receive the same $11 million benefit as those that do ratify the treaty, and thus would have an incentive to free ride. Even so, the eleven participating countries have no incentive to drop out because they are better off with the treaty than without it.[58] These states represent what game theorists call a "minimum viable coalition."[59]

In the real world, of course, both the costs and benefits of regulatory agreements are subject to tremendous uncertainty. Thus, states cannot calculate precisely the entry-into-force requirements needed for a minimum viable coalition; they must set these requirements in a more rough-and-ready way. Moreover, because some states contribute more to environmental problems than others, entry-into-force requirements cannot be stated simply as a number of states, but rather as a variable that reflects the magnitude of different states' contribution to a problem. The Kyoto Protocol, for example, required ratification by fifty-five states representing 55 percent of developed country greenhouse gas emissions,[60] while MARPOL required ratification by fifteen states representing at least 50 percent of global shipping tonnage.[61] Such entry-into-force requirements help ensure reciprocity by requiring participation by states that account for a significant share of the problem.

In contrast to regulatory treaties, constitutive treaties do not impose costly requirements. States, in deciding whether to join, do not therefore need to worry about ensuring a minimum viable coalition. Instead, entry-into-force requirements reflect a different concern—political credibility. Constitutive agreements aim to establish a governance structure for a given issue. To be credible, these governance arrangements need a critical mass of participants. For example, a framework convention on climate change that had only five participating states would not be credible. Moreover, to the extent that states like to be charter members of a regime, in order to have a say in the start-up decisions about rules of procedure, financial arrangements, and so forth, then a lax entry-into-force requirement can undermine this incentive to join by allowing a treaty to come into force quickly, with only a few participants who get to make the initial decisions. Ultimately, in the case of the climate change convention, states chose to make entry into force contingent on a significant but not overwhelming number of ratifications—fifty—the midpoint of the various numbers initially proposed.[62]

SUBSTANTIVE SCOPE

International agreements vary widely in their substantive as well as their participatory scope, ranging from broadly comprehensive agreements such as the UN Convention on the Law of the Sea and the Biological Diversity Convention, to very specific agreements such as those protecting polar bears or controlling the use of anti-fouling paints on ships. Each approach has its pros and cons. Comprehensive agreements can take account of the interdependence between different environmental issues and allow states to address them in a holistic manner, making appropriate trade-offs and issue linkages. In contrast, more narrowly focused agreements create the potential for fragmentation, duplication of effort, and even conflict. In addressing one environmental problem, they may exacerbate another. But narrowly focused agreements also have a significant, compensatory advantage: they allow states to target problems and develop specific, meaningful responses.

The early history of the climate change negotiations illustrates these tensions. In the late 1980s, when climate change first emerged onto the international agenda, some suggested developing a general agreement on the "law of the atmosphere," modeled on the Law of the Sea Convention, which would serve as an umbrella for subsequent agreements on more specific issues such as global warming, acid rain, and ozone depletion. This general model was adopted for the other treaty negotiated during the run-up to the Rio conference, the Biodiversity Convention. The urgency of the climate change issue led states to adopt a more focused approach, which they thought would be more manageable and would produce more significant results.

Depth

STRINGENCY

A second issue in treaty design is depth, which, as suggested earlier, is a function of two variables—stringency and strength. The stringency of a commitment is the "extent to which it requires states to depart from what they would have done in its absence."[63] All other things being equal, a requirement to cut emissions by 20 percent is deeper than a requirement to cut emissions by 10 percent. The absolute numbers themselves, however, are not necessarily determinative, because stringency is a function of change from business as usual. A strict whaling quota today, when only a few whalers remain, may have less bite than a more generous quota forty years ago, during the so-called Whale Olympics.

Constitutive agreements are by their nature shallow; they aim to establish a general system of governance and impose few, if any, requirements. In contrast, regulatory agreements vary widely in their stringency. As Kal Raustiala notes, "Some accords are deep: they require states to make major changes in policy. Others are shallow: they codify what states are already doing or demand only minor changes in behavior."[64] The 1985 Sulfur Protocol's requirement that states reduce their emissions by 30 percent is an example of a shallow commitment, since emissions were already coming down for other reasons.[65] In contrast, the decision of the

Montreal Protocol parties to eliminate the use of methyl bromide was comparatively deep, at least for countries such as Israel that make extensive use of methyl bromide as a fumigant.

A number of treaty design features affect the stringency of its commitments:

- *Flexible/contextual commitments*—Typically, the more flexible the treaty commitment, the lower its sovereignty and compliance costs. A provision that requires states to promote the wise use of wetlands "as far as possible"[66] gives parties considerable discretion in deciding the appropriate level of protection, and means that the treaty lacks any determinate level of stringency. Similarly, under the Long-Range Transboundary Air Pollution Convention (LRTAP), the Nitrous Oxides (NO_X) Protocol provided states with more flexibility than the 1985 Sulfur Dioxide (SO_2) Protocol by allowing them some discretion in the choice of base year from which to calculate their emission reductions.[67]
- *Differential standards*—Treaties can also differentiate the stringency of the commitments for different classes of countries, establishing more stringent commitments for some and weaker commitments for others. The Montreal Protocol, for example, gives developing countries an additional ten years to comply.[68] The Kyoto Protocol goes much further, differentiating between developed countries (which have emission limitation targets) and developing countries (which do not). By avoiding any new requirements for developing countries, the Kyoto Protocol made it essentially costless for them to join.
- *Reservations*—Rather than establish differential standards directly, a treaty can allow states to differentiate their obligations unilaterally through reservations.[69] Few multilateral environmental agreements do so, however, perhaps because reservations appear inconsistent with the constitutive function of establishing general governance arrangements.[70]

STRENGTH

In contrast to stringency, which measures the distance between the status quo and an international commitment, strength measures the intensity of a commitment. Both the stringency and strength of an agreement raise the agreement's costs, but they do so in different ways: *the stringency of an agreement increases the expected costs of compliance; the strength of an agreement increases the potential costs of non-compliance.* The more stringent an agreement, the bigger the required changes in behavior and the more costly compliance becomes. In contrast, the more intense the commitment, the bigger the limits to sovereignty and the higher the costs if a state fails to comply.

In essence, design elements that limit the strength of an agreement's commitments represent risk management strategies, preserving more of a state's freedom of action in case an agreement does not work out as expected.[71] These elements include:

- *Legal form*—All other things being equal, a legally binding agreement represents a deeper commitment than a non-binding pledge.[72] First, it signals a greater intensity and seriousness of intent, and hence has greater credibility. There is a difference between saying that one will *try* to do something and *committing* to doing it, particularly when the commitment is made at the highest levels of government. Second, in countries that require legislative approval of treaties, legal agreements depend on greater domestic buy-in than non-binding agreements, making them more resistant to backsliding. A pledge by President Carter to return the Panama Canal would have been easier for President Reagan to reverse than a treaty commitment. Finally, to the extent that legalized methods of dispute resolution exist, such as adjudication before the International Court of Justice, legal agreements can get whatever benefit these international procedures provide.
- *Precision*—A second element of a commitment's strength is its precision. All other things being equal, more precise norms constrain states more tightly than vague ones, by making violations more apparent. Compare, for example, a requirement to reduce emissions by 20 percent with a requirement to reduce emissions "significantly," or a requirement that cars get 30 miles to the gallon with a requirement that states adopt "reasonable" fuel efficiency standards.
- *Opt-out clauses*—Multilateral environmental agreements that establish ongoing regulatory systems create special sovereignty risks because of the danger that the regulatory regime will adopt decisions with which a state disagrees. In joining the International Whaling Convention, for example, Japan arguably thought that it was joining an agreement to promote the whaling industry, only to discover, thirty years later, that the International Whaling Commission had evolved into a whale protection regime.[73] Most environmental agreements lessen this risk by allowing states to opt out of

decisions with which they disagree. This is a one-time right, however; if a state does not opt out within the specified period of time, then it is bound.

- *Duration*—The longer and more determinate an agreement's duration, the greater its strength. By lengthening the shadow of the future, an agreement with an indefinite duration helps limit short-term defections and promote stronger cooperation.[74] In doing so, however, it imposes higher sovereignty costs than an agreement that lasts only a few years or allows states to withdraw after providing notice.[75] Although most international environmental agreements have an indefinite duration, some put time limits on particularly costly provisions. For example, the Kyoto Protocol's emissions targets apply to only the five-year period 2008–2012,[76] and the Antarctic Environment Protocol's moratorium on mineral exploration could potentially be changed after fifty years.[77] In addition, most if not all environmental agreements give states the right to exit after the expiration of some minimum period of time, usually simply by providing notice. This mechanism allows a state to avoid its treaty commitment at a lower cost to its reputation than breach.[78] In practice, however, this right to exit may be more theoretical than real because withdrawal tends to be politically costly. As a result, relatively few states appear to utilize exit clauses in environmental agreements.[79] Even Japan, which has vociferously criticized the international whaling regime and threatened to withdraw, has remained inside the agreement.
- *International supervision and enforcement*—Finally, treaties that provide for international supervision and enforcement reflect a stronger level of commitment than those that do not. As we shall explore in Chapter 11, they raise the costs of non-compliance by increasing the likelihood of detection and, in some cases, by helping to organize an international response.

Promoting Participation

As we saw in Chapter 7, participation in international environmental regimes is driven by many exogenous factors—for example, dramatic events like oil spills that raise public awareness and increase domestic pressure to join a treaty;[80] domestic political factors such as elections, which bring a new political party to power;[81] or technological developments that reduce the costs of complying with a treaty's requirements.[82] But a treaty can also seek to encourage greater participation endogenously through design elements that lower the costs of participation or raise the costs of non-participation, thereby changing the cost-benefit calculation for states in deciding whether to participate.

One common way to conceptualize the problem of participation is in terms of a trade-off between the breadth of an international agreement and its depth: the more a treaty demands of states, the fewer that will be willing to join; the more the treaty aspires to broad participation, the less ambitious it can be.[83] Do states, in fact, make such trade-offs between the breadth of an international agreement and its depth? Are they more willing to participate in shallow agreements than deep ones? And within the dimension of depth, do they trade off the stringency and the strength of commitments? Are they more likely to assume a stringent commitment if it is weak, or a strong commitment if it is lax?

The answers to these questions are not self-evident. On the one hand, shallow agreements impose lower compliance costs on participating states than stringent ones, though they provide lower benefits as well. Similarly, weaker forms of commitment provide a hedge against potential compliance costs, while also lessening the assurance that other states will take reciprocal actions, on which the benefits of the agreement depend. So the cost-benefit calculations are complex and uncertain.

With respect to trade-offs between strength and stringency, a former head of the United Kingdom's international environmental law division concluded that states trade off the strength of review mechanisms and the stringency of substantive commitments: the stronger the compliance system, the shallower the substantive commitments, and vice versa.[84] If true, this trade-off suggests that states are more worried about preserving their own flexibility in complying than about ensuring reciprocal action by others.[85] But the World Trade Organization (WTO) dispute settlement procedure reflects a very different dynamic, in which the new WTO developed a stronger compliance system to complement its more stringent commitments. Similarly, the strengthening of the European Union's substantive rules has been accompanied by a strengthening of its enforcement machinery. And in the negotiations over the Kyoto Protocol rules, most commentators argued that ambitious commitments required a stronger compliance system in order to provide states with an assurance that their actions would be reciprocated by others. One recent comparative study concluded that, when a commitment requires irreversible investments, stringency and strength are positively rather than negatively correlated: states are more willing to incur irreversible costs themselves, the greater the credibility of the commitment and hence the stronger the assurance that others will do so as well.[86]

If the trade-off between stringency and strength is uncertain, the conventional wisdom seems correct with respect to the more general trade-off between breadth and depth. States are more willing to participate in shallow agreements than deep ones because even comparatively strong international agreements may not provide states with a sufficient assurance of reciprocity to justify undertaking costly actions.[87] States are reluctant to join deep agreements because the benefits of the bargain are too uncertain to incur the costs. By comparison, shallow agreements involve less risk, increasing their attractiveness. Other states are more likely to comply with a shallow agreement because the costs of doing so are low. Thus, a state that joins is more likely to get whatever benefits the agreement provides. Moreover, even if other states fail to comply and a state receives no benefit from joining the agreement, at least it hasn't lost very much either.

International agreements seek to encourage participation through a variety of design elements that we considered earlier, which loosen either the stringency or the strength of commitments. Some of these elements make an agreement shallower for the parties in general—for example, flexible and contextual standards, which qualify commitments with such phrases as "to the extent possible" or "as the circumstances permit"; non-legal form; weak review mechanisms; and opt-out and withdrawal provisions. Others aim to encourage participation by a particular group of countries by establishing differential (asymmetrical) standards.[88] For example, a number of agreements, including the Montreal Protocol and the UN Framework Convention on Climate Change, contain differential standards for developing countries to encourage them to join. In addition, some agreements create special deals for individual countries to address their particular national circumstances.[89]

In some cases, international environmental agreements also try to encourage participation by directly subsidizing the costs of joining or imposing costs for staying out. China and India, for example, were persuaded to join the Montreal Protocol only on the condition that developed countries establish a Multilateral Fund to provide developing countries with assistance to comply with the treaty. Similarly, the UN Framework Convention on Climate Change makes compliance by developing countries with their one specific commitment—namely, to submit national reports—contingent on full funding by Western countries.[90] In these cases, states with a strong interest in the treaty in essence assumed a greater commitment themselves in order to lower the costs for other states. In a regime that establishes an emissions trading system, one potentially powerful means of subsidizing participation would be to allocate countries additional allowances that they could sell to others. This idea has been proposed in particular as a means of persuading developing countries to join the climate change regime.[91]

Conversely, an agreement can also encourage participation by raising the costs of staying out. Although international environmental law relies more heavily on carrots than on sticks, several agreements use trade measures to encourage participation. The Basel Convention on the Transboundary Movements of Hazardous Wastes, for example, allows parties to trade with non-parties only if the non-party has a control system similar to that of Basel.[92] CITES imposes a similar restriction on trade in endangered species with non-parties, requiring documentation comparable to that required by CITES itself.[93] Finally, the Montreal Protocol prohibits trade with non-parties of ozone-depleting substances and products containing these substances.[94]

Strategies for Building a Treaty Regime over Time

The design elements we have been examining thus far take a static perspective, examining the possible trade-offs between breadth and depth at a single point in time, when an agreement is negotiated. But environmental regimes are not static; they display a remarkable dynamism. Most start modestly, but some develop into highly effective instruments. So perhaps the more important question is, how can states trade off breadth and depth over time in order to promote stronger international cooperation?

Our earlier discussion of breadth and depth suggests two general strategies:

- First, proceed in an incremental fashion, beginning with relatively modest commitments, in order to encourage participation, and then ratchet up the level of ambition.
- Second, aim high from the outset, through a coalition of the willing, and then over time try to build out by attracting more participants.

These strategies are not mutually exclusive. A regime can proceed in a stepwise fashion, developing at times by strengthening the commitments of its existing members, at others times by broadening its membership. This has essentially been the approach of the European Union, which began with a relatively limited agreement among a small number of countries and has undergone a remarkable transformation in both breadth and depth.

Starting Deep and Broadening

One approach to building a regime is to start with a comparatively deep agreement among like-minded states and then attempt to broaden the agreement through the addition of new members and new subject areas. Sometimes, starting with a regional arrangement may make sense because the states within a region are comparatively like-minded. In other cases, shared socioeconomic interests or values may provide the basis for a coalition of the willing.

A narrow but deep approach has several benefits. First, the initial group is able to design the agreement the way it likes. The participants need to reach agreement only among themselves rather than attempting to satisfy a wider group of states, which would result in compromises that weaken or water down the outcome. Second, the comparatively small membership makes the decision-making process more manageable and improves the quality of the likely results. The regime grows in membership not by making compromises that weaken it, but by proving that it works.

The European Union is perhaps the best example of this general approach. It began in the 1950s with relatively deep agreements among a small number of states (six), addressing only economic integration. Today, it has grown to twenty-seven members, with competence over a wide array of economic, social, and environmental policies. Although agreement was not always easy even with six members, the limited breadth of the initial agreements made possible much deeper commitments than if the participants had tried to include other Western European states from the outset.[95]

In a similar way, although neither the General Agreement on Tariffs and Trade (GATT) nor the Montreal Protocol ever attempted to exclude countries, they both benefited from relatively small memberships in their early years, which facilitated agreement and allowed them to develop. The same is true of the Antarctic Treaty regime. It began with an agreement among a comparatively small number of countries on a few key issues (in particular, the territorial status of Antarctica), but has broadened over the years in both membership and functional scope.

The narrow but deep approach works well for problems involving "club goods," where the participating states can capture the benefits of the agreement and thereby come out ahead, even if the agreement has only limited membership. This approach is more problematic, however, with respect to public goods problems such as climate change. In these cases, why might states decide to form a coalition of the willing and proceed on their own with a deeper agreement, even if this means fewer participants initially? One possible answer is that a group of states believes that the agreement is the "right" thing to do; they follow a logic of appropriateness rather than a logic of consequences. Another answer is that the group, though limited in size, still represents a minimum viable coalition and leaves each of the participants better off than before. Perhaps most importantly, the participating states may view their actions as part of a long-term process, not as a one-time event. They may believe that, if they exercise leadership now, others will eventually follow. Indeed, exercising leadership may not only be the right thing to do, but may give them an advantage over the long term by allowing them to shape the regime in advantageous ways. Whether this calculation proves correct is, of course, uncertain. The European Union pushed for the completion and entry into force of the Kyoto Protocol in the belief that if it led the way and showed that the Protocol works, the United States would eventually change its mind and join. Even now, however, with the Bush Administration gone, there is no guarantee that this will happen.

Starting Broad and Deepening

Rather than starting deep and broadening, international environmental law has more typically proceeded the other way around. It has started with relatively modest agreements that are broad but shallow, and then progressively deepened them. This has proceeded along two different routes: first, from soft law to hard law, and second, from framework conventions to protocols.

One route has been to start with a non-binding instrument and convert it into a binding instrument later. In regulating trade in chemicals and pesticides, for example, states initially negotiated the FAO Code of Conduct on the Distribution and Use of Pesticides and the London Guidelines for the Exchange of Information on Chemicals in International Trade, which became the basis for the 1998 Rotterdam Convention. Precisely because soft law instruments impose lower sovereignty costs on states, they may be attractive, particularly when uncertainties are high.[96] In essence, a non-legal instrument allows a state to see if a particular approach works, without risking significant costs if it later changes its mind. For the same reason, non-legal instruments can make it easier for states to adopt ambitious, precise commitments, as they did in the North Sea Declarations, by lowering the potential costs of non-compliance.

A second route from shallow to deep agreements is the framework convention-protocol approach, which has been used to address acid rain, ozone depletion, and climate change, as well as to protect the marine environment of regional seas.[97] Initially, states negotiate a framework convention, which establishes the general architecture of the regime, including, for example, its objective, principles, basic obligations, and institutions. Then, protocols are negotiated that build on the parent agreement through the elaboration of more specific (and costly) commitments. In the environmental field, the first framework convention was the 1976 Barcelona Convention for the Protection of the Mediterranean Sea Against Pollution, negotiated under the auspices of UNEP. This Convention now has protocols addressing the dumping of hazardous wastes, land-based sources of marine pollution, emergency response to oil spills, and specially protected areas.[98] Other prominent examples of the framework convention-protocol approach include the Long-Range Transboundary Air Pollution Convention and its seven protocols,[99] the Vienna Ozone Convention and the Montreal Protocol, the UN Framework Convention on Climate Change and the Kyoto Protocol, and the 1979 Bonn Convention on Migratory Species and its seven subagreements and seventeen memoranda of understanding (MOUs).[100]

The framework convention-protocol approach allows states to address a problem in a step-by-step manner rather than all at once. States tend to be willing to join a framework convention because it does not contain stringent obligations. As a result, they can begin to address a problem without waiting for a consensus to emerge on appropriate response measures. For example, when both LRTAP and the Vienna Ozone Convention were adopted, many states remained unconvinced of the need for action. Nevertheless, even skeptical states acquiesced in the adoption of these conventions, since the conventions did not commit them to take any specific actions.

Although framework conventions are themselves shallow, they can create positive feedback loops that facilitate the deepening of the regime through the adoption of protocols containing specific substantive commitments. First, the framework convention can help reduce uncertainties and produce agreement about the relevant facts—about who is doing what to whom—by requiring states to submit national reports and by encouraging scientific research and assessments. The institutions established by the framework convention often play a catalytic role in this process by collecting data, providing technical assistance, and issuing reports. Second, the framework convention (and, in particular, the regular meetings of the parties) can help generate normative consensus by providing an ongoing forum for discussion and negotiation, serving as a focal point for international public opinion, and building trust among participants. Finally, when states eventually decide to act, framework conventions increase their capacity to do so by putting in place basic institutions and decision-making processes.

The theory is that, once a framework convention is adopted, the international lawmaking process begins to take on a momentum of its own. States that were initially reluctant to undertake substantive commitments, but that acquiesced in the seemingly innocuous process set in motion by the framework convention, will feel increasing pressure not to fall out of step as that process gains momentum. The degree to which framework conventions actually have this effect and lead to stronger international cooperation is the subject of debate.[101] Even critics agree, however, that the framework convention-protocol is an attractive model. In practice, it remains the leading strategy for developing international environmental law.

Ensuring Agreements Stay Up to Date

Regardless of which development path is chosen, environmental agreements have an unusual need for flexibility, in order to take account of developments in our scientific understanding of environmental problems as well as the changing nature of the problems themselves. Species that were once abundant become threatened from overhunting or habitat loss; chemicals that were once deemed safe are revealed as dangerous; and technologies emerge that pose new risks. In the case of the 1987 Montreal Protocol, knowledge of the problem changed so quickly that, according to a knowledgeable observer, "the CFC-reduction rates agreed . . . in September 1987 were already obsolete by the time the protocol entered into force" in 1989.[102] In order to avoid obsolescence, international agreements need to be able to respond flexibly both to new information and to new problems.

Non-legal agreements have traditionally had an edge over treaties in this regard because they can be amended by a simple decision of the participating states. In contrast, treaties require parties to ratify each new amendment. Consider, for example, the PIC procedure for trade in hazardous chemicals, which requires exporters to obtain the prior informed consent of the importing state. States initially adopted the PIC procedure in a voluntary instrument that could be amended by a simple vote of the UNEP Governing Council. Now that the Rotterdam Convention has converted the PIC procedure into a treaty commitment, amendment would require ratification by three-quarters of the treaty parties and would then apply only to the ratifying states.[103]

International environmental agreements often include two design elements intended to keep them up to date. First, some agreements provide for periodic reviews. The Montreal Protocol, for example, provides for quadrennial assessments of its control measures, based on the available scientific, environmental, technical, and economic information.[104] Similarly, the UN Framework Convention on Climate Change required a review of the adequacy of its commitments at its first meeting of the parties,[105] which led to the initiation of the Kyoto Protocol negotiations.

Second, most international environmental agreements segregate their detailed regulatory provisions, which are likely to require periodic updating and revision, by putting them in an annex or schedule that can be amended more easily than the rest of the treaty. For example, the detailed regulations on whaling adopted by the International Whaling Commission—establishing catch limits, equipment requirements, open and closed seasons, and so forth—are included in a schedule to the Whaling Convention, which can be amended by a three-quarters majority vote.[106] Similarly, the endangered and threatened species that receive protection against trade under CITES are listed in appendices, which can be amended by a two-thirds qualified majority vote, in response to changing circumstances and information.[107] As a result, if a species becomes endangered, the parties to CITES can simply vote to include it in Appendix I (thereby prohibiting commercial trade), without waiting for the affirmative consent of each CITES party.

In essence, these flexible amendment procedures vest treaty regimes with ongoing regulatory authority. Although this allows the treaty regime to respond to new information and dangers, it also creates potential dangers. Without appropriate safeguards, it represents a threat to state sovereignty and undermines the consensual basis of international environmental law.

To guard against this possibility, one safeguard found in many environmental agreements is a requirement that amendments to technical annexes have a scientific basis. As the Whaling Convention illustrates, however, states can easily ignore this requirement.[108] More recent agreements, such as the Stockholm Convention on Persistent Organic Pollutants (POPs), have tried to institutionalize the role of science by making a detailed scientific assessment of proposed new chemicals the first step in the procedure to add new chemicals to the Convention.[109]

Ultimately, however, the real safeguard of state sovereignty is the right of states to opt out of regulatory decisions with which they disagree. This right is included in most flexible amendment procedures except the Montreal Protocol's adjustment process (and the specialized procedures established by regional fisheries management treaties).[110] In effect, these procedures represent a balance, removing the need for affirmative consent by states but still ensuring at least tacit consent.

Conclusion

International environmental law is largely treaty law. When new problems emerge, states address them through negotiations, usually resulting in an international agreement.

Although most international environmental norms have a treaty basis, not all of them are found in the text of a treaty itself. In essence, many environmental treaties serve as mini-constitutions, establishing ongoing regulatory regimes with complex institutional structures. The treaty provides the underlying basis for the regime, but central elements of the regime are developed by subsequent decisions of the parties. Some of these decisions have a legal form: for example, the addition of new species to the CITES appendices, or the ratcheting up of regulatory requirements under the Montreal Protocol. Other decisions are non-legal or quasi-legal. The detailed rules for operationalizing the Kyoto Protocol, totaling hundreds of pages of text, were adopted by a simple decision of Kyoto parties, leaving their legal status unclear. Similarly, the CITES compliance procedure, which has imposed trade suspensions against countries with general implementation problems, was developed by the conference of the parties. The same is true of the wise use guidelines for wetlands developed under the Ramsar Convention and the criteria for listing world heritage sites.

Despite their dynamism, some argue that consensually based negotiations will ultimately prove too weak to address environmental problems such as climate change or loss of biodiversity. In their view, stronger, non-consensual decision-making methods will be required.[111] From a political standpoint, such a development seems unlikely. Perhaps more interestingly, however, it would also raise serious issues of legitimacy. Domestically, democracy serves as the touchstone of legitimacy. Democratic decision making, in which the minority accepts the will of the majority, depends on a sense of community, which has yet to develop internationally. Unless some other basis of legitimacy can be found, negotiated agreements based on state consent will likely remain a defining feature of the international law-making process.[112]

Recommended Reading

Scott Barrett, *Environment and Statecraft: The Strategy of Environmental Treaty-Making* (Oxford: Oxford University Press, 2003).

Richard B. Bilder, *Managing the Risks of International Agreement* (Madison: University of Wisconsin Press, 1981).

Pamela S. Chasek, *Earth Negotiations: Analyzing Thirty Years of Environmental Diplomacy* (Tokyo: United Nations University Press, 2001).

George W. Downs, Kyle W. Danish, and Peter N. Barsoom, "The Transformational Model of International Regime Design: Triumph of Hope or Experience?" *Columbia Journal of Transnational Law* 38 (2000), pp. 465–514.

Thomas Gehring, *Dynamic International Regimes; Institutions for International Environmental Governance* (Frankfurt: Peter Lang, 1994).

Andrew T. Guzman, "The Design of International Agreements," *European Journal of International Law* 16 (2005), pp. 579–612.

Barbara Koremenos, Charles Lipson, and Duncan Snidal, "The Rational Design of International Institutions," *International Organization* 55 (2001), pp. 761–799.

Kal Raustiala, "Form and Substance in International Agreements," *American Journal of International Law* 99 (2005), pp. 581–614.

Peter H. Sand, *Lessons Learned in Global Environmental Governance* (Washington, DC: World Resources Institute, 1990).

Bertram I. Spector, Gunnar Sjöstedt, and I. William Zartman, eds., *Negotiating International Regimes: Lessons Learned from the United Nations Conference on Environment and Development (UNCED)* (London: Graham and Trotman, 1994).

CHAPTER NINE

Customary (and Not So Customary) Norms

[M]ost of what we perversely persist in calling customary
international law is not only *not* customary law: it does not
even faintly resemble a customary law.

Robert Jennings, "The Identification of International Law"

THE EXPLOSION OF international environmental treaty-making
over the last thirty years suggests a diminished role for other
types of international law, including custom and general principles. Nevertheless, many writers still consider non-treaty norms an important source of international environmental law, and claims regarding
them are not uncommon. Authors argue, for example, that:

- States must take precautionary actions against environmental risks,
  rather than await scientific certainty.[1]
- States have a duty to prevent significant transboundary harm, and
  to provide notice and engage in consultations concerning possible
  harms.[2]
- States must take steps to protect endangered species[3] (or, more
  fancifully, whales have an emerging right to life under customary
  international law).[4]
- The current generation owes a duty to future generations to
  preserve and transmit the Earth's natural assets.

Meanwhile, expert groups have expended considerable time and effort
attempting to codify what they regard as the general (non-treaty) norms
of international environmental law.[5]

This chapter draws from Daniel Bodansky, "Customary (and Not So Customary) International Environmental Law," *Indiana Journal of Global Legal Studies*
3 (1995), pp. 105–119.

In contrast to treaties, which fit comfortably within the positivist account of law, the two main types of non-treaty norms—customary law and general principles—are not created through purposeful acts of lawmaking and do not have a canonical form. Instead, they emerge through less well-defined, more informal processes and raise a host of theoretical puzzles:

- How do non-treaty norms emerge? To what extent, for example, do customary norms emerge as a result of calculations by states of their rational self-interest? To what extent are they imposed by powerful states? To what extent do they reflect psychological needs for order and regularity? These are causal questions, focusing on the social, economic, psychological, and political processes that account for the development of customary international law.
- Do non-treaty norms have any effect on behavior, and, if so, how and why? This, too, is a causal question.
- What does it mean to say that a norm is part of customary international law or is a general principle of law? Where does the "binding" character of these norms come from? These are jurisprudential questions about the conditions of legal validity of non-treaty norms, focusing on the "formal sources" of law.
- Finally, should non-treaty norms be followed? Are they legitimate sources of obligation? Do they have any claim to obedience? In contrast to the explanatory questions of how norms emerge and affect behavior, these are normative rather than empirical questions, which demand an inquiry into the basis of legal obligation.

What Is Customary International Law?

Although the concept of customary international law is often viewed as mystifying,[6] the emergence and application of social norms through informal, decentralized processes is a commonplace occurrence.[7] Language provides a good illustration. Every time we speak, we apply a complex set of customary rules of grammar and usage. These rules are not legislated or enforced by any centralized body (the attempts of the French Academy notwithstanding!).[8] Instead, they emerge and evolve through the regular practice of language users and are enforced through a diffuse set of social sanctions. Like other social norms, they are observable facts that need to be identified and learned if one is to be able to participate effectively in society.

In the domestic arena, we ordinarily distinguish social norms from law on the basis that social norms emerge through informal, spontaneous processes; they do not have a canonical form; and they rely on decentralized, community sanctions. But these features, which serve to differentiate social norms from many domestic legal norms, are exactly the characteristic features of customary international law. So theories of social norms provide a useful starting point for thinking about custom.

Anthropologists and sociologists have long recognized the importance of social norms enforced through community pressure. Recently, political scientists—and, in particular, rational choice theorists—have become interested in social norms as well, using game theory to explain how informal norms might emerge in the absence of centralized governmental authority.[9] More recently still, the continuing role of such norms in contemporary society has become a significant focus of legal scholarship, stemming from Robert Ellickson's seminal book, *Order without Law*.[10]

The causal mechanisms by which social norms develop either among individuals or states are not well understood. Many different factors may be involved:

- In some cases, a norm may emerge through the interactions of rational actors, all pursuing their individual interests, in what amounts to a "market for norms."[11] The rules of diplomatic immunity may perhaps be explicable in these terms.
- Some norms may have psychological roots, reflecting a need for order and regularity.
- In addition, "norm entrepreneurs" may play an important role,[12] proposing norms for various self-interested, altruistic, or ideological reasons. Examples include religious leaders in the nineteenth century who believed that the slave trade was immoral; the Truman Administration in 1945 when it claimed the resources of the continental shelf on behalf of the United States; and environmentalists in the 1990s concerned about the risks of persistent organic pollutants. How successful these norm entrepreneurs are in getting others to go along may depend on additional factors, including not only the norm's attractiveness to others but also the power and reputation of the norm entrepreneur itself. The fact that the continental shelf doctrine, for example, was advanced by the world's most powerful nation presumably helped in its acceptance.
- Finally, knowledge may influence the development of norms, particularly in areas such as the environment, by identifying new threats that require a normative response.

All of these are plausible causal stories that help explain the emergence of social norms. Until more empirical work is completed,[13] however, they remain only stories, and in some cases "just so stories" at that.[14]

If the causal explanation of custom is challenging, so too is the question of its binding force. What constitutes a customary norm as "law"? As we discussed in Chapter 5, this question about the bases of legal validity—or, as we called it there, the "formal" sources of law—is very different from the causal question of how law develops. It is one thing to ask, why did the precautionary principle or the polluter-pays principle emerge, and quite another to ask, what makes them valid legal norms.

According to the orthodox account of customary international law, the customary lawmaking process involves two elements: first, consistent state practice and, second, a sense of legal obligation (or *opinio juris*).[15] When many states behave in a consistent manner for a significant period of time, and when this consistent, long-standing practice manifests a belief about what the law requires, then customary international law is created. For example, states generally grant immunity to foreign diplomats; they assert control over a particular territory and population; they refrain from exercising law enforcement functions in the territory of other states; and they do not interfere with foreign vessels on the high seas. These represent significant regularities of behavior—apparently normatively based—amidst the extremely complex and often *ad hoc* interactions among states.

In discussions of the customary lawmaking process, the relative importance of state practice and *opinio juris* has been a central and continuing source of controversy. Some writers see state practice as the critical element in the creation of customary international law;[16] others *opinio juris*;[17] and still others suggest that the two should be taken in combination: the more there is of one, the less is needed of the other.[18] Regardless of which view they adopt, however, most writers see the creation of custom as governed by a "secondary" lawmaking rule, accepted by states and other international actors, which specifies how valid custom is generated.[19] Although they disagree about the content of the secondary rule, they agree that the test of whether, say, the precautionary principle represents customary law is whether it conforms to the accepted secondary rule governing customary lawmaking.

To the extent, however, that custom is simply a species of social norm, this traditional account of customary law appears misconceived. Just as it would be a mistake to ask what is the secondary rule that creates a norm of fashion or etiquette, it would be wrong to analyze customary international law in terms of secondary rules. The validity of a norm of fashion or etiquette does not depend on its being adopted "in the right way," according to some rule. Indeed, the very concept of "validity" does not make sense with respect to such norms. Instead, rules of fashion and etiquette depend simply on acceptance by a relevant community of actors. To the extent that custom is a type of social norm, then it too represents what H. L. A. Hart called a "primitive" legal system, created not according to defined rules accepted as having law-creating effect, but rather through direct acceptance of the customary norm.[20]

On this view of custom, what is the role of state practice? State practice is not a formal source of custom, as in the traditional account of custom, since a norm's status as custom depends simply on whether it is treated as such. Instead, state practice matters for its causal and evidentiary roles. First, state practice can provide the historical background—the raw material—for the emergence of customary rules. As one sociologist observes, "when many people engage in the same behavior, that behavior comes to be associated with a sense of oughtness."[21] What is normal in a descriptive sense tends to become seen as normal in an evaluative sense.[22] Thus consistent state practice can *cause* a sense of legal obligation to develop, even if it is not a *reason* to accept the obligation.

In addition, state practice plays an evidentiary role. In order to identify the customary norms of a community, one ordinarily starts by identifying its regularities of behavior. Although any given regularity of behavior may reflect mere habit or independent responses to a common stimulus (like people all putting up umbrellas when it rains), the fact that behavior is regular at least *suggests* that it may be rule-governed.[23]

Which of these two contrasting accounts of custom is correct, the traditional one that sees custom as a formal source of law, created through regular state practice accompanied by *opinio juris*, or the theory that custom is a species of social norm? Is there an accepted customary lawmaking process, the products of which represent valid custom, as the traditional approach suggests? If there is a dispute about customary law—whether, say, there is a customary norm against whaling—can we provide legal reasons, based on the secondary rule, as to why an asserted norm should be regarded as customary law? Or is custom simply a social fact, dependent on acceptance by a given community of actors such as states?

The answer to this question need not be either-or. As we discussed in Chapter 5, the binding force of any norm depends ultimately on its acceptance as binding by a community of actors, whether directly (as is true of social norms) or indirectly because the norm was generated through an accepted lawmaking process. Consequently, which perspective on custom is correct depends ultimately on which is accepted by states or other international actors; in other words, it depends on what H. L. A. Hart referred to as a social fact. To the extent that different groups of actors accept customary norms in different ways, then each account of custom could be true for a particular group.

Although custom is usually treated as a single phenomenon, a pluralist view is probably more accurate,[24] which accepts that customary norms operate differently in different communities of actors, in some cases as a formal source and in others as a social norm. International jurists, for example, clearly believe that custom is created according to a secondary rule, which determines whether an asserted norm has the status of customary law. It would be impossible to account for the practice of the International Court of Justice (or other international and domestic courts) in any other way. More generally, to the extent that the traditional account of custom represents the prevailing view among the "invisible college of international lawyers,"[25] then one would expect it to accurately describe the practice of that community. It is far more questionable, however, whether states accept a secondary rule of customary lawmaking, the products of which they recognize as law.[26]

What difference does it make which perspective about custom we adopt? One reason is that the answer determines the kinds of legal arguments available about custom. If a state rejects a purported customary norm—say, a rule against whaling—what kinds of arguments can one make in response? If the traditional view that custom develops through an accepted lawmaking process is correct, then one can make a content-independent, process-based argument for the prohibition of whaling. Namely, we can say that the prohibition was adopted through this accepted process, through consistent practice accompanied by *opinio juris*. If customary rules are social norms, however, then this type of process-based argument is not available. Instead, one must justify the prohibition on commercial whaling on substantive grounds—for example, on the ground that it reflects a principle of justice or promotes economic efficiency. The fact that other states generally accept the rule may *cause* a recalcitrant state to follow it, in order to avoid community sanctions (including loss of reputation). But consistent state practice does not provide a *reason* to accept the rule. In this respect, customary law differs from treaty law, where, in response to the question, "why should I accept a rule?" it is possible to give a process-based answer, "because you consented."

Regardless of which view of custom is correct, compliance should, in general, be unproblematic rather than a mystery requiring explanation. The fact that a significant behavioral regularity has emerged suggests either that actors have fully internalized the norm (in which case they do not even see it as a constraint on their behavior), or they accept the norm as a guide to action. Ordinarily, we don't decide whether to comply with a rule of etiquette or fashion or grammar—we just comply.

In some cases, an actor might violate a norm because it makes a mistake about what the norm requires. For example, a state might mistakenly believe that the customary norms of diplomatic immunity do not cover household servants. Or it might violate a norm because the norm's role as a guide to behavior is overridden by other considerations—for example, domestic political pressures to punish diplomats who flout the law. Or it might commit a violation because it does not accept the norm in the first place—for example, because it is a rogue state, such as Iran in 1979, when it seized the U.S. embassy in Tehran and held U.S. diplomats hostage. The existence of a customary norm does not imply perfect uniformity of behavior.[27] Mistakes and violations are possible, but these must represent the exception rather than the rule. If they become prevalent, this suggests that the norm is breaking down and is no longer generally accepted by the group as a standard of behavior.

Are International Environmental Norms Customary in Nature?

Whether or not state practice represents a formal source of custom, it serves an important evidentiary function in determining the customary rules of international law. In ascertaining customary law, our task is similar to that of a legal anthropologist who wishes to determine how an alien society works, or of someone trying to understand a strange game or a foreign language. We must observe what actors do.[28] In watching a football game, for example, we might notice that players' actions seem to be divided into discrete units or plays; one side has the ball for several such plays in a row; during each play, the ball can be advanced by running or passing or kicking; and so on. Similarly, in learning a foreign language, we could try to observe how natives regularly use and combine words. This is presumably how infants learn vocabulary (if not grammar): through induction from observed behavior.

To what degree have social (customary) norms developed relating to international environmental protection? Do the purported norms of customary international environmental law, such as the prohibition on transboundary harm or the precautionary principle, represent regularities (if not perfect uniformities) of state behavior? Would the proverbial Martian coming to Earth[29] be able to induce these norms by observing what international actors do?

To a significant degree, the honest answer is, we do not know. To provide an answer, one would need to undertake a systematic survey of state behavior. For example, with respect to the duties to assess activities that may cause transboundary harm and to notify potentially affected states, one would need to identify the set of activities that pose a significant risk of transboundary harm and then examine how often states undertake assessments and provide notifications. Similarly, with regard to the duty to prevent significant transboundary pollution, one would need to determine whether states ordinarily take action to limit the pollution escaping their borders.

Needless to say, attempting to induce the rules of customary international law directly from state practice would be a Herculean task.[30] One would need to determine whose and which kinds of behavior count, and then survey that behavior among the 190-plus states of the world. Generally, although writers claim to adhere to the traditional account of customary international law, they do not base their assertions about customary international law on systematic surveys of state practice.[31] Nor does their training as lawyers equip them for this task. Thus, even when surveys of state practice are undertaken (e.g., by committees of the International Law Association), the reliability of these efforts is open to doubt. If we really wanted systematic empirical studies of state practice, anthropologists or historians would likely do a better job.

I observed this first-hand when I served on an International Law Association committee examining coastal state jurisdiction over marine pollution. As the U.S. member, I was responsible for reporting on U.S. practice. Initially, I expected this would be a relatively straightforward task. The problem of coastal state jurisdiction is an old one, and government officials are well aware of it and might be expected to keep detailed records. Nonetheless, it proved surprisingly difficult to obtain systematic information about pollution incidents by foreign vessels in U.S. coastal waters. If this information is unavailable for the United States, think how much more difficult it must be to obtain for most other states. By necessity, my report focused on U.S. legislation, with only anecdotal information about actual incidents.

To the extent that we can venture an opinion about whether the principles of international environmental law reflect regularities of behavior, the short answer seems to be "no."[32] Consider, for example, the duty to prevent transboundary pollution, which has been called the cornerstone of international environmental law[33] and is generally seen as its most firmly established customary norm. Although I am not aware of any systematic empirical study of this issue, transboundary pollution seems much more the rule than the exception in interstate relations. Pollutants are carried across most international borders continuously through the air and by rivers and ocean currents. Even dramatic examples of transboundary pollution, such as the Chernobyl accident, go unchallenged legally.[34] As Schachter concludes, "To say that a state has no right to injure the environment of another seems quixotic in the face of the great variety of transborder environmental harms that occur every day."[35]

If the putative rules of customary international environmental law reflected behavioral regularities, then they would allow us to predict how a state would ordinarily behave when considering an activity with potential transboundary effects: the state would undertake an assessment, provide notice to and engage in consultations with potentially affected states, and not proceed if a significant risk of harm existed. Indeed, according to the precautionary principle, one would expect states to refrain from actions that have the potential to cause substantial, irreversible harm, even if significant uncertainties exist. Would these be sound predictions of state behavior? Quite the contrary. If one were a government lawyer providing advice to policymakers, then relying on the purported norms of customary international environmental law as the basis of one's predictions would constitute malpractice.

As a growing number of international legal scholars recognize, there is a disparity between the traditional theory of customary law, which emphasizes consistent and uniform state practice, and the norms generally espoused as "customary."[36] Robert Jennings, a former president of the International Court of Justice, put it well when he observed: "most of what we perversely persist in calling customary international law is not only *not* customary law: it does not even faintly resemble a customary law."[37] Torture is said to be prohibited by customary international law,[38] even though it is widespread throughout the world.[39] Prompt, adequate, and effective compensation in expropriation cases was held to be required by customary international law,[40] even though this formula has seldom if ever been applied by states in actual expropriation cases in the absence of a treaty.[41] Similarly, scholars characterize the duty to prevent transboundary pollution and the precautionary principle as customary obligations, when there is little support for them in the actual behavior of states. As Jennings concludes, "Perhaps it is time to face squarely the fact that the orthodox tests of custom—practice and *opinio juris*—are often not only inadequate but even irrelevant for the identification of much new law today."[42]

General Principles

If principles such as the duty to prevent transboundary harm and the precautionary principle do not reflect behavioral regularities, and therefore do not qualify as customary norms, then what is their status? Do they have any effect on behavior? Should we care about them at all? In my view, the answer to the last two questions is a qualified "yes." Although these principles do not reflect behavioral regularities, they do show attitudinal regularities among states and other international actors. They articulate collective aspirations that play an important role over the longer term, framing both discussions about the development of international law and negotiations to develop more precise norms.

That the principles of international environmental law represent attitudinal rather than behavioral regularities is apparent from the methodology used to identify them. In writing about these principles, international lawyers usually base their arguments on what states and other international actors say rather than what they do. They examine both written and oral texts, produced in some cases by states, but often by non-state actors such as international courts and arbitral panels,[43] intergovernmental and non-governmental organizations,[44] and legal scholars. Their methodology is to collate these texts in order to see whether a critical mass of authority exists in support of a given norm. At most, scholars cite one or two celebrated incidents but provide little or no analysis of whether these incidents typify state behavior. The International Law Association (ILA), for example, cited only seven examples of state practice in support of its conclusion that the duty to inform is a norm of customary international law,[45] out of the presumably countless instances in which states have undertaken activities with a significant risk of transboundary harm. Instead, the ILA's analysis emphasized the various resolutions and treaties in which the putative customary norm appeared.[46]

Discussions of the duty to prevent transboundary pollution are similar. In analyzing this duty, writers generally begin by citing *Trail Smelter*,[47] which after more than fifty years is still the only case in which a state was held internationally responsible for causing transboundary environmental harm.[48] Writers then cite Principle 21 of the Stockholm Declaration, now joined by the reiteration of this principle (very slightly modified) in the 1992 Rio Declaration and the pronouncement of the International Court of Justice (ICJ) in its *Nuclear Weapons* advisory opinion (although the ICJ simply said in this opinion that the duty is part of the corpus of general international law rather than of customary law in particular).[49] For good measure, references are also usually included to the Organisation for Economic Cooperation and Development (OECD) Council Recommendation Concerning Transfrontier Pollution, UN General Assembly resolutions, the International Law Association's Montreal Rules of International Law Applicable to Transfrontier Pollution, and various treaties, as well as to the numerous international law scholars who have asserted that customary law imposes a duty to prevent transboundary environmental harm.[50]

What do all of these references establish? Certainly not a behavioral regularity. Rather, they establish, at most, how states and other international actors speak to one another. They provide evidence of the evaluative standards that states and non-state actors use to justify their actions and to criticize the actions of others. Writers tend to persist in characterizing these norms as "customary," the catch-all term generally applied to any non-treaty norm, but it would be more accurate to describe them as general principles of law,[51] or, as one writer has suggested, "declarative law."[52]

To what extent do these norms influence behavior? Or are they merely "cheap talk," without any effect? In thinking about this question, two preliminary observations are in order.

First, because general principles are not generated by any accepted lawmaking process, they must be justified on content-based rather than source-based grounds. States and international tribunals apply general principles, if at all, not because the principles emanate from a valid source, but because they believe the principles are substantively correct. In *Trail Smelter*, for example, the arbitral tribunal cited little actual evidence of state practice or *opinio juris* in support of its conclusion that states have a duty to prevent transboundary harm. Instead, it ruled in favor of the duty to prevent transboundary harm because it felt that this was the right result (and phrased its conclusion at such a high level of generality that everyone could agree). By the same token, if a skeptical government official were to ask, "why should we follow the precautionary principle?" one could not answer—because the principle was adopted by such and such a forum. The better answer would be—because the precautionary principle represents the right approach to the problem of uncertainty.[53]

Second, principles such as the duty to prevent transboundary harm and the precautionary principle operate primarily to channel future decision making rather than to govern behavior directly; that is, they represent standards rather than rules.[54] The distinction between rules and standards is a familiar one, which we examined in Chapter 5. A rule defines precisely what conduct is permissible or impermissible; in contrast, a standard sets forth more open-ended tests, whose application depends on the exercise of judgment or discretion. In essence, a rule requires *ex ante* decision making about what facts should yield what results, whereas standards allow *ex post* decision making, leaving a significant part of the decision making to subsequent decision makers.[55]

A norm such as the precautionary principle represents a standard rather than a rule. It encourages states to act in a precautionary way rather than await scientific certainty, but leaves many issues open. What level of information is required to justify precautionary action, for example? What level of risk triggers application of the principle? What types of actions should a state take in response? All of these questions are left for subsequent elaboration.[56]

How big an effect do international environmental principles have? It is useful here to distinguish three different types of effects: first, on the behavior of states directly; second, on the behavior of courts; and, finally, on the ongoing process of legal development through negotiations.

In terms of the first of these—the influence of general principles on the behavior of states—the answer seems to be, not much, although much more empirical work is needed to answer this question definitively. States acknowledge a duty to prevent significant transboundary harm but go on causing such harm. They accept resolutions recommending assessments and notification, but they do not necessarily act accordingly; and so forth and so on. Even if state actors felt an internal sense of obligation to prevent transboundary harm or to take precautionary measures, these principles leave states with huge leeway in deciding what to do. International environmental law, for example, tells states to avoid significant transboundary pollution, but what constitutes "significant"? States ought to undertake precautionary action, but in what circumstances and to what degree? Virtually any behavior that a state might wish to engage in, for self-interested reasons, could be reconciled with very general standards such as these. Thus, states are able to interpret these norms in self-serving ways, with little cost to their reputation.

International environmental principles might also exercise influence through courts or other third-party dispute resolution mechanisms. In the domestic context, where courts wield significant power, principles such as due process and equal protection play a huge role through their application by courts in particular cases. Indeed, in his famous essay, "The Path of the Law," Oliver Wendell Holmes even suggested that law is nothing more than a prediction of how courts will decide.[57] To the extent that one is able to convince a court that a given norm represents the law, then the court can apply and enforce the norm.

In my view, most writers on customary international law instinctively assume a state of affairs where third-party dispute resolution is available and subconsciously address their arguments to legal decision makers such as courts and arbitrators. These legal decision makers are the real target audience for the voluminous writings on customary international environmental law. The problem is that courts and arbitral tribunals still play only a minor role in addressing international environmental problems. That is why the few cases that have been decided thus far, such as *Trail Smelter*, must carry such a heavy load in current scholarship on customary international law. The establishment of new international tribunals, and the accompanying uptick in the number of cases heard, may signal the emergence of a greater judicial role. At present, however, legal discourse that presupposes a judicial audience plays to a largely empty house.

The primary way internationally that broad standards get converted into specific rules is through negotiations. Here is where general standards such as the duty to prevent transboundary pollution are likely to have the greatest influence. These principles operate as meta-rules, which establish the context within which bargaining takes place to develop more specific norms, usually in treaties. They set bounds for the types of proposals and arguments that can be made. Although they do not determine the result, they channel the negotiations by setting the terms of the debate, providing evaluative standards, and serving as a basis to criticize other states' proposals. In the U.S.-Canada acid rain dispute, for example, the duty to prevent transboundary harm did not directly constrain the United States, but it arguably had an indirect effect by providing a shared normative framework for the negotiations that led ultimately to the 1991 U.S.-Canada Air Quality Agreement.[58] To the extent it influenced state behavior, it was through this indirect mechanism.

Conclusion

The process of normative development in international environmental law involves both the elaboration of specific rules of behavior and the broader development of a common ethical framework. The decentralized and uncoordinated nature of customary lawmaking makes it ill-suited for the first of these tasks. Instead, the elaboration of specific rules of behavior (for example, to regulate greenhouse gas emissions, hazardous materials, or trade in endangered species) has proceeded through purposive negotiations, resulting in a treaty or other type of agreed instrument. In contrast, the emergence of broader principles, such as the precautionary principle and the duty to prevent transboundary pollution, has proceeded in a more decentralized, informal way. These principles do not directly guide behavior. Instead, they set boundary conditions for the development of more precise behavioral rules. They serve to frame the debate rather than to govern conduct. Although this role is more intangible and difficult to measure than that of treaties, this does not mean that it is any less real.

Recommended Reading

Pierre-Marie Dupuy, "Overview of the Existing Customary Legal Regime Regarding International Pollution," in Daniel Barstow Magraw, ed., *International Law and Pollution* (Philadelphia: University of Pennsylvania Press, 1991), pp. 61–89.

Amanda Perreau-Saussine and James Bernard Murphy, eds., *The Nature of Customary Law: Legal, Historical and Philosophical Perspectives* (Cambridge: Cambridge University Press, 2007).

Nicolas de Sadeleer, *Environmental Principles: From Political Slogans to Legal Rules* (Oxford: Oxford University Press, 2002).

Oscar Schachter, "The Emergence of International Environmental Law," *Journal of International Affairs* 44 (1991), pp. 457–493.

G. J. H. van Hoof, *Rethinking the Sources of International Law* (Deventer, Netherlands: Kluwer, 1983).

CHAPTER TEN

How and Why Do States Implement Their Commitments?

There is a Kafkaesque aspect to implementation . . . [I]t is a
crucial area, yet people act as if it did not exist.

Walter Williams, *Policy Analysis*, Vol. 1, p. 458 (1975)

THE EXPLOSION OF lawmaking over the past several decades
makes it easy to fall prey to the view that the development of
international environmental agreements, in itself, represents
progress—that texts matter and that stronger texts mean better environmental protection. But words on paper are not enough. Although they
represent an important first step, what matters, in the final analysis, is
not the number of treaties that have been negotiated or even ratified, but
rather their effectiveness in improving the quality of the environment.

The effectiveness of international environmental law is a function of
many factors, but implementation is first and foremost. This chapter thus
begins our consideration of effectiveness by focusing on national implementation, asking how and why it occurs. Chapter 11 then considers the
role of the international system in the implementation process. As we
shall see, although national action remains primary, international environmental regimes have increasingly focused, not just on the adoption of
new standards, but on the implementation of existing ones. Chapter 12
concludes by considering the question of effectiveness in more general
terms.

The Challenge of Implementation

Implementation is the process by which policies get translated into action.[1] It can encompass a wide range of measures, such as elaborating a
policy through more specific laws or regulations, educating people about
what a rule requires, building a new power plant that emits less pollution,

and monitoring and enforcing compliance. In a broad sense, all of these measures can be considered part of the implementation process.[2]

In some cases, implementation can be comparatively straightforward. When the state itself is the regulatory target, it can implement a rule simply by performing (or not performing) the prescribed action. For example, a state can implement the Antarctic Treaty's prohibition against establishing military bases or testing weapons in Antarctica simply by refraining from these activities. And it can implement an obligation to report on its national legislation regarding trade in endangered species simply by preparing and submitting the required report.[3] In these cases, implementation involves nothing more than compliance, and we may not even think of "implementation" as a separate category at all.

The term *implementation* is usually reserved for situations in which the relationship between an international rule and the behavior it aims to change is more attenuated. The bigger the gap between the two, the more that must be filled in through a process of further policy elaboration. The Kyoto Protocol, for example, requires Japan to reduce its emissions of greenhouse gases by 6 percent from 1990 levels during the 2008–2012 commitment period.[4] Japan cannot comply with this requirement the way it can comply with the prohibition on the use of force contained in the UN Charter by simply forbearing from the prohibited activity. Most greenhouse gas emissions are the result of activities by companies and individuals, who are not directly bound by Kyoto. Thus, to translate its 6 percent reduction target into reality, Japan must elaborate a set of national (and possibly international) policies, such as voluntary agreements with industry, appliance efficiency standards, and investments in renewable energy sources.

Translating policy into action is notoriously difficult. Many policies are characterized, as Richard Elmore once quipped, by "grand pretensions, faulty execution, puny results."[5] Critics often bemoan the lack of implementation of international environmental law, as if such problems were unique to the international level. However, implementation problems plague domestic law as well, even in a country such as the United States with its strong rule-of-law tradition and extensive administrative resources. According to one estimate,

> [T]hrough 1990 the EPA [Environmental Protection Agency] had managed to meet only 14 percent of the deadlines for environmental improvement mandated by Congress. . . . Eleven years after the passage of the Clean Air Act Amendments of 1970, 87 percent of the nation's integrated iron and steel facilities, 54 percent of its primary smelters, and 19 percent of its petroleum refineries did not meet federal and state emissions limits. A decade

after the passage of the 1972 Clean Water Act, only half of the nation's lakes and streams had met the water quality standards established by this legislation.[6]

As another study concluded, "[i]n many instances the implementation process appears never-ending. Commitments are adopted; efforts are made to implement; the commitments are adjusted. Problems are managed rather than eliminated—implementation is part of a perpetual cycle of policy that is driven by new information, experience, and political pressures."[7]

Because international environmental law typically aims to control not merely state conduct but private conduct, its implementation poses a particular challenge. Success depends on a wide variety of factors, including:

- The depth or stringency of the commitment—the bigger the required change from the status quo, the more likely it is that implementation will be costly and will conflict with entrenched interests.
- The type of commitment involved—commitments to engage in particular conduct (for example, adopting an oil pollution discharge standard) are more directly under a party's control than commitments to achieve some general result (reducing national emissions by a specified amount, as in the Kyoto Protocol example above, or making the nation's navigable waters "fishable" and "swimmable"), which depend on a multitude of factors that may be difficult to change.
- The capacity of the state—implementation generally requires resources and expertise to draft laws, monitor behavior, administer a permitting scheme, prepare reports, bring prosecutions, and so forth.
- The degree to which implementation converges with other domestic policy objectives—for example, a country is more likely to implement a commitment to reduce carbon dioxide emissions if doing so will also reduce urban air pollution or contribute to energy security.

Despite the importance of the implementation process, only in recent times has it received sustained analysis. And much of the work to date has been done by political scientists[8] rather than lawyers.[9]

The subsequent sections of this chapter focus on three questions, which might be referred to as the *who,* the *how,* and the *why* of implementation. First, *who* is primarily responsible for implementing international environmental law? Second, *how* do these actors go about implementing a state's international obligations, and what are the alternatives available to them? Finally, to the extent that actors undertake implementation efforts, *why* do they do so? What factors explain their behavior?

Who Is Responsible for Implementing International Environmental Law?— The Primacy of National Implementation

As in most areas of international law, states serve as the primary transmission belt for putting international environmental rules into effect. International environmental agreements impose obligations on states and rely on states to implement their commitments.[10] For this reason, the success of treaties such as the Montreal Protocol, the Kyoto Protocol, and the Convention on International Trade in Endangered Species (CITES) depends on the degree to which they are "domesticated."[11] Some treaties spell out the duty to implement explicitly.[12] Even in the absence of any explicit provision, the rule of *pacta sunt servanda*—the foundation of international treaty law—requires states to do whatever is necessary to implement their treaty obligations.[13]

Reliance on national implementation seems so natural that it is easy to forget that it represents a choice rather than a necessary feature of international environmental regimes. A treaty could, in theory, give substantial implementation responsibilities to non-governmental groups, as some bilateral arrangements and private codes of conduct do.[14] Or, conceivably, a treaty could bypass states altogether and regulate private conduct directly, assigning to an international institution such as UNEP the various tasks of implementation, including developing technical regulations, performing inspections, and initiating enforcement proceedings. Or rather than requiring states to establish national permitting schemes, CITES could establish an international permitting process to limit trade in endangered species, administered directly by an international institution.[15]

Federal systems such as the United States and the European Union illustrate the potential choice between centralized and decentralized implementation models. In the United States, some federal environmental laws follow the decentralized model of international environmental law. These laws establish broad requirements and then require states to develop the necessary implementation measures. The Clean Air Act, for example, provides for the establishment of federal air quality standards and then requires states to develop state implementation plans (SIPs) to achieve these federal standards.[16] As environmental law emerged in the United States in the 1970s, however, the federal government did not rely wholly on state implementation. Instead, it created the Environmental

Protection Agency and gave this new federal agency authority not only to oversee state implementation, but also to implement federal environmental standards directly through administrative rule-making, monitoring, and enforcement.[17]

In contrast, international environmental law has yet to develop centralized institutions with similar implementation responsibilities. Although many environmental regimes establish implementation mechanisms (discussed in Chapter 11), these play a secondary role, facilitating, and (to a limited degree) policing national implementation. They do not change the fundamental character of international law—that is, a decentralized, horizontal system that imposes obligations on states and then relies on them to put into practice the policies to which they have agreed internationally.

In part, the reliance on national implementation reflects the persistent, deeply ingrained conception of international law as a system of rules applicable to states. Yet even if international environmental law were to regulate private conduct directly, it would still mostly likely rely on national implementation, given the weakness of international institutions. Implementation depends on the capacity to control the conduct of individuals and firms—for example, to induce whalers to stop whaling, consumers of ozone-depleting substances to adopt substitutes, or electric utilities to switch to renewable energy sources. This requires legislative, executive, and judicial powers that international organizations typically lack and that states are reluctant to cede. As the continued smuggling of ozone-depleting substances illustrates, implementation is not an easy task, even for a government such as the United States, with considerable administrative resources at its disposal, much less an international organization.

International environmental law's reliance on national implementation raises the question: which state should be responsible for implementing which obligations with respect to which actors and activities? In general, international law is territorially based; its obligations apply to activities within a state's borders. The United States must reduce consumption of ozone-depleting substances within its territory and Germany within its territory. But how about environmental problems involving areas beyond national jurisdiction, such as the high seas or Antarctica? These problems raise more difficult questions.

If there is no territorial basis for jurisdiction, international law usually looks next to nationality. Implementation of vessel-source pollution standards and fisheries regulations, for example, is generally the responsibility of flag states. Similarly, the Antarctic Treaty makes parties responsible for controlling the conduct of their nationals.

Beyond this, international law sometimes allows states to exercise jurisdiction based on temporary presence. For example, the Law of the Sea Convention permits port states to implement marine pollution standards by inspecting and detaining vessels,[18] and the 1995 UN Fish Stocks Agreement calls for more effective enforcement by flag, port, and costal states of international conservation measures.[19] In much the same way, the states from which Antarctic tour boats depart could be given responsibility for implementing and enforcing international standards for Antarctic tourism.

In saying that states have the primary responsibility for implementing international environmental law, this is the beginning and not the end of the story. It represents an oversimplification in two important respects. First, as noted earlier, states are not unitary actors. They are divided both horizontally among the legislative, executive, and judicial branches of government and vertically between the central government and political subdivisions. In federal states, where the central government has limited authority, a question may even arise as to whether it has the competence to implement the issues addressed by a treaty and, if not, whether the country's constitutional system gives the central government the special ability to implement international agreements.[20] As we will explore in the next section, in states with a separation of powers between the legislative, executive, and judicial branches, national implementation raises questions about each branch's specific roles in the implementation process.

Second, implementation is not merely a technical, top-down process, involving directives from the government. It is a political process in which industry groups and environmental organizations all participate to varying degrees. Industry can contribute positively by providing expertise in designing technically feasible and cost-effective approaches, but it may also seek to weaken implementation measures in order to reduce its own adjustment costs.

Public participation is an increasingly integral part of the national implementation process and has gained international legal recognition in the Aarhus Convention.[21] In some international agreements, such as MARPOL and CITES, non-governmental groups perform specific implementation functions. In the oil pollution regime, for example, classification societies (which inspect ships) and insurance companies play important roles in implementing the design and construction standards of MARPOL, aimed at limiting oil pollution.[22] Similarly, CITES relies heavily on the non-governmental group, TRAFFIC, for monitoring and reporting functions. And the Johannesburg Summit more generally encouraged voluntary ("Type II") partnerships between non-governmental organizations and industry, which may in some cases bypass states altogether.[23] Conceptualizing implementation as a state-driven process can be a useful simplification, but one must always keep in mind that for most obligations, implementation ultimately depends on a variety of domestic and transnational actors.

Methods of Implementation

Assume that a state becomes a party to an international environmental agreement, such as the Kyoto Protocol, CITES, or the Basel Convention on the Transboundary Movements of Hazardous Wastes. What are its options to implement its new obligations? The answer depends on the interaction of two factors: the requirements of the treaty itself and rules of the state's own legal system.

The substantive obligations imposed by the treaty provide the starting point of our analysis. CITES, for example, requires each party to

- establish a permitting system for imports and exports of listed species.
- designate national scientific and management authorities to determine whether exports will be detrimental to the survival of a protected species, and whether the import of an endangered species is primarily for commercial purposes.
- inspect shipments entering and leaving its territory to determine whether they contain species listed in CITES and, if so, whether they conform to the CITES requirements.
- prohibit and penalize trade in violation of the Convention.
- confiscate illegally traded specimens.

These requirements specify a variety of implementation tasks but leave open the means by which they must be accomplished. A permitting system, for example, could be established through legislative or administrative action. Similarly, violations could be penalized through criminal prosecutions or administrative proceedings.

Treaties vary considerably in how much freedom they give states in the choice of implementation methods. At one end of the spectrum, some agreements set forth quite specific obligations of conduct that leave little discretion. For example, MARPOL requires flag states to prescribe precise rules for the construction and design of oil tankers, and to prohibit and sanction violations of these standards by vessels operating under their authority.[24] Similarly, the 1993 Food and Agriculture Organization (FAO) Fisheries Compliance Agreement and the 1995 UN Fish Stocks

Agreement both define a state's implementation responsibilities in considerable detail.[25]

Often, however, international law does not specify any particular implementation method, leaving it up to each state to decide how it will fulfill its international obligations in accordance with its own domestic law. A typical formulation on implementation, found in many treaties, simply requires states to take "appropriate" measures.[26] This allows each state to take into account its own legal system, regulatory culture, and other national circumstances in determining what measures are "appropriate." At the far extreme, treaties establishing an obligation to achieve some overall result, such as the national emissions targets in the Kyoto Protocol, give states almost complete flexibility in determining how they will reach the required outcome—whether by means of taxes, product standards, emission limits, voluntary agreements with industry, subsidies, education, and so forth.

The choice among implementation methods depends not only on the terms of a treaty but also on a state's domestic legal system. Separation of powers principles, for example, may assign particular tasks to particular branches or levels of government. Some domestic legal systems allow courts to implement international agreements directly; others make judicial implementation dependent on prior enactment of a treaty into domestic law.[27] Similarly, a country's constitutional law may give the executive branch particular powers or may require legislation for certain types of measures, such as imposing taxes, appropriating money, or criminalizing an activity. As a result, under their domestic constitutions, different countries may need to implement the same treaty obligations in different ways.

Legislative Implementation[28]

A threshold issue in treaty implementation is whether implementation requires legislation.[29] For a variety of reasons, sometimes the answer is no. A treaty may focus on governmental actions such as reporting, which can be performed by the executive branch on its own authority, without any need for legislative approval. Or, under a country's constitution, treaties may have the force of domestic law directly, making additional legislative implementation unnecessary. Or existing legislation may provide the necessary authority to implement a treaty's obligations.[30]

Consider, for example, the UN Framework Convention on Climate Change, which the United States ratified in 1992. In joining this agreement, the United States did not enact implementing legislation, partly because most of the Convention's obligations are very general and do not require specific acts of implementation, and partly because the Convention's more specific requirements, such as the obligation to submit periodic reports on national greenhouse gas emissions, can be performed directly by the executive branch. Even if the United States had decided to ratify the Kyoto Protocol, it might have been able to implement its obligations on the basis of existing law, given the Supreme Court's decision in *Massachusetts v. EPA*, which held that the Clean Air Act gives the EPA authority to regulate emissions of carbon dioxide from cars.[31]

Although not all international environmental agreements need legislative implementation, many do, particularly when they seek to control private or substate actors. For example, CITES mandates that states prohibit individuals from importing or exporting endangered species without a permit. So, unless a country's domestic law already regulates trade in endangered species, it will need to enact new legislation.[32] Similarly, MARPOL requires states to prohibit MARPOL violations under their domestic law.[33] In both cases, the treaties establish obligations of conduct that are legislative in nature and thus require legislative implementation.

Even when a treaty does not require it, countries often choose to enact implementing legislation in order to provide a stronger assurance of compliance.[34] The Kyoto Protocol, for example, does not necessitate implementing legislation. Its emissions reduction targets establish "obligations of result" that states could, in principle, achieve through non-regulatory means such as education and exhortation. Although a few states such as Japan emphasize voluntary measures, most rely on regulation (and other mandatory measures such as taxes) to change private behavior. Similarly, the United States has implemented its obligations under the Montreal Protocol to phase out the consumption and production of ozone-depleting substances, not through persuasion but through enactment of two pieces of legislation: Title VI of the 1990 Amendments to the Clean Air Act, which sets forth a schedule for phasing out the production and consumption of ozone-depleting substances,[35] and the Omnibus Budget Reconciliation Act of 1989, which imposes an excise tax on ozone-depleting substances.[36]

The pitfalls of choosing to forego legislative implementation are illustrated in the human rights field. The European Convention on Human Rights requires that states "secure to everyone within their jurisdiction" various human rights but does not mandate that states do so by legislative means. Until recently, the United Kingdom chose not to adopt any implementing legislation for the European Convention, in the belief that its domestic law already contained sufficient human rights protections. As a result, individuals could not pursue claims for violations of the European Convention in British courts, but instead had to resort to the international petition procedure, a costly and time-consuming process. Despite these costs, the number of complaints filed against the United Kingdom was significant, not because Britain had a particularly poor human rights record, but because the absence of domestic implementing legislation meant that an international complaint was the only means of raising a treaty violation. To reduce the need for international implementation, the United Kingdom finally adopted legislation that gives direct effect to the European Convention in its domestic law.[37]

Although adoption of implementing legislation is typically only the first step in the implementation process and does not in itself ensure compliance, even this initial step can prove difficult. As of 2007, for example, the CITES Secretariat found that more than half of the CITES parties still lacked fully adequate implementing legislation.[38] In some cases, difficulties in adopting implementing legislation can delay or even prevent ratification of a treaty. The United States, for example, is generally unwilling to ratify international environmental agreements until the necessary implementing legislation is in place. As a result, it has been unable to join the Basel Convention, even though the Senate has given its advice and consent to ratification, because the implementing legislation for Basel has been mired in a broader domestic dispute about hazardous substances regulation.

To avoid compounding these problems, legislation designed to implement treaties with flexible amendment procedures may provide for the direct incorporation of treaty amendments into domestic law, eliminating the need for further legislative action. For example, the U.S. Clean Air Act authorizes the EPA to adjust its phaseout schedule for ozone-depleting substances in accordance with changes in the international phaseout schedule under the Montreal Protocol.[39] Such delegations of authority avoid the need for new implementing legislation every time a new pollutant is regulated by a treaty (or, in the case of wildlife treaties, a new species is protected) and thereby serve as an important complement to the flexible amendment procedures described in Chapter 8.

Executive/Administrative Implementation

The adoption of implementing legislation is usually only the first step in the implementation process. Most treaties require various types of administrative implementation, such as further rule-making to give greater specificity to general legislative mandates, monitoring and assessment, preparation of reports, issuance of permits, and the investigation and prosecution of alleged violations. Consequently, as a recent study of implementation observed, "[o]ne cannot simply read domestic legislation to determine whether countries are complying. . . . [Compliance] involves assessing the extent to which governments follow through on the steps that they have taken."[40]

Different agreements vary considerably in the types of administrative implementation they entail. For example:

- Under MARPOL, states must inspect oil tankers flying their flag and bring prosecutions against substandard vessels.
- Under Ramsar, states must provide for the adequate wardening of wetlands within their territory.
- Under the Espoo Convention, states must perform environmental impact assessments of activities that pose a significant risk of transboundary harm.
- Under the London (Dumping) Convention, states must administer a permitting system for the dumping of hazardous wastes at sea.
- Under the UN Framework Convention on Climate Change, states must prepare inventories of their greenhouse gas emissions.

Typically, these administrative functions are performed not by a state's foreign ministry, but by the government agency with domestic responsibility for the issue in question. In the United States, for example, EPA has primary responsibility for implementing the Montreal Ozone Protocol, the Fish and Wildlife Service for implementing CITES, and the National Science Foundation for implementing the Antarctic Environment Protocol. Whether a state effectively implements its obligations under a treaty depends largely on the capabilities and priorities of the domestic agencies responsible for the treaty's implementation. For treaties such as CITES, where effective administration requires significant resources and expertise—for example, by customs officials to determine whether a particular specimen comes from a protected species—administrative implementation may pose a greater challenge to a treaty's effectiveness than legislative implementation.

Implementation of an international environmental agreement sometimes involves collaboration between national administering agencies—for example, through training programs for environmental enforcement officials, sharing of information about criminal violations of oil pollution standards through the International Criminal Police Organization (INTERPOL), mutual recognition of import and export permits under CITES, or coordination by port states of ship inspections under the Paris

Memorandum of Understanding on Port State Control.[41] This is part of a broader development of transgovernmental regulatory networks[42] and what some have called an emerging global administrative law.[43]

Judicial Implementation

In most cases, the courts become involved in the implementation process through their role in applying a state's domestic law. Assume, for example, that a state determines that an oil tanker has discharged oil in violation of the limits imposed by MARPOL, or that a garbage company has dumped medical wastes at sea, or that a shipper has imported elephant ivory without the necessary permits. In each case, the state might implement its treaty commitments by bringing a prosecution in its domestic courts, under its domestic implementing legislation. Indeed, some agreements require states to enforce their national implementing legislation in this manner.

In applying domestic law, courts play an important but subsidiary function in the implementation process. Just as a state's bureaucracy contributes to its capacity to implement international law, so do its courts. The primary steps in the implementation process, however, are the enactment of domestic legislation and the enforcement of that legislation by the executive. Once they have done so, a court's role is the same as when it enforces any piece of national legislation. In essence, it serves as one of the tools by which a state controls private conduct.

In contrast, courts play a more independent role in the implementation process when they apply international law directly or use it to interpret national law. This is especially true in cases against the government, where non-governmental actors allege that the political branches have failed to implement international environmental law.[44] In these contexts, national courts serve not merely as a tool to effectuate national policies, but as "an agent of an emerging international system of order," in the words of Richard Falk.[45] For example:

- In *Vellore Citizens Welfare Forum v. Union of India,* the Indian Supreme Court found that untreated discharges from tanneries violated the precautionary principle, the polluter-pays principle, and the principle of sustainable development, which the Court held are part of customary international law.[46]
- In *Minors Oposa,* the Philippine Supreme Court applied the principle of intergenerational equity to allow a group of children to challenge licenses to harvest timber.[47]

- In *Defenders of Wildlife, Inc. v. Endangered Species Scientific Authority*, a U.S. Court of Appeals held that the government's administrative guidelines for granting permits to export bobcats were contrary to CITES. In doing so, the court rejected the notion that, "in the absence of further congressional implementation, compliance with the Convention is left to the political branch of the government."[48]
- In the *Tasmanian Dam* case, an Australian court upheld a federal challenge to Tasmania's proposal to build a dam on the grounds that the dam would have destroyed a World Heritage site that Australia was obligated to protect.
- In a Canadian case, environmental groups alleged that the federal ministries of environment and health violated Canada's obligations under the Kyoto Protocol.[49]
- In a decision concerning the Athens Protocol for the Protection of the Mediterranean Sea against Pollution from Land-Based Sources, the European Court of Justice held that the agreement has direct effect "so that any interested party is entitled to rely on those provisions before the national courts."[50]

Decisions such as these illustrate the potential role of domestic courts in implementing international environmental law directly. Thus far, however, this role has been largely unrealized. Judicial implementation has been quite rare, particularly in comparison to human rights law, where courts have played a central role in implementation.[51] In a surprising number of environmental decisions to date, courts have not even indicated how they were using international law—indirectly, as an aid in interpreting national law, or directly, as a rule of decision.[52]

Several factors have hindered the application of international environmental law by national courts. First, in so-called dualist countries, which draw a sharp separation between international and national law, domestic courts can apply only a state's implementing legislation, not international law directly. Even in nominally "monist" countries such as the United States, where the Constitution proclaims treaties to be part of the "supreme law of the land," courts have tended to reach the same result, finding that environmental agreements are "non-self-executing" and cannot be applied by courts directly. In one U.S. case concerning the London Dumping Convention, even the plaintiffs conceded that the Convention does not have any independent effect and that the EPA's obligations derive solely from U.S. domestic implementing legislation.[53] Second, courts have been reluctant to apply international environmental norms such as the precautionary principle and sustainable development on the ground that they are highly indeterminate and do not "set forth any specific proscriptions."[54] Finally, in lawsuits that attempt to enforce international environmental law against non-state actors, courts have generally found that international environmental law creates duties only for states, not for private parties.[55]

The net effect of these doctrines has been to limit the independent role of courts in implementing international environmental law. Decisions by national courts have been "too sporadic" to play a "significant deterrent role."[56] Instead, the political branches have predominated in translating international norms into action, with courts serving an adjutant function.

Why Do States Implement International Environmental Law?

When a state implements its international commitments, it self-complies. Of course, sometimes states fail to do so, making international compliance mechanisms necessary (a topic that we will explore in the next chapter). But international environmental law typically does not depend on international enforcement; instead, it relies on self-implementation and self-compliance by states.[57] The United States implements its commitments under the Montreal Ozone Protocol, for example, not out of fear of international sanctions. Rather, it self-complies through regulation of ozone-depleting substances under Title VI of the Clean Air Act and has progressively ratcheted up its regulatory requirements in response to the adoption of new control measures under the Protocol.[58] As of early 2009, for example, the Food and Drug Administration banned the use of chlorofluorocarbons (CFCs) in asthma inhalers to implement U.S. obligations under the Montreal Protocol, even though the substitute inhalers cost consumers an average of three times more.[59]

Why do states generally self-comply? Why don't they join international environmental agreements and then violate those agreements with impunity, whenever this suits their interests? Particularly when implementation is costly, why don't states simply free ride on the efforts of others?

A multitude of factors contribute to self-compliance; the reasons vary from state to state and from issue to issue. All ultimately rest on some combination of the two basic behavioral models we examined earlier: a logic of appropriateness and a logic of consequences, normative feelings of obligation and instrumental calculations of self-interest. To some degree, one can think about these at the level of the state. In understanding implementation, however, one also needs to look inside the state and consider the wide variety of actors that help determine how states behave. That is, one needs to consider the domestic policy process.[60]

Preexisting Reasons

As a starting point, one simple explanation of self-compliance is that states do so for the same reasons they enter into a commitment in the first place:

- The required actions might reflect what a state was already doing or planned to do. For example, the 1991 U.S.-Canada Air Quality Agreement merely codified what the United States and Canada had decided to do domestically.[61] Thus, additional implementation was unnecessary.[62]
- A state might believe that the required actions are in its interest, regardless of what others do; that is, it might have an interest in unilateral compliance. A state might, for example, think that it has an independent interest in conserving energy to reduce dependence on foreign oil or in conserving wetlands because of the ecosystem services that wetlands provide. Although the state could conceivably do these things even in the absence of a treaty, the treaty-making process can help states better appreciate their interests, serve as a catalyst to overcome inertia, or provide leverage to overcome opposition from domestic interest groups.
- A state might believe that the required actions are in its interest in exchange for reciprocal actions by others, and fear that, if it fails to implement the agreement, others will violate the agreement in retaliation, causing it to lose the benefit of the bargain. In other words, it might have what Ron Mitchell calls an "interdependent" rather than an "independent" interest in implementation.[63]
- State actors might believe that the treaty furthers their values. They might believe, for example, that they have a moral responsibility to future generations (or to poor, vulnerable countries) to prevent climate change. Therefore, they might enter into, and comply with, a treaty to reduce emissions because this is the "right" thing to do.
- Finally, environmental groups, scientific experts, and other domestic actors might push state decision makers first to accept an agreement and then to implement it. One study concluded, for example, that public concern is "[o]ften the most important factor in determining whether international regimes can be effective."[64]

In all of these cases, states act in good faith in joining a treaty; they are what Beth Simmons calls "sincere ratifiers."[65] They enter into the agreement intending to implement and comply with it because it reflects their interests and/or values. As long as the state's *ex ante* views are borne out, then implementation is not surprising.[66]

Interestingly, these explanatory factors, which focus on a state's reasons for joining an agreement, do not necessarily hinge on the agreement's legal status. As long as a state believes, for whatever reason, that acting in a particular way makes sense, one would expect it to continue acting that way, whether or not it has assumed an obligation. That is why, in some cases, states go further than what a treaty requires (i.e., they overcomply) or even implement an agreement by which they are not legally bound.

Often, overcompliance is interpreted as an indication that the actor would have behaved the same anyway, even in the absence of the agreement. In other words, it is taken as a sign that the agreement is epiphenomenal. This does not necessarily follow, however. An agreement might make a difference in helping to spur action, even if the resulting action is not performed out of a sense of legal commitment. A significant number of U.S. cities, for example, have pledged to implement the U.S. emissions target under the Kyoto Protocol, even though the United States is not a party to Kyoto and even though cities have no obligations under the agreement. Although the cities are not acting out of a sense of legal obligation, it is hard to imagine that they would have behaved in the same way if Kyoto had never existed. Kyoto established a norm of appropriate behavior that the cities accept. In pledging to meet the Kyoto target, the cities demonstrate that they are the kind of actor that is willing to do its fair share to combat climate change.

Existence of a Legal Commitment

As we have seen, the reasons that lead a state to join an agreement also, typically, lead to implementation. What if circumstances change, however, and the reasons that led a state to join an agreement no longer apply? What if the costs of the agreement turn out to be higher than expected, or the benefits lower? Or what if new leaders come to power with different views about the merits of the agreement? It is in these kinds of circumstances that the existence of a legal obligation becomes important. In the absence of an obligation, a state might not otherwise be inclined to do what the agreement requires. The obligation changes the implementation equation and helps "lock in" the required behavior.[67]

First, from a logic of appropriateness, a state might feel it "ought" to implement its international obligations (or, more precisely, its leaders might feel this way). For example, a state might reduce its emissions of sulfur dioxide pursuant to LRTAP, or regulate the import of hazardous wastes pursuant to the Basel Convention because it promised to do so and it regards consent as a legitimate basis of obligation. In other words, it might take seriously the fundamental principle of treaty law, *pacta sunt servanda* (treaties must be obeyed), and, accordingly, enact implementing legislation as a matter of course when it joins a multilateral environmental agreement.[68]

Over time, the norms in an agreement might also exercise a deeper normative effect.[69] Through a process of socialization, actors within a state might internalize the agreement's norms. As a result, they might no longer see them as an external constraint, which they follow out of a sense of legal obligation, but rather as providing the appropriate standards of conduct.

Alternatively, a state might self-implement a commitment based on a logic of consequences.[70] For example, it might believe that it has a long-term interest in a world where commitments are generally kept and thus have meaning. Alternatively, it might believe that it benefits from a reputation for reliability, and fear that, if it failed to implement a treaty, its reputation as a good citizen would decline, making it more difficult to enter into cooperative arrangements in the future. These types of instrumental factors represent the second basic way in which the existence of an obligation might change the implementation equation.

The two accounts of implementation, one based on a logic of appropriateness and the other on a logic of consequences, are often portrayed as competitors, but they are in fact complementary and indeed interdependent.[71] Consider a key component of instrumental theories of compliance: reputation. One instrumental reason a state might implement its commitments is that it fears a loss of reputation if it acts otherwise. But part of this reputational loss may itself depend on the belief by others that states *ought* to fulfill their commitments. To the extent that some states (or the public) take international obligations seriously, they are likely to judge a country harshly for failing to live up to its commitments. So the normative belief in commitments by some states may give other states, which do not hold these normative views, an instrumental reason to comply.

Domestic Factors

Thus far, we have been treating states as unitary actors that have feelings of legal obligation and that calculate their interests. As a shorthand, it is sometimes useful to say, for example, that the United States prohibits imports of elephant ivory because of the obligation imposed by CITES. But, of course, states are abstractions; it is in fact individuals who have interests and feelings of legal obligation. Thus a richer account of implementation must explore more fully the different actors who play a role in the implementation process.

The sense of obligation is likely to be strongest, for example, among those in the executive branch who actually negotiate an international agreement and thereby put their own personal reputations on the line. It tends to be weakest among those harmed by an international environmental agreement, who may view the domestic implementation process as a fresh opportunity to refight the battle. Legislators may share a belief that their country should live up to its commitments, but since they are not generally involved in treaty negotiations, their normative sense of commitment may be weak. In any event, legislators are heavily influenced by domestic political considerations, which in turn are driven by private actors, some of whom are motivated by a logic of consequences (e.g., companies that bear high adjustment costs) and others by a logic of appropriateness.

Just as decisions about whether to join a treaty reflect, in part, the relative political power of the domestic winners and losers, the same is true of decisions about implementation and compliance. Even if an international environmental agreement imposes costs on a country as a whole, it may leave particular domestic constituencies such as environmental activists and green businesses better off. To the extent that these winners have greater influence in the domestic policy process than the losers (e.g., because they are more numerous or are better financed), a country is more likely to implement its treaty commitments.[72]

Influence over implementation is a function not only of political clout, but of expertise. As one study concluded, "Becoming an influential participant in the implementation phase is a costly undertaking that bears fruit only after years of investment."[73] For this reason, expert networks (or "epistemic communities," as they are sometimes called) often play a particularly influential role in the implementation process.[74]

The domestication of an international commitment through implementing legislation brings additional factors into play. In countries with a strong, professional bureaucracy, implementation tends to become routinized. Officials simply undertake the quotidian tasks of implementation as a matter of course rather than engage in instrumental calculations of interest. Over time, a "culture of compliance develops," as normative factors are internalized.[75] "[C]ompliance becomes an automatic response," as one studied concluded, "rather than a matter requiring an assessment of costs and benefits on a case-by-case basis."[76]

Similarly, to the limited extent that international environmental norms can be applied by judges, either directly or by means of implementing legislation, this gives domestic supporters an additional avenue to promote compliance. Moreover, in this process of judicial implementation, normative factors predominate, since the role of judges is to apply rules *qua* rules rather than as part of an instrumental calculation of interests.

Conclusion

To be effective, international environmental norms must be implemented. Implementation does not guarantee effectiveness; a weak norm, even if perfectly implemented, will not do much to improve the environment. But although implementation is not a sufficient condition for effectiveness, it is a necessary one. Given the weakness of international institutions, the heavy lifting of implementation must take place at the national level.

Implementation can involve a wide variety of tasks: incorporating international norms into national law, translating them into rules regulating firms and individuals, monitoring behavior, training officials, adjudicating cases, and prosecuting and punishing violations. In most cases, international law gives states significant discretion as to the choice of implementation methods. States are allowed to implement their international obligations in a manner that is compatible with their domestic legal and administrative systems.

Even in the absence of international enforcement, many if not most states implement their international environmental obligations almost as a matter of course: they establish permitting systems under the London Convention and CITES, regulate exports of hazardous wastes under Basel, and adopt rules requiring the phaseout of ozone-depleting substances under the Montreal Protocol. Many causal factors help account for this process of self-implementation: calculations of self-interest, a sense of normative commitment, bureaucratic routines, or pressure (or even litigation) by environmental groups. Their relative importance in explaining implementation varies from country to country and treaty to treaty. Implementation is a messy, complex process and is beyond our ability to explain—at least thus far—through simple models.[77]

Recommended Reading

Michael Anderson and Paolo Galizzi, eds., *International Environmental Law in National Courts* (London: British Institute of International and Comparative Law, 2002).

Abram Chayes and Antonia Handler Chayes, *The New Sovereignty: Compliance with International Regulatory Agreements* (Cambridge, MA: Harvard University Press, 1995).

Kenneth Hanf and Arild Underdal, "Domesticating International Commitments: Linking National and International Decision-Making," in Arild Underdal, ed., *The Politics of International Environmental Management* (Dordrecht, Netherlands: Kluwer, 1998), pp. 149–170.

Kal Raustiala and Anne-Marie Slaughter, "International Law, International Relations and Compliance," in Walter Carlsnaes, Thomas Risse, and Beth A. Simmons, eds., *Handbook of International Relations* (London: Sage, 2002), pp. 538–557.

Catherine Redgwell, "National Implementation," in Daniel Bodansky, Jutta Brunnée, and Ellen Hey, eds., *The Oxford Handbook of International Environmental Law* (Oxford: Oxford University Press, 2007), pp. 922–946.

Alexei Roginko, "Domestic Compliance with International Environmental Agreements: A Review of Current Literature," Working Paper WP-94–128 (Laxenburg, Austria: International Institute for Applied Systems Analysis, 1994).

UNEP, *Manual on Compliance with and Enforcement of Multilateral Environmental Agreements* (Nairobi: UNEP, 2006), www.unep.org (accessed 2/4/09).

David G. Victor, Kal Raustiala, and Eugene B. Skolnikoff, eds., *The Implementation and Effectiveness of International Environmental Commitments: Theory and Practice* (Cambridge, MA: MIT Press, 1998).

Edith Brown Weiss and Harold K. Jacobson, eds., *Engaging Countries: Strengthening Compliance with International Environmental Accords* (Cambridge, MA: MIT Press, 1998).

CHAPTER ELEVEN

International Carrots and Sticks

> [C]ovenants, without the sword, are but words and of no
> strength to secure a man at all.
>
> Thomas Hobbes, *Leviathan,* Pt. II, Ch. XVII

I N 1949, THE International Whaling Commission set a quota on
the killing of humpback whales, and, in the mid-1960s, it banned
the hunting of humpback whales altogether. But rather than recover, humpback whale populations fell precipitously. What accounted
for this decline? The mystery was not solved until the 1990s, after the
dissolution of the Soviet Union, when archival records came to light revealing that Soviet whalers had systematically violated the IWC quotas,
killing more than 100,000 *excess* whales during the period from 1948 to
1987.[1]

The Soviet violation of the International Whaling Convention quotas
was perhaps unusual in its egregiousness but not its occurrence. Although most states may comply with most of their international commitments most of the time (as Louis Henkin famously proclaimed),[2] violations remain a problem. For example,

- In 2001, the Taliban government of Afghanistan dynamited the
  giant Buddhas at Bamiyan, despite their protected status under the
  World Heritage Convention.
- In 2002, Canada ratified the Kyoto Protocol on climate change,
  which requires it to reduce its emissions of carbon dioxide and
  other greenhouse gases by 6 percent from 1990 levels during the
  2008–2012 commitment period. Instead, Canada's emissions have
  continued to rise and will clearly exceed its Kyoto target.
- As of 2007, three decades after its entry into force, more than
  half of the parties to the Convention on International Trade in

Endangered Species of Wild Flora and Fauna (CITES) had still failed to enact implementing legislation that fully satisfies the treaty's requirements.[3]

As these cases remind us, we cannot rely on states to implement their international environmental commitments. Even comparatively easy, procedural commitments, such as the obligation to file reports, often go unfulfilled by states. International measures are also needed to make international environmental law effective.

Addressing the issue of non-compliance is crucial not simply because violations harm the environment directly, but because they erode the capacity for international cooperation more generally by undermining trust. Environmental agreements are built on reciprocity: each state agrees to act in exchange for action by others. However, if a state lacks confidence that others will do what they say, then it has no incentive to take action itself. Canada's violation of the Kyoto Protocol may not in itself negate the reciprocal benefits of the agreement because Canada's emissions are a relatively small part of the problem. Yet if Canada can violate its commitments under the Kyoto Protocol and get away with it, what assurance is there that others will comply?

Although some observers criticize international environmental law as a "negotiating system" that pays insufficient attention to implementation,[4] international environmental regimes have in fact developed a wide variety of institutions and mechanisms to address the problem of compliance.[5] Some of these are specified in the treaty text itself, others have been elaborated through decisions of the parties, and still others have developed more informally through practice over time.[6]

International implementation measures raise a variety of doctrinal, explanatory, and policy questions. What role can the international community play in promoting better implementation? What are the options? Which of these alternatives are most effective? What approaches do international environmental regimes employ and why? And how might these be improved?

One potential response to the problem of non-compliance is enforcement. But enforcement has never been the strong suit of international law.[7] In contrast to domestic legal systems, which can enforce rules through the centralized application of sanctions, international law is a decentralized system that has traditionally relied on self-help by the injured state. Such "private" enforcement can be successful in addressing problems that result in concentrated harm to particular states, which have an incentive to retaliate.[8] Without international oversight, however, private enforcement is easily subject to abuse and can exacerbate tensions. Moreover, it is ill suited to global environmental problems such as climate change or ozone depletion, which injure the international community as a whole. In such cases, individual states have little incentive to act because most of the benefits of enforcement flow to the international community rather than to the state taking action. In essence, enforcement provides a public good, and, as economic theory teaches, public goods are typically underproduced.

In some areas of international law, efforts have been made to replace private enforcement with public enforcement—for example, through the Security Council or the World Trade Organization's dispute settlement body. Thus far, however, multilateral environmental agreements contain few enforcement mechanisms. Moreover, proposals to provide stronger enforcement meet resistance from states seeking to protect their sovereignty.

Rather than focus on enforcement, international environmental regimes have taken a different tack, attempting to encourage and facilitate compliance, rather than to deter and prevent non-compliance. For example:

- The CITES Secretariat helps countries draft implementing legislation, so that they can satisfy their treaty requirements.
- The World Heritage Convention Secretariat has produced a 150+ page manual setting forth operational guidelines for the implementation of the Convention.[9]
- The Montreal Protocol Multilateral Fund provides financial assistance to help defray the additional costs of ozone-friendly technologies.

Even the procedures established by many recent agreements to identify and respond to cases of non-compliance have a primarily facilitative rather than an enforcement function. Few "punish" violators with anything more than international exposure and embarrassment. Instead, they seek to determine the cause of non-compliance and work with the state concerned to rectify the problem.[10]

Are facilitative approaches such as these enough? Thus far, they have helped to produce better implementation of international environmental norms, if not perfect compliance. But skeptics attribute this comparative success not to the strength of the compliance systems, but to the weakness of the commitments that states have negotiated.[11] Facilitative approaches, they argue, may be sufficient to encourage implementation of relatively shallow commitments, which do not require significant changes in behavior. Deeper, more demanding commitments will depend on an enforcement system with "teeth," which can force states to comply through the threat of sanctions. In their view, the present lack of strong enforcement is the Achilles' heel of international environmental law.[12]

Although this concern should not be dismissed lightly, it depends on an assumption about state behavior that is at least open to question—namely, that treaty violations reflect deliberate decisions by states based on instrumental calculations of national interest. For this reason, I will begin by investigating the potential sources of non-compliance with international environmental law. Then, I will examine the potential international responses, focusing on the familiar questions of why, who, and how: Why have an international response—what is the purpose or goal? Who are the potential actors? And how might they respond—what are the options?

Causes of Non-Compliance

Why do states sometimes fail to comply with their international obligation? Why do they make commitments and then fail to do what they promised? Many reasons are possible: bad faith, changed circumstances, poor planning, domestic politics, and lack of capacity.

In some cases, states may ratify an agreement with no intention to comply. Not to put too fine a point on it, they may lie.[13] What would a state hope to gain from doing so? First, its decision to ratify might sucker more honorable states into ratifying, bringing the agreement into force and thereby providing the bad-faith ratifier with environmental benefits. Second, even if an insincere ratifier received no environmental benefit from a treaty, it might gain a competitive advantage over sincere ratifiers if implementation proves costly. Third, ratification typically brings good publicity and thus provides reputational benefits. These gains may prove short-lived if a state's violations of an agreement become apparent. Like the former Soviet Union in the whaling and dumping cases, however, a state might hope that its violations will go undetected. Or its leaders might have a short time horizon, preferring the immediate gains from ratification over the more distant costs of non-compliance. Moreover, a state might hope that its violations, even if discovered, will not be enough to provoke others to pull out. After all, most states have stuck with Kyoto, despite Canada's expected non-compliance.

Critics of international law often seem to assume that bad-faith ratification is common—that many world leaders behave like Saddam Hussein or Kim Jong-Il, making commitments that they have no intention of keeping. In classroom simulations of the prisoner's dilemma, students often engage in this kind of bad-faith behavior: they promise to cooperate in the next round of the game, only to defect. One should be cautious, however, about putting too much stock in these classroom simulations, for the students' behavior may be an artifact of their knowledge that they are engaged in a game and that chronic defection will not really harm their reputation. Empirical studies suggest that, in real life, states typically do intend to implement the agreements they ratify. In other words, insincere ratification represents the exception rather than the norm.[14]

Even if a state ratifies an agreement in good faith, it might later change its mind. This represents a more likely scenario than insincere ratification. After all, if the constellation of factors that led a state to ratify changes, it is only natural that a state's propensity to comply would change as well. New leaders might come to power with different values—for example, the Taliban in Afghanistan, whose Muslim fundamentalism made preservation of the giant Buddhas at Bamiyan under the World Heritage Convention seem an apostasy rather than a duty. Or an environmental agreement might develop in ways that a state views as illegitimate, weakening the state's sense of normative obligation. (If Japan were to violate the International Whaling Convention by resuming commercial whaling, this would be the likely explanation.) Or the benefits of violation might simply prove irresistible, overwhelming any perceived duty to comply.

One can conceptualize these scenarios in terms of a balance between the factors weighing for and against compliance. In the former category are the factors we examined in the last chapter that support implementation: a state's environmental values, the perceived benefits of the agreement, a state's sense of normative commitment, domestic politics, and bureaucratic routine. Added to these are whatever costs might be associated with violation, such as loss of reputation, which the state wants to avoid. Together these determine a state's willingness to comply.

On the other side of the scale are the costs of compliance (or what amounts to the same thing—the benefits of violation). These include both the direct costs of implementing an agreement, such as retrofitting oil tankers, installing pollution control equipment, and training game wardens and customs inspectors, as well as the opportunity costs of not being able to engage in a productive activity such as selling elephant ivory, hunting whales, or developing wetlands. As the costs of compliance wax, or the willingness to comply wanes, the likelihood of non-compliance increases.

To the extent that a violation results, it may represent an act of omission rather than commission; that is, it may result from insufficient will to comply rather than from an affirmative intent to renege. Consider the following familiar scenario. A state ratifies an agreement with a general intent to comply but without any plan for how it will do so. Later, when compliance proves more difficult than expected—when the true costs become apparent—it lacks the political will necessary to adopt costly implementing measures. The factors that proved sufficient for ratification are too weak to overcome the domestic resistance to implementation. The state never intends to violate the agreement, but it ends up doing so, as a result of poor planning or miscalculation. In broad terms, this describes Canada's performance under the Kyoto Protocol.[15] According to one comparative study, most cases of non-compliance can be explained in this manner. They are the "product of incomplete planning and miscalculation rather than a willful act."[16]

Further complicating the picture, both the willingness to comply and the costs of compliance differ for different actors within a country. So whether a state complies depends on the distribution as well as the magnitude of costs and benefits. The executive branch may ratify an agreement fully intending to comply but may then be unable to convince the legislature to enact the necessary implementing legislation, possibly because powerful domestic constituencies oppose it. Or a domestic court may decide a case in a manner that results in a treaty violation, as in the *Shrimp/Turtle* case, where a U.S. court ordered the State Department to adopt turtle conservation measures that initially were found to violate the General Agreement on Tariffs and Trade (GATT).[17] In these situations, non-compliance does not reflect a deliberate national decision that the benefits of violation outweigh the costs. Rather, it is the product of a country's domestic political and legal systems.

Yet another source of non-compliance is lack of capacity. Even when a state wishes to comply with its international commitments, it may lack the wherewithal to do so. For example, it may have insufficient expertise and personnel to draft implementing legislation, prepare reports, carry out inspections, or prosecute those responsible for violating a treaty.[18] Or it may lack the financial resources needed to adopt new technologies or build new, greener facilities.

Some commentators suggest that lack of capacity should be seen differently from other sources of non-compliance in that it represents a type of "good faith" or unintentional non-compliance.[19] However, apart from the first basis of non-compliance we examined above—strategic ratification with no intent to comply—the other sources of non-compliance do not fit neatly into the categories of "good" or "bad" faith. If a state ratifies an agreement without any plan for implementation, or if it makes some efforts to comply but fails to do more when the going gets tough, does this constitute bad faith? How about cases where the executive wishes to implement a treaty but fails to get its proposed measures enacted by the legislature, or is ordered by the courts to do something that violates the treaty? Conversely, is a state that violates an agreement due to lack of capacity entirely blameless? Does a state act in good faith if it ratifies an agreement with which it cannot comply?

As these questions suggest, lack of capacity does not represent an entirely different basis of non-compliance than other causes; it fits into the general calculus of non-compliance that we discussed earlier. Even poor states, with relatively few resources, could comply with many environmental standards if they wanted to do so badly enough. Compliance is usually a function not simply of capacity, but rather of capacity and willingness together.

Consider, for example, Japan's performance under the Kyoto Protocol. Under the Protocol, Japan is required to reduce its greenhouse gas emissions by 6 percent from 1990 levels during the 2008–2012 commitment period.[20] If Japan misses this target, as appears likely,[21] will this violation represent a lack of capacity or a lack of willingness to comply? By all indications, Japan entered into the Kyoto agreement with every intention of complying and would be willing to do so if compliance were not too costly. Indeed, it has already taken steps to implement the treaty and is, to some degree, trying to comply. But is it trying hard enough? Achieving its 6 percent emissions reduction target would be technically possible but difficult, given Japan's historically high rates of efficiency and low rates of emissions. In the end, if it fails to comply, this will be the result of both lack of capacity and lack of willingness.

Finally, states sometimes violate agreements inadvertently—by mistake so to speak. The implementation measures a state adopts may fail to have the expected effect on private behavior. For example, an unexpectedly cold winter may increase demand for home heating oil and thereby increase carbon dioxide emissions, causing a state to miss its Kyoto target. Or a treaty provision may be unclear, so that a state believes that it is complying, only to find out later that the treaty requires something else. In these cases, the phrase "good-faith" non-compliance seems truly appropriate.

Goals in Addressing Non-Compliance

In addressing the problem of non-compliance, what should be our goal? In general, there are three (often complementary) possibilities: punish the violator, compensate the victim, and promote future compliance. To the extent that states (or individuals) act in bad faith—for example, by joining an agreement that they have no intent to implement—one tempting response is to punish the wrongdoer. International law has occasionally given way to this desire for retributive justice (or, depending on one's point of view, revenge). The reparations imposed on Germany after World War I under the Versailles Treaty and the Nuremberg prosecutions after World War II are two prominent examples. Thus far, however, international environmental law has not included punishment in its repertoire of responses to non-compliance, even in egregious cases such as the 1991 Gulf War, when Iraq purposefully inflicted massive environmental damage as it was withdrawing from Kuwait. Some have proposed defining environmental crimes such as "ecocide," but, at present, the International Criminal Court Statute establishes criminal responsibility for environmental damage only in very limited circumstances during wartime.[22]

Another possible goal of international remedies is to compensate victims. Like retribution, compensation is backward looking, although, unlike retribution, it focuses on helping the victims rather than punishing the perpetrators. The 1992 Oil Pollution Fund Convention, which provides money to victims of oil pollution damage, is compensatory in purpose,[23] as (in part) are the liability regimes established by a number of international agreements.[24]

These examples aside, international environmental law generally seeks to promote future compliance rather than to remedy past non-compliance. To the limited extent that international law imposes sanctions (e.g., through trade restrictions), it does so for deterrent or preventive rather than for retributive purposes. It aims to influence future behavior rather than to settle old scores. Some international mechanisms reflect this positive, forward-looking orientation by referring to themselves as compliance systems rather than non-compliance systems.

Compliance, however, represents merely a floor. As we will discuss in Chapter 12, the fact that states are complying with a treaty does not necessarily mean that the treaty is changing anyone's behavior or is actually helping the environment. Perhaps the key states responsible for a problem are not parties to the treaty or have opted out of important regulatory decisions, such as the moratorium on commercial whaling. Or perhaps a treaty's obligations fall short of ensuring its environmental objective. Establishing a permitting system under CITES, for example, is a start, but only a start, in the effort to control illegal trade in wildlife. If a state does not adequately train or pay its customs inspectors, then they may fail to detect illegal trade due to incompetence or corruption.

For these reasons, international efforts often aim at more than mere compliance: they seek to promote effectiveness more generally. This intent is made explicit in the U.S. Pelly Amendment, which authorizes the president to impose trade sanctions against countries that "diminish the effectiveness" of an international conservation program, even if no legal violation has occurred.[25] In the 1980s, the United States threatened to use this provision against Japan and Norway, not in response to an actual violation of the International Whaling Convention, but to dissuade them from exercising their legal right to opt out of the International Whaling Commission's decision to impose a moratorium on commercial whaling. Similarly, the goal of international financial assistance, training programs, and other forms of capacity building is often to promote the general effectiveness of a regime, not simply compliance.

General Tasks of International Compliance Mechanisms

In promoting implementation and compliance, international mechanisms have thee basic tasks:

- To obtain accurate information about the performance of states and other actors (for example, oil tanker operators or whalers).
- To encourage and enable future compliance through financial and technical assistance.
- To identify and respond to cases of non-compliance or lack of effective implementation *ex post*.

Before considering these tasks in more detail, it is useful to discuss who might perform them, as well as two general models of international implementation.

Who's Who in International Implementation

A multitude of actors play important roles in providing information, triggering international procedures, providing assistance, and responding to cases of non-compliance. These include international institutions, non-governmental groups, private actors, and other states. Some of their roles are official in nature. The UN Framework Convention on Climate Change, for example, designates the Global Environment Facility to administer its financial mechanism, and the North American Free Trade Agreement (NAFTA) allows individuals to bring complaints regarding non-enforcement of national laws. Many actors play unofficial roles as well. In the whaling regime, for example, Greenpeace serves as an unofficial source of information about infractions; the United States has threatened unilateral trade measures against countries that undermine the effectiveness of the whaling regime; and non-governmental organizations (NGOs) organized an international boycott of Icelandic fish products in an effort to force Iceland to stop its whaling activities.

Other states.   In cases where an environmental problem significantly affects particular states, as in a transboundary pollution case, the affected states have a clear incentive to act in order to promote compliance. But even when an environmental problem damages the global commons and enforcement produces primarily public goods, states occasionally undertake enforcement measures. This suggests that a broader array of causal factors than self-interest influence state behavior. The United States' threats to impose trade measures to enforce the whaling moratorium, for example, are difficult to explain in terms of self-interest. Rather, they illustrate the role of domestic politics and, in particular, the influence of non-governmental groups over state actions.[26]

International institutions.   Because of the public goods character of international implementation and enforcement, states often choose to act collectively through international institutions rather than individually. In general, enforcement measures by international institutions are seen as more legitimate than those by individual states acting unilaterally because international institutions are subject to a measure of community control. Many regimes have established implementation or compliance committees to review issues of non-compliance and make recommendations or decisions. Most regimes also establish some kind of financial mechanism, often relying on international financial institutions such as the Global Environment Facility. Although many key institutions such as compliance committees are made up mostly of government officials, treaty secretariats sometimes play a significant role in the implementation process. The Convention on International Trade in Endangered Species (CITES) Secretariat, for example, evaluates the adequacy of national implementing legislation, organizes country visits, and prepares reports.

Non-governmental actors.   Environmental groups typically have a more single-minded focus than governments and hence are more willing to invest in implementation and enforcement measures. They monitor behavior, publicize violations, mobilize public opinion against delinquent states, and provide technical and financial assistance. Usually, non-governmental organizations play these roles informally, but a few international regimes give NGOs and individuals an official role in the implementation process. TRAFFIC, for example, provides information about trade in endangered species under CITES.[27] The North American Agreement on Environmental Cooperation (NAAEC) goes further, establishing a citizen suit procedure under which private actors can bring claims that a state has failed to enforce its own environmental laws.[28]

What explains the creation of these non-state mechanisms? Conceivably, states might allow individual compliance procedures because they recognize that NGOs and individuals have a greater incentive to undertake enforcement than they do. This kind of functionalist account helps explain, for example, the creation of individual petition procedures in human rights regimes. In contrast, in the environmental arena, domestic factors, especially lobbying by domestic NGOs, seem to have played a larger role in the creation of individual petition procedures and other non-state mechanisms.[29]

Enforcement and Managerial Models

In seeking to promote compliance and effectiveness, what means should international environmental law use? At the risk of oversimplification, we can think about the potential responses in terms of two general models, usually referred to as the enforcement and managerial models. These models reflect different assumptions about state behavior, the causes of non-compliance, and the role of the international system in responding.

To the extent that states deliberately violate their international commitments, this suggests the need for an enforcement approach that induces states to comply. Enforcement can work in two ways. In its ideal-typical form, enforcement involves compulsion: for example, a policeman overpowering a criminal and putting him in handcuffs or the authorities garnishing a person's bank account. Although international environmental law does not establish any enforcement mechanisms in this strong sense, some international environmental regimes operate in a similar manner by limiting a state's ability to commit violations. The trade suspensions imposed under CITES against countries with persistent compliance problems exemplify this approach. The purpose of these trade measures is to prevent countries with compliance problems from committing additional violations.[30]

Much of what we characterize as enforcement, however, does not literally *compel* compliance. Rather than depriving the actor of volition, it seeks to influence an actor's decision-making process by increasing the costs of non-compliance, so that non-compliance becomes more expensive

Box 11.1.   Two Models of International Implementation

Enforcement Model	Managerial Model
Assumptions about State Behavior	
• States are rational utility maximizers. • States will violate treaties if the benefits of violation outweigh the costs.	• States are engaged in a cooperative venture. • States internalize treaty norms and are likely to comply unless there are strong countervailing circumstances. • Non-compliance usually results from lack of capacity or clarity rather than from willful disobedience.
Theory of Compliance	
• Coerced compliance to prevent violations. • Treaty must raise the costs of violation by imposing sanctions.	• Treaty regimes play an active role in modifying state preferences. • Non-compliance is a problem to be solved through mutual consultation and deliberation. • Treaties help to encourage compliance by promoting transparency and building national capacity.

Source: Daniel Bodansky, *What Makes International Agreements Effective? Some Pointers for the WHO Framework Convention on Tobacco Control,* WHO/NCD/TF/99.4 (Geneva: WHO, 1999), p. 33.

than compliance. Consider, for example, the trade restrictions the United States threatened against Japan in the early 1980s for Japan's failure to accept the whaling moratorium. The threatened measures did not compel Japan to stop whaling; instead, they sought to raise the costs Japan would incur by not accepting the moratorium decision in order to make Japan change its mind. Other sanctions wielded by international environmental regimes, such as limitations on membership, have a similar deterrent function. The deeper the commitments imposed by a treaty and the greater the temptation to violate, the stronger the penalties needed to deter defection effectively.

Interestingly, some of the most powerful enforcement tools in international environmental politics are wielded not by international institutions but by individual states and NGOs, which can act unilaterally, without having to get agreement from others. The threatened U.S. trade measures against Japan fall into this category. Similarly, non-governmental groups such as Greenpeace have threatened boycotts of Icelandic fish products in retaliation for Iceland's decision to resume whaling, and have even taken direct action to thwart whaling operations. Such unilateral action, particularly by states, can produce conflict and thus be disruptive to the international system. Nevertheless, unilateralism has an important role to play, given the weakness of multilateral enforcement mechanisms. In cases where more facilitative approaches prove inadequate and no viable multilateral enforcement option is possible, the choice is not between unilateralism and multilateralism, but between unilateralism and doing nothing.[31]

In contrast to the enforcement model, the managerial model of compliance starts from very different assumptions about state behavior.[32] The enforcement model views states as unitary, rational actors that will violate an agreement when doing so suits their interests. In contrast, the managerial approach sees states as complex organizations that have a propensity to comply with treaties unless strong countervailing circumstances are present. This approach explains most non-compliance as the result of mistakes, changes in circumstances, or lack of capacity rather than of a deliberate decision to violate.[33] In this view, the function of a compliance system is not to punish non-compliance, but rather to encourage and facilitate compliance. To a significant degree, the managerial approach to compliance predominates in international environmental law.[34] The response to Russia's non-compliance with the Montreal Protocol in the mid-1990s provides an illustration. Rather than recommend sanctions, the other parties (through the Protocol's Implementation Committee) in essence negotiated a phaseout plan with Russia, involving subsidies from the World Bank to close the Russian facilities that produced CFCs.[35] As a result, Russia closed its last production facility in 2002, thereby coming into compliance with the Protocol.

Although the managerial model is sometimes described as reflecting a logic of appropriateness rather than a logic of consequences, it is eclectic, positing a variety of causal mechanisms. For example, international institutions can promote implementation by

- Providing financial and technical assistance to states, thereby lowering the costs of compliance—an instrumental, cost-benefit explanation.
- Clarifying the content of international obligations—for example, by developing model implementing legislation—thereby strengthening the parties' sense of normative commitment.
- Requiring states to file reports and prepare national implementation plans, which help mobilize and empower domestic constituencies—a mechanism that focuses on domestic politics.
- Entering into a constructive dialogue with governments about implementation issues, in the context of reviewing national reports—a process that gives a treaty's domestic supporters an additional lever with which to influence government policies.

The managerial model is not necessarily incompatible with the enforcement model. The two models proceed from different, but not mutually exclusive, premises. States may generally be predisposed to comply with their international obligations, as the managerial theory presupposes; but they may also violate their obligations when the temptations prove too great, as the enforcement model assumes. The managerial model does differ from the enforcement model in downplaying the role of sanctions,[36] but it does not preclude a role for sanctions. Indeed, the soft sanction of exposure figures prominently in managerial accounts. The managerial account differs from the enforcement model only in claiming that compliance usually does not depend on additional, more stringent types of sanctions. Enforcement plays a part, but it represents the exception rather than the rule.

Assessing Implementation and Compliance: Sources of Information

As the Soviet whaling case illustrates, no matter what the approach to compliance, obtaining accurate information is a critical first step. States that deliberately violate an agreement will be deterred by sanctions only to the extent that they fear discovery. The efficacy of enforcement measures is thus a function not only of the magnitude of the sanctions but also of the likelihood of detection.

Generally, national reporting is the primary source of information concerning implementation and effectiveness. In many regimes, this is supplemented by other sources of information as well as by international verification mechanisms.

Self-Reporting by States[37]

National reporting requirements are almost certainly the most ubiquitous obligations in multilateral environmental agreements.[38] In some cases, reporting is the only specific action required of states. Reporting requirements typically focus on the steps states have taken to implement their international commitments, including information on implementing legislation as well as on national measures to implement and enforce this legislation (permits issued, investigations undertaken, prosecutions brought, etc.).

Self-reporting might seem a curious, even poor, means of evaluating compliance, but misreporting is more difficult than it might appear, especially in states with open and participatory political processes and with professional bureaucracies that are relatively insulated from political pressures. Even when states are less than forthright in their reports, the formal presentation of a report to an international body presents NGOs and other critics with a convenient target. It facilitates evaluation of a country's performance by providing a focal point for others to assess and criticize the information provided.

Although national reporting serves primarily an informational function, it plays other roles as well. In situations in which a state joins an agreement in good faith, national reporting can perform a policy reform function by encouraging self-examination. Even when a state is less than sincere, the process of preparing a national report may have a catalytic effect in promoting internal policy reform by mobilizing and empowering actors both within and outside the government. Through the sharing of information in reports, states may also learn about policy options or technologies they had not previously considered.

National reporting can serve a legislative function as well. A notable feature of environmental regimes is their dynamic quality. Reporting can contribute to this norm-making process in two ways: first, by furthering our scientific understanding of a problem (for example, national inventories of greenhouse gas emissions give a better picture of what is actually taking place in the atmosphere); and second, by allowing an assessment of the overall performance of a regime in achieving its objectives (sometimes referred to as regime review).

In general, reporting requirements track the substantive obligations detailed in an agreement. Agreements that establish a performance standard require states to report on their performance; agreements that establish permitting systems require parties to provide information on the permits granted; and agreements that require states to punish violations require them to provide information on the number of prosecutions brought.[39] The more specific the underlying obligation in a regime, the more specific the reporting requirement. General obligations have corresponding general reporting requirements.[40] Conversely, specific obligations usually carry with them more specific reporting requirements.[41]

To help ensure both the quality and comparability of reports, most international environmental regimes establish reporting guidelines or standardized formats—sometimes in very elaborate detail, as the climate change regime illustrates. Although states may still submit incomplete or inaccurate data, detailed guidelines and common templates at least make misreporting easier to detect and hence a less appealing option.

Other Sources of Information

Although national reporting remains the principal source of information in most environmental regimes, many regimes draw on other sources of information as well. Such information is particularly vital for an enforcement model, which assumes that states sometimes act in bad faith. If a state deliberately decides to violate its substantive obligations, the information it provides in its national reports can hardly be trusted. More likely, a state will try to hide its violations, as the Soviets did in the whaling and ocean dumping cases. Thus, an enforcement approach depends on the availability of independent sources of information.

The various sources of information on environmental performance can be assessed along two dimensions:

- First, the source can be public or private, centralized or decentralized. International institutions such as treaty secretariats are centralized, public actors, reflecting the community of states, whereas non-governmental organizations and individuals are decentralized, private actors.
- Second, information can be gathered on a routine or episodic basis. It can result, for example, from ongoing monitoring programs, such as aerial surveillance of shipping lanes to detect oil spills, or from a random observation by a passing ship.

The distinction drawn by some analysts between police patrols and fire alarms[42] focuses on two possible combinations of these elements—public-routine vs. private-episodic—but other combinations are possible.

International monitoring and inspections.   International inspections are a major source of information in some arenas, such as arms control. Perhaps the most robust example is the International Atomic Energy Agency's role under the nuclear non-proliferation regime. Although environmental agreements do not give international institutions as extensive powers of inspection, a few establish monitoring or observer programs. Perhaps the most systematic is the European Monitoring and Evaluation Programme (EMEP), which monitors emissions and transboundary flows of the pollutants that cause acid rain.[43] On a more episodic basis, some fisheries regimes provide for international observer programs, and CITES authorizes its secretariat to make country visits and to prepare reports on national performance.

Independent experts.   In the human rights field, international institutions such as the UN Human Rights Commission (now the Human Rights Council) often designate an independent expert as *rapporteur* for a particular subject, such as torture or the death penalty. The *rapporteur* studies the subject, gathers information on the performance of individual countries, and prepares a report. Although international environmental regimes have used independent experts to verify national reports (discussed below), thus far they have not used independent experts to engage in more open-ended studies and reporting.

Business actors.   Business actors are often the ultimate target of international environmental standards and have the best access to much of the relevant data. Only a few international environmental agreements, however, require reporting directly by private actors. A rare example is the International Convention for the Prevention of Pollution from Ships (MARPOL), which requires oil tankers to have oil discharge monitoring equipment and to keep an oil record book of all discharges during a voyage.

Non-governmental actors.   In practice, NGOs are often the main independent source of information about implementation and compliance. Greenpeace, for example, monitors whaling activities and trade in hazardous wastes, whereas TRAFFIC gathers information on illegal trade in wildlife products.[44] Some agreements provide for NGO participation in the preparation of national reports, but most do not officially recognize NGO information. For example, at International Whaling Commission meetings, Greenpeace must find a friendly government to present its data on infractions because it lacks any official status. One exception to this general rule is CITES, which allows the secretariat to receive information directly from TRAFFIC.[45] The citizen submission procedure under the

NAEEC similarly allows individuals to submit information about national performance. As Raustiala notes, individuals may have an advantage over centralized institutions in obtaining environmental information because the information tends to be widely dispersed.[46]

International Review

Comparatively few international environmental agreements have formal procedures for the review of national reports, but many have more informal arrangements either to review the accuracy of the information provided in national reports (a process usually referred to as verification) or to use that information to evaluate performance. In general, international review can serve three functions:[47]

- *Implementation review* assesses a country's implementation efforts. What laws and regulations has it adopted? What criminal penalties does it impose for violations? Which institutions have which implementation responsibilities? What steps has a country taken to enforce its laws? How many inspections has it performed? How many prosecutions have been brought? The list could go on and on.
- *Compliance review* typically includes a review of implementation but focuses more narrowly on a country's compliance with its legal obligations.
- *Effectiveness review* is the broadest function, examining the adequacy of an agreement more generally, including the adequacy of its commitments, rather than focusing on individual countries' performance.

Traditionally, multilateral environmental agreements provided only for effectiveness review, not for implementation or compliance review. For example, LRTAP provides that the Executive Body (the equivalent of the conference of the parties) shall "review the implementation of the present Convention," but it does not authorize the Executive Body to review individual national reports or request additional information.[48] Examining the aggregate performance of the parties in achieving a treaty's objectives is useful in assessing whether adjustments or amendments are needed, and thus serves an important legislative function.[49] But it does not allow an evaluation of the performance of individual countries.

Increasingly, environmental regimes have begun to allow implementation and compliance reviews, either by experts or other states. Beginning in 1979, for example, the CITES Secretariat has submitted Infraction Reports to the Conference of the Parties. Based on these reports, the CITES

Standing Committee may recommend trade suspensions against persistent violators. The 1994 Nuclear Safety Convention takes a somewhat different approach, establishing a peer review process to consider how the participating states can improve the safety of their nuclear installations. The climate change regime establishes perhaps the most detailed review process to date, involving review of individual developed country reports by expert review teams, including through country visits.[50] These processes of implementation review not only increase transparency and provide the factual basis for possible non-compliance responses, but they also "redistribute political power to domestic actors that favour full implementation and compliance" and promote learning by the state itself.[51]

Facilitating Compliance through Financial and Technical Assistance

Multilateral environmental agreements generally take a proactive approach: they do not merely respond to non-compliance *ex post*, but actively seek to promote compliance *ex ante* through the provision of financial and technical assistance. A study done for the 1992 Earth Summit gave a rough estimate of $600 billion per year for the total costs necessary to implement Agenda 21 in developing countries.[52] This is a huge number compared to existing development assistance (which currently totals only about $100 billion annually),[53] but it is still comparatively modest in the context of overall world gross domestic product of $48 trillion in 2006.[54]

Implementation assistance can take the form not only of financial aid, but also of technical support to draft legislation, train personnel, develop environmental management tools, adapt technologies to local conditions, provide information, and, in general, build the capacity of local institutions. A wide variety of institutions provide such assistance: bilateral developments agencies such as the U.S. Agency for International Development (USAID), international financial institutions such as the World Bank, and specialized programs such as UNEP, the UN Development Programme, and the UN Institute for Training and Research (UNITAR).

The principal international financial institution with an exclusively environmental orientation is the Global Environment Facility, or GEF, which was established in 1991 by a group of donor countries under the auspices of the World Bank, but has developed into an independent institution with a global membership and its own governing agreement. Since 1991, it has provided over $8 billion in grants and generated over $33 billion in cofinancing—a small amount given the magnitude of the needs, but large relative to other sources.[55]

Virtually all multilateral environmental agreements provide some implementation assistance. In some cases, MEAs give only quite limited support, for example, to prepare reports or provide training; in other cases they provide much more significant assistance to implement substantive requirements designed to reduce pollution or conserve resources. Beginning with the 1973 World Heritage Convention, multilateral environmental agreements have often established special funds to assist with implementation. The World Heritage Fund is quite small, with an annual budget of only about $4 million to help countries identify and propose sites for inclusion on the World Heritage List, prepare management plans, and train personnel.[56] In contrast, the Montreal Protocol's Multilateral Fund provides more than $150 million per year (and more than $2 billion since its inception in 1990) to support specific projects to phase out the use of ozone-depleting substances, including through technology transfer.[57]

Assistance not only enables countries to implement and comply with their existing commitments, but it can also provide an incentive for countries to join an agreement in the first place by lowering the expected costs of compliance. China and India agreed to ratify the Montreal Protocol, for example, only on the condition that industrialized countries establish the Multilateral Fund. Similarly, the inclusion of a financial mechanism in the UN Framework Convention on Climate Change was one of the key demands of developing countries.

Implementation assistance raises a host of design questions: who pays, to whom, for what, why, and how (that is, through what mechanisms)? And who decides these questions? The question that drives all of the others is "why?" What is the rationale for assistance? Answering this question is critical in determining who provides what assistance to whom, through what mechanisms, and with what governance arrangements.

Unlike traditional development assistance, environmental assistance benefits the global community as a whole rather than just the recipient countries. For example, environmental assistance helps protect World Heritage sites, preserve the ozone layer, and prevent climate change.[58] Thus, it should not be seen as charity. Instead, it represents a contribution by donor countries to the production of global public goods, which allows developing countries to take action against environmental problems.

This distinctive character of environmental assistance has important implications for the design of financial mechanisms:

- *Governance*—Traditionally, donor countries have controlled decisions about official development assistance. Just as individuals decide which charities to support, donor countries decide how their development assistance is spent. In the World Bank, for example, voting rights are weighted based on the size of a donor's contribution. To the extent, however, that environmental assistance contributes to the provision of a public good, arguably all countries should have a say in the decision-making process. This is reflected in the novel governance arrangements of both the GEF and the Montreal Protocol Multilateral Fund, which make decisions dependent on a double-majority vote of both donor and recipient countries.

- *Eligible costs*—If environmental assistance is given to produce global public goods, then it is necessary to distinguish between project costs that provide global benefits and are hence eligible for assistance, and costs that produce national benefits and hence are not eligible. GEF, for example, funds only "incremental costs"— that is, the costs associated with "transforming a project with national benefits into one with global environmental benefits."[59]

- *Mandatory or voluntary funding*—Traditionally, development assistance has been voluntary. Each country decides how much, if anything, it wishes to give. Arguably, however, all countries have an obligation to contribute to the production of global public goods inasmuch as all countries benefit from them.[60] Although GEF continues to be funded through a voluntary pledging process, the Montreal Protocol Multilateral Fund was drafted to "convey the impression of at least a tacit commitment," by creating a "'scale of contributions.'"[61]

Responding to Non-Compliance

Traditional Dispute Settlement

Historically, international law sought to address issues of non-compliance through dispute settlement initiated by the injured against the culpable state. In the *Trail Smelter* case, for example, the United States claimed that Canada had breached its duty not to cause transboundary harm. More recently, in the *Gabčíkovo Dam* case, Hungary alleged that a dam being built along the Danube by Slovakia would cause irreversible ecological damage and endanger plant and animal life. And in the *MOX* case, Ireland brought an arbitral proceeding against the United Kingdom, alleging that the United Kingdom had breached its duty to provide Ireland with access to information about a potentially harmful nuclear facility, pursuant to a regional treaty dealing with the North-East Atlantic.

Dispute resolution is sometimes characterized as an enforcement method,[62] but this characterization can be a bit misleading. In domestic legal systems, we associate dispute settlement with enforcement because judicial decisions can themselves be enforced through seizure of assets, contempt proceedings, and ultimately the police. Similarly, the dispute settlement system of the World Trade Organization (WTO) can appropriately be called an enforcement system because its decisions can be enforced through trade restrictions imposed by the winning state against the loser. In contrast, international dispute settlement procedures rarely establish any special enforcement mechanisms. Instead, they rely on the losing party to voluntarily comply with a decision. These procedures are significant not because they represent an additional sanction, but because they reinforce and amplify the reputational costs of violating international law. In the absence of dispute settlement, a violator could argue that it is, in fact, complying, thereby muddying the waters and diluting any reputational costs the violator might suffer. An authoritative finding of non-compliance by a dispute resolution body precludes this option. Furthermore, if the dispute settlement procedure is itself binding, then a state that fails to comply with the outcome of that binding process commits another violation of international law, incurring additional reputational costs. Now it has violated not only its underlying environmental obligation, but also its duty to comply with the decisions of the international tribunal.

The law of state responsibility provides the conceptual architecture for interstate dispute settlement.[63] Although it took the International Law Commission (ILC) more than forty years to work out the details, the basic rules of state responsibility can be simply stated:

- A state is responsible for conduct attributable to it that breaches its international obligations.
- State responsibility gives rise to a duty to make reparations, usually through the provision of compensation.
- An injured state may invoke state responsibility through dispute settlement.
- If the responsible state does not cease its wrongful conduct, the injured state can engage in self-help (referred to as countermeasures).

Virtually all multilateral environmental agreements provide for dispute settlement of some kind (usually arbitration), and, in recent years, international tribunals have proliferated.[64] In addition to the International Court of Justice, the UN Convention on the Law of the Sea established the International Tribunal on the Law of the Sea (ITLOS), and the Permanent Court of Arbitration (which, international lawyers like to joke, is neither permanent nor a court) adopted special rules for environmental dispute settlement.

Although *Trail Smelter* has been much celebrated, and the last decade has witnessed a modest rise in environmental litigation,[65] traditional dispute settlement still plays a negligible role in the implementation of international environmental law. The law of state responsibility is geared primarily to bilateral enforcement by the "injured state" against the non-compliant state. In theory, this makes sense because the injured state is the one with the greatest interest in responding. In practice, however, injured states have rarely resorted to dispute settlement. Even an environmental catastrophe such as Chernobyl did not lead to any legal claims. Bringing a legal claim can be costly, not only financially but also to relations with the state against whom the claim is brought. *Trail Smelter* notwithstanding, few states have been willing to incur these costs to pursue the uncertain benefits of litigation.

States are even less likely to use traditional dispute settlement to address global commons problems such as ozone depletion or climate change, where the harms are widely distributed and where, as a result, no individual state is likely to have a sufficient incentive to undertake enforcement actions. As a result, despite efforts to modernize the law of state responsibility to address harms to the international community as a whole, the provisions in multilateral environmental agreements regarding traditional dispute resolution have gone almost completely unused.[66]

Should the lack of traditional dispute settlement be a source of concern? Probably not. Even in its revised form, the law of state responsibility remains ill suited to global environmental problems:

- The law of state responsibility is legalistic, focusing on whether a state has committed an "internationally wrongful act," rather than on whether states are implementing their commitments effectively.
- It tends to sees the world in static terms, focusing on restoration of the *status quo ante* rather than on promoting environmental effectiveness going forward (although the *Trail Smelter* case is an exception and resulted in a remedial regime to reduce future air pollution).
- Finally, it is formalistic, focusing on the fact that a state has breached an international obligation, not on why it has done so.

Multilateral Non-Compliance Procedures

Rather than rely on traditional dispute settlement to address the problem of non-compliance, a better way to promote the effectiveness of international environmental law is through flexible, political approaches, involving a wider variety of actors, which investigate the sources of non-compliance in a particular case and find appropriate responses. This has been the trend in international environmental law. Increasingly, international environmental agreements have established treaty-based compliance systems, each with its own specialized compliance or implementation committee. The Montreal Protocol's Non-Compliance Procedure, the first such procedure,[67] served as the model for several other agreements. Perhaps the most elaborate procedure is the Kyoto Protocol's Compliance Committee, which includes both a facilitative and an enforcement branch. Today, most multilateral environmental agreements have either already adopted a non-compliance procedure or are considering doing so.[68]

These treaty-based compliance systems operate in fundamentally different ways from traditional dispute settlement:

- They are political and pragmatic, not legalistic.[69]
- They are forward- not backward-looking. Their goal is to manage environmental problems in order to achieve a reasonable level of compliance in the future, not to establish legal rights and duties or to rectify past breaches.
- They are non-adversarial rather than contentious in nature. In many cases thus far, the non-compliant state itself has initiated proceedings.
- They view compliance and non-compliance as part of a continuum, not in all-or-nothing terms. On this continuum, the difference between a small and a big violation, or between bare compliance and overcompliance, may be more significant than the difference between compliance and breach.

These fundamental differences between traditional dispute settlement and treaty-based compliance systems manifest themselves in interesting ways. First, compliance bodies are often composed of government negotiators rather than independent experts, reflecting their political nature. Second, the procedures are collective rather than bilateral in nature. Any state may initiate a case, with no need to show injury. Third, cases may concern not only actual but potential non-compliance. Finally, since the goal is to bring a state back into compliance, one of the principal responses to non-compliance is to provide assistance[70]—an approach that seems bizarre from the perspective of traditional dispute settlement because it arguably rewards a state for its internationally wrongful act.

Most multilateral compliance procedures rely more on positive incentives for compliance than on sanctions for non-compliance. According to a recent UNEP study, fewer than a quarter make any provision for the imposition of sanctions.[71] Typically, the most significant "sanction" imposed by international environmental regimes is exposure. Although exposure may seem to be a modest penalty, it can result in significant costs. It subjects a state to adverse publicity both at home and abroad, it makes future treaty negotiations more difficult, and it can "infect other aspects of the relationship between the parties"[72] and even a state's status as a member in good standing of the international community.[73] In addition to exposure, some international environmental regimes require delinquent states to develop compliance action plans that detail how they will bring themselves back into compliance, on the assumption that non-compliance is usually the result of poor planning and lack of capacity.

What additional sanctioning mechanisms might be possible? Trade measures offer a potential lever, and the Montreal Protocol provides for trade restrictions as a response to both non-participation and non-compliance. The use of trade measures to promote participation and compliance has proven highly controversial, however, and other international environmental agreements have thus far not followed the Montreal Protocol's lead.

Financial penalties are also sometimes suggested as a sanction, but they have proven to be politically unacceptable. In any event, they would not solve the enforcement problem because they themselves require enforcement. (If a state violates an environmental commitment, what reason is there to think that it will comply with an obligation to pay a financial penalty?) At most, non-compliance may result in a loss of eligibility for existing funding, rather than the imposition of penalties. But even that penalty is unusual because states fear that cutting assistance will exacerbate rather than solve non-compliance. So, in practice, non-compliance more often leads to greater rather than less financial assistance—exactly the opposite of an enforcement model.

A final possibility would be to impose sanctions directly on the individuals responsible for violating international environmental law, rather than on the state. Whether criminal punishment would be appropriate is debatable, however, since most environmental problems result from everyday activities rather than from "bad" actors. Even with respect to deliberate, widespread environmental damage, which might merit criminal punishment, proposals to designate "ecocide" as an international crime have attracted little support. Individual criminal responsibility for environmental offenses is rare even in domestic law and seems unlikely anytime soon at the international level.

In contrast to these sanctioning approaches, some international environmental regimes seek to prevent states from being able to commit violations in the first place by suspending their privilege to engage in potentially harmful activities. Consider, for example, the trade suspensions authorized by CITES against countries that lack adequate implementing legislation or that have a persistent pattern of violations. These trade measures preclude the target countries from engaging in potentially illegal trade in endangered species. Although these measures do not involve compulsion, they work in a similar manner, independently of the violator's volition, by preventing delinquent countries from further undermining the treaty. The Kyoto Protocol similarly seeks to contain the consequences of noncompliance by providing that, if a country lacks an adequate national system for estimating emissions or misses its emission targets, it loses its eligibility to participate in emissions trading.[74] In essence, the Protocol views an adequate national reporting system as a condition precedent for trading (the same way passing a driving exam and obtaining a license is a condition precedent for driving). Such a system is designed to ensure that emission trading does not undermine the integrity of Kyoto's targets. In the cases of both CITES and Kyoto, limiting trade prevents violations resulting from trade itself.[75]

In certain respects, MARPOL takes a similar approach except that it focuses on compliance by private parties, especially oil tanker operators and owners. Like CITES and Kyoto with their trade restrictions, MARPOL seeks to prevent violations from occurring in the first place by making it difficult to insure a vessel unless the ship has been certified as meeting MARPOL's construction, design, and equipment requirements.[76]

Conclusion

International compliance mechanisms are more successful in encouraging the average state than in coercing the truly bad one. They do so by strengthening a state's sense of normative commitment, encouraging it to engage in better planning, and giving it the wherewithal to comply, rather than by making a legal finding of violation.

Some see the trend from traditional dispute settlement to more political compliance procedures in a negative light. As Jan Klabbers notes, in compliance procedures, "flexibility is the name of the game—flexible norms, flexible baseline values, flexible implementation, and flexible assistance."[77] Critics worry that this flexibility erodes the special status of law as a mode of social ordering.[78]

But legal and non-legal approaches to controlling behavior form a continuum. Different points along this continuum are appropriate for different sorts of problems. Human rights law, for example, tends to be more legalistic in nature. Once an issue is conceived in terms of rights, it is removed from the political arena of competing interests and policies. Perhaps for this reason, the paradigmatic institution established by human rights treaties is the expert committee, composed largely of lawyers. The paradigmatic non-compliance tool is the individual complaint procedure, which aims to achieve a just result in the individual case rather than an acceptable level of compliance overall.

In contrast, international environmental law is a fundamentally political process of balancing competing interests, which blurs the distinction between law and politics. Therefore, it should not be surprising that a more political, pragmatic approach is taken to non-compliance issues. This flexible approach mirrors developments in national law, which put greater emphasis on negotiated solutions to compliance problems than on purely legal enforcement.[79] In international environmental law, the goal is to produce an acceptable level of compliance, not perfect compliance—an objective that is ultimately more political than legal in character.[80]

Recommended Reading

Ulrich Beyerlin, Peter-Tobias Stoll, and Rüdiger Wolfrum, eds., *Ensuring Compliance with Multilateral Environmental Agreements: A Dialogue Between Practitioners and Academia* (Leiden: Martinus Nijhoff, 2006).

James Cameron, Jacob Werksman, and Peter Roderick, eds., *Improving Compliance with International Environmental Law* (London: Earthscan, 1996).

Abram Chayes and Antonia Handler Chayes, *The New Sovereignty: Compliance with International Regulatory Agreements* (Cambridge, MA: Harvard University Press, 1995).

Martti Koskenniemi, "Breach of Treaty or Non-Compliance? Reflections on the Enforcement of the Montreal Protocol," *Yearbook of International Environmental Law* 3 (1992), pp. 123–162.

Kal Raustiala, *Reporting and Review Institutions in 10 Multilateral Environmental Agreements* (Nairobi: UNEP, 2001).

Cesare P. R. Romano, *The Peaceful Settlement of International Environmental Disputes: A Pragmatic Approach* (London: Kluwer Law International, 2000).

UNEP, *Compliance Mechanisms under Selected Multilateral Agreements* (Nairobi: UNEP, 2007), www.unep.org (accessed 2/8/09).

Rüdiger Wolfrum, "Means of Ensuring Compliance with and Enforcement of International Environmental Law," *Recueil des Cours* 272 (1998), pp. 9–154.

CHAPTER TWELVE

Is International Environmental Law Effective?

> Failure is simply the opportunity to begin again,
> this time more intelligently.
>
> Henry Ford

SHORTLY AFTER THE 1992 Rio Conference, an environmental scientist expressed the concern that the "the 1990s may be remembered as the decade of empty pledges, when nations met, pontificated on environmental problems, signed agreements and then went home but little action followed."[1] Has this fear proved correct? Is international environmentalism merely epiphenomenal or, even worse, counterproductive, by giving the illusion of progress and thereby reducing pressure for real change?[2] Or has it solved—or, at least, ameliorated—important problems such as loss of biodiversity, depletion of the stratospheric ozone layer, and global warming?

Since the Rio Conference, political scientists and lawyers have devoted considerable attention to these questions, but there is still little consensus about the answers.[3] Assessing the effectiveness of international environmental regimes poses significant methodological challenges. Often it is difficult to gather reliable evidence about the basic facts—for example, the amount of oil pollution from ships, the number of acres deforested in the Amazon, or the number of species becoming extinct. So, we may not be sure whether environmental quality improved following the adoption of a treaty. Even when an environmental problem shows signs of improvement, it is difficult to determine the cause. Sulfur dioxide emissions in Europe, for example, declined significantly following the adoption in 1979 of the Long-Range Transboundary Air Pollution Convention (LRTAP). Many analysts argue, however, that the reductions had little to do with LRTAP and would have occurred anyway, due to a variety of economic and political changes, including a shift in domestic energy sources from coal to natural gas.[4]

Having examined both national and international implementation of international environmental norms, this chapter will consider the problem of effectiveness in more general terms. To begin with, what do we mean by "effectiveness," and what are the different ways of measuring it? To what degree have international environmental regimes been effective? Finally, why do some agreements work better than others? What explains the relative effectiveness (or ineffectiveness) of different regimes?

Three Meanings of Effectiveness[5]

In thinking about the question of effectiveness, it is useful, initially, to distinguish three different meanings of the term:[6]

- *Legal effectiveness* focuses on the issue of compliance—that is, whether outcomes conform to what a legal rule requires. If a treaty sets forth obligations of conduct—a duty to establish a permitting system for trade in endangered species or to submit reports on greenhouse gas emissions—then it is legally effective to the degree that states act consistently with its requirements. In contrast, if it sets forth obligations of result—a duty to reduce carbon dioxide emissions by 10 percent, for example—then it is legally effective if emissions decline by the required amount.
- *Behavioral effectiveness* focuses on the role of international environmental law in causing states and individuals to modify their behavior in the "right" direction—that is, toward achieving the regime's objective.[7] A treaty is behaviorally effective if it influences an actor's behavior—if, *but for the treaty,* the actor would have behaved differently—even if the actor does not fully comply with the treaty's obligations.
- Finally, *problem-solving effectiveness* focuses on the degree to which a treaty achieves its objectives or, more generally, solves the environmental problem it addresses.

The difference between these three meanings of effectiveness can be illustrated by a simple example. The 1987 Montreal Protocol on Substances that Deplete the Ozone Layer limits the consumption and production of ozone-depleting substances (ODS). The Protocol is legally effective to the extent that states reduce their consumption and production of ODS by the required amounts. It is behaviorally effective to the extent that these reductions are a result of the Protocol and would not have occurred otherwise. And it has problem-solving effectiveness to the extent that it stops and reverses depletion of the stratospheric ozone layer.

Legal Effectiveness: Compliance

Lawyers tend to concentrate on the issue of legal effectiveness. They often view a treaty as effective if it achieves compliance and ineffective if states fail to meet their obligations.

Compliance is a function of two factors: first, the obligations established by a rule (what the rule requires states or other actors to do or to achieve) and, second, the actual conduct or results of those subject to these obligations. The Kyoto Protocol, for example, requires the European Union to reduce its emissions of greenhouse gases by 8 percent from 1990 levels for the 2008–2012 period.[8] So, we can compare the EU's actual emissions with its Kyoto obligation to determine whether the EU is in compliance.

To the extent that the obligations established by a rule are unclear, it may be difficult or even impossible to identify the required (or prohibited) conduct and, consequently, to categorize behavior as "compliant" or "non-compliant." For example, Article 4.1(b) of the UN Framework Convention on Climate Change (UNFCCC) requires states to formulate national climate change programs. However, this obligation is so general and subject to so many caveats ("taking into account their specific national and regional development priorities, objectives and circumstances")[9] that it is difficult to imagine what conduct by a party would constitute non-compliance. As a result, in such cases, the concept of "compliance" lacks much bite.

Although lawyers tend to focus on compliance, compliance by itself is a poor indicator of a treaty's value because it is neither a necessary nor a sufficient condition for behavioral or problem-solving effectiveness. A high degree of compliance (or even perfect compliance) might mean only that an international environmental regime is unambitious and does not require states to do much, if anything, to change their behavior.[10] Conversely, a low-compliance rate might result from overly ambitious treaty goals, not from the treaty's lack of positive effect.

Consider, for example, the International Whaling Convention, which authorizes the International Whaling Commission (IWC) to adopt conservation regulations, including quotas on the number of whales that can be killed. During the 1960s, when whaling states engaged in the so-called Whaling Olympics, killing 50,000 to 60,000 whales per year, they did so in full compliance with the IWC quotas. The high rate of compliance demonstrated the laxness rather than the strength of the Whaling Convention.[11]

In a much celebrated dictum, Louis Henkin opined that "[i]t is probably the case that almost all nations observe . . . almost all of their obligations almost all of the time."[12] Even if true, this would not show what Henkin thought, namely, that international law is effective. Rather, it is equally consistent with the view espoused by realist scholars of international relations that international law is merely epiphenomenal, reflecting rather than influencing behavior.[13]

Behavioral Effectiveness

To make the concept of compliance more meaningful, political scientists often distinguish between "mere" compliance and "treaty-induced" compliance. The latter moves us from the world of purely legal effectiveness to that of behavioral effectiveness. In order for compliance to be treaty-induced, the treaty must have some causal effect: it must influence a state to act differently than the state would have acted otherwise; for example, it must lead a state to kill fewer whales or to reduce its consumption of ozone-depleting substances.

At root, assessing the contribution of international environmental law is a causal question: How much difference has international environmental law made? How much has it improved the *status quo ante*? As Myrick Freeman notes in connection with water pollution, "The relevant question is not how much some measure of water quality has changed over time at some location; this is a before-versus-after question. The right question is a with-versus-without question: How much better was actual water quality . . . than it would have been . . . without the cleanup requirements . . . but with the same economic conditions, weather, rainfall, and so forth?"[14] The answer depends not only on compliance, but also on the degree to which international environmental law requires states to depart from business as usual.

Behavioral effectiveness is more difficult to measure than legal effectiveness. Legal effectiveness requires us merely to compare what a norm requires with what actually takes place. For example, if the Kyoto Protocol requires an 8 percent reduction in emissions, we can simply look to see whether emissions in fact went down by this amount. In contrast, behavioral effectiveness requires us to compare what takes place with what would have occurred in the absence of the treaty. That requires us to enter the subjunctive world of counterfactuals. We can read a treaty such as the Kyoto Protocol to determine what it requires; we can observe emissions to see what happens (even if only indirectly, through various indicators); but we cannot observe what would have happened if the world were different and Kyoto did not exist. As a result, skeptics can question even an apparent success story such as the Montreal Protocol, on the ground that ozone-depleting substances might have been phased out anyway.[15]

Problem-Solving Effectiveness

Behavioral change is a necessary precondition for effectiveness. Ultimately, however, we assess international environmental law in terms of its success in improving the environment. Has the International Whaling Convention, for example, saved whales from extinction? Has the Ramsar Convention on Wetlands of International Importance protected wetlands from destruction? Has the Long-Range Transboundary Air Pollution Convention reduced acid rain in Europe? Has the Montreal Protocol helped repair the ozone layer? These are the bottom-line issues.

Evaluating a norm's problem-solving effectiveness depends, of course, on how we define the problem. Is the problem addressed by CITES illegal trade in threatened species or protection of biodiversity more generally? If illegal trade in threatened species is the problem, then CITES would score high on problem-solving effectiveness to the extent it succeeded in eliminating illegal trade. If we instead define the problem more generally as preservation of biological diversity, then even if CITES ended illegal trade completely, it might still be ineffective because trade constitutes only a small part of the more general problem of species extinctions. Indeed, elephants now face a bigger threat from habitat loss than from poaching.

In the case of the Whaling Convention, the Convention itself defines its goal as "safeguarding for future generations the great natural resources represented by the whale stocks,"[16] which it seeks to accomplish through restrictions on whaling. But what if the Convention's assumption is wrong that whales can be saved by regulating whaling? For example, what if whales succumb to some other threat such as marine pollution or collisions with ships (now the primary threat to right whales)? In that case, the Whaling Convention would have a low degree of problem-solving effectiveness even if it succeeded in eliminating whaling altogether.

The concept of problem-solving effectiveness requires us to look further down the causal chain. We must examine not simply how an international norm affects behavior, but also how these behavioral changes affect environmental outcomes (Figure 12.1).[17] Consider, for example, the Kyoto Protocol, which requires developed countries to reduce their emissions of greenhouse gases by specified amounts during the 2008–

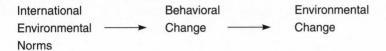

Figure 12.1 From Norms to Environmental Outcomes

2012 period (the EU by 8 percent from 1990 levels, Japan by 6 percent and so forth). Kyoto will be legally effective to the extent that developed states make the required reductions, and it will be behaviorally effective if the emission reductions result from the treaty obligation. But if polluting industries respond to the Protocol by moving to India or China, which are not subject to any emissions limitations, then the Protocol might have no effect whatsoever on overall global emissions; that is, it might make no contribution to solving the climate change problem.

Similarly, CITES requires participating states to adopt a permitting system for the import and export of threatened and endangered species. To the extent that states, in response to the treaty, adopt and implement the required permitting system, then CITES would be legally and behaviorally effective. Nevertheless, its problem-solving effectiveness might still be low if traders are able to smuggle animal parts across borders illegally, thus evading the treaty's controls.

As these cases illustrate, problem-solving effectiveness depends on more than compliance or even behavioral change. It also depends on the issues we examined in Chapter 8: first, the depth and nature of an agreement's commitments (do they target the right behavior and are they sufficiently ambitious?), and second, the degree to which the states that contribute most to a problem participate.

How should we measure the problem-solving effectiveness of international environmental law? Commentators have suggested several possibilities (Figure 12.2):[18]

- *How far have we come?*—One measure of achievement is to compare environmental outcomes with and without the regime. Here, the question is: How much improvement has the regime made from what would have occurred otherwise? To what degree, for example, has the Biodiversity Convention slowed the rate of species extinctions or the UNFCCC reduced greenhouse gas emissions? This requires the kind of counterfactual evaluation we discussed earlier in relation to behavioral effectiveness, except with a focus on environmental outcomes rather than on behavioral change.

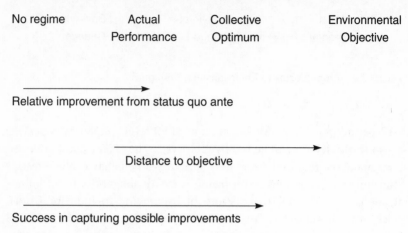

Figure 12.2   Measures of Environmental Effectiveness

- *How close have we gotten to where we want to end up?*—An alternative way to measure a regime's achievement is to compare its results with where we need to end up in order to solve the problem. How close have we come to achieving our objectives? Have we reduced greenhouse gas emissions enough to prevent dangerous climate change? Have we protected species from extinction? Have we repaired the ozone layer? On this score, even the Montreal Protocol—which has apparently reversed the depletion of the ozone layer—still has a long way to go and may never restore the ozone layer completely to predepletion levels.[19]
- *How successful have we been in exploiting the available opportunities?*—A third possibility, which lies somewhere between the other two, is to ask: How much of the potential gains from cooperation has a regime captured? Has the regime "left money on the table," or has it fully exploited the available possibilities for cooperation, given existing knowledge and values?[20] Answering this question requires us to determine the outcome that could be achieved assuming perfect cooperation (the so-called collective optimum) and then to compare this optimal result with what a regime has actually achieved.[21] This definition of success is fraught with conceptual and empirical difficulties and depends on normative choices that are not objectively determinable.[22] Moreover, it views regimes in static terms and fails to consider a regime's dynamic effects on knowledge and values, which can expand the scope for cooperation—the collective optimum—by changing actors' perceptions of their own interests.

Evaluating the Effectiveness of International Environmental Regimes

Now that international environmental law has developed a longer track record, several large-scale empirical research projects have attempted to evaluate its effectiveness in more systematic terms. The task poses significant methodological difficulties. In theory, effectiveness could be studied quantitatively, using statistical techniques such as regression analysis, which allow one to determine the importance of different causal factors in explaining behavioral or environmental change.[23] This approach, however, would require identifying and quantifying not only the relevant changes in behavior and environmental outcomes (the so-called dependent variables in the regression analysis), but also the range of causal factors that might account for these changes (the "independent variables"). Such tasks are extremely difficult to perform rigorously.

An alternative approach is to rely on expert assessments rather than direct measurement to quantify the relevant variables.[24] But this approach is also open to serious question because even supposed experts may not have reliable knowledge about a regime's effectiveness. As we have seen, experts often make quite different assessments of the effectiveness of the same regime.[25] Thus it is questionable whether their ratings of effectiveness (in terms of a numerical scale) provide a sound basis for quantitative analysis.

Perhaps in recognition of these difficulties, most of the studies of effectiveness to date have been qualitative, involving a limited number of detailed case studies. One study compared how nine political units (eight countries plus the European Union) have implemented five international agreements.[26] Another used a "process tracing" model to identify cause-and-effect relationships—in essence, the method of history.[27]

In general, these studies reveal a mixed picture. International environmental law has been neither a complete triumph nor an abject failure. In some cases, it has had impressive results:

- In 1972, when the Oslo Convention on dumping in the North Sea was adopted, "national legislation on dumping and permitting procedures were, in most cases, completely absent. . . . [A]nyone could dump anything without interference from national authorities or international bodies."[28] Three decades later, virtually no hazardous waste is disposed of in the North Sea.
- Since the adoption of the International Convention for the Prevention of Pollution by Ships (MARPOL), oil pollution from routine tanker operations has declined from more than 1,080,000 tons in

1975 to 158,600 tons in 1990 to an estimated 36,000 tons in 2002.[29] Although the decline is attributable to several causes (including reduction in seaborne oil trade and increased oil prices), the equipment and construction standards set forth in MARPOL have apparently been a significant factor, especially the requirements that oil tankers have segregated ballast tanks and crude oil washing equipment.[30]

- Between 1986 and 1995, global consumption and production of ozone-depleting substances declined by more than 75 percent,[31] and the rate of depletion of the stratospheric ozone layer has begun to slow (see Figure 12.3). Scientists now believe that by the middle of the century the ozone layer will have recovered to pre-1980 levels.[32]
- In the late nineteenth and early twentieth centuries, the population of North Pacific fur seals declined from more than 2 million to less than 150,000. Following the adoption in 1911 of the North Pacific Fur Seals Treaty, the population quickly recovered. Within six years, it had tripled, and by 1940 the population had returned to its pre-hunt levels.[33]

Counterbalancing these successes is the failure of international environmental law to do much to solve other problems:

- Despite the adoption of the Convention on Biological Diversity in 1992, an estimated 50 to 150 species continue to be lost every day.[34] The World Conservation Union estimates that almost one in four mammals and one in eight birds face a high risk of extinction in the near future.[35]
- Almost two decades after the emergence of global warming as a significant political issue, global emissions of greenhouse gases continue to grow at a rate of roughly 1.9 percent per year, and the entry into force of the Kyoto Protocol in February 2005 has done little to slow this trend.[36]
- An estimated 12 million hectares are lost to deserts each year, despite the adoption in 1994 of a treaty to combat desertification.[37]

Although many questions remain, the studies thus far suggest a few preliminary conclusions. First, while compliance is imperfect, the general trend has been toward greater compliance. According to one study, "viewed against the assessment of compliance with national laws and regulations ... the record at the international level is comparable or better."[38]

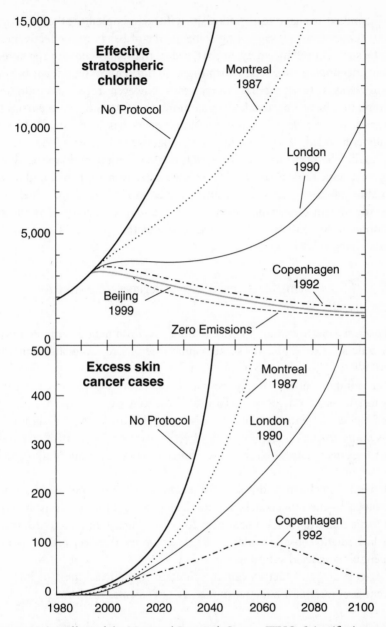

Figure 12.3 Effect of the Montreal Protocol. *Source:* WHO, Scientific Assessment of Ozone Depletion (2006).

Second, states have made increasing efforts to implement their international commitments, suggesting some degree of behavioral effectiveness. To be sure, compliance may, in part, reflect the shallowness of the agreements negotiated by states, which often do not require significant behavioral changes. Over the past thirty years, however, implementation and compliance have improved, even as more states have become parties to treaties and the depth of treaty commitments has increased.[39] As one study concluded, "[r]egimes do make a significant difference."[40]

Finally, the performance of international environmental law has been weakest with respect to problem-solving effectiveness. It has had some notable successes, most importantly, the Montreal Protocol, which has already had an observable effect on the abundance of chlorine in the atmosphere. But thus far it has failed to solve other problems such as climate change and biodiversity loss.

Why Are Some International Environmental Regimes More Effective than Others?

The mixed performance of international environmental regimes raises the crucial issue: Why have some regimes been more successful than others? What factors help explain the differential rates of success? The answer is important not simply from an explanatory perspective, but from an instrumental one as well. To the extent that we can improve the effectiveness of treaties "endogenously," through better legal design, then this could help us negotiate more effective treaties. Even if we conclude that the effectiveness of a treaty is a function of "exogenous" factors that are beyond the control of the treaty negotiators—the nature of the environmental problem addressed, for example, or the types of countries involved[41]—then this conclusion too has important implications. It helps us focus our attention on problems for which international environmental law might actually make a difference rather than on problems not amenable to a legal solution.

A wide array of factors can contribute to the effectiveness or ineffectiveness of international environmental agreements:[42]

Nature of the problem.   To begin with, some problems are easier to address than others.[43] According to game theory, for example, we would expect regimes addressing so-called coordination problems to be more effective than those addressing "cooperation" problems.[44] The reason is that in a coordination game, participants have no incentive to cheat, whereas in a cooperation game states can gain an advantage by free riding on the efforts of others. Other scholars have attempted to identify a wider range of differences between "benign" and "malign" problems.[45] Problems are usually easier to address when a strong scientific consensus exists, when the costs of addressing the problem are low and do not affect a country's competitiveness relative to other countries, when relatively few countries are involved (whose behavior is easy to monitor), and when countries' interests are aligned. On this score, climate change is an extremely difficult problem: it involves a large number of countries, often with very different interests; it requires countries to take costly actions now to avoid long-term and uncertain damage; and the high costs of action give countries a significant incentive to cheat and raise serious competitiveness concerns. Oil pollution from ships is an easier problem, given the incentive for common international standards governing the construction and design of oil tankers, and the mobile nature of the pollution source, which allows enforcement by a large number of states, as an oil tanker moves from port to port.

International political system. Features of the international political system may also have an important effect on the success of international environmental regimes. For example, a regime is more likely to be successful if it is backed by a powerful state such as the United States and less likely to be successful if it is opposed by a powerful state; the whaling and oil pollution regimes fall into the first category, the Biological Diversity Convention into the second. Regimes are also likely to be more successful if they involve states bound together by a sense of community, sharing common values, a common history, and cooperation in other spheres. Witness the remarkable development of the European Union.

Characteristics of the countries involved. Characteristics of the individual countries involved in a regime can also influence its implementation and effectiveness. Because changing behavior is usually costly, an international regime is likely to have a bigger effect on prosperous states, which have both the administrative and financial capacity to implement their commitments, than on poorer ones. Some writers argue that a country's political system also makes a difference and that the public participation and accountability characteristic of liberal democracies makes them more likely to implement and comply with international commitments than non-democratic states.[46] Similarly, an active NGO movement, which can help mobilize public opinion, serve as a watchdog, publicize information, and put pressure on government actors, improves prospects for compliance. To the extent a regime is able to take advantage of these factors, by assigning implementation responsibilities to those countries most likely to comply, then it improves its prospects for success, as we will explore further below.

Design of the regime.   International lawyers tend to believe, as an article of faith, that a regime's institutional and legal characteristics play an important role. This belief in the importance of regime design issues is increasingly shared by political scientists with an institutionalist bent.[47] We have already identified many of these design issues in earlier chapters. They include:

- *Legality*—As discussed in Chapter 8, the assumption behind most treaty negotiations is that binding instruments have a greater influence on state behavior than non-binding instruments. They demonstrate a stronger sense of commitment by states and are more costly to violate. The relationship between legalization and effectiveness is not invariant, however. In some circumstances, non-binding instruments may be more effective than binding ones, by allowing states to adopt clear and ambitious commitments even when they are not sure they will be able to comply. This is particularly true in the early stages of a regime, when states can profit from "learning by doing."[48]
- *Precision*—The effectiveness of an international instrument may also depend on the precision of its rules, a factor we examined in Chapter 5. By reducing ambiguity about what an agreement requires, precise rules provide greater guidance to states and make violations more apparent and therefore costly.
- *Legitimacy*—Rules regarding participation and decision making are another important design feature. In general, states are more likely to feel an obligation to comply with an agreement that results from a process they regard as legitimate, containing rules that they regard as fair.[49]
- *Type of commitments*—The choice of regulatory instrument can also be important, as we explored in Chapter 4. For example, in the oil pollution regime, equipment and design standards proved much more effective than discharge standards because they required compliance only at a single point in time (when the vessel was built) and could be easily verified.[50]
- *Assignment of implementation responsibilities*—To the extent that some types of countries have greater capacity and inclination to comply, placing more of the implementation burden on them is likely to improve effectiveness. Consider, for example, trade in

endangered species. Most of the demand for products such as rhino horn or elephant ivory comes from comparatively prosperous countries, which have greater ability to police their borders than the poor, developing countries where the endangered species originate. Imposing permitting requirements under CITES on importing countries is therefore likely to increase compliance and effectiveness. Conversely, the Basel Convention was motivated largely by concerns about shipments of hazardous wastes from developed to developing countries. Although developing countries could, in theory, protect themselves by controlling imports, they may lack the capacity to do so. So putting the onus for implementation on exporting countries improves the prospects for the Basel Convention's effectiveness.[51]

- *Empowerment of domestic supporters*—A regime is more likely to be effective if it is able to empower domestic stakeholders, for example, by giving them a foothold in the domestic policy process.
- *Institutions*—As Chapter 6 discussed, establishing institutions, such as a regular meeting of the parties, can help keep attention focused on an issue, build trust, and enmesh states in a web of collective expectations.[52]
- *International implementation procedures*—Finally, as we examined in Chapter 11, many regimes establish specific mechanisms and institutions to promote implementation and effectiveness. These include reporting and review procedures aimed at promoting transparency, mobilizing domestic constituency groups, and embarrassing free riders; financial assistance to encourage and help states comply; penalties such as trade sanctions to discourage non-compliance; and dispute settlement and non-compliance procedures.

Although these regime design issues are by no means the only important determinants of effectiveness, they are the ones most directly under our control and hence have the greatest implications for policy development. Because they are interlinked, they cannot be considered in isolation. Pushing in one place may simply cause a weakening in another. For this reason, issues of legal design must be approached holistically, a point to which I will return in the concluding chapter.

Conclusion

Do international environmental regimes matter? Although the issue is still much debated, the evidence suggests a qualified "yes." Most international environmental regimes make a "significant difference," as one study concluded,[53] although they fall short of achieving complete solutions. They are behaviorally effective even if not fully effective in a problem-solving sense.

What determines a regime's effectiveness? The answer is complex and inadequately understood. Effectiveness is the product of many factors, some of which are intrinsic to the problem itself and others to the international political system at a given time. Of particular interest to international lawyers are the ways that a regime's design can enhance its behavioral and problem-solving effectiveness by changing states' calculations of costs and benefits, helping to mobilize domestic constituency groups, promoting social learning and changes in values, and establishing rules perceived to be legitimate, which give states a normative reason to comply.

Recommended Reading

Thomas Bernauer, "The Effect of International Environmental Institutions: How Might We Learn More," *International Organization* 49 (1995), pp. 351–377.

Helmut Breitmeier, Oran R. Young, and Michael Zürn, *Analyzing International Environmental Regimes: From Case Study to Database* (Cambridge, MA: MIT Press, 2006).

George W. Downs, David M. Rocke, and Peter N. Barsoom, "Is the Good News about Compliance Good News about Cooperation?" *International Organization* 50 (1996), pp. 379–406.

Edward L. Miles, Arild Underdal, Steinar Andresen, Jørgen Wettestad, Jon Birger Skjærseth, and Elaine M. Carlin, *Environmental Regime Effectiveness: Confronting Theory with Evidence* (Cambridge, MA: MIT Press, 2002).

Ronald B. Mitchell, "Compliance Theory: Compliance, Effectiveness, and Behavior Change in International Environmental Law," in Daniel Bodansky, Jutta Brunnée, and Ellen Hey, eds., *The Oxford Handbook of International Environmental Law* (Oxford: Oxford University Press, 2007), pp. 893–921.

Kal Raustiala, "Compliance and Effectiveness in International Regulatory Cooperation," *Case Western Reserve Journal of International Law* 32 (2000), pp. 387–440.

Edith Brown Weiss and Harold K. Jacobson, eds., *Engaging Countries: Strengthening Compliance with International Environmental Accords* (Cambridge, MA: MIT Press, 1998).

Jørgen Wettestad, *Designing Effective Environmental Regimes: The Key Conditions* (Cheltenham, UK: Edward Elgar, 1999).

Oran R. Young, ed., *The Effectiveness of International Environmental Regimes: Causal Connections and Behavioral Mechanisms* (Cambridge, MA: MIT Press, 1999).

Oran R. Young, "Evaluating the Success of International Environmental Regimes: Where Are We Now?" *Global Environmental Change* 12 (2002), pp. 73–77.

Conclusion: Taking Stock

A S THE INTERNATIONAL community continues to grapple with environmental issues such as climate change, it is important to step back and ask, are we generally on the right track? Is the existing paradigm of international environmental law adequate? Or is more radical change required? Where do we go from here?

Some writers, surveying the record of international environmental law, see failure. Gus Speth, former dean of Yale's School of Forestry and Environmental Studies and president of the World Resources Institute, concludes that, despite the negotiation of numerous treaties, "efforts to protect the global environment have largely failed in the sense that the trends in environmental deterioration have not improved and that more of the same will not get us where we want to be in time to head off an era of unprecedented environmental decline."[1]

To my mind, this is an overly harsh assessment. Yes, the looming threat of global warming, the deterioration of many ecosystems, and the high rates of species extinctions should disabuse us of too optimistic an outlook. At the same time, international environmental law has had significant successes—the Montreal Ozone Protocol and the North Pacific Fur Seals Convention, to name two—so we should not write it off either.

To the extent that international environmental law falls short, what is the solution? One possibility would be to create a new global environmental institution to consolidate the existing disparate regimes.[2] This approach assumes that the weakness of international environmental law stems, at least in part, from its *ad hoc* and fragmented quality. In this view, the lack of coordination between different treaty regimes and international organizations creates the potential for conflicts, gaps, and overlapping, inefficient requirements, or what some have referred to as "treaty congestion." As one report observes, "There are too many organizations engaged in environmental governance in too many different places, often with duplicative mandates."[3] A new international environmental organization could help address these problems by ensuring that issues are addressed in a holistic manner, that the requirements of different agreements complement and reinforce one another, and that states are not subject to overlapping mandates.[4] This is a comparatively modest agenda, which could improve the efficiency of international environmental law, but at the expense of the creativity spawned by the current multiplicity of treaty regimes. Given the inertia within existing institutions (reflected in the unhappy record of UN reform),[5] it is questionable whether the benefits of this approach justify the investment of political capital necessary to bring it about.

A more ambitious reform agenda would create a new environmental organization with greater lawmaking and enforcement authority in order to deter free riding and overcome the collective action problems that plague current efforts at environmental regulation.[6] Of course, a Hobbesian Leviathan that could compel states to cooperate is utopian (or dystopian, depending on one's perspective). But the Security Council and the World Trade Organization illustrate the possibility of international institutions with binding decision-making and dispute resolution powers.

This perspective has much to recommend it. International environmental law does suffer from a decision-making deficit, which hobbles its effectiveness. Over the long term, it is difficult to see how a problem such as climate change could be addressed without giving international institutions greater standard-setting and enforcement authority. Nevertheless, efforts to do so would raise major practical and theoretical challenges. From a practical standpoint, states are extremely jealous of their sovereignty. Ceding authority requires trust, which takes time to develop. That is why institution-building is ordinarily a slow, incremental process. A crisis can produce a more rapid realignment in what Bruce Ackerman has termed a "constitutional moment." For many environmental problems, however, by the time a crisis occurs, it may already be too late to respond, given the inertia of physical systems such as climate and the irreversible nature of some environmental harms. Proposals for greater global governance also raise the more theoretical question: what would be the basis of legitimacy for a new, more powerful institution? In the absence of a global community, the one compelling answer, democracy, is unavailable. And at the moment, we lack any clear alternative.[7]

Some go further still in their diagnosis of the current crisis, arguing that the state system is incorrigible and cannot be reformed. What is needed, they maintain, is no less than a transformation in people's values and consciousness, leading to a single global constitution[8]—"an international movement of citizens and scientists, one capable of dramatically advancing the political and personal actions needed for the transition to sustainability."[9]

Perhaps. But I think that the solutions to environmental problems will depend as much, if not more, on the painstaking, incremental, often frustrating work described in this book as on a radical transformation of human consciousness.

In its brief history, international environmental law has failed to solve many pressing problems, but it has also had some notable successes. In doing so, it has displayed impressive ingenuity, developing a wide range of mechanisms to set standards and promote implementation. Whether or not one believes that more radical changes will be necessary, much can be done with these existing tools.

On the standard-setting side, international environmental law has promoted the development of environmental regimes through:

- Regular scientific assessments to help produce "consensus" knowledge.
- Soft law instruments such as codes of conduct and guidelines.
- The framework convention-protocol approach to allow step-by-step progress and to catalyze further action.
- Tacit amendment procedures to allow regimes to develop in a flexible manner, in response to new information and new concerns.
- Differential standards, to take account of differences between states in historical responsibility and capacity.
- Elaboration through decisions of the parties that are not formally binding but are, in practice, accepted as authoritative.

Similarly, on the compliance side, the picture also looks quite different from the standard approach of international law, which focuses on the concepts of breach, state responsibility, invocation of responsibility by the injured state, dispute settlement, and remedies such as restitution and compensation. In contrast to this traditional model, international environmental regimes have developed their own *sui generis* arrangements, aimed not so much at determining state responsibility and imposing remedies as at making the regime more effective in the future.

Finally, in terms of institutions, the central international environmental institution—the conference of the parties—represents a new form of international cooperation. From the perspective of general international law, it is neither an intergovernmental conference nor a traditional international organization but a combination of the two.

Together, these changes have transformed international environmental law into a distinct field, with its own characteristic methodologies and techniques.[10] In the process, they have blurred not only the (already fuzzy) line between international law and politics, but also the lines between public and private, and international and domestic. In international environmental law, the private sector engages in the quintessential public task of general standard setting through regimes such as the International Organization for Standardization and the Forest Stewardship Council. And in MARPOL, private-sector actors play a key role in the compliance process through the inspection and certification of oil tankers.

Some express concern about these developments, fearing that they erode the fundamental distinctiveness of law as a social instrument. However, the emergence of new approaches to standard setting and compliance represents an understandable and appropriate response to the distinctive characteristics of international environmental problems:

- These problems are physical as well as legal and political and involve a great deal of technical complexity.
- They result primarily from private rather than governmental conduct.
- They are highly uncertain and rapidly changing.

In order to address international environmental problems, we therefore need to develop dynamic regulatory regimes that can respond flexibly to new knowledge and problems, and that take a pragmatic and forward-looking approach to issues of compliance and effectiveness.

As we have seen, in designing environmental regimes, international environmental lawyers can consider many variables, including choice of forum, substantive scope, legal or non-legal form, choice of regulatory instrument, stringency of commitments (both in general and for particular countries); precision; voting rules, financial incentives, reporting and review procedures, non-compliance institutions, minimum participation requirements, and ease of exit through reservations or withdrawal.

Recent work by international relations-oriented scholars has done much to introduce greater rigor to the analysis of these design elements.[11] In doing so, these scholars have called into question some conventional wisdom—for example, that legal instruments are always better than non-legal ones, that a more stringent non-compliance system is necessarily better than a weaker one, and that restricting the ability of states to exit an agreement is necessarily better than permitting exit.[12] Ultimately, the effectiveness of an environmental regime is a function not only of the stringency of its commitments, but of the degree to which states participate and comply. A strong agreement in which few states participate might be less effective than a weaker one with wider participation. To the extent that states trade off different design elements against one another, we cannot analyze these elements in isolation; we need to consider them as a whole.[13]

But although political science has helped identify potential trade-offs, it has not yet been able to tell us how to make them. Should we include, say, strong enforcement measures in a new climate agreement? The answer is uncertain. A strong enforcement system may scare off states worried about their own potential non-compliance. At the same time, it may also reassure them that others will comply. So, depending on which possibility states are more concerned about—their own non-compliance or non-compliance by other states—they may prefer a weaker or stronger approach. The same reasoning applies to many other design elements that affect the strength of a commitment. For example, a withdrawal provision that allows a state to exit a treaty simply by providing notice reduces the risk associated with the agreement but also makes the agreement less credible.[14]

Our inability to resolve these questions of treaty design in a determinate way is one reason that international environmental law remains more an art than a science. Interestingly, some political scientists agree. As one study concluded, there is "no reliable technology for telling us what design strategy is best for a given set of circumstances. Any single design strategy may speed the evolution of cooperation in some cases, but it seems certain to slow it in others."[15] Deciding on the right approach depends on practical judgment rather than on any simple formula.

In the end, international environmental law aims to find, not the optimal outcome, but rather the skillful compromise that bridges the gap between competing positions and advances the ball, even if only a little. This view of international environmental law is admittedly more prosaic than heroic. It counsels us to resist the tempting oversimplification. It accepts that international environmental law, like politics, is the art of the possible—and seeks to find the "sweet spot," which goes as far as possible but not beyond. Above all, it sees the discipline of international environmental law, not as a panacea, but rather as an art and a craft.

Notes

Preface

1. Philippe Sands, *Principles of International Environmental Law* (Cambridge: Cambridge University Press, 2d ed. 2003).
2. Kluwer's series, *International Environmental Law and Policy*, began in the late 1980s under the editorship of Stanley Johnson.
3. Bernd Rüster and Bruno Simma, eds., *International Protection of the Environment: Treaties and Related Documents* (Dobbs Ferry, NY: Oceana Publications, 1st ser. 1975–1982; 2d ser. 1990–1995).
4. *E.g.*, Patricia Birnie, Alan Boyle, and Catherine Redgwell, *International Law and the Environment* (Oxford: Oxford University Press, 3d ed. 2009); Sands, *Principles.*
5. Jon Elster, *Nuts and Bolts for the Social Sciences* (Cambridge: Cambridge University Press, 1989), p. vii.
6. Ibid.
7. Robert V. Percival et al., *Environmental Regulation: Law, Science, and Policy* (Boston: Little, Brown, 1992), p. 67 (contrasting "moral outrage" and "cool analysis").

1. What Is International Environmental Law?

1. Neo-Malthusians are modern-day successors to Thomas Malthus, who theorized in the early nineteenth century that population grows exponentially and eventually outstrips natural resources. Neo-Malthusian writings include Donella H. Meadows et al., *The Limits to Growth: A Report for the Club of Rome's Project on the Predicament of Mankind* (New York: Universe Books, 1972) and Paul R. Ehrlich, *The Population Bomb* (New York: Ballantine Books, 1968).

2. In Greek mythology, cornucopia was the horn of plenty, containing an endless supply of food and drink. So-called Cornucopians stress the role of technology in freeing humans from natural limits to growth imposed by the environment. Cornucopian writings include Julian L. Simon and Herman Kahn, eds., *The Resourceful Earth: A Response to Global 2000* (Oxford: Blackwell, 1984) and Julian L. Simon, *The Ultimate Resource* (Princeton, NJ: Princeton University Press, 1981).

3. *See, e.g.,* Anthony D'Amato and Sudhir K. Chopra, "Whales: Their Emerging Right to Life," *American Journal of International Law* 85 (1991), pp. 21–62.

4. For a critical examination of the "litany," see Bjørn Lomborg, *The Skeptical Environmentalist: Measuring the Real State of the World* (Cambridge: Cambridge University Press, 2001).

5. *E.g.,* Piers Forster et al., "Changes in Atmospheric Constituents and in Radiative Forcing," in Susan Solomon et al., eds., *Climate Change 2007: The Physical Science Basis* (Cambridge: Cambridge University Press, 2007), pp. 129–234, at 137; Eystein Jansen et al., "Paleoclimate," in ibid., 433–497, at 435.

6. Millennium Ecosystem Assessment, *Ecosystems and Human Well Being: Biodiversity Synthesis* (Washington, DC: World Resources Institute, 2005), pp. 2–3, 43; *see also* International Union for the Conservation of Nature (IUCN), "Red List of Threatened Species," www.iucnredlist.org (accessed 5/17/09) (estimating that almost 17,000 known species are threatened with extinction).

7. Food and Agriculture Organization (FAO), *The State of the World Fisheries and Aquaculture 2006* (Rome: FAO, 2007), pp. 3, 29. A study published in 2006 in the journal *Science* projected a "global collapse" of all species currently being fish. *See* Boris Worm et al., "Impacts of Biodiversity Loss on Ocean Ecosystem Services," *Science* 314 (2006), pp. 787–790. U.S. government fisheries experts, however, report that only about 20 percent of the fish stocks that they monitor are overfished. *See* Cornelia Dean, "Study Sees 'Global Collapse' of Fish Species," *New York Times,* November 3, 2006, p. A21.

8. Millennium Ecosystem Assessment, *Ecosystems,* 5.

9. FAO, *Global Forest Resources Assessment 2005: Progress Towards Sustainable Forest Management* (Rome: FAO, 2006), p. 13. A hectare equals about 2.5 acres. Six million hectares is equal to about 23,000 square miles.

10. Millennium Ecosystem Assessment, *Ecosystems,* 2.

11. *E.g.,* James Gustave Speth, *Red Sky at Morning: America and the Crisis of the Global Environment* (New Haven, CT: Yale University Press, 2004), p. 14; Pesticide Action Network, *PAN Pesticide Database,* www.pesticideinfo.org (accessed 5/17/09).

12. *E.g.,* World Bank, *World Development Report: Development and the Environment* (Oxford: Oxford University Press, 1992), p. 5; World Health Organization, *WHO Air Quality Guidelines for Particulate Matter, Ozone, Nitrogen Dioxide and Sulphur Dioxide: Global Update 2005—Summary of Risk Assessment* (Geneva: WHO Press, 2006), p. 5.

13. *E.g.*, World Wide Fund for Nature (WWF), *Living Planet Report 2004* (Gland, Switzerland, 2004), p. 16; Millennium Ecosystem Assessment, *Ecosystems: Overall Synthesis*, 13, 106.

14. United Nations International Children's Emergency Fund (UNICEF), *Progress for Children: A Report Card on Water and Sanitation* (New York: UNICEF, 2006), p. 1.

15. These three approaches correspond to those that Anthony Kronman associates with Max Weber's sociology of law, which Kronman labels the dogmatic, the moral, and the sociological approaches. Anthony T. Kronman, *Max Weber* (Stanford, CA: Stanford University Press, 1983).

16. For example, an economically minded judge might interpret "significant transboundary pollution" to mean situations in which the marginal costs of the polluting activity exceed the marginal benefits, whereas a more ecologically minded judge might set some fixed threshold of harm that should not be crossed, regardless of the perceived benefits of the polluting activity.

17. D'Amato and Chopra, "Whales."

18. Mark Allan Gray, "The International Crime of Ecocide," *California Western International Law Journal* 26 (1996), pp. 215–271. Gray's reasoning illustrates a common fallacy, namely that international environmental law must in fact include a particular norm because the norm is functionally or morally necessary. Ibid., 270 ("Criminalization of ecocide will occur because it must.").

19. Michael J. Glennon, "Has International Law Failed the Elephant?" *American Journal of International Law* 84 (1990), pp. 1–41, at 30.

20. *See, e.g.*, Rüdiger Wolfrum, "Purposes and Principles of International Environmental Law," *German Yearbook of International Law* 33 (1990), pp. 308–330, at 313; *Restatement (Third) of the Foreign Relations Law of the United States*, §601, comment e; *compare* Daniel G. Partan, "The 'Duty to Inform' in International Environmental Law," *Boston University International Law Journal* 6 (1988), pp. 43–88, at 83 (stating that duty to inform "has finally emerged as a legal duty of all states under general international law," although its customary law status is open to doubt).

21. For a general survey on realism, see Robert O. Keohane, ed., *Neorealism and Its Critics* (New York: Columbia University Press, 1986); *see also* John J. Mearsheimer, "The False Promise of International Institutions," *International Security* 19 (1994/1995), pp. 5–49.

22. *See, e.g.*, Robert O. Keohane, *After Hegemony: Cooperation and Discord in the World Political Economy* (Princeton, NJ: Princeton University Press, 1984); Stephen D. Krasner, ed., *International Regimes* (Ithaca, NY: Cornell University Press, 1983). A game theoretic version of instrumentalism is found in Scott Barrett, *Environment and Statecraft: The Strategy of Environmental Treaty-Making* (Oxford: Oxford University Press, 2003).

23. *See, e.g.*, Andrew Moravcsik, "Taking Preferences Seriously: A Liberal Theory of International Politics," *International Organization* 51 (1997), pp. 513–533.

24. *See, e.g.*, Peter M. Haas, *Saving the Mediterranean: The Politics of International Environmental Cooperation* (New York: Columbia University Press,

1990); Martha Finnemore and Kathryn Sikkink, "International Norm Dynamics and Political Change," *International Organization* 52 (1998), pp. 887–917. For an international law approach, see Jutta Brunnée and Stephen J. Toope, "International Law and Constructivism: Elements of an Interactional Theory of International Law," *Columbia Journal of Transnational Law* 39 (2000), pp. 19–74.

25. *See, e.g.*, Oran R. Young, *International Governance: Protecting the Environment in a Stateless Society* (Ithaca, NY: Cornell University Press, 1994); Peter M. Haas, Robert O. Keohane, and Marc A. Levy, eds., *Institutions for the Earth: Sources of Effective International Environmental Protection* (Cambridge, MA: MIT Press, 1993).

26. Lynton Keith Caldwell, *International Environmental Policy: Emergence and Dimensions* (Durham, NC: Duke University Press, 2d ed. 1990), p. 197 (referring to development); *see also, e.g.*, Philippe Sands, *Principles of International Environmental Law* (Cambridge: Cambridge University Press, 2d ed. 2003), p. 16 (stating that the term "'environment' does not have a generally accepted usage as a term of art under international law"); Gordon J. MacDonald, "Environment: Evolution of a Concept," *Journal of Environment and Development* 12 (2003), pp. 151–176, at 151 ("The modern concept of environment encompasses ecological, economic, aesthetic, and ethical concerns.").

27. Andy Crump, *Dictionary of Environment and Development: People, Places, Ideas and Organizations* (Cambridge, MA: MIT Press, 1993).

28. Council Directive 79/117, art. 2(10), 1979 O. J. (L 33) 36 (EC).

29. *See* Alan Gilpin, *Dictionary of Environmental Law* (Northampton, MA: Edward Elgar, 2000), p. 92. The 1977 Environmental Modification Convention defines "environmental modification techniques" as techniques for changing, "through the deliberate manipulation of natural processes, the dynamics, composition or structure of the Earth, including its biota, lithosphere, hydrosphere and atmosphere, or of outer space." ENMOD Convention art. II.

30. In a few cases, international environmental agreements also seek to protect certain aspects of the human world—in particular, historical and cultural sites such as the Egyptian pyramids or the Great Wall, which are protected under the 1972 World Heritage Convention.

31. *See* Daniel C. Esty, "A Term's Limits," *Foreign Policy* (Sept./Oct. 2001), pp. 74–75 (characterizing sustainable development as "a buzzword largely devoid of content"). For more on sustainable development, see Chapter 2, fourth section.

32. As Frank Biermann notes, "Despite two decades of debate on sustainable development, few examples of integrated ministries of sustainable development can be found. Most countries maintain the differentiation between their economic (or development) ministries and their environmental ministries." Frank Biermann, "Reforming Global Environmental Governance: From UNEP Towards a World Environment Organization," in Lydia Swart and Estelle Perry, eds., *Global Environmental Governance: Perspectives on the Current Debate* (New York: Center for UN Reform Education, 2007), pp. 103–123, at 115.

33. The *Trail Smelter* case arose in the 1920s, and involved a claim by the United States against Canada for damage caused by fumes from a giant zinc and lead smelter located in Trail, British Columbia, about 7 miles north of the U.S. border. In one of the most-frequently quoted passages in international environmental law, the arbitral tribunal found that "no State has the right to use or permit the use of its territory in such a manner as to cause injury by fumes in or to the territory of another or the properties or persons therein, when the case is of serious consequence and the injury is established by clear and convincing evidence." *Trail Smelter Case,* at 1965.

34. In addition, people in other countries value the continued existence of elephants, so elephant conservation has what I refer to below as positive psychological spillovers.

35. In the long term, loss of habitat due to population growth probably constitutes the ultimate threat to the African elephant. Douglas H. Chadwick, *The Fate of the Elephant* (San Francisco: Sierra Club Books, 1992), pp. 467–468.

36. For a vivid account, see Joe Kane, *Savages* (New York: Knopf, 1995).

37. *See* Tseming Yang and Robert V. Percival, "The Emergence of Global Environmental Law," www.ssrn.com (accessed 5/17/09).

38. For contrasting explanations of environmental policy convergence by political scientists and sociologists, *compare* Katharina Holzinger, Christoph Knill, and Thomas Sommerer, "Environmental Policy Convergence: The Impact of International Harmonization, Transnational Communication and Regulatory Competition," *International Organization* 62 (2008), pp. 553–587 (illustrating the political science perspective that emphasizes harmonization and transnational communication) *with* David John Frank, Ann Hironaka, and Evan Schofer, "The Nation-State and the Natural Environment over the Twentieth Century," *American Sociological Review* 65 (2000), pp. 96–116 (illustrating the sociological perspective that emphasizes acculturation).

39. As we shall see in Chapter 9, the recognized sources of international law include, in addition to treaties: (1) regular patterns of practice by states, accepted as law, which create customary international law, and (2) general principles of law recognized by civilized nations. Statute of the International Court of Justice art. 38(1).

40. UNFCCC art. 4.2.

41. G. A. Res. 46/215, U.N. Doc. A/RES/46/215 (December 20, 1991).

42. Donald R. Rothwell, "The General Assembly Ban on Driftnet Fishing," in Dinah Shelton, ed., *Commitment and Compliance: The Role of Non-Binding Norms in the International Legal System* (Oxford: Oxford University Press, 2000), pp. 121–146.

43. *See, e.g.,* Jack L. Goldsmith and Eric A. Posner, *The Limits of International Law* (New York: Oxford University Press, 2005).

44. Geoffrey Palmer, "An International Regime for Environmental Protection," *Washington University Journal of Urban and Contemporary Law* 42 (1992), pp. 5–19, at 17.

45. Daniel Bodansky, "The Legitimacy of International Governance: A Coming Challenge for International Environmental Law?" *American Journal of International Law* 93 (1999), 596–624.
46. Thomas Gehring, *Dynamic International Regimes: Institutions for International Environmental Governance* (Frankfurt: Peter Lang, 1994).
47. Abram Chayes and Antonia Handler Chayes, "On Compliance," *International Organization* 47 (1993), pp. 175–205.

2. How We Got Here

1. Wolfgang Friedmann, *The Changing Structure of International Law* (New York: Columbia University Press, 1964), pp. 152–187.
2. Ian Brownlie, *Principles of Public International Law* (Oxford: Clarendon Press, 3d ed. 1979). In contrast, the sixth edition of Brownlie's treatise, published in 2003, included a brief chapter on "Legal Aspects of the Protection of the Environment."
3. *See generally* Friedmann, *Changing Structure.*
4. As we shall see, however, because the interests of states and other actors often differ, interest in environmental protection is not always shared.
5. *See generally* Clive Ponting, *A Green History of the World: The Environment and the Collapse of Great Civilizations* (New York: Penguin Books, 1991).
6. *See* Jared Diamond, *Collapse: How Societies Choose to Fail or Succeed* (New York: Viking, 2005). *But see* Terry L. Hunt, "Rethinking the Fall of Easter Island," *American Scientist* 94 (2006), pp. 412–419 (calling into question Diamond's account).
7. Robert Boardman, *International Organization and the Conservation of Nature* (Bloomington: Indiana University Press, 1981), p. 13.
8. Ponting, *Green History,* 164.
9. *See* Aaron Sachs, *The Humboldt Current: Nineteenth Century Exploration and the Roots of American Environmentalism* (New York: Viking, 2006).
10. Philip Shabecoff, *A Fierce Green Fire: The American Environmental Movement* (Washington, DC: Island Press, 2003).
11. George Perkins Marsh, *Man and Nature; Or, Physical Geography as Modified by Human Action* (New York: Scribner, 1864), p. 36.
12. Anthony Downs, "Up and Down with Ecology: The 'Issue-Attention Cycle,'" *Public Interest* 28 (1972), pp. 38–50; *see also, e.g.,* John McCormick, *Reclaiming Paradise: The Global Environmental Movement* (Bloomington: Indiana University Press, 1989), pp. 64–65; Tony Brenton, *The Greening of Machiavelli: The Evolution of International Environmental Politics* (London: Earthscan, 1994), pp. 15–24.
13. Cf. Michael E. Colby, *Environmental Management in Development: The Evolution of Paradigms,* World Bank Discussion Paper WBDP-80 (Washington, DC: World Bank, 1990).
14. Classical international law is usually dated back to the Peace of Westphalia in 1648 and is often referred to as the Westphalian system.

15. Tuomas Kuokkanen, *International Law and the Environment: Variations on a Theme* (New York: Kluwer Law International, 2002).

16. For an excellent discussion of the fur seals issue, see Scott Barrett, *Environment and Statecraft: The Strategy of Environmental Treaty-Making* (Oxford: Oxford University Press, 2003), pp. 19–39.

17. Several other treaties could plausibly claim that title, including the 1900 African Wildlife Convention.

18. Hawks, the eagle owl, and ducks were among the birds listed as harmful. The 1900 African Wildlife Convention was similarly limited to species of wildlife that are useful or inoffensive to humans.

19. The early twentieth-century conservation movement also considered the related issue of trade in endangered species, which already posed a significant threat to tropical birds in Victorian times, due to demand for plumage by the hat industry. In 1869 alone, for example, Brazil exported 170,000 birds. In 1897, Britain proposed regulation of the international ivory trade, due to concerns about overhunting in Africa—a precursor to the eventual ban on ivory trade adopted by the international community almost a century later.

20. Simon Lyster, *International Wildlife Law* (Cambridge: Grotius Publications, 1985), p. 124 (characterizing the Western Hemisphere Convention as the "sleeping treaty").

21. Lynton Keith Caldwell, *International Environmental Policy: Emergence and Dimensions* (Durham, NC: Duke University Press, 2d ed. 1990), p. 40.

22. *See generally* Lyster, *International Wildlife Law.*

23. Other leading works of the environmental revolution included: Stewart Udall, *The Quiet Crisis* (New York: Holt, Rinehart and Winston, 1963); Paul R. Ehrlich, *The Population Bomb* (New York: Ballantine Books, 1968); Barry Commoner, *The Closing Circle: Nature, Man, and Technology* (New York: Knopf, 1971); and Donella H. Meadows et al., *The Limits to Growth: A Report for the Club of Rome's Project on the Predicament of Mankind* (New York: Universe Books, 1972).

24. Brenton, *Greening of Machiavelli,* 19.

25. "Issue of the Year: The Environment," *Time,* January 4, 1971.

26. McCormick, *Reclaiming Paradise,* 38. Many detractors viewed conservationism as "the amiable eccentricity of a number of people who had to be humored." Ibid., 39 (quoting Max Nicholson).

27. R. Michael M'Gonigle and Mark W. Zacher, *Pollution, Politics, and International Law: Tankers at Sea* (Berkeley: University of California Press, 1979).

28. Brenton, *Greening of Machiavelli,* 36.

29. Caldwell, *International Environmental Policy,* 59.

30. Brenton, *Greening of Machiavelli,* 42.

31. One apparently jaded participant in the Rio Conference delineated the "life cycle" of these conferences: "Each one is born out of a political need to be seen to be doing something about a visible current problem. The announcement of the conference then generates high, if imprecise, public expectations. As preparations get under way it becomes clear to the negotiators, although not yet to the public at large, that the words which are, after all,

all the conference will produce, will have to embrace a widely divergent range of national views, significantly diluting their eventual operational content. Current political differences which have little to do with the purposes of the conference will complicate, and may occasionally dominate, the negotiation. Governments will protest their attachment to the future welfare of humanity in public, while firmly (and, in their view, consistently) defending their national interests in private. As the preparatory period ticks away negotiators will start looking for some concrete decisions (normally institutional or financial) which can be used to meet the public appetite for concrete action. By this time ministerial speeches will be dwelling less on the unique importance of the conference and more on its role as part of a process. In a period of panic at the end compromise texts are cobbled together in which generalized language has often had to replace precise commitment, but in which large sums of money and eye-catching new institutions will, if possible, also figure. A grandiloquent package is presented to the waiting world and participants return to their capitals. It is left to a skeptical press to assess quite how much impact the whole affair has made on the problem it was originally designed to solve." Brenton, *Greening of Machiavelli*, 35–36.

32. *See generally* Louis B. Sohn, "The Stockholm Declaration on the Human Environment," *Harvard International Law Journal* 14 (1973), pp. 423–515.

33. *Nuclear Weapons Advisory Opinion*, at §§ 27–29.

34. Brenton, *Greening of Machiavelli*, 45–46.

35. *See* David John Frank, Ann Hironaka, and Evan Schofer, "The Nation-State and the Natural Environment over the Twentieth Century," *American Sociological Review* 65 (2000), pp. 96–116.

36. Brenton, *Greening of Machiavelli*, 67.

37. World Commission on Environment and Development, *Our Common Future* (Oxford: Oxford University Press, 1987).

38. Ibid., 43.

39. For example, would cutting down and exporting all the trees on a desert island and then using the "proceeds to set up schools, homes and factories for a new Hong Kong" constitute sustainable development? "Inheriting the Earth," *Economist*, September 16, 1989, p. 109. Depending on whether one views natural resources and human resources as substitutable, the answer would be different. According to some counts, more than one hundred definitions of "sustainable development" have been proposed. For an economist's attempt to make sense of the concept, see Robert M. Solow, "Sustainability: An Economist's Perspective," in Robert Dorfman and Nancy S. Dorfman, eds., *Economics of the Environment: Selected Readings* (New York: Norton, 3rd ed. 1993), pp. 179–187.

40. *See* Philippe Sands, *Principles of International Environmental Law* (Cambridge: Cambridge University Press, 2d ed. 2003), pp. 799–800.

41. Jim MacNeill, "The Greening of International Relations," *International Journal* 45 (1989–1990), pp. 1–35.

42. The third direct output of the conference was a Non-Legally Binding Statement of Forest Principles.

43. UNCED also called for the negotiation of a third treaty, the UN Convention to Combat Desertification, which was adopted two years later, in 1994.
44. I explore the issue of effectiveness further in Chapter 12.

3. Diagnosing the Causes of Environmental Problems

1. Although this chapter argues that causal analysis is important, it is not necessarily a precondition for effective action. Even when the cause of an illness is unknown, a doctor may still be able to treat the symptoms. Similarly, it may sometimes be easier to address the surface manifestations of an environmental problem, rather than its underlying causes.
2. According to the World Conservation Monitoring Centre (WCMC), species introduction accounts for 39 percent of the animal extinctions with known causes, habitat destruction for 36 percent, and hunting for 23 percent. WCMC, *Global Biodiversity: Status of the Earth's Living Resources* (London: Chapman & Hall, 1992), p. 199. *See also* James Gustave Speth, *Red Sky at Morning: America and the Crisis of the Global Environment* (New Haven, CT: Yale University Press, 2004), pp. 30–36 (identifying habitat loss as the most significant cause of biotic impoverishment).
3. *See* Paul R. Ehrlich and John P. Holdren, "Impact of Population Growth," *Science* 171 (1971), pp. 1212–1217.
4. Exponential growth in population has been most characteristic of the modern period, although, as discussed below, population levels have now stabilized in Western industrialized countries. In many earlier periods of human history, population grew relatively slowly, if at all.
5. Bill McKibbin, "A Special Moment in History," *Atlantic Monthly,* May 1998, pp. 55–78, at 55–56.
6. *See, e.g.,* Joel E. Cohen, *How Many People Can the Earth Support?* (New York: W. W. Norton, 1995).
7. *E.g.,* Jared Diamond, *Collapse: How Societies Choose to Fail or Succeed* (New York: Viking, 2005); Clive Ponting, *A New Green History of the World: The Environment and the Collapse of Great Civilizations* (New York: Penguin Books, 2007).
8. Speth, *Red Sky,* 124.
9. Ibid., 20–21.
10. McKibbin, "Special Moment," 57.
11. Speth, *Red Sky,* 21.
12. World Commission on Environment and Development, *Our Common Future* (Oxford: Oxford University Press, 1987), p. 14.
13. As of 2006, China emitted about 6 billion metric tons of carbon dioxide; *see* Energy Information Administration (EIA), "World Carbon Dioxide Emissions from the Consumption and Flaring of Fossil Fuels," www.eia.doe.gov (accessed 1/16/09). Its energy use per capita was about one-fifth that of the United States. *See* EIA, "World Per Capita Total Primary Energy Consumption, 1980–2006," www.eia.doe.gov (accessed 1/16/09). As of 2006, global carbon

dioxide emissions were about 28 billion metric tons. EIA, "World Carbon Dioxide Emissions."

14. Christopher Case-Dunn, *Global Formation: Structures of the World Economy* (Lanham, MD: Rowman & Littlefield, 1998), p. xxv.

15. I say, "in part" a technological problem because we can also conceive of climate change as an economic problem, caused by improper incentives, or as a moral problem. I explore these two perspectives later in the chapter.

16. James E. Scarff, "The International Management of Whales, Dolphins, and Porpoises: An Interdisciplinary Assessment," *Ecology Law Quarterly* 6 (1977), pp. 323–427, at 346.

17. Helmut Haberl et al., "Quantifying and Mapping the Human Appropriation of Net Primary Production in Earth's Terrestrial Ecosystems," *Proceedings of the National Academy of Sciences* 104 (2007), pp. 12942–12947, at 12942.

18. These natural limits are emphasized by ecological economists such as Herman Daly. *See, e.g.,* Herman E. Daly, *Steady-State Economics* (Washington, DC: Island Press, 2d ed. 1991).

19. *E.g.,* Phillip Longman, "The Global Baby Bust," *Foreign Affairs,* May/June 2004, pp. 64–79, at 65; *World Population Prospects: The 2006 Revision* (New York: United Nations, 2007), p. xxi.

20. Although *Limits to Growth* is often portrayed as discredited, one recent study found that its scenarios (which did not predict global collapse until the middle of the twenty-first century) have been largely accurate thus far. Graham M. Turner, "A Comparison of *Limits to Growth* with 30 Years of Reality," *Global Environmental Change* 18 (2008), pp. 397–411, at 410.

21. *See, e.g.,* Gregg Easterbrook, *A Moment on the Earth: The Coming Age of Environmental Optimism* (New York: Viking, 1995); Bjørn Lomborg, *The Skeptical Environmentalist: Measuring the Real State of the World* (Cambridge: Cambridge University Press, 2001).

22. *See, e.g.,* Amartya Sen, *Poverty and Famines: An Essay on Entitlement and Deprivation* (Oxford: Oxford University Press, 1982); Jeffrey D. Sachs, *Common Wealth: Economics for a Crowded Planet* (New York: Penguin, 2008) (attributing recent food crises in significant part to political failures).

23. John O'Connor and David Orsmond, "The Recent Rise in Commodity Prices: A Long-Run Perspective," *Reserve Bank of Australia Bulletin,* April 2007, pp. 1–9, at 1–2.

24. *See* Mark Sagoff, "Do We Consume Too Much?" *Atlantic Monthly,* June 1997, pp. 80–96.

25. Similarly, although technological developments helped revive the whaling industry in the twentieth century, earlier they had helped end the U.S. whaling industry, first through the discovery of crude oil in the mid-nineteenth century, which reduced demand for whale oil, and then through the development of corset-free fashion lines in the early twentieth century, which reduced demand for whale bone for corset stays. Eric Jay Dolan, *Leviathan: The History of Whaling in America* (New York: W. W. Norton, 2007).

26. In contrast to traditional economists, who view natural and manufactured (technological) capital as substitutable, ecological economists argue that

natural capital is not fully substitutable and therefore imposes constraints on growth that technology cannot overcome. *See generally* Michael Common and Sigrid Stagl, *Ecological Economics: An Introduction* (Cambridge: Cambridge University Press, 2005).

27. John S. Dryzek, *The Politics of the Earth: Environmental Discourses* (Oxford: Oxford University Press, 2d ed. 2005), p. 32 (discussing Lester Brown, *The Twenty-Ninth Day* [New York: W. W. Norton, 1978]); *see also* Nassim Nicolas Talem, *The Black Swan: The Impact of the Highly Improbable* (New York: Random House, 2007) (arguing that people assume too readily that past events will repeat).

28. Dryzek, *Politics of the Earth*, 70.

29. David I. Stern et al., "Economic Growth and Environmental Degradation: The Environmental Kuznets Curve and Sustainable Development," *World Development* 24 (1996), pp. 1151–1160, at 1152. In general, affluence and population growth also seem to be inversely correlated: as societies get wealthier, their rate of population growth goes down, in some cases eventually becoming negative. Jean-Claude Chesnais, *The Demographic Transition: Stages, Patterns, and Economic Implications,* trans. Elizabeth Kreager and Philip Kreager (Oxford: Oxford University Press, 1993).

30. Meanwhile, others label this claim a "myth." *See* David Sattherwaite, "The Ten and a Half Myths That May Distort the Urban Policies of Governments and International Agencies," www.ucl.ac.uk (accessed 1/13/09).

31. *See* Paul R. Ehrlich, *The Population Bomb* (New York: Ballantine, 1968).

32. *E.g.,* William Ophuls, *Ecology and the Politics of Scarcity* (San Francisco: W. H. Freeman, 1977); Garrett Hardin, "The Tragedy of the Commons," *Science* 162 (1968), pp. 1243–1248, at 1246.

33. *E.g.,* Julian Simon, *The Ultimate Resource* (Princeton, NJ: Princeton University Press, 1981). As noted in Chapter 1, in Greek mythology, the *cornucopia* was the horn of plenty, containing an endless supply of food and drink.

34. *E.g.,* Dryzek, *Politics of the Earth,* 36–38, 191 (discussing the views of Robert Heilbroner and William Ophuls on the need for spiritual transformation).

35. Nebojša Nakicenovic et al., eds., *Emissions Scenarios* (Cambridge: Cambridge University Press, 2000).

36. Donald Worster, *The Wealth of Nature: Environmental History and the Ecological Imagination* (New York: Oxford University Press, 1993), p. 27.

37. For example, in 2006, per capita energy consumption in the United States was about twice that of France and Japan, more than 20 times higher than India, and more than 70 times higher than Bangladesh. EIA, "World Per Capita Total Primary Energy Consumption, 1980–2006," www.eia.doe.gov (accessed 1/16/09).

38. The environmental damage wrought by Saddam Hussein at the end of the 1991 Gulf War, when he burned Kuwaiti oil wells, is a dramatic exception.

39. A typical example of this way of thinking is the Stern Report's characterization of climate change as "the greatest example of market failure we have ever seen." Nicholas Stern, *The Economics of Climate Change: The Stern Review* (Cambridge: Cambridge University Press, 2007), p. 1.

40. *See* David W. Pearce and R. Kerry Turner, *Economics of Natural Resources and the Environment* (Baltimore, MD: Johns Hopkins University Press, 1990), pp. 61–69 (discussing "optimal" level of pollution).

41. See Chapter 4 for a further discussion of discount rates.

42. As we will explore in Chapter 6, the assumption of rationality is even more questionable in the case of states, whose policies are often the products of domestic politics, not rational calculations of self-interest. That is one reason why, contrary to our initial assumption about Roberta Crusoe, nations often do "foul their nests," mismanaging domestic environmental resources.

43. See Chapter 2 for a further discussion of the *Trail Smelter* case.

44. Keith Bradsher and David Barboza, "Pollution from Chinese Coal Casts Shadow around Globe," *New York Times*, June 11, 2006, p. A1.

45. In the case of the Amazon, deforestation also produces physical externalities by affecting the climate on a regional, and possibly global, basis. Roni Avissar and David Werth, "Global Hydroclimatological Teleconnections Resulting from Tropical Deforestation," *Journal of Hydrometeorology* 6 (2005), pp. 134–145.

46. *See* Ronald H. Coase, "The Problem of Social Cost," *Journal of Law and Economics* 3 (1960), pp. 1–44.

47. An outcome is Pareto superior if it leaves at least one individual better off and no one worse off.

48. Like Einstein, who won his Nobel Prize in Physics not for his most famous work, on relativity theory, but rather for his work on the photoelectric effect, Coase won his Nobel Prize in Economics for his work on the theory of the firm rather than for the Coase Theorem.

49. Todd Sandler, *Global Challenges: An Approach to Environmental, Political, and Economic Problems* (Cambridge: Cambridge University Press, 1997), p. 42.

50. Hardin, "Tragedy," 1244.

51. *See, e.g.,* Elinor Ostrom, *Governing the Commons: The Evolution of Institutions for Collective Action* (Cambridge: Cambridge University Press, 1990); Susan Jane Buck Cox, "No Tragedy of the Commons," *Environmental Ethics* 7 (1985), pp. 49–61.

52. The 1982 UN Convention on the Law of the Sea now imposes additional conditions on high seas fishing, UNCLOS arts. 116–119, and high seas fishing is also regulated by a variety of other international agreements, including the 1995 Fish Stocks Agreement.

53. The collapse of the Atlantic cod fishery in the 1970s is a well-known example. *See* Michael Harris, *Lament for an Ocean: The Collapse of the Atlantic Cod Fishery* (Toronto: McClelland & Stewart, 1998).

54. Robert Dorfman, "Some Concepts from Welfare Economics," in Robert Dorfman and Nancy S. Dorfman, eds., *Economics of the Environment: Selected Readings* (New York: W. W. Norton, 3d ed. 1993), pp. 79–96, at 82.

55. Sandler, *Global Challenges,* 43.

56. In academic economics, the deference to personal preferences has a methodological rationale: it reflects the view that economics cannot try to answer

every question. Why people have the preferences that they do—why they prefer SUVs, for example, to compact cars—is a question for psychology or sociology or perhaps even biology. The role of economics is simply to determine how to maximize the satisfaction of people's preferences.

57. *See, e.g.,* A. Myrick Freeman III, "The Ethical Basis of the Economic View of the Environment," in Donald VanDeVeer and Christine Pierce, eds., *The Environmental Ethics and Policy Book: Philosophy, Ecology, Economics* (London: Wadsworth, 2d ed. 1997), pp. 293–300, at 294 (stating that many economists assume "individuals . . . have . . . absence of limits on wants") .

58. For classic expositions of this view, see Thorsten Veblen, *The Theory of the Leisure Class: An Economic Study of Institutions* (New York: Macmillan Co., 1899); John Kenneth Galbraith, *The Affluent Society* (Boston: Houghton Mifflin, 1958).

59. Victor Lebow, "Price Competition in 1955," *Journal of Retailing* 31 (1955), pp. 5–10, 42, 44, at 7.

60. Lynn White Jr., "The Historical Roots of Our Ecological Crisis," *Science* 155 (1967), pp. 1203–1207, at 1205.

61. *E.g.,* Shepard Krech III, *The Ecological Indian: Myth and History* (New York: W. W. Norton, 1999).

62. Barbara Arnn, "Ad Expenditures Continue Global Growth, New Media Lead Way," January 5, 2005, http://multichannelmerchant.com (accessed 1/16/09).

63. J. R. McNeill, *Something New under the Sun: An Environmental History of the Twentieth Century* (New York: W. W. Norton, 2000), p. 336.

64. Speth, *Red Sky,* 192–193.

65. White, "Historical Roots," 1207.

4. Prescribing the Cure

1. Viewing policy problems from the perspective of a single, rational decision maker is common in policy analysis. *See, e.g.,* Edith Stokey and Richard Zeckhauser, *A Primer for Policy Analysis* (New York: W. W. Norton, 1978), p. 3. In his analysis of global environmental regulation, Wiener refers to this approach as "unitary fiat." Jonathan Baert Wiener, "Global Environmental Regulation: Instrument Choice in Legal Context," *Yale Law Journal* 108 (1999), pp. 677–800.

2. *E.g.,* Abruja Declaration on Roll Back Malaria, Abuja, Nigeria, April 25, 2000, Doc. No. WHO/CDS/RBM/2000.17; cf. John Luke Gallup and Jeffrey D. Sachs, "The Economic Burden of Malaria," *American Journal of Tropical Medicine and Hygiene* 64 (2001), pp. 85–96. Like many factoids, this estimate of $12 billion is difficult to pin down. *See* R. I. Chima, C. A. Goodman, and A. Mills, "The Economic Impact of Malaria in Africa: A Critical Review of the Evidence," *Health Policy* 63 (2003), pp. 17–36; Randall M. Packard, "Roll Back Malaria, Roll in Development? Reassessing the Economic Burden of Malaria," *Population and Development Review* 35 (2009), pp. 53–87.

3. *See* Olivia Judson, "A Bug's Death," *New York Times,* September 25, 2003.

4. Clive Ponting, *A Green History of the World: The Environment and the Collapse of Great Civilizations* (New York: Penguin Books, 1991), p. 164.

5. Daniel A. Farber, *Eco-Pragmatism: Making Sensible Environmental Decisions in an Uncertain World* (Chicago: University of Chicago Press, 1999), p. 39.

6. Robert V. Percival et al., *Environmental Regulation: Law, Science, and Policy* (Boston: Little, Brown, 1992), p. 67 (contrasting "moral outrage" and "cool analysis").

7. *See, e.g.,* UNCLOS art. 1(4) (defining pollution of the marine environment as "the introduction by man, directly or indirectly, of substances or energy . . . which results or is likely to result in . . . deleterious effects"); Allen L. Springer, *The International Law of Pollution: Protecting the Global Environment in a World of Sovereign States* (Westport, CT: Quorum Books, 1983), pp. 64–84 (discussing possible criteria to define "legally significant pollution").

8. The threshold below which environmental harm does not occur is generally referred to as the environment's "assimilative capacity." *See, e.g.,* ibid., 76–77.

9. 1994 Sulfur Protocol art. 1.8 (defining "critical load") and art. 2.1 (requiring states to reduce sulfur emissions).

10. *See* ibid., annex II.

11. Following *Tennessee Valley Authority v. Hill*, 437 U.S. 153 (1978). Congress amended the ESA to provide for consideration of economic factors. *See* 16 U.S.C. § 1533 (b)(2) (2008).

12. Bjørn Lomborg, *The Skeptical Environmentalist: Measuring the Real State of the World* (Cambridge: Cambridge University Press, 2001), p. 334.

13. *See generally* Alan Boyle and Michael Anderson, eds., *Human Rights Approaches to Environmental Protection* (Oxford: Oxford University Press, 1996).

14. James Salzman and Barton H. Thompson, Jr., *Environmental Law and Policy* (New York: Foundation Press, 2003), p. 27.

15. *See, e.g.,* Haw. Const. art. XI, § 9 ("Every person has the right to a clean and healthful environment . . ."); Mass. Const. art. XCVII ("The people shall have the right to clean air and water . . . and the natural, scenic, historic, and esthetic qualities of their environment."); Mont. Const. art. II, § 3 ("All persons . . . have certain inalienable rights. They include the right to a clean and healthful environment . . ."); Pa. Const. art. I, § 27 ("The people have a right to clean air, pure water, and to the preservation of the natural, scenic, historic and esthetic values of the environment.") The Aarhus Convention on Access to Information, Public Participation in Decision-Making and Access to Justice in Environmental Matters adopts a rights-based approach with respect to procedural issues (rights of access to information, public participation in decision making, and access to justice) but does not create substantive environmental rights.

16. *See, e.g., López Ostra v. Spain* (1994) (holding pollution to be violation of the right to respect for home and for private and family life); *Guerra v. Italy* (1998) (holding same); *Öneryildiz v. Turkey* (2004) (holding pollution to be

violation of the right to life). Even in these cases, however, the European Court of Human Rights did not take an absolutist approach. Rather, it found that the government had failed to strike a fair balance between the individual's rights and the interests of the community to economic well-being. *See generally* Svitlana Kravchenko and John E. Bonine, *Human Rights and the Environment: Cases, Law, and Policy* (Durham, NC: Carolina Academic Press, 2008).

17. Aldo Leopold, *A Sand County Almanac, and Sketches Here and There* (Oxford: Oxford University Press, 1949), pp. 224–225.

18. Although, interestingly, Leopold himself recognized that "economic feasibility limits the tether of what can or cannot be done for land." Ibid., 225.

19. For critical analyses of the precautionary principle, see, *e.g.*, Jonathan B. Wiener, "Precaution," in Daniel Bodansky, Jutta Brunnée, and Ellen Hey, eds., *The Oxford Handbook of International Environmental Law* (Oxford: Oxford University Press, 2007), pp. 597–612; Daniel Bodansky, "Deconstructing the Precautionary Principle," in David D. Caron and Harry N. Scheiber, eds., *Bringing New Law to Ocean Waters* (Leiden: Brill, 2004), pp. 381–391.

20. Christopher D. Stone, "Is There a Precautionary Principle?" *Environmental Law Reporter* 31 (2001), pp. 10790–10799, at 10799.

21. *See* Tina Rosenberg, "What the World Needs Now Is DDT," *New York Times,* April 11, 2004, p. F38. Rosenberg quotes a former WHO official as saying, "In tropical Africa, if you don't use DDT, forget it." The Persistent Organic Pollutants (POPs) Convention resolves this dilemma by allowing countries to continue using DDT for malaria control when safe, effective, and affordable alternatives are not available. POPs Convention annex B, pt. II.

22. *See* David W. Pearce and R. Kerry Turner, *Economics of Natural Resources and the Environment* (Baltimore, MD: Johns Hopkins University Press, 1990), pp. 61–69. The Copenhagen Consensus project, organized in 2004 by Bjørn Lomborg, attempts to apply cost-benefit analysis to compare the severity of a wide variety of global problems relating to development, poverty, and the environment, and then to assess the cost-effectiveness of different solutions. A group of about fifty top economists was given the question, "Imagine you had $75 [billion] to donate to worthwhile causes. What would you do, and where should we start?" requiring them to prioritize both problems and potential solutions. *See, e.g.,* www.copenhagenconsensus.com (accessed 1/23/09); Bjørn Lomberg, ed., *Solutions for the World's Biggest Problems: Costs and Benefits* (Cambridge: Cambridge University Press, 2007).

23. Of course, in some cases, we can get direct evidence of how much individuals are willing to pay for an environmental benefit; for example, we can observe how much people are willing to pay to visit a national park. But often environmental benefits are public goods for which there is no market. The ecosystem functions provided by biological diversity are one example.

24. *See, e.g.,* Paul R. Portney, "The Contingent Valuation Debate: Why Economists Should Care," in Robert N. Stavins, ed., *Economics of the Environment:*

Selected Readings (New York: W. W. Norton, 4th ed. 2000), pp. 253–267; W. Michael Hanemann, "Valuing the Environment Through Contingent Valuation," in ibid., 268–294; Peter A. Diamond and Jerry A. Hausman, "Contingent Valuation: Is Some Number Better than No Number?," in ibid., 295–315.

25. *See, e.g.,* V. Kerry Smith, "Nonmarket Valuation of Environmental Resources: An Interpretive Appraisal," in ibid., 219–252, at 224–227.

26. For example, in the climate change debate, many environmentalists argue that there is a significant potential to reduce greenhouse gas emissions through "no regrets" measures—for example, more efficient technologies—that pay for themselves in the long run and therefore make sense whether or not climate change proves to be a real problem. However, many economists are skeptical about the extent of no-regrets measures.

27. *See* Stokey and Zeckhauser, *Primer,* 159–176. In addition to this "pure time" discount rate, which compares how much we value current versus future generations, people in the future are likely to be richer than those in the present, assuming continued economic growth, and therefore will be able to afford to pay more for environmental protection.

28. Tariq Banuri et al., "Technical Summary," in Bert Metz et al., eds., *Climate Change 2001: Mitigation* (Cambridge: Cambridge University Press, 2001), pp. 15–71, at 52. For example, the much-cited Stern Review on the Economics of Climate Change assumed a discount rate of only 0.1 percent and therefore found that we should invest a great deal now (1 percent of global GDP) to reduce the impact of global warming. Nicholas Stern, *The Economics of Climate Change: The Stern Review* (Cambridge: Cambridge University Press, 2007), pp. 35–37, 49–59, 184, 262. But assuming a discount rate of 3 percent, the optimal emissions reduction by 2050 drops from 25 percent to 14 percent. Lucy Odling-Smee, "Climate Change 2007: What Price a Cooler Future?" *Nature* 445 (2007), pp. 582–583, at 583.

29. In the lingo of economics, the behavior of investors "reveals" their preferences as between the present and the future. A rational investor will not be willing to make an investment if the internal rate of return is not greater than his or her private discount rate.

30. Kirsten Halsnæs et al., "Framing Issues," in Bert Metz et al., eds., *Climate Change 2007: Mitigation of Climate Change* (Cambridge: Cambridge University Press, 2007) pp. 117–167, at 137–138.

31. *See, e.g.,* Mark Sagoff, *The Economy of the Earth: Philosophy, Law, and the Environment* (Cambridge: Cambridge University Press, 2d ed. 2008), pp. 46–66. Behavioral economics makes a similar point. As Daniel Ariely notes, "we live in two worlds: one characterized by social exchanges and the other characterized by market exchanges. And we apply different norms to these two kinds of relationships." Dan Ariely, *Predictably Irrational: The Hidden Forces that Shape Our Decisions* (New York: HarperCollins, 2008), p. 76.

32. *See, e.g.,* Frank Ackerman and Lisa Heinzerling, *Priceless: On Knowing the Price of Everything and the Value of Nothing* (New York: New Press, 2004); Steven Kelman, "Cost-Benefit Analysis: An Ethical Critique," *AEI Journal on Government and Society Regulation,* January/February 1981, pp. 33–40,

reprinted in Stavins, ed., *Economics of the Environment*, 355–365. In his "Ballad of Ecological Awareness," Kenneth E. Boulding wrote,

So cost-benefit analysis is nearly always sure,
To justify the building of a solid concrete fact,
While the Ecological Truth is left behind in the Abstract.

M. Taghi Farvar and John P. Milton, eds., *The Careless Technology: Ecology and International Development* (Garden City, NY: Natural History Press, 1972), p. 157.

33. *See* Robert M. Solow, "Reply to Steven Kelman," *AEI Journal on Government and Society Regulation*, March/April 1981, pp. 40–41, reprinted in Stavins, ed., *Economics of the Environment*, 367–368, at 368.

34. Stokey and Zeckhauser, *Primer*, 135–158.

35. Jason Merchey, *Values of the Wise: Humanity's Highest Aspirations* (W. Conshohocken, PA: Infinity Publishing, 2004), p. 63.

36. "Letter to Joseph Priestley, Sept. 19, 1772," in *Franklin: Writings*, ed. J. A. Leo Lemay (New York: Library of America, 1987), p. 878. I am indebted to Andy Keeler for this reference.

37. According to one analysis, the estimated cost per life saved has varied in different federal regulations from $200,000 to $6 trillion. Kenneth Arrow et al., "Is There a Role for Benefit-Cost Analysis in Environmental, Health, and Safety Regulation?" *Science* 272 (1996), pp. 221–222, reprinted in Stavins, ed., *Economics of the Environment*, 319–324, at 320.

38. Indeed, "is responsible for" is often used synonymously with "cause."

39. Cf. Scott Barrett, *Environment and Statecraft: The Strategy of Environmental Treaty-Making* (Oxford: Oxford University Press, 2003), p. 345.

40. The various conventions that establish liability regimes for oil spills and nuclear accidents also create liability standards for private actors.

41. Similarly, the 1949 International Whaling Convention authorizes the International Whaling Commission to adopt rules governing allowable catch, open and closed seasons, size limits, equipment restrictions, and so forth. But rather than applying these requirements directly to private whalers, the Convention relies on national implementation, requiring each participating state to "take appropriate measures to ensure the application of the provisions of this Convention and the punishment of infractions . . . in operations carried out by persons or by vessels under its jurisdiction." Ibid., art. IX(1).

42. For an excellent survey, see Richard B. Stewart, "Instrument Choice," in Bodansky, Brunnée, and Hey, eds., *Oxford Handbook of International Environmental Law*, 147–181.

43. *See generally* Wesley A. Magat and W. Kip Viscusi, *Informational Approaches to Regulation* (Cambridge, MA: MIT Press, 1992).

44. The same is true if people's actions reflect their sense of identity rather than their economic interests. If I learn, for example, that I am individually responsible for (literally) tons of carbon dioxide emissions per year, this may cause me to change my behavior, not because this would make me better off, but because it does not square with my own self-image as a responsible

member of the community. Information thus plays a positive role regardless of what behavioral model we subscribe to, a logic of consequences or a logic of appropriateness.

45. *See also* Principle 17 of the 1992 Rio Declaration, which articulates a general duty on national governments to undertake EIAs "for proposed activities that are likely to have a significant adverse impact on the environment and are subject to a decision of a competent national authority."

46. MARPOL 78 annex III (addressing harmful substances carried in packaged form).

47. *See, e.g.,* Rio Declaration principle 18; UNCLOS art. 198; Convention on Biological Diversity art. 14(1)(d).

48. Louis D. Brandeis, *Other People's Money and How the Bankers Use It* (New York: Frederick A. Stokes, 1914), p. 92.

49. *See, e.g.,* Espoo Convention art. 3.

50. Peter H. Sand, "Information Disclosure as an Instrument of Environmental Governance," *Heidelberg Journal of International Law* 63 (2003), pp. 487–502, at 487–488.

51. Aarhus Convention art. 4.

52. The Kiev Protocol on Pollutant Release and Transfer Registries, adopted by the parties to the Aarhus Convention on May 21, 2003, is loosely modeled on the U.S. Toxics Release Inventory, which requires industry to disclose toxic releases. *Compare* Kiev Protocol, www.unece.org (accessed 1/23/09) *with* TRI Program, www.epa.gov (accessed 1/23/09). The United States has declined to join the Protocol on the ground that it does not go as far as U.S. law.

53. *See* Bruce A. Ackerman and Richard B. Stewart, "Reforming Environmental Law," *Stanford Law Review* 37 (1985), pp. 1333–1365, at 1335–1338.

54. Although specification standards can be differentiated, this puts huge informational demands on regulators to determine the appropriate technology or design for each regulated entity.

55. Howard Latin, "Ideal versus Real Regulatory Efficiency: Implementation of Uniform Standards and 'Fine-Tuning' Regulatory Reforms," *Stanford Law Review* 37 (1985), pp. 1267–1332, at 1271.

56. *See generally* Ronald B. Mitchell, *Intentional Oil Pollution at Sea: Environmental Policy and Treaty Compliance* (Cambridge, MA: MIT Press, 1994).

57. Scott Barrett, "An Economic Theory of International Environmental Law," in Bodansky, Brunnée, and Hey, eds., *Oxford Handbook of International Environmental Law*, 231–261, at 254–255.

58. Ibid., 255.

59. OILPOL art. III(1).

60. Comprehensiveness enhances not only cost-effectiveness but also environmental effectiveness, by preventing "leakage"—that is, the shifting of production from regulated gases and industries to unregulated ones. Richard B. Stewart and Jonathan B. Wiener, "The Comprehensive Approach to Global Climate Policy: Issues of Design and Practicality," *Arizona Journal of International and Comparative Law* 9 (1992), pp. 83–113, at 91.

61. *See* 33 U.S.C. § 1251(a)(2)-(3) (2000).
62. *See* Jon Birger Skjærseth, "Cleaning Up the North Sea: The Case of Land-Based Pollution Control," in Edward L. Miles et al., *Environmental Regime Effectiveness: Confronting Theory with Evidence* (Cambridge, MA: MIT Press, 2002), pp. 175–196.
63. One exception is the 1978 Great Lakes Water Quality Agreement, which has used environmental quality standards as its principal regulatory instrument. The 1978 Agreement was further elaborated by a protocol in 1987 and has been implemented primarily through the adoption of reduction action plans by each of the participating states.
64. UNFCCC art. 2.
65. UN Environmental Programme, *A Guide to Emissions Trading* (Roskilde, Denmark: UNEP, 2002), pp. 36–37.
66. *See* Jutta Brunnée, "Of Sense and Sensibility: Reflections on International Liability Regimes as Tools for Environmental Protection," *International and Comparative Law Quarterly* 53 (2004), pp. 351–367, at 365–366 (stating there is no empirical evidence that existing international liability regimes affect polluter behavior).
67. *E.g.,* 1969 Civil Liability Convention for Oil Pollution; 1963 Vienna Convention on Civil Liability for Nuclear Damage.
68. *E.g.,* Antarctic Environment Protocol annex VI; Basel Protocol on Liability and Compensation.
69. *E.g.,* Raymond Kopp, Richard Morgenstern, and William Pizer, *Something for Everyone: A Climate Policy that Both Environmentalists and Industry Could Live With,* September 29, 1997, www.weathervane.rff.org (accessed 1/23/09); Warwick J. McKibbin and Peter J. Wilcoxen, "A Better Way to Slow Global Climate Change," *Brookings Policy Brief No. 20,* June 1997.

5. Varieties of Environmental Norms

1. Conference of the Parties to the United Nations Framework Convention on Climate Change on Its First Session, Berlin, March 28–April 7, 1995, *Decision 1/CP.1 (Berlin Mandate),* UN Doc. FCCC/CP/1995/7/Add.1 (June 6, 1995).
2. Broad consensus to negotiate legally binding emission targets was reached in 1996. *See* Conference of the Parties to the United Nations Framework Convention on Climate Change on Its Second Session, Geneva, Switzerland, July 8–19, 1996, *Geneva Ministerial Declaration,* UN Doc. FCCC/CP/1996/15/ Add.1 Annex I (October 29, 1996).
3. Kyoto Protocol art. 18.
4. The "Non-Legally Binding Authoritative Statement of Principles for a Global Consensus on the Management, Conservation and Sustainable Development of All Types of Forests," United Nations Conference on Environment and Development, Rio de Janeiro, Brazil, June 3–14, 1992, UN Doc. A/CONF.151/26 Annex III (June 13, 1992)—a document whose title reads like a caricature of UN-speak—raises similar perplexities. In what sense is the statement "authoritative" but not "legally binding"?

5. *See, e.g.,* Robert C. Ellickson, *Order Without Law: How Neighbors Settle Disputes* (Cambridge, MA: Harvard University Press, 1991), p. 126. In using the term *prescriptive,* however, it is important to remember that there need not be any prescribing agent.

6. Alf Ross, *Directives and Norms* (London: Routledge & Kegan Paul, 1968), p. 34 (identifying a directive as "an action-idea conceived as a pattern of behavior").

7. *Compare* Peter Winch, *The Idea of a Social Science and Its Relation to Philosophy* (London: Routledge & Kegan Paul, 2d ed. 1990), p. 32 ("[T]he point of the concept of a rule is that it should enable us to *evaluate* what is being done.").

8. Joseph Raz, *Practical Reasons and Norms* (Oxford: Oxford University Press, 1999), p. 9.

9. Ross, *Directives and Norms,* 82–92.

10. John Searle, *Expression and Meaning: Studies in the Theory of Speech Acts* (Cambridge: Cambridge University Press, 1979), p. 13 (listing the taxonomy of illocutionary acts). H. L. A. Hart uses the term *imperatives* to refer to this linguistic form. H. L. A. Hart, *The Concept of Law* (Oxford: Oxford University Press, 2d ed. 1994), pp. 18–19.

11. John R. Searle and Daniel Vanderveken, *Foundations of Illocutionary Logic* (Cambridge: Cambridge University Press, 1985), pp. 198–205; *see also* Frederick Schauer, "Prescription in Three Dimensions," *Iowa Law Review* 82 (1997), pp. 911–922, at 912. Directives can also be expressed by the use of what Alf Ross calls "deontic expressions" such as "ought to," "have to," "must," "are obliged to," "are bound to," and "have a right to." Ross, *Directives and Norms,* 36.

12. Searle, *Expression and Meaning,* 13.

13. Normative language such as "ought" and "should" is used in connection not only with directives but also with promises, contracts, assurances, and the like—what linguistic philosophers refer to as "commissives." As the term suggests, a commissive "commit[s] the speaker (again in varying degrees) to some future course of action." Ibid., 14. "[W]hereas the point of a promise is to commit the speaker to doing something . . . the point of a [directive] is to try to get the hearer to do something." Ibid. The two types of illocutionary acts are linked in that a promise, contract, or other commissive provides the basis for a directive of the type: "you ought to (or must or should) keep your promise."

14. John R. Searle, *Speech Acts: An Essay in the Philosophy of Language* (Cambridge: Cambridge University Press, 1969), p. 33.

15. Ibid., 33–34.

16. Hart, *Concept of Law,* 81. Like the rules of a game, secondary rules also define (and thereby limit) how those powers may be exercised.

17. Often instruments contain both constitutive and regulatory norms. The Kyoto Protocol, for example, is both regulatory (limiting emissions of greenhouse gases) and constitutive (establishing the Clean Development Mechanism and a compliance committee). Indeed, few documents are purely regulatory or

constitutive. The International Whaling Convention Schedule is an example of a purely regulatory document, whereas the agreement creating the GEF is purely constitutive. But, more typically, even primarily constitutive documents, such as the United Nations Charter or the Vienna Convention on the Protection of the Ozone Layer, contain at least some regulatory norms. Conversely, primarily regulatory documents such as the Montreal Protocol on Substances that Deplete the Ozone Layer usually include constitutive elements.

18. Hart, *Concept of Law,* 56–57.
19. Frederick Schauer, *Playing by the Rules: A Philosophical Examination of Rule-Based Decision-Making in Law and in Life* (Oxford: Clarendon Press, 1991), pp. 121–122.
20. Martha Finnemore and Kathryn Sikkink, "International Norm Dynamics and Political Change," *International Organization* 52 (1998), pp. 887–917, at 898.
21. *See generally* Schauer, *Playing by the Rules.*
22. UN Charter preamble, para. 1.
23. This discussion is drawn from my article, "International Law in Black and White," *Georgia Journal of International and Comparative Law* 34 (2006), pp. 285–304.
24. Thomas Franck described this feeling of constraint as a norm's "compliance pull." *See* Thomas M. Franck, *The Power of Legitimacy among Nations* (Oxford: Oxford University Press, 1990).
25. *See* Hart, *Concept of Law,* 86.
26. Internalization figured prominently in Durkheim's sociological theory and is today reflected in constructivist accounts of international relations. For the difficulties of conceptualizing internalization, see Robert E. Scott, "The Limits of Behavioral Theories of Law and Social Norms," *Virginia Law Review* 86 (2000), pp. 1603–1647.
27. Finnemore and Sikkink, "International Norm Dynamics," 904.
28. *Compare* Winch, *Idea of a Social Science,* 58 ("[T]he test of whether a man's actions are the application of a rule is not whether he can *formulate* it but whether it makes sense to distinguish between a right and a wrong way of doing things.").
29. James G. March and Johan P. Olson, *Rediscovering Institutions: The Organizational Basis of Politics* (New York: Free Press, 1989) (introducing the concepts of a logic of consequences and of appropriateness).
30. Oliver Wendell Holmes, "The Path of the Law," *Harvard Law Review* 10 (1897), pp. 457–478, at 459.
31. *See, e.g.,* Andrew T. Guzman, *How International Law Works: A Rational Choice Theory* (Oxford: Oxford University Press, 2008).
32. *See, e.g.,* Jack L. Goldsmith and Eric A. Posner, *The Limits of International Law* (New York: Oxford University Press, 2005).
33. Holmes, "Path of the Law," 459 ("You can see very plainly that a bad man has as much reason as a good one for wishing to avoid an encounter with the public force, and therefore you can see the practical importance of the distinction between morality and law.").

34. *E.g.*, Guzman, *How International Law Works;* Edward T. Swaine, "Rational Custom," *Duke Law Journal* 52 (2002), pp. 559–627. This is the basis of rule-utilitarianism.

35. *See, e.g.*, Guzman, *How International Law Works,* 16, 19.

36. *See, e.g.*, Goldsmith and Posner, *Limits,* 39 ("A state's compliance . . . has nothing to do with acting from a sense of legal obligation.").

37. For example, a study of compliance by parents with a day care center's norm establishing a required pick-up time illustrates the limitations of a purely instrumental account of behavior. It found that, when the day care center added a fine to enforce the required pickup time, compliance decreased rather than increased. Apparently, the deterrent effect of the fine was less than its effect in undermining the normative force of the rule, by making parents feel that it was permissible to violate the norm if they paid the fine. Dan Ariely, *Predictably Irrational: The Hidden Forces that Shape Our Decisions* (New York: Harper-Collins, 2008), pp. 76–77.

38. *See, e.g.*, Tom R. Tyler, *Why People Obey the Law* (New Haven, CT: Yale University Press, 1990). In their best-selling book, *Freakonomics,* Steven Levitt and Stephen Dubner cite experimental data suggesting that people comply with the moral norm against stealing 87 percent of the time, even in the absence of any enforcement. Steven D. Levitt and Stephen J. Dubner, *Freakonomics: A Rogue Economist Explores the Hidden Side of Everything* (New York: HarperCollins, 2005), pp. 45–51.

39. Hart, *Concept of Law,* 56. Similarly, sociological theorists who focus on norm internalization also recognize the important role of sanctions in enforcing social norms. *E. g.*, Christine Horne, "Sociological Perspectives on the Emergence of Social Norms," in Michael Hechter and Karl-Dieter Opp, eds., *Social Norms* (New York: Russell Sage Foundation, 2001), pp. 3–34, at 5.

40. London Guidelines for the Exchange of Information on Chemicals in International Trade (1987).

41. The FAO International Code of Conduct on the Distribution and Use of Pesticides was originally adopted in 1985 and was amended in 1989 to include a PIC procedure. FAO Res. 6/89 (November 29, 1989).

42. The principal cases are collected in Karen Lee, ed., *International Environmental Law Reports: Volume 5, International Environmental Law in International Tribunals* (Cambridge: Cambridge University Press, 2007).

43. *Lac Lanoux Case,* 281–317.

44. These national court decisions are discussed further in Chapter 10.

45. *E.g.*, International Law Commission, *Draft Articles on Prevention of Transboundary Harm from Hazardous Activities,* UN GAOR, 56th Sess., Supp. No. 10, UN Doc. A/56/10 (2001); International Law Association, *Montreal Rules of International Law Applicable to Transfrontier Pollution* art. 3(1) (1982); Institut de Droit International, *Resolution on Transboundary Air Pollution* art. 2 (1987). Although the International Law Commission (ILC) was created by the UN General Assembly and has an official status, the International Law Association and the Institut de Droit International are purely private associations of international lawyers.

46. *See generally,* Dinah Shelton, ed., *Commitment and Compliance: The Role of Non-Binding Norms in the International Legal System* (Oxford: Oxford University Press, 2000); Michael Bothe, "Legal and Non-Legal Norms—A Meaningful Distinction in International Relations?" *Netherlands Yearbook of International Law* 11 (1980), pp. 65–95.

47. To distinguish them from formal sources, international lawyers sometimes refer to causes as "material sources."

48. Finnemore and Sikkink, "International Norm Dynamics."

49. Expert initiatives can also serve as a "material" (or causal) source of new law. For example, state officials may read an expert report, find it persuasive, and incorporate it into a subsequent treaty. In this example, however, the treaty is the formal source of law; the expert initiative is merely part of the causal explanation for the development of the treaty. The International Law Commission's (ILC's) mandate to codify and progressively develop international law illustrates the dual role of expert initiatives. In codifying international law, ILC studies serve as evidence of existing law; in contrast, in progressively developing international law, the ILC serves as a material source of new customary or treaty norms.

50. *See* Bruno Simma and Philip Alston, "The Sources of Human Rights Law: Custom, Jus Cogens, and General Principles," *Australian Yearbook of International Law* 12 (1988/1989), pp. 82–108.

51. *Trail Smelter Case,* 1965.

52. *See, e.g.,* Pierre-Marie Dupuy, "Soft Law and the International Law of the Environment," *Michigan Journal of International Law* 12 (1991), pp. 420–435; Christine M. Chinkin, "The Challenge of Soft Law: Development and Change in International Law," *International and Comparative Law Quarterly* 38 (1989), pp. 850–866. Though commonly used, the term *soft law* can create confusion because it is sometimes used to refer to several different features of norms: their legal vs. non-legal character, their precision, their mandatory vs. hortatory language, and their implementation mechanisms. Some have criticized it for this reason as well as because it blurs the distinction between law and non-law. Kal Raustiala, "Form and Substance in International Agreements," *American Journal of International Law* 99 (2005), pp. 581–614, at 586 ("There is no such thing as 'soft law.' "). I use the term *soft law* in this passage to refer only to non-legal norms, and I consider other dimensions of norms (including their precision, mandatory quality, and implementation mechanisms) separately in the final section of the chapter.

53. *See* Jutta Brunnée, "COPing with Consent: Law-Making under Multilateral Environmental Agreements," *Leiden Journal of International Law* 15 (2002), pp. 1–52.

54. *See* Christopher C. Joyner, "The Legal Status and Effect of Antarctic Recommended Measures," in Shelton, ed., *Commitment and Compliance,* 163–196.

55. AIDS Summit, Paris, France, December 1, 1994, *Paris Declaration.*

56. For a similar criticism regarding instruments to limit biological weapons, see William J. Broad, "Sowing Death: A Special Report; How Japan Germ Terror

Alerted World," *New York Times,* May 26, 1998, p. A1 (criticizing Australia Group's call for measures to prevent biological weapons because it "came in the form of recommendations, not rules"). *See generally* Raustiala, "Form and Substance," 596 (discussing preference of environmental groups for binding agreements).

57. See Chapter 11.

58. Pelly Amendment to the United States Fishermen's Protective Act, 22 U.S.C. § 1978.

59. Even domestically, however, a judicial remedy is not necessarily available for the violation of every legal norm. This is perhaps most apparent in the national security and foreign affairs arenas, where constitutional provisions regarding the war power and the treaty power are, in most cases, judicially unenforceable.

60. However, we would still need to investigate how much difference judicial application makes, given the lack of sanctions in most cases.

61. For a similar typology, see Judith Goldstein, Miles Kahler, Robert O. Keohane, and Anne-Marie Slaughter, eds., *Legalization and World Politics* (Cambridge, MA: MIT Press, 2001), which focuses on three variables: legal form, precision, and what they call "delegation," which refers to third-party implementation mechanisms.

62. Ibid.

63. Of course, by consenting to the UN Charter, states accept the process by which Security Council decisions are adopted. But this basis of consent is much more attenuated than consent to a particular norm.

64. *See* Jeffrey D. Kovar, "A Short Guide to the Rio Declaration," *Colorado Journal of International Environmental Law and Policy* 4 (1993), pp. 119–140.

65. Laurence R. Helfer, "Nonconsensual International Lawmaking," *University of Illinois Law Review* (2008), pp. 71–125, at 82–83.

66. *See* Boockmann and Paul W. Thurner, "Flexibility Provisions in Multilateral Environmental Treaties," *International Environmental Agreements: Politics, Law and Economics* 6 (2006), pp. 113–135.

67. Montreal Protocol art. 2(9). The possibility of non-consensual decision making is more theoretical than real, however, since adjustments to the Montreal Protocol have in fact always been adopted by consensus.

68. As Searle notes, directives "may be very modest 'attempts' as when I invite you to do [something] or suggest that you do it, or they may be very fierce attempts as when I insist that you do it." Searle, *Expression and Meaning,* 13.

69. G. A. Res. 46/215, §§ 3(c)-4, UN Doc. A/RES/46/215 (December 20, 1991).

70. NO_x Protocol art. 10.

71. Ibid., tech. annex, para. 3.

72. This dimension can easily be confused with a different feature of a norm, namely, the degree to which it is particular or general. The two aspects are distinct, however. A particular norm may be vague ("David, play reasonably!"), and a general norm precise ("No one may smoke cigarettes on airplanes."). What gives rise to the confusion is the belief that the opposite of precision is generality rather than vagueness. *See* Schauer, "Prescription in

Three Dimensions," 913 ("Not all general classes (or categories) are vague. The category 'insects,' for example, is very large, including literally trillions of particular insects, but it is still reasonably specific in the sense of *precise.* As to a very large percentage of the trillions of insects, there is little doubt as to whether a particular creature is or is not an insect. Perhaps there are some borderline cases, but there are not many, and thus the dimension of the size (generality) of a class is not necessarily the dimension of specificity or vagueness.").

73. MARPOL annex 1, regulations 9, 13.

74. *See, e.g.,* Louis Kaplow, "Rules Versus Standards: An Economic Analysis," *Duke Law Journal* 42 (1992), pp. 557–629; Duncan Kennedy, "Form and Substance in Private Law Adjudication," *Harvard Law Review* 89 (1976), pp. 1685–1778; Pierre Schlag, "Rules and Standards," *UCLA Law Review* 33 (1985), pp. 379–430. For an application of the rules vs. standards issue to international law, see Daniel Bodansky, "Rules vs. Standards in International Environmental Law," in *Proceedings of the 98th Annual Meeting of the American Society of International Law* (2004), pp. 275–280.

75. Kaplow, "Rules Versus Standards."

76. Decisions of the parties elaborating a treaty standard supplement a vague legal norm with a precise non-legal one.

77. *See generally* Bodansky, "Rules vs. Standards."

78. Erika B. Schlager, "A Hard Look at Compliance with 'Soft' Law: The Case of the OSCE," in Shelton, ed., *Commitment and Compliance,* 346–371, at 355–359.

6. Who's Who in the Legal Process

1. Press Release, UNFCCC Secretariat, "UN Breakthrough on Climate Change Reached in Bali" (December 15, 2007).

2. The primacy of the state system is usually dated to the Peace of Westphalia in 1648, which ended the Thirty Years War. Today, the state system seems so "natural" that it is easy to forget that other modes of social organization exist—for example, feudalism, which was organized based on personal loyalties between lord and vassal.

3. The European Union, of course, represents the principal exception to this general rule. It has shared competence with its member states to enter into and implement international agreements. Although the EU, of course, is not a state, it shares many of the same characteristics. For this reason, in this chapter and throughout the book, in referring to "states" I generally mean to include the European Union. In addition, some liability treaties create rights and duties for private actors. Moreover, to the extent there is a human right to a clean environment, this is an individual right.

4. Pamela S. Chasek, David L. Downie, and Janet Welsh Brown, *Global Environmental Politics* (Boulder, CO: Westview, 4th ed. 2006), pp. 42–43.

5. These international relations approaches are reflected in the legal literature, respectively, by Jack L. Goldsmith and Eric A. Posner, *The Limits of*

International Law (New York: Oxford University Press, 2005) and Andrew T. Guzman, *How International Law Works: A Rational Choice Theory* (Oxford: Oxford University Press, 2008).

6. *See, e.g.*, Joseph M. Grieco, "Anarchy and the Limits of Cooperation: A Realist Critique of the Newest Liberal Institutionalism," *International Organization* 42 (1988), pp. 485–507, at 487; John J. Mearsheimer, "The False Promise of International Institutions," *International Security* 19 (1994/1995), pp. 5–49.

7. *See, e.g.*, George W. Downs, David M. Rocke, and Peter N. Barsoom, "Is the Good News about Compliance Good News about Cooperation?" *International Organization* 50 (1996), pp. 379–406.

8. Although particular economic sectors (and individuals) within a country might lose as a result of international trade, they too could come out ahead if some of the gains from international trade were used to compensate them.

9. A Pareto improvement refers to a development that leaves at least one of the participants better off and none worse off. It is named for the Italian economist, Vilfredo Pareto (1848–1923).

10. *See, e.g.*, Scott Barrett, *Environment and Statecraft: The Strategy of Environmental Treaty-Making* (Oxford: Oxford University Press, 2003), pp. 228–230 (citing the EPA calculation that the Montreal Protocol would produce a payoff to the United States of more than $3 trillion); Todd Sandler, *Global Challenges: An Approach to Environmental, Political, and Economic Problems* (Cambridge: Cambridge University Press, 1997).

11. Detlef Sprinz and Tapani Vaahtoranta, "The Interest-Based Explanation of International Environmental Policy," *International Organization* 48 (1994), pp. 77–105.

12. Ibid., 79. As this model suggests, in the European acid rain regime, the "importers" of transboundary pollution (the Scandinavian states) pushed for emissions reductions, whereas the "exporters" of acid rain (the United Kingdom and Germany) initially opposed international regulation.

13. In particular, a state's economic costs of pollution abatement (or natural resources conservation) and its environmental vulnerability. *See, e.g.*, ibid., 78.

14. James G. March and Johan P. Olsen, *Rediscovering Institutions: The Organizational Basis of Politics* (New York: Free Press, 1989) (introducing the concepts of a logic of consequences and of appropriateness).

15. Jonathan Baert Wiener, "On the Political Economy of Global Environmental Regulation," *Georgetown Law Journal* 87 (1999), pp. 749–794, at 751–752 (quoting Robert D. Putnam, "Diplomacy and Domestic Politics: The Logic of Two-Level Games," *International Organization* 42 (1988), pp. 427–460).

16. See Ian H. Rowlands, "Explaining National Climate Change Policies," *Global Environmental Change* 5 (1995), pp. 235–249.

17. For a classic analysis of the role of bureaucratic politics in foreign affairs, see Graham T. Allison, *Essence of Decision: Explaining the Cuban Missile Crisis* (Boston: Little, Brown, 1971).

18. In saying this, I do not mean to suggest that we consciously intended to do things contrary to Administration policy, but rather that we did not want

political appointees getting involved in all of the multitudinous, often rather technical issues that arise in every negotiation.

19. Byrd-Hagel Resolution, S. Res. 98, 105th Cong. (1997) (adopted 95–0).

20. For example, Ford's commitment to build hybrid cars is often attributed to the environmentalism of the company's chief executive officer, Bill Ford, Jr. On the role of management styles, see Neil Gunningham, Robert A. Kagan, and Dorothy Thornton, *Shades of Green: Business, Regulation, and Environment* (Stanford, CA: Stanford University Press, 2003), pp. 95–134.

21. As a result, diplomacy is what Robert Putnam has called a "two-level game," involving domestic as well international politics. Putnam, "Diplomacy and Domestic Politics."

22. *See* Stephen Jay Gould, *The Panda's Thumb: More Reflections in Natural History* (New York: W. W. Norton, 1980).

23. In a series of recent cases, for example, the United States has been put into violation of the Vienna Convention on Consular Relations due to the failure by state police to notify aliens who have been detained of their right to speak with their consular representatives. *See, e.g., Medellin v. Texas,* 552 U.S. ___, 128 S. Ct. 1346 (2008); *Sanchez-Llamas v. Oregon,* 548 U.S. 331 (2006).

24. The sources of state influence are complex, however, and do not always reflect size, economic weight, or military might. In the 1980s and early 1990s, for example, a proposal made by two small island states—Nauru and Kiribati—to ban ocean disposal of low-level radioactive wastes was ultimately adopted by the parties to the London (Dumping) Convention, Res. LC 51(16) (November 12, 1993), despite the initial opposition of the United States, United Kingdom, France, and Japan. *See* Lasse Ringius, *Radioactive Waste Disposal at Sea: Public Ideas, Transnational Policy Entrepreneurs, and Environmental Regimes* (Cambridge, MA: MIT Press, 2000), pp. 21–34.

25. *See* Steve Charnovitz, "A World Environment Organization," *Columbia Journal of Environmental Law* 27 (2002), pp. 323–362.

26. *See generally* Jacob Werksman, ed., *Greening International Institutions* (London: Earthscan, 1996).

27. *See* José E. Alvarez, *International Organizations as Law-makers* (Oxford: Oxford University Press, 2005), pp. 4–16.

28. Adil Najam, Mihaela Papa, and Nadaa Taiyab, *Global Environmental Governance: A Reform Agenda* (Winnipeg, Canada: International Institute for Sustainable Development, 2006), p. 12.

29. The Commission on Sustainable Development—the principal institutional outcome of the Rio Conference twenty years later—also has a general mandate but has become largely a talk shop, with few tangible achievements.

30. *See* Robin R. Churchill and Geir Ulfstein, "Autonomous Institutional Arrangements in Multilateral Environmental Agreements: A Little-Noticed Phenomenon in International Law," *American Journal of International Law* 94 (2000), pp. 623–659.

31. The Antarctic Treaty Consultative Meetings are a rare exception to this general rule. They give full voting rights only to Antarctic Treaty parties that demonstrate their interest in Antarctica by conducting substantial research

activities and that thereby have what is referred to as "consultative status." Antarctic Treaty art. IX(2).

32. UNEP serves as the institutional home for the treaty secretariats of the Montreal Protocol, the Convention on Biological Diversity, the Basel Convention, and the Convention on International Trade in Endangered Species (CITES). Other international organizations that provide secretariat services for MEAs include the IMO for marine pollution agreements such as MARPOL and the London (Dumping) Convention, and the UN Economic Commission for Europe (UNECE) for the Long-Range Transboundary Air Pollution Convention. At least one MEA—the Ramsar wetlands treaty—designates an NGO, the International Union for the Conservation of Nature, as its secretariat, although this has been somewhat problematic and the parties are considering switching the secretariat from IUCN, so that it has the same international legal status as other environmental secretariats.

33. The International Whaling Convention Secretariat, for example, is an independent institution.

34. *See generally* Jan Klabbers, *An Introduction to International Institutional Law* (Cambridge: Cambridge University Press, 2002).

35. For a description and critique of functionalist approaches, see Michael Barnett and Martha Finnemore, "The Power of Liberal International Organizations," in Michael Barnett and Raymond Duvall, eds., *Power in Global Governance* (Cambridge: Cambridge University Press, 2005), pp. 161–184. The term *functionalism* is also used in a narrower way in international relations literature to refer to the approach associated with David Mitrany in the 1930s, who stressed the common interests of states in global integration. *See* David Mitrany, *The Progress of International Government* (New Haven, CT: Yale University Press, 1933).

36. Duncan Snidal, "International Political Economy Approaches to International Institutions," in Jagdeep S. Bhandari and Alan O. Sykes, eds., *Economic Dimensions in International Law: Comparative and Empirical Perspectives* (Cambridge: Cambridge University Press, 1997), pp. 477–512, at 494–495.

37. *See* Frank Biermann and Steffen Bauer, "Assessing the Effectiveness of Intergovernmental Organisations in International Environmental Politics," *Global Environmental Change* 14 (2004), pp. 189–193.

38. Simon Lyster, *International Wildlife Law* (Cambridge: Grotius Publications, 1985), p. 124 (referring to the Western Hemisphere Convention as the "sleeping treaty").

39. Because the Ramsar Convention, as originally adopted, did not provide for amendments, the parties had to use a two-stage process, first adopting a protocol that established an amendment procedure and then using this new procedure to adopt an amendment that provided for regular meetings of the Ramsar parties.

40. Prior to the establishment of the Antarctic Treaty Secretariat, secretariat services had been performed on a rotating basis by the state scheduled to host the next meeting of the parties. This is still the case for the International Coral Reef Initiative.

41. Rosemary Sandford, "International Environmental Treaty Secretariats: Stage-Hands or Actors?" in Helge Ole Bergesen and Georg Parmann, eds., *Green Globe Yearbook of International Cooperation on Environment and Development 1994* (Oxford: Oxford University Press, 1994), pp. 17–29.

42. Frank Biermann and Bernd Siebenhüner, "Managers of Global Change: The Core Findings of the MANUS Project," *Global Governance Working Paper No. 25* (Amsterdam: Global Governance Project, July 2007), p. 25.

43. CITES art. XII.

44. *See, e.g.*, Michael N. Barnett and Martha Finnemore, "The Politics, Power, and Pathologies of International Organizations," *International Organization* 53 (1999), pp. 699–732.

45. Barnett and Finnemore, "Power of Liberal International Organizations," 169–175.

46. Wolfgang E. Burhenne, "The Role of NGOs," in Winfried Lang, ed., *Sustainable Development and International Law* (London: Graham & Trotman, 1995), pp. 207–211, at 207.

47. The total number of non-governmental organizations of all types worldwide has been estimated to be 51,509, although almost 24,000 of these may be categorized as inactive or nonconventional. Union of International Associations, ed., *Yearbook of International Organizations: Guide to Global Civil Society Networks, 2005/2006, vol. 5: Statistics, Visualizations and Patterns* (München, Germany: K. G. Saur, 2005), p. 3.

48. In recognition of this fact, the climate change regime now distinguishes between ENGOs (environmental NGOs) and RNGOs (research NGOs).

49. Kal Raustiala and David G. Victor, "Conclusions," in David G. Victor, Kal Raustiala, and Eugene B. Skolnikoff, eds., *The Implementation and Effectiveness of International Environmental Commitments: Theory and Practice* (Cambridge, MA: MIT Press, 1998), pp. 659–707, at 664–665.

50. In the last years of the Clinton Administration, for example, the leading officials on climate change at the Environmental Protection Agency (EPA) and the Energy Department had NGO backgrounds.

51. *See*, generally Grant Jordan, *Shell, Greenpeace and Brent Spar* (Basingstoke, U.K.: Palgrave Macmillan, 2001). Brent Spar was an abandoned oil storage and tanker loading buoy in the North Sea, operated by Shell. In 1995, Shell applied to sink the platform in deep waters off the Scottish coast, arguing that this was the safest option. Greenpeace organized a worldwide campaign against the plan and occupied Brent Spar for several weeks. Eventually, Shell withdrew its application.

52. *See, e.g.*, Raymond Bonner, *At the Hand of Man: Peril and Hope for Africa's Wildlife* (New York: Vintage, 1994).

53. In opposing the U.S.–Peru Free Trade Agreement, for example, several environmental groups wrote a letter to Congress that began, "[o]n behalf of our one million members, we urge you to oppose the U.S.-Peru Free Trade Agreement." Letter by Defenders of Wildlife, Friends of the Earth, Sierra Club, Center for International Environmental Law, and Earthjustice to Congress (March 10, 2006).

54. *See* Peter J. Spiro, "New Global Potentates: Nongovernmental Organizations and the 'Unregulated' Marketplace," *Cardozo Law Review* 18 (1996), pp. 957–969.

55. Daniel C. Esty, "Non-Governmental Organizations at the World Trade Organization: Cooperation, Competition, or Exclusion," *Journal of International Economic Law* 1 (1998), pp. 123–147, at 132.

56. Thomas Princen and Matthias Finger, *Environmental NGOs in World Politics: Linking the Local and the Global* (London: Routledge, 1994), p. 34.

57. *See* Peter J. Spiro, "Non-Governmental Organizations and Civil Society," in Daniel Bodansky, Jutta Brunnée, and Ellen Hey, eds., *The Oxford Handbook of International Environmental Law* (Oxford: Oxford University Press, 2007), pp. 770–790.

58. For an interesting case study involving congressional lobbying, see Barbara J. Bramble and Gareth Porter, "Non-Governmental Organizations and the Making of US International Environmental Policy," in Andrew Hurrell and Benedict Kinsbury, eds., *The International Politics of the Environment: Actors, Interests, and Institutions* (Oxford: Oxford University Press, 1992), pp. 313–353, at 325–336. Bramble and Porter describe the efforts of U.S. NGOs in the 1970s to push the U.S. government to support environmental reform in the World Bank. NGOs began by lobbying congressional staffers to hold hearings about the World Bank's environmental performance. At the hearings, the NGOs presented evidence about World Bank projects that caused significant environmental harm. Working with congressional staffers, NGOs developed recommendations for the Treasury Department, which represents the United States on the World Bank's Board of Governors, and continued to build public pressure on the executive through use of the media to publicize the Bank's environmental failures. They also developed alliances with NGOs in developing countries to support World Bank reform. Whether as a result of their efforts or for independent reasons, the World Bank has, in fact, become greener. It established an Environment Department in 1988, an environmental assessment procedure in 1989, and an inspection panel procedure (which can hear complaints by individuals) in 1993. In 2001 it adopted a comprehensive environmental strategy. Similarly, Kal Raustiala attributes the success of U.S. environmental groups in lobbying the Clinton Administration for inclusion of a citizens submission process under the North American Agreement on Environmental Cooperation (NAAEC) to the fact that the Administration needed congressional approval of the NAAEC. Kal Raustiala, "Police Patrols and Fire Alarms in the NAAEC," *Loyola of Los Angeles International and Comparative Law Review* 26 (2004), pp. 389–413, at 401.

59. *Japan Whaling Association v. American Cetacean Society,* 478 U.S. 221 (1986).

60. *Earth Island Institute v. Christopher,* 20 Ct. Int'l Trade 1221 (1996), *vacated, Earth Island Institute v. Albright,* 147 F.3d 1352 (Fed. Cir. 1998) (holding that the Court of International Trade lacked jurisdiction to rule on a motion by environmental and animal protection organizations to enforce prior judgment).

61. *See generally* Jonas Ebbesson, "Public Participation," in Bodansky, Brunnée, and Hey, eds., *Oxford Handbook of International Environmental Law*, 681–703.

62. The Aarhus Convention on Access to Information, Public Participation in Decision-Making and Access to Justice in Environmental Matters was adopted in 1998 by the UN Economic Commission for Europe, which includes as members not only European states but also the United States and Canada, as well as several Asian states that were formerly part of the Soviet Union.

63. *See* Alan Boyle and Christine Chinkin, *The Making of International Law* (New York: Oxford University Press, 2007), p. 57.

64. Second Meeting of the Parties to the Convention on Access to Information, Public Participation in Decision-Making and Access to Justice in Environmental Matters, Almaty, Kazakhstan, May 25–27, 2005, *Decision II/4: Promoting the Application of the Aarhus Convention in International Forums*, UN Doc. ECE/MP.PP/2005/2/Add.5 (June 20, 2005).

65. The CITES Secretariat has entered into a formal arrangement with TRAFFIC, pursuant to art. XII(1), which authorizes the secretariat to work with "suitable" NGOs.

66. Article 7.6 of the UN Framework Convention on Climate Change is fairly typical. It allows any non-governmental body to participate in the COPs as observers, unless at least one-third of the parties object.

67. The World Bank Inspection Panel is a three-member body created in 1993 to improve the Bank's accountability and to ensure that it adheres to its social and environmental policies and procedures. The Inspection Panel can hear claims from people who believe that they have been harmed by Bank projects. The Panel functions as a fact-finding body, conducting investigations of alleged violations by the Bank of its own policies and procedures. In addition to the World Bank Inspection Panel, several international agreements allow individuals to trigger international review mechanisms. Under the North American Agreement on Environmental Cooperation art. 14, individuals can make submissions to the Commission on Environmental Cooperation about a party's failure to enforce its own environmental laws. Similarly, under Article 15 of the 1998 Aarhus Convention, individuals may make submissions directly to the Compliance Committee about alleged cases of non-compliance.

68. Benjamin Cashore, Graeme Auld, and Deanna Newsom, *Governing through Markets: Forest Certification and the Emergence of Non-State Authority* (New Haven, CT: Yale University Press, 2004); Errol E. Meidinger, "The New Environmental Law: Forest Certification," *Buffalo Environmental Law Journal* 10 (2002–2003), pp. 211–300; http://www.fsc.org/ (accessed 2/3/09).

69. The World Commission on Dams operated from 1998 to 2000, and included members from government, international organizations, industry, NGOs and academia.

70. For an excellent analysis on the role of business, to which this section is much indebted, see Stephen R. Ratner, "Business," in Bodansky, Brunnée, and Hey, eds., *Oxford Handbook of International Environmental Law*, 807–828.

71. Gunningham, Kagan, and Thornton, *Shades of Green*.

72. Ibid.
73. Of course, industry does not act in isolation; it has a symbiotic relation with individuals, both responding to and helping to shape their demands.
74. For a critique of what he calls the "orthodox" view that international law does not impose duties on states, see Ratner, "Business," 812.
75. *See* Richard L. Herz, "Litigating Environmental Abuses under the Alien Tort Claims Act: A Practical Assessment," *Virginia Journal of International Law* 40 (2000), pp. 545–638.
76. Marc Gunther, "The Green Machine," *Fortune,* July 31, 2006.
77. Michael P. Vandenbergh, "The New Wal-Mart Effect: The Role of Private Contracting in Global Governance," *UCLA Law Review* 54 (2007), pp. 913–970.
78. In Japan, industry influence on the whaling issue is so great that a Japanese Whaling Association member has often headed the Japanese delegation to the International Whaling Commission. Chasek, Downie, and Brown, *Global Environmental Politics,* 89.
79. www.equator-principles.com (accessed 1/30/09).
80. www.iccwbo.org (accessed 1/30/09).

7. Overcoming Obstacles to International Cooperation

1. Mario J. Molina and F. S. Rowland, "Stratospheric Sink for Chlorofluoromethanes: Chlorine Atom-Catalysed Destruction of Ozone," *Nature* 249 (1974), pp. 810–812.
2. Daniel Bodansky, "Prologue to the Climate Change Convention," in Irving M. Mintzer and J. A. Leonard, eds., *Negotiating Climate Change: The Inside Story of the Rio Convention* (Cambridge: Cambridge University Press, 1994), pp. 45–74.
3. R. Michael M'Gonigle and Mark W. Zacher, *Pollution, Politics and International Law: Tankers at Sea* (Berkeley: University of California Press, 1979).
4. Some ozone-depleting substances, such as chlorofluorocarbons (CFCs) and hydrochlorofluorocarbons (HCFCs), are also greenhouse gases, which leads to a partial overlap between the two issues.
5. Daniel J. Fiorino, *Making Environmental Policy* (Berkeley: University of California Press, 1995), pp. 3–4.
6. John D. Graham and Jonathan B. Wiener, eds., *Risk vs. Risk: Tradeoffs in Protecting Health and the Environment* (Cambridge, MA: Harvard University Press, 1995), p. 234.
7. Paul Slovic, Baruch Fischhoff and Sarah Lichtenstein, "Rating the Risks," *Environment* 21 (April 1979), pp. 14–20, 36–39. For reasons that are sometimes obvious and sometimes difficult to understand, these factors play out differently in different countries, depending on the issue. Genetically modified organisms (GMOs) are a bigger issue in Europe than the United States. Conversely, ozone depletion became a policy priority in the United States before Europe. *See, e.g.,* Sheila Jasanoff, *Risk Management and Political Culture: A Comparative Study of Science in the Policy Context* (New York: Russell Sage Foundation, 1986); Norman J. Vig and Michael G. Faure, eds., *Green Giants?:*

Environmental Policies of the United States and the European Union (Cambridge, MA: MIT Press, 2004); David Vogel, "The Politics of Risk Regulation in Europe and the United States," *Yearbook of European Environmental Law* 3 (2003), pp. 31–42.

8. David A. King, "Climate Change Science: Adapt, Mitigate, or Ignore?" *Science* 303 (January 9, 2004), pp. 176–177.

9. *E.g.*, Bjørn Lomborg, *The Skeptical Environmentalist: Measuring the Real State of the World* (Cambridge: Cambridge University Press, 2001); Aaron Wildavsky, *But Is It True?: A Citizen's Guide to Environmental Health and Safety Issues* (Cambridge, MA: Harvard University Press, 1997).

10. In 2000, the National Academy of Sciences issued a report concluding that the surface warming trend is "undoubtedly real" and that "[t]he disparity between surface and upper air trends in no way invalidates the conclusion that surface temperature has been rising." National Research Council, *Reconciling Observations of Global Temperature Change* (Washington, DC: National Academy Press, 2000), p. 2. Nonetheless, the debate has continued. *See, e.g.,* Richard S. Lindzen and Constantine Giannitsis, "Reconciling Observations of Global Temperature Change," *Geophysical Research Letters* 29 (2002), 10.1029/2001GL014704.

11. Richard B. Alley et al., "Summary for Policymakers," in Susan Solomon et al., eds., *Climate Change 2007: The Physical Science Basis* (Cambridge: Cambridge University Press, 2007), pp. 1–18, at 10 (emphasis in original). "Very likely" corresponds to a greater than 90 percent probability in the IPCC's estimate. Susan Solomon et al., "Technical Summary," in Solomon et al., eds., *Climate Change 2007,* 19–91, at 23.

12. According to a Rasmussen Reports poll in January 2009, only 41 percent of the American public think global warming is due to human causes, and 44 percent think it is due to natural planetary trends. www.rasmussenreports.com (accessed 2/4/09).

13. If the economy grows quickly, for example, emissions will tend to increase; if lower-emitting technologies progress, however, emissions will tend to decrease.

14. William A. Nitze, "Acid Rain: A United States Policy Perspective," in Daniel Barstow Magraw, ed., *International Law and Pollution* (Philadelphia: University of Pennsylvania Press, 1991), pp. 329–343. Net exporters of acid rain in Europe played the same game, opposing emissions controls on the ground that more research was needed. Jørgen Wettestad, "The Convention on Long-Range Transboundary Pollution," in Edward L. Miles et al., *Environmental Regime Effectiveness: Confronting Theory with Evidence* (Cambridge, MA: MIT Press, 2002), pp. 197–221, at 206.

15. *See* Lomborg, *Skeptical Environmentalist.*

16. David Broder, "Beyond Folk Songs and Flowers," *Washington Post,* April 22, 1990, p. B7.

17. *See* Daniel Bell, *The End of Ideology* (New York: Free Press, 1960); Francis Fukuyama, *The End of History and the Last Man* (New York: Free Press, 1992).

18. Quoted in Jonathan Baert Wiener, "On the Political Economy of Global Environmental Regulation," *Georgetown Law Journal* 87 (1999), pp. 749–794, at 765 note 73.
19. UNFCCC art. 2.
20. Wettestad, "Convention on Long-Range Transboundary Pollution," 205–207.
21. For example, in the European negotiations on acid rain in the 1980s, exporters of acid rain pollution, such as England and Germany, initially opposed controls and called for more research, while Scandinavian countries, who are big importers of pollution, supported an agreement. Ibid., 206.
22. Detlef Sprinz and Tapani Vaahtoranta, "The Interest-Based Explanation of International Environmental Policy," *International Organization* 48 (1994), pp. 77–105, at 80–81.
23. This same conflict between individual and collective interests can arise even in bilateral contexts (as the two-person prisoner's dilemma game teaches us). For simplicity, I focus here on the global level because, in bilateral cases, (1) more of the pollution damage is likely to be incurred domestically, giving states an individual (as opposed to just a collective) interest to stop polluting (in the U.S.-Canada acid rain case, for example, U.S. acid rain caused significant damage to the northeastern part of the United States), and (2) agreement is easier to achieve with fewer parties, as I discuss below.
24. *See* Steven J. Brams and Alan D. Taylor, *Fair Division: From Cake-Cutting to Dispute Resolution* (Cambridge: Cambridge University Press, 1996). Although fair division games suggest that the actors apply a logic of appropriateness, one could also attempt to explain them in terms of a consequentialist logic by assuming that the players care more about relative than absolute gains. In this case, a small piece of cake might well leave the second player worse off, relative to the other player, than before the game began.
25. The classic work on this subject is Mancur Olson, *The Logic of Collective Action* (Cambridge, MA: Harvard University Press, 1965).
26. Elinor Ostrom, *Governing the Commons: The Evolution of Institutions for Collective Action* (Cambridge: Cambridge University Press, 1990).
27. For an outstanding analysis of the strategic issues involved in international cooperation, see generally Barrett, *Environment and Statecraft.*
28. The Bush Administration's announcement in March 2001 that it was rejecting Kyoto responded to expressions of concern by industry that the Administration might be prepared to renegotiate Kyoto.
29. Dennis C. Mueller, *Public Choice III* (Cambridge: Cambridge University Press, 2003).
30. *See, e.g.*, Wiener, "Political Economy of Global Environmental Regulation," 754–758 (critiquing this rent-seeking view); Daniel Farber, "Politics and Procedure in Environmental Law," *Journal of Law, Economics, and Organization* 8 (1992), pp. 59–81, at 60 (same).
31. For example, some conservatives explain environmental regulation on the basis that it provides concentrated benefits to environmental special interest groups, while imposing larger but more diffuse costs on the general public, through the drag that it imposes on the economy. *See, e.g.*, Michael S. Greve

and Fred L. Smith Jr., eds., *Environmental Politics: Public Costs, Private Rewards* (New York: Praeger, 1992). Or, alternatively, environmental regulations could be explained in public choice terms as providing disguised benefits to some industries at the expense of others. These theories are described and criticized in Farber, "Politics and Procedure."

32. Wiener, "Political Economy of Global Environmental Regulation," 769. Of course, states still seek outcomes that serve their private interests—for example, through the adoption of a regulatory approach that they already use or that favors their industry—and sometimes may bamboozle benighted states into going along. Ibid., 771–773.

33. George W. Downs, David M. Rocke, and Peter N. Barsoom, "Is the Good News about Compliance Good News about Cooperation?" *International Organization* 50 (1996), pp. 379–406.

34. For example, Farber argues that the early 1970s, when many of the major U.S. environmental statutes were enacted, represents a "republican moment," when civil republicanism dominated. Farber, "Politics and Procedure," 66. Hybrid approaches try to synthesize public choice and civic republicanism by explaining environmental regulation as an alliance between "Baptists and bootleggers"—that is, between those seeking to provide public goods and those seeking to garner private benefits. Wiener, "Political Economy of Global Environmental Regulation," 760.

35. *See generally* Oran R. Young and Gail Osherenko, eds., *Polar Politics: Creating International Environmental Regimes* (Ithaca, NY: Cornell University Press, 1993), pp. 8–20 (analyzing explanations of regime formation based on power, interests, and knowledge).

36. Peter M. Haas, *Saving the Mediterranean: The Politics of International Environmental Cooperation* (New York: Columbia University Press, 1990) (emphasizing the role of "epistemic communities").

37. For an excellent history of this process, see M'Gonigle and Zacher, *Pollution, Politics, and International Law.*

38. Elizabeth R. DeSombre, *Domestic Sources of International Environmental Policy: Industry, Environmentalists, and U.S. Power* (Cambridge, MA: MIT Press, 2000), pp. 39–47. On the ozone case, see generally Richard Elliot Benedick, *Ozone Diplomacy: New Directions in Safeguarding the Planet* (Cambridge, MA: Harvard University Press, enlarged ed. 1998).

39. Martha Finnemore and Kathryn Sikkink, "International Norm Dynamics and Political Change," *International Organization* 52 (1998), pp. 887–917, at 898.

40. *See generally* DeSombre, *Domestic Sources.*

41. Anthony Bergin, "The Politics of Antarctic Minerals: The Greening of White Australia," *Australian Journal of Political Science* 26 (1991), pp. 216–239 (concluding that the Australian position was "largely determined" by domestic politics).

42. *E.g.,* Oran R. Young, "Political Leadership and Regime Formation: On the Development of Institutions in International Society," *International Organization* 45 (1991), pp. 281–308; Gunnar Sjöstedt, "Leadership in Multilateral

Negotiations: Crisis or Transition?" in Peter Berton, Hiroshi Kimura, and I. William Zartman, eds., *International Negotiations: Actors, Structure/Process, Values* (New York: St. Martin's Press, 1999), pp. 223–253.

43. Finnemore and Sikkink, "International Norm Dynamics," 895, 902 (borrowing a term from Cass Sunstein).

44. The three functions are described as the "three C's" by Peter Haas, Robert Keohane, and Marc Levy in *Institutions for the Earth*. They suggest that international institutions (1) raise concern about international environmental issues, and thus play an agenda-setting role; (2) enhance the contractual environment, making possible agreements; and (3) build capacity to implement solutions, particularly in developing countries. Peter M. Haas, Robert O. Keohane, and Marc A. Levy, eds., *Institutions for the Earth: Sources of Effective International Environmental Protection* (Cambridge, MA: MIT Press, 1993). Abram Chayes and Antonia Handler Chayes take a similar approach in *The New Sovereignty: Compliance with International Regulatory Agreements* (Cambridge, MA: Harvard University Press, 1995).

45. Miles et al., *Environmental Regime Effectiveness*, 467–468 (concluding that two-thirds of the regimes they studied fostered transnational learning, in some cases helping to redefine a problem and making it less intractable).

46. Wettestad, "Convention on Long-Range Transboundary Air Pollution," 208.

47. Chayes and Chayes, *New Sovereignty*.

48. Barrett, *Environment and Statecraft*.

49. Brenton attributes Japanese acceptance of the Montreal Protocol, in part, to a fear of trade sanctions. Tony Brenton, *The Greening of Machiavelli: The Evolution of International Environmental Politics* (London: Earthscan, 1994), p. 140.

50. James K. Sebenius, "Negotiation Arithmetic: Adding and Subtracting Issues and Parties," *International Organization* 37 (1983), pp. 281–316, at 282.

51. J. H. Dales, *Pollution, Property and Prices: An Essay in Policy-Making and Economics* (Toronto: Toronto University Press, 1968).

8. Negotiating Agreements

1. Ronald B. Mitchell, *International Environmental Law Database Project*, http://iea.uoregon.edu (accessed 2/8/09).

2. *See generally* Edith Brown Weiss, "International Environmental Law: Contemporary Issues and the Emergence of a New World Order," *Georgetown Law Journal* 81 (1993), pp. 675–710, at 697.

3. *See generally* Thomas Gehring, *Dynamic International Regimes: Institutions for International Environmental Governance* (Frankfurt: Peter Lang, 1994).

4. Kal Raustiala, "Form and Substance in International Agreements," *American Journal of International Law* 99 (2005), pp. 581–614, at 582–583.

5. *E.g.*, Kenneth W. Abbott and Duncan Snidal, "Hard and Soft Law in International Governance," *International Organization* 54 (2000), pp. 421–456, at 441–444; Charles Lipson, "Why Are Some International Agreements Informal?" *International Organization* 45 (1991), pp. 495–538.

6. For example, President Ford made an explicit statement when adopting the 1975 Helsinki Accords that the agreement was not legally binding. "European Security Conference Discussed by President Ford," 73 *Department of State Bulletin* (1975), pp. 204–206, at 205 ("I would emphasize that the document . . . is [not] . . . legally binding.").

7. An amusing personal story illustrates this point. As a junior lawyer at the State Department, I was once sent to negotiate an agreement on whaling but, by mistake, failed to go through the proper formalities to obtain negotiating authority (what is known in the State Department as Circular-175 authority, after the instrument that lays out the required procedures). In the midst of the negotiations, I realized my oversight. My solution? I proposed changing the word "shall" to "will" throughout the document, to make the agreement purely factual in character (in effect, a statement of intent about what the parties "will" do), thereby depriving it of any legally binding effect.

8. Vienna Convention on the Law of Treaties art. 34.

9. Although treaties based on coercion are invalid, treaty law defines coercion very narrowly. Ibid., arts. 51–52.

10. *See* www.fsc.org (accessed 2/10/09).

11. *See, e.g., Trans World Airlines, Inc. v. Franklin Mint Corp.,* 466 U.S. 243, 253 (1984) ("A treaty is in the nature of a contract between nations"). In distinguishing between legal and non-legal agreements, Raustiala uses the terms *contracts* and *pledges,* reflecting the contractual character of treaties. Raustiala, "Form and Substance," 581.

12. For example, treaty law does not include any doctrine of consideration. *See generally, e.g.,* Friedrich Kratochwil, "The Limits of Contract," *European Journal of International Law* 5 (1994), pp. 465–491; Evangelos Raftopoulos, *The Inadequacy of the Contractual Analogy in the Law of Treaties* (Athens: Hellenic Institute of International and Foreign Law, 1990).

13. *See* Pamela S. Chasek, *Earth Negotiations: Analyzing Thirty Years of Environmental Diplomacy* (Tokyo: United Nations University Press, 2001), pp. 30–31.

14. *Cf.* Joost Pauwelyn, "A Typology of Multilateral Treaty Obligations: Are WTO Obligations Bilateral or Collective in Nature?," *European Journal of International Law* 14 (2003), pp. 907–951 (distinguishing between bilateral and collective treaties).

15. Kratochwil, "Limits of Contract," 472.

16. Reinhold Niebuhr, *Moral Man and Immoral Society: A Study in Ethics and Politics* (New York: Charles Scribner's Sons, 1932), p. 84 (quoting Haller).

17. Although, as discussed in a later section of this chapter, the situation is more complicated for multilateral treaties that can come into effect without universal participation and have negative effects for non-parties. In such cases, a state's preferred outcome might be no treaty, but given the existence of the treaty, it prefers party to non-party status. This issue is explored in Lloyd Gruber, *Ruling the World: Power Politics and the Rise of Supranational Institutions* (Princeton, NJ: Princeton University Press, 2000).

18. The range of possible agreements that would leave both sides better off is usually referred to as the contract zone or zone of agreement. *See generally* Howard Raiffa, *The Art and Science of Negotiation: How to Resolve Conflicts and Get the Best out of Bargaining* (Cambridge, MA: Harvard University Press, 1982).

19. Ibid., 33, 131.

20. Scott Barrett, *Environment and Statecraft: The Strategy of Environmental Treaty-Making* (Oxford: Oxford University Press, 2003), pp. 79–80.

21. This is the result we examined in Chapter 3 in discussing the Coase Theorem. Under the 1976 Bonn Convention on the Protection of the Rhine Against Chemical Pollution, for example, the state furthest downstream (the Netherlands) pays the largest share of the abatement costs, whereas the state furthest upstream (Switzerland) pays the least, by a ratio of almost 6 to 1. Ibid., 129–131. Similarly, the Montreal Protocol on Substances that Deplete the Ozone Layer involves side payments (that is, financial assistance) to developing countries to encourage them to participate.

22. A similar dynamic seems to have been at work in the recent controversy over the U.S.-Colombian Free Trade Agreement, *available at* www.ustr.gov (accessed 2/10/09), which would provide for the mutual elimination of tariffs and other barriers to trade. At first glance, the debate over this agreement appears bizarre. On the one hand, Colombia currently imposes duties on U.S. goods, which it would have to eliminate; on the other hand, the United States has already removed most of its tariffs on Colombian goods and is thus already doing what the treaty would require. So, ordinarily, one might expect the United States to support the agreement and Colombia to oppose it. But, in fact, the reverse was true: Colombia strongly supported the agreement and congressional Democrats opposed it, insisting that they would consent to the agreement only if Colombia agreed to reform its labor laws. What might account for these seemingly odd positions? One plausible explanation is that congressional Democrats opposed the agreement because it would limit the ability of the United States to reintroduce tariffs in the future and Colombia wanted the agreement for this very same reason.

23. Detlef Sprinz and Tapani Vaahtoranta, "The Interest-Based Explanation of International Environmental Policy," *International Organization* 48 (1994), pp. 77–105.

24. I discuss these entry-into-force issues in a later section.

25. *See* Gruber, *Ruling the World.*

26. Barrett, *Environment and Statecraft,* 33–37.

27. In the language of game theory, the current participants in the Kyoto Protocol do not represent a "minimum viable coalition": without the participation of the United States and China, the Kyoto Protocol does not provide them with sufficient environmental benefits to justify their implementation costs.

28. Barrett, *Environment and Statecraft,* 228.

29. Marc A. Levy, "European Acid Rain: The Power of Tote-Board Diplomacy," in Peter M. Haas, Robert O. Keohane, and Marc A. Levy, eds., *Institutions*

for the Earth: Sources of Effective International Environmental Protection (Cambridge, MA: MIT Press, 1993), pp. 75–132

30. Scott Barrett (private communication with author).

31. For this reason, Putnam characterizes international negotiations as "two-level games," with both an international and a domestic component. Robert D. Putnam, "Diplomacy and Domestic Politics: The Logic of Two-Level Games," *International Organization* 42 (1988), pp. 427–460.

32. Different theories of domestic politics posit different mechanisms for transmission of individual preferences to government actors. In a democracy, elected officials are likely to win because they share the values and preferences of their constituents. Even when they do not, they may believe that they have a duty to reflect the views of their constituents or may simply do so out of a self-interested desire to be reelected.

33. This hypothesis is at best only a partial explanation and does not account for why the United States led Europe in the Montreal Protocol negotiations.

34. For an application of this lock-in theory to human rights law, see Andrew Moravcsik, "The Origins of Human Rights Regimes: Democratic Delegation in Postwar Europe," *International Organization* 54 (2000), pp. 217–252.

35. On precommitment theory generally, see Steven R. Ratner, "Precommitment Theory and International Law: Starting a Conversation," *Texas Law Review* 81 (2003), pp. 2055–2081.

36. For an excellent analysis of the different phases in treaty negotiations, see Chasek, *Earth Negotiations.* For general analysis, see Bertram I. Spector, Gunnar Sjöstedt, and I. William Zartman, eds., *Negotiating International Regimes: Lessons Learned from the United Nations Conference on Environment and Development (UNCED)* (London: Graham and Trotman, 1994).

37. This is for the moment purely hypothetical, as the UN General Assembly decided to put off discussion of a forest convention until 2015. Non-legally Binding Instrument on All Types of Forests, G. A. Res. 62/98, UN Doc. A/RES/62/98 (January 31, 2008).

38. Berlin Mandate, Conference of the Parties to the UN Framework Convention on Climate Change on its First Session (COP-1), Berlin, March 28–April 7, 1995, *Final Report,* Dec. 1/CP.1 para. 2(b), UN Doc. FCCC/CP/1995/7/Add.1 (June 6, 1995).

39. Bali Action Plan, Conference of the Parties to the UN Framework Convention on Climate Change on its Thirteenth Session (COP-13), Bali, December 3–15, 2007, *Final Report,* Dec. 1/CP.13 UN Doc. FCCC/CP/2007/6/ Add.1 (March 14, 2008).

40. As Pamela Chasek notes, "The formation of groups or alliances is one of the means of managing the complexities inherent in large-scale multilateral negotiations." Chasek, *Earth Negotiations,* 139.

41. In United Nations forums, developing countries usually negotiate as a single bloc—the so-called Group of 77 (or G-77), named for the seventy-seven original participants. To maintain their collective influence, they have generally stuck together in the climate change negotiations, even though their interests span the entire spectrum, from small-island states, which risk devastation

from sea-level rise, to oil-producing states, which oppose any actions that might limit demand for oil.

42. *See* Arnold N. Pronto, "Some Thoughts on the Making of International Law," *European Journal of International Law* 19 (2008), pp. 601–616, at 607 (discussing emphasis on consensus adoption procedure in contemporary international law in Alan Boyle and Christine Chinkin, *The Making of International Law* [New York: Oxford University Press, 2007]).

43. For examples of each technique, see Daniel Bodansky, "The United Nations Framework Convention on Climate Change: A Commentary," *Yale Journal of International Law* 18 (1993), pp. 451–558, at 492–493.

44. In the UN Framework Convention on Climate Change negotiations, for example, states were unable to agree even that they should be required to "report" because some thought the term *report* suggested an intrusive, interventionist process. As a result, the Convention uses the phrase "communication of information" instead.

45. Jonas Ebbesson, "The Notion of Public Participation in International Environmental Law," *Yearbook of International Environmental Law* 8 (1997), pp. 51–97.

46. Vienna Convention on the Law of Treaties art. 18(a).

47. Peter H. Sand, *Lessons Learned in Global Environmental Governance* (Washington, DC: World Resources Institute, 1990), pp. 15–16.

48. For a negotiations theory analysis of the problem of breadth, see James K. Sebenius, "Negotiation Arithmetic: Adding and Subtracting Issues and Parties," *International Organization* 37 (1983), pp. 281–316; *see also* Barrett, *Environment and Statecraft,* 153–158.

49. In general, treaties determine who may participate through their signature provision, which defines which states are eligible to sign the treaty.

50. Cartagena Convention arts. 25, 27(2).

51. Antarctic Treaty art. IX(2) (limiting full participation to states that demonstrate their interest in Antarctica "by conducting substantial scientific research activity there"). Although the Treaty couches this requirement in terms of "demonstrating an interest" in Antarctica, it can also be conceptualized in terms of expertise.

52. Whaling Convention preamble, para. 8.

53. This is the approach of the North Atlantic Marine Mammal Commission (NAMMCO), which was established by Norway, Iceland, and Greenland in 1992.

54. Game theorists refer to the number of countries affected by an externality as N and describe different games as N-number games. Barrett, *Environment and Statecraft,* 153–155.

55. Fish Stocks Agreement art. 8.

56. Antarctic Treaty art. IX(2).

57. Whaling Convention preamble, para. 2.

58. This discussion draws on the excellent analysis by Scott Barrett in "An Economic Theory of International Environmental Law," in Daniel Bodansky, Jutta Brunnée, and Ellen Hey, eds., *The Oxford Handbook of International*

Environmental Law (Oxford: Oxford University Press, 2007), pp. 231–261, at 247–249.

59. In the case of a so-called tipping treaty, the minimum entry-into-force requirements should be set at the tipping point, where network externalities kick in and give other states an incentive to join. Ibid., 254–255.

60. Kyoto Protocol art. 25.1.

61. MARPOL art. 15(1).

62. UNFCCC art. 23.1.

63. George W. Downs, David M. Rocke, and Peter N. Barsoom, "Is the Good News about Compliance Good News about Cooperation?" *International Organization* 50 (1996), pp. 379–406, at 383.

64. Raustiala, "Form and Substance," 584.

65. Barrett, *Environment and Statecraft*, 8–11.

66. Ramsar Convention art. 3(1).

67. *Compare* 1985 Sulphur Protocol art. 2 (setting 1980 base year) *with* 1988 NO_x Protocol art. 2(1) (allowing states to specify any year prior to 1987 as their base year); *see* Barrett, *Environment and Statecraft*, 162 (explaining U.S. participation in the NO_x but not the SO_2 Protocol on this basis).

68. Montreal Protocol art. 5(1). To qualify for this ten-year grace period, a developing country's consumption of ozone-depleting substances must also be below a specified per capita level.

69. Edward T. Swaine, "Reserving," *Yale Journal of International Law* 31 (2006), pp. 307–366.

70. *See* M. H. Mendelson, "Reservations to the Constitutions of International Organizations," *British Yearbook of International Law* 45 (1971), pp. 137–171 (reservations generally not allowed for constitutional agreements).

71. *See generally* Richard B. Bilder, *Managing the Risks of International Agreement* (Madison: University of Wisconsin Press, 1981).

72. *See generally* Abbott and Snidal, "Hard and Soft Law," 427–430; Raustiala, "Form and Substance," 598.

73. *See generally* M. J. Peterson, "Whalers, Cetologists, Environmentalists, and the International Management of Whaling," *International Organization* 46 (1992), pp. 147–186.

74. *See* John K. Setear, "Ozone, Iteration, and International Law," *Virginia Journal of International Law* 40 (1999), pp. 193–309, at 200–203.

75. Barbara Koremenos, "Loosening the Ties that Bind: A Learning Model of Agreement Flexibility," *International Organization* 55 (2001), pp. 289–325. As Helfer notes, exit clauses "function as an insurance policy, providing a hedge against uncertainty that allows a state to renounce its commitments if the anticipated benefits of cooperation turn out to be overblown." Laurence R. Helfer, "Exiting Treaties," *Virginia Law Review* 91 (2005), pp. 1579–1648, at 1591.

76. Kyoto Protocol art. 3.1.

77. Antarctic Environment Protocol arts. 7, 25 (prohibition on mineral resource activities in Article 7 can be amended only by review conference held at least fifty years after the Protocol's entry into force).

78. Helfer, "Exiting Treaties," 1621–1629.
79. Iceland's temporary withdrawal from the International Convention on the Regulation of Whaling is a notable example. Helfer does not provide statistics specifically on environmental agreements, but cites some examples in his study of treaty exit. *See* Helfer, "Exiting Treaties."
80. The development of MARPOL illustrates this point.
81. As discussed earlier, for example, the 2007 Australian election brought the Labor Party to power, which ratified the Kyoto Protocol.
82. For example, DuPont's development of affordable substitutes for chlorofluorocarbons helped make possible the Montreal Protocol.
83. For an example of this argument, see George W. Downs, David M. Rocke, and Peter N. Barsoom, "Managing the Evolution of Multilateralism," *International Organization* 52 (1998), pp. 397–419.
84. Patrick Szell, "The Development of Multilateral Mechanisms for Monitoring Compliance," in Winfried Lang, ed., *Sustainable Development and International Law* (London: Graham & Trotman, 1995), pp. 97–109, at 107. Similarly, Helfer argues that the easier it is for states to exit an agreement, the more willing they will be to negotiate stringent commitments. Helfer, "Exiting Treaties," 1599.
85. Raustiala, "Form and Substance," 602–603.
86. Boockmann and Paul W. Thurner, "Flexibility Provisions in Multilateral Environmental Treaties," *International Environmental Agreements* 6 (2006), pp. 113–135.
87. The most notable counterexample—the Montreal Protocol—is, arguably, the exception that proves the rule. Despite the depth of its commitments, it has attracted near universal participation. According to the Ozone Secretariat website, as of January 29, 2009, the Protocol had 194 parties, leaving only two non-parties: San Marino and Timor-Leste. http://ozone.unep.org (accessed 2/10/09). One factor that may help account for this unusual combination of breadth and depth is the strength of the Protocol's compliance system. For an outstanding analysis of the relation of compliance and participation in the Montreal Protocol regime, see Barrett, *Environment and Statecraft.*
88. Interestingly, multilateral environmental agreements generally specify whatever differential standards apply to different countries, rather than allow states to differentiate their commitments unilaterally through reservations.
89. For example, art. 2(6) of the Montreal Protocol created grandfather rights for facilities under construction by the Soviet Union. Michael Gilligan argues that, in general, in regimes that involve differentiated rather than identical commitments, there is no trade-off between depth and breadth. Michael J. Gilligan, "Is There a Broader-Deeper Trade-off in International Multilateral Agreements?" *International Organization* 58 (2004), pp. 459–484.
90. UNFCCC arts. 4.3, 12.5.
91. *See* Jonathan Baert Wiener, "Global Environmental Regulation: Instrument Choice in Legal Context," *Yale Law Journal* 108 (1999), pp. 677–800.
92. Basel Convention arts. 4(5), 11(1).

93. CITES art. X. In contrast, although the Biosafety Protocol also addresses trade with non-parties, it sets a lower standard for such trade, which needs to be consistent only with the "objectives" of the Protocol. Biosafety Protocol art. 24(1).

94. Montreal Protocol art. 4.

95. For a general history and analysis of the deepening and widening of the European Union, see Richard E. Baldwin, "Sequencing and Depth of Regional Economic Integration: Lessons for the Americas from Europe," *World Economy* 31 (2008), pp. 5–30; *see also* Downs et al., "Managing the Evolution" (discussing advantages of this approach).

96. *E.g.*, Abbott and Snidal, "Hard and Soft Law," 441; Raustiala, "Form and Substance," 593.

97. For an excellent analysis and critique of the framework convention-protocol approach, see George W. Downs, Kyle W. Danish, and Peter N. Barsoom, "The Transformational Model of International Regime Design: Triumph of Hope or Experience?" *Columbia Journal of Transnational Law* 38 (2000), pp. 465–514.

98. *See* www.unepmap.org (accessed 2/11/09) (providing the history and text of Barcelona Convention and its Protocols).

99. *See* www.unece.org (accessed 2/11/09) (providing the history and text of LRTAP and its Protocols).

100. *See* www.cms.int (accessed 2/11/09) (providing the history and text of Convention on Migratory Species, subagreements, and MOUs).

101. Downs, Danish, and Barsoom, "Transformational Model," 503–506.

102. Sand, *Lessons Learned,* 15.

103. Rotterdam Convention art. 21.

104. Montreal Protocol art. 6.

105. UNFCCC art. 4.2(d).

106. Whaling Convention art. III(2).

107. CITES art. XV(1)(b).

108. The Scientific Committee of the International Whaling Convention has repeatedly questioned the need for the current moratorium on commercial whaling. In 1993, the chairman of the Scientific Committee resigned in protest, asking "what is the point of having a Scientific Committee if its unanimous recommendations on a matter of primary importance are treated with such contempt?" Letter of Resignation by Philip Hammond, Chairman of the Scientific Committee of the International Whaling Commission, to Dr. Ray Gambell, Secretary of the International Whaling Commission (May 26, 1993).

109. POPs Convention art. 8.

110. Some regional fisheries management regimes now allow legally binding rules for the conduct of fisheries to be adopted by decisions of the parties.

111. *E.g.*, Geoffrey Palmer, "New Ways to Make International Environmental Law," *American Journal of International Law* 86 (1992), pp. 259–283.

112. Daniel Bodansky, "The Legitimacy of International Governance: A Coming Challenge for International Environmental Law?" *American Journal of International Law* 93 (1999), pp. 596–624.

9. Customary (and Not So Customary) Norms

1. *See generally* Arie Trouwborst, *Evolution and Status of the Precautionary Principle in International Law* (The Hague: Kluwer Law International, 2002).
2. *See, e.g.,* Rüdiger Wolfrum, "Purposes and Principles of International Environmental Law," *German Yearbook of International Law* 33 (1990), pp. 308–330, at 313; Restatement (Third) of the Foreign Relations Law of the United States § 601 (1987), comment e; *compare* Daniel G. Partan, "The 'Duty to Inform' in International Environmental Law," *Boston University International Law Journal* 6 (1988), pp. 43–88, at 83 (stating that duty to inform "has finally emerged as a legal duty of all states under general international law," although its customary law status is open to doubt).
3. Michael J. Glennon, "Has International Law Failed the Elephant?" *American Journal of International Law* 84 (1990), pp. 1–41, at 30–32.
4. Anthony D'Amato and Sudhir K. Chopra, "Whales: Their Emerging Right to Life," *American Journal of International Law* 85 (1991), pp. 21–62.
5. *See, e.g.,* Experts Group on Environmental Law of the World Commission on Environment and Development, *Environmental Protection and Sustainable Development: Legal Principles and Recommendations* (London: Graham & Trotman, 1987). For a general discussion of principles of international environmental law, see Philippe Sands, *Principles of International Environmental Law* (Cambridge: Cambridge University Press, 2d ed. 2003).
6. *See, e.g.,* Anthony A. D'Amato, *The Concept of Custom in International Law* (Ithaca, NY: Cornell University Press, 1971), p. 4 ("The questions of how custom comes into being and how it can be changed or modified are wrapped in mystery and illogic"); G. J. H. van Hoof, *Rethinking the Sources of International Law* (Deventer, Netherlands: Kluwer, 1983), p. 85 (noting that "it has become almost customary to start off a discussion of the nature of customary international law with some kind of lamentation signaling to the reader that he is about to embark upon an extremely intricate and complex subject"); Karol Wolfke, *Custom in Present International Law* (Dordrecht, Netherlands: Martinus Nijhoff, 2d rev. ed. 1993), p. xiii (stating that "international custom and customary law still raise the greatest number of doubts and controversies" of any type of international law). According to Manley O. Hudson, even the drafters of the International Court of Justice and International Law Commission statutes "had no very clear idea as to what constituted international custom." *Summary Records of the Second Session,* Yearbook of the International Law Commission 1 (1950), p. 6, UN Doc. No. A/CN.4/Ser. A/1950.
7. *See generally* Michael Hechter and Karl-Dieter Opp, eds., *Social Norms* (New York: Russell Sage Foundation, 2001).
8. The French Academy was founded in 1635 by Cardinal de Richelieu and publishes an "official" dictionary of the French language, the *Dictionnaire de l'Académie française.*

9. *E.g.*, Edna Ullmann-Margalit, *The Emergence of Norms* (Oxford: Oxford University Press, 1977); Robert Axelrod, *The Evolution of Cooperation* (New York: Basic Books, 1984), pp. 73–87; Jon Elster, *The Cement of Society: A Study of Social Order* (Cambridge: Cambridge University Press, 1989).

10. Robert C. Ellickson, *Order Without Law: How Neighbors Settle Disputes* (Cambridge, MA: Harvard University Press, 1991); *see generally* Richard H. McAdams, "The Origin, Development and Regulation of Norms," *Michigan Law Review* 96 (1997), pp. 338–433. Social norms had earlier been studied by law and society scholars, such as Stewart Macauley's seminal work on social norms of contracting. Stewart Macauley, "Non-Contractual Relations in Business: A Preliminary Study," *American Sociological Review* 28 (1963), pp. 55–67.

11. *See, e.g.*, Axelrod, *Evolution of Cooperation*, 73–87 (using game theory to explain the development of informal rules of trench warfare during World War I); *see generally* Robert C. Ellickson, "The Evolution of Social Norms: A Perspective from the Legal Academy," in Hechter and Opp, eds., *Social Norms*, 35–75.

12. Martha Finnemore and Kathryn Sikkink, "International Norm Dynamics and Political Change," *International Organization* 52 (1998), pp. 887–917, at 895–898.

13. Hechter and Opp, eds., *Social Norms*, xiii ("Because of the dearth of empirical research on the emergence of social norms, much of the relevant literature is speculative.").

14. Jon Elster, *Nuts and Bolts for the Social Sciences* (Cambridge: Cambridge University Press, 1989), p. 8 (characterizing functionalist explanations as "just so" stories).

15. *See, e.g., Asylum* Case, 277 (describing custom as a "constant and uniform usage, accepted as law"); Restatement (Third) of the Foreign Relations Law of the United States § 102(2) (1987) ("Customary international law results from a general and consistent practice of states followed by them from a sense of legal obligation.").

16. *E.g.*, Lazare Kopelmanas, "Custom as a Means of the Creation of International Law," *British Yearbook of International Law* 18 (1937), pp. 127–151; Paul Guggenheim, "Les deux éléments de la coutume en droit international," *La Technique et les Principe du Droit Public: Études en l'Honneur de Georges Scelle* 1 (1950), pp. 275–280.

17. *E.g.*, Andrew T. Guzman, *How International Law Works: A Rational Choice Theory* (Oxford: Oxford University Press, 2008), pp. 194–201; Harlan Grant Cohen, "Finding International Law: Rethinking the Doctrine of Sources," *Iowa Law Review* 93 (2007), pp. 65–129; Bin Cheng, "United Nations Resolutions on Outer Space: 'Instant' International Customary Law?" *Indian Journal of International Law* 5 (1965), pp. 23–48.

18. *E.g.*, Frederic L. Kirgis, Jr., "Custom on a Sliding Scale," *American Journal of International Law* 81 (1987), pp. 146–151; *compare* Anthea Elizabeth Roberts, "Traditional and Modern Approaches to Custom: A Reconciliation," *American Journal of International Law* 95 (2001), pp. 757–791; John Tasioulas,

"Customary International Law and the Quest for Global Justice," in Amanda Perreau-Saussine and James Bernard Murphy, eds., *The Nature of Customary Law: Legal, Historical and Philosophical Perspectives* (Cambridge: Cambridge University Press, 2007), pp. 307–335.

19. *See, e.g.,* Thomas M. Franck, *The Power of Legitimacy among Nations* (New York: Oxford University Press, 1990), p. 189 ("[T]here is widespread acceptance by states of the notion that time-and-practice-honored conduct—pedigreed custom—has the capacity to bind states, even when they prefer to act inconsistently with such a customary rule.").

20. H. L. A. Hart, *The Concept of Law* (Oxford: Clarendon Press, 2d ed. 1994), pp. 54–61 (distinguishing between habits and rules).

21. Christine Horne, "Sociological Perspectives on the Emergence of Social Norms," in Hechter and Opp, eds., *Social Norms,* 3–34, at 6.

22. What converts a general practice into a legal norm, however, is not the amount or the consistency of the practice, but whether relevant actors accept the norm as reflecting a legal obligation—whether *opinio juris* develops.

23. Some have criticized the formulation of customary law in Article 38(1)(b) of the Statute of the International Court of Justice (ICJ), which identifies, as a source of international law, "international custom as evidence of a general practice accepted as law," on the grounds that this formulation gets matters backward—a general practice accepted as law is evidence of custom, not the other way around. *E.g.,* Rosalyn Higgins, *Problems and Process: International Law and How We Use It* (Oxford: Oxford University. Press, 1994), p. 18. But our analysis suggests that the ICJ statute gets the matter right: a "general practice accepted as law" constitutes a legal norm, and custom is evidence of the existence of such a norm.

24. *See* Paul Schiff Berman, "Global Legal Pluralism," *Southern California Law Review* 80 (2007), pp. 1155–1237.

25. Oscar Schachter, "The Invisible College of International Lawyers," *Northwestern University Law Review* 72 (1977), pp. 217–226.

26. I once heard the State Department's legal adviser observe that he never made an argument to the secretary of state based on customary international law because the argument would not carry any weight. And this was during a Democratic Administration that was, in theory, committed to the rule of international law!

27. *See Case Concerning Military and Paramilitary Activities in and Against Nicaragua,* 98 ("The Court does not consider that, for a rule to be established as customary, the corresponding practice must be in absolutely rigorous conformity with the rule. . . . [T]he Court deems it sufficient that the conduct of states should, in general, be consistent with such rules.").

28. *Compare* Georg Schwarzenberger, "The Inductive Approach to International Law," *Harvard Law Review* 60 (1947), pp. 539–570 (emphasizing study of judicial and arbitral decisions).

29. *See* Franck, *Power of Legitimacy,* 41–42.

30. *Compare* Ronald Dworkin, *Taking Rights Seriously* (Cambridge, MA: Harvard University Press, 1977), p. 105 (naming his ideal judge "Hercules").

Zamora comments that only the International Law Commission "in permanent session with armies of researchers could gather and sift through all the relevant evidence to establish, in a manner acceptable to social scientists, the existence of a rule of customary international law." *See* Stephen Zamora, "Is There Customary International Economic Law?," *German Yearbook of International Law* 32 (1989), pp. 9–42, at 38.

31. Schwarzenberger's comment, that "the immense material from which 'international custom' . . . may be gathered has hardly yet been touched by international lawyers," still rings true today. *See* Schwarzenberger, "Inductive Approach," 563–564.

32. *See, e.g.,* Thomas W. Merrill, "Golden Rules for Transboundary Pollution," *Duke Law Journal* 46 (1997), pp. 931–1019, at 937 ("With isolated exceptions, transboundary pollution as such is subject to very little effective regulation."); Oscar Schachter, "The Emergence of International Environmental Law," *Journal of International Affairs* 44 (1991), pp. 457–493, at 462–463 (admitting that there is only fragmentary evidence that international environmental principles are supported by state practice and *opinio juris*).

33. Günther Handl, "Transboundary Impacts," in Daniel Bodansky, Jutta Brunnée, and Ellen Hey, eds., *The Oxford Handbook of International Environmental Law* (Oxford: Oxford University Press, 2007), pp. 531–549, at 548.

34. Merrill, "Golden Rules," 958–959.

35. Schachter, "Emergence of International Environmental Law," 463.

36. *See, e.g.,* Hiram E. Chodosh, "Neither Treaty Nor Custom: The Emergence of Declarative International Law," *Texas International Law Journal* 26 (1991), pp. 87–124; N. C. H. Dunbar, "The Myth of Customary International Law," *Australian Yearbook of International Law* 8 (1978–1980), pp. 1–19; J. Patrick Kelly, "The Twilight of Customary International Law," *Virginia Journal of International Law* 40 (2000), pp. 449–543; Zamora, "Is There Customary International Economic Law?," 9.

37. Robert Y. Jennings, "The Identification of International Law," in Bin Cheng, ed., *International Law: Theory and Practice* (London: Stevens, 1982), p. 5 (emphasis in original).

38. *See, e.g., Filartiga v. Pena-Irala,* 630 F.2d 876, 884 (2d Cir. 1980) ("Having examined the sources from which customary international law is derived the usage of nations, judicial opinions and the works of jurists we conclude that official torture is now prohibited by the law of nations.").

39. *See* Bruno Simma and Philip Alston, "The Sources of Human Rights Law: Custom, Jus Cogens, and General Principles," *Australian Yearbook of International Law* 12 (1988–1989), pp. 82–108, at 91–92.

40. Patrick M. Norton, "A Law of the Future or a Law of the Past? Modern Tribunals and the International Law of Expropriation," *American Journal of International Law* 85 (1991), pp. 474–505, at 488.

41. Generally, expropriation cases have been resolved through lump-sum settlements in which considerably less than full compensation has been paid. Richard B. Lillich and Burns H. Weston, *International Claims: Their Settlement by Lump Sum Agreements* (Charlottesville: University of Virginia Press, 1975).

42. Robert Y. Jennings, "What Is International Law and How Do We Tell It When We See It?," *Annuaire Suisse de Droit International* 37 (1981), pp. 59–88, at 67.

43. *See* Norton, "Law of the Future," 498 (stating that "[v]irtually all of the recent opinions [of the Iran-US Claims Tribunal] placed their principal reliance on judicial and arbitral precedents").

44. The International Law Association and the Institute of International Law are examples.

45. *See* Partan, "Duty to Inform," 51. Three of these examples were based on treaties. Even with respect to the four instances of notification not based on treaty, whether they were made out of a sense of international legal obligation is, according to Partan, "'problematical'" and "'entirely speculative.'" Ibid., 54.

46. Ibid., 51–53.

47. *Trail Smelter Case*, 1965 (stating that "no State has the right to use or permit the use of its territory in such a manner as to cause injury . . . in or to the territory of another or the properties or persons therein, when the case is of serious consequence and the injury is established by clear and convincing evidence").

48. The *Corfu Channel Case*, also cited by most scholars in support of the duty to prevent transboundary environmental harm, did not involve transboundary pollution. Instead, it enunciated the more general principle that a state may not knowingly allow its territory to be used to injure another state.

49. *Nuclear Weapons Advisory Opinion*, 241–42 (characterizing the duty to prevent transboundary harm as "part of the corpus of international law relating to the environment," without specifying whether the norm is part of customary law or a general principle).

50. *See, e.g.*, Patricia W. Birnie and Alan E. Boyle, *International Law and the Environment* (Oxford: Oxford University Press, 2d ed. 2002), pp. 104–109. Dupuy, for example, cites the *Trail Smelter* and *Corfu Channel* cases, Stockholm Principle 21, several UN General Assembly resolutions, OECD Council recommendations, the Helsinki Final Act, and the UNEP Draft Principles of Conduct on Shared Natural Resources. Pierre-Marie Dupuy, "Overview of the Existing Customary Legal Regime Regarding International Pollution," in Daniel Barstow Magraw, ed., *International Law and Pollution* (Philadelphia: University of Pennsylvania Press, 1991), pp. 61–89 at 63–65. As far as "concrete cases" of state practice are concerned, however, he notes that states "seem partly to ignore" the rule. Ibid., 66.

51. Undercutting this claim that international environmental norms are "general principles of law," within the meaning of Article 38 of the ICJ Statute, is the fact most international environmental principles do not fit within any of the proposed theories of "general principles of law." They are not principles of legal logic. Nor do they appear to represent principles common to most national legal systems. Although traces of the precautionary principle can be found in U.S. and European environmental law, generalizing from this to the

rest of the world reflects a Eurocentric view. Finally, they do not represent principles of natural law.

52. Chodosh, "Neither Treaty Nor Custom," 89.

53. Indeed, I am inclined to think that, even when the principle has been incorporated into a treaty, as in the UN Framework Convention on Climate Change, this does not make a significant difference.

54. See Chapter 5 for additional discussion of the distinction between rules and standards.

55. *See generally* Louis Kaplow, "Rules Versus Standards: An Economic Analysis," *Duke Law Journal* 42 (1992), pp. 557–629.

56. *E.g.,* Christopher D. Stone, "Is There a Precautionary Principle?" *Environmental Law Reporter* 31 (2001), pp. 10790–10799; Daniel Bodansky, "Deconstructing the Precautionary Principle," in David D. Caron and Harry N. Scheiber, eds., *Bringing New Law to Ocean Waters* (Leiden: Martinus Nijhoff, 2004), pp. 381–391.

57. *Harvard Law Review* 10 (1897), pp. 457–478, at 461.

58. *See* Don Munton, "Acid Rain and Transboundary Air Quality in Canadian-American Relations," *American Review of Canadian Studies* 27 (1997), pp. 327–358.

10. How and Why Do States Implement Their Commitments?

1. The verb "implement" is defined as to "carry out, accomplish; *especially:* to give practical effect to and ensure actual fulfillment by concrete measures." Merriam-Webster Online Dictionary, www.merriam-webster.com (accessed 2/5/09).

2. The United Nations Environment Programme (UNEP) Guidelines on Compliance with and Enforcement of Multilateral Environmental Agreements define "implementation" as "all relevant laws, regulations, policies, and other measures and initiatives, that contracting parties adapt and/or take to meet their obligations under a multilateral environmental agreement." UNEP, *Manual on Compliance with and Enforcement of Multilateral Environmental Agreements* (Nairobi: UNEP, 2006), Annex I, para. 9. The UNEP Governing Council at the Seventh Special Session/Global Ministerial Environment Forum adopted the Guidelines in Decision SS.VII/4 on February 13–15, 2002. *See* UNEP/GCSS. VII/6 (March 5, 2002).

3. These statements represent oversimplifications because they treat the state as a unitary actor rather than a complex system of individuals and organizational entities (departments, offices, etc.). To some extent, a state may need to undertake measures to implement even the Antarctic Treaty's prohibition on military activities—for example, to ensure that its military units are all aware of this prohibition and to guard against behavior by rogue officers. Similarly, obligations to report require some acts of implementation, including designating the agency (and ultimately the people) responsible for preparing and submitting the report, and ensuring that they have adequate incentives and resources.

4. Kyoto Protocol annex B.

5. Richard F. Elmore, "Organizational Models of Social Program Implementation," *Public Policy* 26 (1978), pp. 185–228, at 186.

6. David Vogel and Timothy Kessler, "How Compliance Happens and Doesn't Happen Domestically," in Edith Brown Weiss and Harold K. Jacobson, eds., *Engaging Countries: Strengthening Compliance with International Environmental Accords* (Cambridge, MA: MIT Press, 1998), pp. 19–37, at 19; *see generally* Jeffrey L. Pressman and Aaron Wildavsky, *Implementation: How Great Expectations in Washington Are Dashed in Oakland; Or Why It's Amazing that Federal Programs Work at All, This Being a Saga of the Economic Development Administration as Told by Two Sympathetic Observers Who Seek to Build Morals on a Foundation of Ruined Hope* (Berkeley: University of California Press, 1973).

7. David G. Victor, Kal Raustiala, and Eugene B. Skolnikoff, "Introduction and Overview," in David G. Victor, Kal Raustiala, and Eugene B. Skolnikoff, eds., *The Implementation and Effectiveness of International Environmental Commitments: Theory and Practice* (Cambridge, MA: MIT Press, 1998), pp. 1–46, at 6.

8. *See, e.g.,* Weiss and Jacobson, eds., *Engaging Countries;* Edward L. Miles et al., *Environmental Regime Effectiveness: Confronting Theory with Evidence* (Cambridge, MA: MIT Press, 2002); Victor et al., eds., *Implementation and Effectiveness.*

9. As Catherine Redgwell notes, implementation is not addressed in detail in most international environmental law texts. Catherine Redgwell, "National Implementation," in Daniel Bodansky, Jutta Brunnée, and Ellen Hey, eds., *The Oxford Handbook of International Environmental Law* (Oxford: Oxford University Press, 2007), pp. 922–946, at 923. To the extent that lawyers have addressed implementation, they have tended to focus on judicial implementation. *See, e.g.,* Michael Anderson and Paolo Galizzi, eds., *International Environmental Law in National Courts* (London: British Institute of International and Comparative Law, 2002).

10. The European Union (EU) represents an exception to this general rule. It plays a major role in the implementation of international environmental agreements such as the Convention on International Trade in Endangered Species (CITES) to which it is not even a party. *See, e.g.,* Council Regulation 338/97, 1997 O. J. (L61) 1 (EC) (implementing CITES). In referring to "states" throughout this chapter, I also mean to include the European Union.

11. Kenneth Hanf and Arild Underdal, "Domesticating International Commitments: Linking National and International Decision-Making," in Arild Underdal, ed., *The Politics of International Environmental Management* (Dordrecht, Netherlands: Kluwer, 1995), pp. 149–170.

12. *E.g.,* Espoo Convention art. 2(2); London Convention art. 7; Basel Convention art. 4(4); *see also* World Charter for Nature, G. A. Res. 37/7, preamble, UN Doc. A/RES/37/7 (October 28, 1982) (recognizing the importance of national implementation).

13. Vienna Convention on the Law of Treaties art. 26 ("Every treaty in force is binding upon the parties to it and must be performed by them in good faith.").

14. For example, the first generation of so-called debt-for-nature swaps gave national non-governmental groups significant implementation responsibilities. Michael S. Sher, "Can Lawyers Save the Rainforest? Enforcing the Second Generation of Debt-for-Nature Swaps," *Harvard Environmental Law Review* 17 (1993), pp. 151–224. Similarly, private companies are responsible for implementing private codes of conduct, such as the Forest and Marine Stewardship Council codes. Indeed, business giants such as Wal-Mart are able to implement environmental standards not only in their own operations, but up and down the supply chain, through supply-chain contracts. Michael P. Vandenbergh, "The New Wal-Mart Effect: The Role of Private Contracting in Global Governance," *UCLA Law Review* 54 (2007), pp. 913–970. However, the UNEP Compliance Guidelines expressly exclude non-governmental activities from its definition of implementation. Redgwell, "National Implementation," 924.

15. A few areas of international law have moved in this direction, most notably international criminal law, which provides for direct prosecutions of individuals in the International Criminal Court. Yet even international criminal law continues to view national prosecutions as the norm, and provides for international prosecutions only in exceptional cases, when states fail to prosecute.

16. SIPs must contain enforceable emission limits, compliance schedules, monitoring procedures, and enforcement measures. Clean Air Act, 42 U.S.C. § 7410 (2006).

17. EU legislation makes a similar distinction between directives, which require substantial implementation by member states in order to become effective, and regulations, which apply directly.

18. UNCLOS art. 218.

19. Fish Stocks Agreement preamble, para. 4.

20. For example, the U.S. Supreme Court held in *Missouri v. Holland* that the federal government had authority to implement a migratory bird agreement with Canada, even though it was unclear whether, in the absence of the treaty, the federal government would have had authority to regulate migratory bird issues. *Missouri v. Holland*, 252 U.S. 416 (1920). The Australian High Court reached a similar result in *Commonwealth of Australia v. State of Tasmania* (1983) 158 C.L.R. 1, finding that the Commonwealth of Australia has the authority to implement the World Heritage Convention. But the Canadian Supreme Court held the opposite way in *R. v. Crown Zellerbach Canada Ltd.* [1988] 1 S.C.R. 401, rejecting any special federal competence to implement international agreements.

21. Aarhus Convention art. 1 (recognizing a right of public participation in environmental decision making).

22. Ronald B. Mitchell, *Intentional Oil Pollution at Sea: Environmental Policy and Treaty Compliance* (Cambridge, MA: MIT Press, 1994).

23. *See* Carl Bruch and John Pendergrass, "Type II Partnerships, International Law, and the Commons," *Georgetown International Environmental Law Review* 15 (2003), pp. 855–886.

24. MARPOL art. 4(1) ("Any violation of the requirements of the present Convention shall be prohibited and sanctions shall be established therefor under the law of the Administration of the ship concerned wherever the violation occurs.").

25. *See* William Edeson, David Freestone, and Elly Gudmundsdottir, *Legislating for Sustainable Fisheries: A Guide to Implementing the 1993 FAO Compliance Agreement and the 1995 UN Fish Stocks Agreement* (Washington, DC: World Bank, 2001).

26. *E.g.,* London Convention art. VII(2).

27. In practice, however, these constitutional differences seem to make little difference. For example, regardless of a country's constitutional system, courts have rarely enforced international environmental rules directly. Daniel Bodansky and Jutta Brunnée, "Introduction: The Role of National Courts in the Field of International Environmental Law," in Anderson and Galizzi, eds., *National Courts,* 1–22.

28. For an excellent discussion of national implementing legislation, see the section on "National Laws and Regulations" in UNEP's online *Manual on Compliance with and Enforcement of Multilateral Environmental Agreements* (Nairobi: UNEP, 2006), www.unep.org (accessed 2/4/09).

29. In the United States, the documents transmitting a treaty to the Senate for advice and consent to ratification typically address this issue expressly, analyzing the extent to which a treaty can be implemented under existing law or requires implementing legislation.

30. For example, U.S. ratification of the London (Dumping) Convention did not require implementing legislation because the Ocean Dumping Act, Pub. L. No. 92–532, 86 Stat. 1060 (1972), 33 U.S.C. §§ 1401–1445 (2007), was already in effect and could be used, with minor amendments, to implement the London Convention's permitting requirements for the disposal of hazardous wastes at sea. Similarly, if the United States were to become a party to the Biological Diversity Convention, the Endangered Species Act, 16 U.S.C. §§ 1531–1544 (2007), might provide sufficient implementing authority. *See* The Convention on Biological Diversity, S. Treaty Doc. No. 103–20 (1994). *See generally* Christian L. Wiktor, *Treaties Submitted to the United States Senate: Legislative History, 1989–2004* (Leiden: Martinus Nijhoff, 2006) (identifying treaties not requiring implementing legislation, including the SPREP Convention on the South Pacific region and the Desertification Convention).

31. *Massachusetts v. EPA,* 549 U.S. 497 (2007).

32. The United States, for example, after signing CITES on March 3, 1973, adopted the Endangered Species Act on December 28, 1973. Endangered Species Act, Pub. L. No. 93–205, §§8A, 9 (c)-(d), 87 Stat. 884, at 892–895 (1973). *See* 16 U.S.C. §§ 1531–1544 (2007).

33. MARPOL art. 4(1).

34. Redgwell notes several other benefits of legislative implementation: national laws and regulations tend to be more transparent than administrative and judicial implementation and can take a preventive and even precautionary approach. Redgwell, "National Implementation," 929.

35. Clean Air Act Amendments, Title VI, Pub. L. No. 101–549 §§ 601–618, 104 Stat. 2399, at 2648–2672 (November 15, 1990), 42 U.S.C. § 7671 (2006). Title VI also establishes an allowance trading regime; imposes labeling, monitoring, and reporting requirements; and requires the EPA administrator to promulgate regulations regarding recycling and government procurement.

36. Pub. L. No. 101–239, Title VII, § 7506(a), 103 Stat. 2106, at 2364 (December 19, 1989), 26 U.S.C. § 4681–4682 (2000).

37. Human Rights Act, 1998, ch. 42 (UK).

38. CITES Secretariat, Fourteenth Meeting of the Conference of the Parties to the Convention on International Trade in Endangered Species of Wild Fauna and Flora, The Hague, June 3–15, 1997, *National Laws for Implementation of the Convention*, CoP14 Doc. 24, pp. 4–5.

39. Clean Air Act Amendments, Pub. L. No. 101–549, § 606(a)(3), 104 Stat. 2399, at 2660 (November 15, 1990), 42 U.S.C. § 7671e (2006). *But see Natural Resources Defense Council v. Environmental Protection Agency,* 464 F.3d 1 (D.C. Cir. 2006) (holding that EPA is not bound under Clean Air Act to implement Montreal Protocol decisions on the "critical use" exemption).

40. Harold K. Jacobson and Edith Brown Weiss, "A Framework for Analysis," in Weiss and Jacobson, eds., *Engaging Countries,* 1–18, at 2, 4.

41. The 1982 Paris MOU is an agreement among twenty-seven maritime administrations in Europe and North America to harmonize and coordinate their inspections of ships in order to ensure compliance with international safety, security, and environmental standards. *See* www.parismou.org (accessed 2/5/09). On coordination among national administrative agencies, see generally Peter H. Sand, *Lessons Learned in Global Environmental Governance* (Washington, DC: World Resources Institute, 1990).

42. Anne-Marie Slaughter, *A New World Order* (Princeton, NJ: Princeton University Press, 2004).

43. Benedict Kingsbury et al., "The Emergence of Global Administrative Law," *Law and Contemporary Problems* 68 (3) (Summer/Autumn 2005), pp. 15–61 (discussing "parallel" and "network" administration).

44. The role of national courts in implementing international environmental law should be distinguished from their role in addressing transboundary environmental issues through the application of national law. Their role in transboundary issues was extensively studied in the 1970s and 1980s both in the Organisation for Economic Cooperation and Development (OECD) and in the U.S.-Canadian context. *See, e.g.,* OECD, *Problems in Transfrontier Pollution* (Paris: OECD, 1974).

45. Richard A. Falk, "The Interplay of Westphalia and Charter Conceptions of International Legal Order," in Richard Falk and Cyril E. Black, eds., *The Future of the International Legal Order,* vol. 1: *Trends and Patterns* (Princeton, NJ: Princeton University Press, 1969), pp. 32–70, at 69.

46. (1996) 5 *Supreme Court Cases* (S.C.C.) 647.

47. *Minors Oposa v. Secretary of Environment and Natural Resources, Supreme Court Reports Annotated* (G. R.) No. 101083, (S.C. July 30, 1993), *reprinted in* 33 I.L.M 174 (1994).

48. 659 F.2d 168, at 175 (D.C. Cir. 1981).
49. *Friends of the Earth v. Canada (Governor in Council)*, 2008 F.C. 1183 (Fed. Ct. Canada 2008), para. 45 (dismissing claim under Kyoto Protocol Implementation Act as non-justiciable, quoting approvingly from earlier opinion that the issues raised are of "an inherently political nature and should be addressed in a political forum rather than in the courts"). On the application of international environmental by Canadian courts, see Jerry V. DeMarco and Michelle L. Campbell, "The Supreme Court of Canada's Progressive Use of International Environmental Law and Policy in Interpreting Domestic Legislation," *Review of European Community and International Environmental Law* 13 (2004), pp. 320–332.
50. Case C-213/03, *Syndicat professionnel coordination des pêcheurs de l'etang de Berre et de la région v. Électricité de France*, 2004 *Report of Cases Before the Court of Justice of the European Communities* (E.C.R.) I-07357, at ¶ 47 (Eur. Ct. Just. 2004); *see* Redgwell, "National Implementation," 928.
51. *See* Harold Hongju Koh, "Why Do Nations Obey International Law?" *Yale Law Journal* 106 (1997), pp. 2599–2659 (explaining compliance in terms of internalization of international norms in the domestic legal process).
52. Bodansky and Brunnée, "Role of National Courts," 12.
53. Daniel Bodansky and Mary Manous, "International Environmental Law in US Courts," in Anderson and Palizzi, eds., *National Courts*, 233–246, at 239 (discussing *National Wildlife Federation v. Costle*, 629 F.2d 118 [D.C. Cir. 1980]).
54. *Amlon Metals, Inc. v. FMC Corp.*, 775 F. Supp. 668, at 671 (S.D.N.Y. 1991).
55. *See, e.g., Beanal v. Freeport-McMoRan, Inc.*, 969 F. Supp. 362, at 371 (E. D. La. 1997).
56. Bodansky and Brunnée, "Role of National Courts," 21–22.
57. The rate of self-compliance with international law has been the subject of considerable dispute. International lawyers tend to assume that self-compliance represents the norm. As Louis Henkin memorably put it, "almost all nations observe almost all principles of international law and almost all of their obligations almost all of the time." *How Nations Behave* (New York: Columbia University Press, 2d ed. 1979), p. 47. The realist, Hans Morgenthau, agreed that "[t]he great majority of the rules of international law are generally observed by all nations without actual compulsion." Hans Morgenthau, *Politics among Nations*, rev. Kenneth W. Thompson (New York: Alfred A. Knopf, 6th ed. 1985), p. 312. But some political scientists respond that self-compliance occurs primarily in easy cases, when a treaty doesn't require states to change their behavior significantly. George W. Downs, David M. Rocke, and Peter N. Barsoom, "Is the Good News about Compliance Good News about Cooperation?" *International Organization* 50 (1996), pp. 379–406. Kal Raustiala and David Victor agree that Henkin's statement is true because "most governments [are] very conservative in the international commitments that they adopt." Kal Raustiala and David G. Victor, "Conclusions," in Victor et al., eds., *Implementation and Effectiveness*, 659–708, at 661.

58. In a major comparative study, Weiss and Jacobson found a general trend toward strengthened implementation, even as treaties such as the Montreal Protocol have become deeper. Harold K. Jacobson and Edith Brown Weiss, "Assessing the Record and Designing Strategies to Engage Countries," in Weiss and Jacobson, eds., *Engaging Countries,* 511–554, at 513.

59. Laurie Tarkan, "Rough Transition to a New Asthma Inhaler," *New York Times,* May 13, 2008, p. D5.

60. Adil Najam, "Learning from the Literature on Implementation: A Synthesis Perspective," Working Paper WP 95–61 (Laxenburg, Austria: International Institute for Applied Systems Analysis, 1995), p. 32.

61. *See* Don Munton, "Acid Rain and Transboundary Air Quality in Canadian-American Relations," *American Review of Canadian Studies* 27 (1997), pp. 327–358.

62. Similarly, as Downs and his co-authors note, states found it easy to comply with the Antarctic Treaty's ban on weapons since, at the time of the treaty's adoption, no states had plans to do so. Downs et al., "Good News," 389. Murdoch and Sandler even make the same claim about the Montreal Protocol, namely, that it merely "codified reductions in CFC emissions that polluters were voluntarily prepared to accomplish." James C. Murdoch and Todd Sandler, "The Voluntary Provision of a Pure Public Good: The Case of Reduced CFC Emissions and the Montreal Protocol," *Journal of Public Economics* 63 (1997), pp. 331–349, at 332.

63. Ronald B. Mitchell, "Compliance Theory: A Synthesis," *Review of European Community and International Environmental Law* 2 (1993), pp. 327–334, at 328–329. In a forthcoming book on compliance with human rights agreements, Beth Simmons draws a similar distinction between what she calls "contingent" and "unilateral" compliance. Beth A. Simmons, *Mobilizing for Human Rights: International Law in Domestic Politics* (Cambridge: Cambridge University Press, forthcoming 2009).

64. Victor et al., "Introduction," 13.

65. Simmons, *Mobilizing for Human Rights.*

66. Raustiala and Victor, "Conclusions," 662 (stating that "legally binding agreements often codify what is already under way or reflect actions that parties are confident they can implement"). Oona Hathaway makes a similar argument about human rights agreements, namely, that "whether states will commit to a treaty depends in significant part on whether they expect to comply with it once they join." Oona A. Hathaway, "Why Do Countries Commit to Human Rights Treaties?" *Journal of Conflict Resolution* 51 (2007), pp. 588–621, at 590.

67. *See generally* Chapter 5 on the role of norms.

68. Detlev F. Vagts, "The United States and Its Treaties: Observance and Breach," *American Journal of International Law* 95 (2001), pp. 313–334, at 324–326 (arguing that sense of honor helps explain treaty compliance). As Chayes and Chayes note, "In common experience, people—whether as a result of socialization or otherwise—accept that they are obligated to obey the law. The existence of legal obligation, for most actors in most situations, translates into a presumption of compliance, in the absence of strong countervailing

circumstances. So it is with states." Abram Chayes and Antonia Handler Chayes, *The New Sovereignty: Compliance with International Regulatory Agreements* (Cambridge, MA: Harvard University Press, 1995), p. 8.

69. This political science school is usually referred to as "constructivism."

70. Andrew T. Guzman provides the most comprehensive account of these instrumental reasons for compliance in his recent book, *How International Law Works: A Rational Choice Theory* (Oxford: Oxford University Press, 2008).

71. *E.g.*, Arild Underdal, "Explaining Compliance and Defection: Three Models," *European Journal of International Relations* 4 (1998), pp. 5–30; Derek Beach, "Why Governments Comply: An Integrative Compliance Model that Bridges the Gap Between Instrumental and Normative Models of Compliance," *Journal of European Public Policy* 12 (2005), pp. 113–142, at 135.

72. Xinyuan Dai, "Why Comply? The Domestic Constituency Mechanism," *International Organization* 59 (2005), pp. 363–398.

73. Raustiala and Victor, "Conclusions," 669. Dai's game theoretic model of domestic compliance comes to a similar conclusion, namely, that a country's compliance decisions reflect not only the "electoral leverage" of domestic constituencies but also their "informational status"—that is, how well informed they are about the domestic policy process. Dai, "Why Comply?" 365.

74. Peter M. Haas, *Saving the Mediterranean: The Politics of International Environmental Cooperation* (New York: Columbia University Press, 1990).

75. For the now classic exposition of this managerial theory of compliance, see Chayes and Chayes, *New Sovereignty; see also* Tom R. Tyler, "Compliance with Intellectual Property Laws: A Psychological Perspective," *NYU Journal of International Law and Politics* 29 (1996–1997), pp. 219–235 (discussing "culture of compliance").

76. Helmut Breitmeier, Oran R. Young, and Michael Zürn, *Analyzing International Environmental Regimes: From Case Study to Database* (Cambridge, MA: MIT Press, 2006), p. 187.

77. A recent study of EU implementation concluded that many different causal factors contribute to predictive success. As the study noted, "when it comes to understanding why states do—or indeed, do not—comply with their treaty obligations to implement MEAs, it would be fair to say that theorization has run ahead of empirical testing. . . . [C]omparatively little research has been undertaken to validate empirically [scholars'] respective predictions." Richard Perkins and Eric Neumayer, "Implementing Multilateral Environmental Directives: An Analysis of EU Directives," *Global Environmental Politics* 7 (3) (August 2007), pp. 13–41, at 34.

11. International Carrots and Sticks

1. Virginia M. Walsh, "Illegal Whaling for Humpbacks by the Soviet Union in the Antarctic, 1947–1972," *Journal of Environment and Development* 8 (1999), pp. 307–327.

2. Louis Henkin, *How Nations Behave: Law and Foreign Policy* (New York: Columbia University Press, 2d ed. 1979), p. 47.

3. CITES Secretariat, Fourteenth Meeting of the Conference of the Parties to the Convention on International Trade in Endangered Species of Wild Fauna and Flora, The Hague, June 3–15, 1997, *National Laws for Implementation of the Convention*, CoP14 Doc. 24, pp. 4–5.

4. Adil Najam, Mihaela Papa, and Nadaa Taiyab, *Global Environmental Governance: A Reform Agenda* (Winnipeg, Canada: International Institute for Sustainable Development, 2006), p. 15 (claiming the existence of an "implementation deficit").

5. *See generally* Kal Raustiala, *Reporting and Review Institutions in 10 Multilateral Environmental Agreements* (Nairobi: UNEP, 2001); *see also* UNEP, *Compliance Mechanisms under Selected Multilateral Agreements* (Nairobi: UNEP, 2007), www.unep.org (accessed 2/4/09).

6. For this reason, in studying international implementation mechanisms, one "need[s] to go beyond treaty text to subsequent decisions and especially to actual practice." Raustiala, *Reporting and Review Institutions*, 3.

7. As Jutta Brunnée notes, the term *enforcement* is not even included in the index of most international law treatises. Jutta Brunnée, "Enforcement Mechanisms in International Law and International Environmental Law," in Ulrich Beyerlin, Peter-Tobias Stoll, and Rüdiger Wolfrum, eds., *Ensuring Compliance with Multilateral Environmental Agreements: A Dialogue Between Practitioners and Academia* (Leiden: Martinus Nijhoff, 2006), pp. 1–23.

8. The trade regime provides an illustration. States injured by trade restrictions have an incentive to take enforcement actions.

9. UNESCO Intergovernmental Committee for the Protection of the World Cultural and Natural Heritage, *Operational Guidelines for the Implementation of the World Heritage Convention* (Paris: UNESCO, 2008), www.whc.unesco.org (accessed 2/6/09).

10. As I once heard an international official involved with a compliance institution put it, the motto of compliance institutions could be put as "hiss don't bite."

11. *E.g.*, George W. Downs, David M. Rocke, and Peter N. Barsoom, "Is the Good News about Compliance Good News about Cooperation?" *International Organization* 50 (1996), pp. 379–406.

12. *E.g.*, Scott Barrett, *Environment and Statecraft: The Strategy of Environmental Treaty-Making* (Oxford: Oxford University Press, 2003).

13. Beth Simmons more politely refers to such states as "insincere ratifiers." Beth A. Simmons, *Mobilizing for Human Rights: International Law in Domestic Politics* (Cambridge: Cambridge University Press, forthcoming 2009).

14. *E.g.*, ibid.; Kal Raustiala and David G. Victor, "Conclusions," in David G. Victor, Kal Raustiala, and Eugene B. Skolnikoff, eds., *The Implementation and Effectiveness of International Environmental Commitments: Theory and Practice* (Cambridge, MA: MIT Press, 1998), pp. 659–708, at 682; David Vogel and Timothy Kessler, "How Compliance Happens and Doesn't Happen Domestically," in Edith Brown Weiss and Harold K. Jacobson, eds., *Engaging*

Countries: Strengthening Compliance with International Environmental Accords (Cambridge, MA: MIT Press, 1998), pp. 19–37.

15. Some writers distinguish between intentional and unintentional noncompliance. *See* Jacobson and Weiss, "Assessing the Record," in Weiss and Jacobson, eds., *Engaging Countries,* 538–539. As this example suggests, the line between the two is blurry, and they can both be analyzed using the same types of causal factors.

16. Raustiala and Victor, "Conclusions," 661.

17. *Earth Island Institute v. Christopher,* 20 Ct. Int'l Trade 1221 (1996), *vacated, Earth Island Institute v. Albright,* 147 F.3d 1352 (Fed. Cir. 1998) (holding that the Court of International Trade lacked jurisdiction to rule on a motion by environmental and animal protection organizations to enforce prior judgment).

18. A study prepared by the CITES Secretariat in the early 1980s, for example, revealed that, owing to mistakes in identifying species and filling out forms, the content of annual reports was generally "so inadequate that the value of those reports which are submitted is highly dubious." Simon Lyster, *International Wildlife Law* (Cambridge: Grotius Publications, 1985), p. 269.

19. *See, e.g.,* Abram Chayes, Antonia Handler Chayes, and Ronald B. Mitchell, "Managing Compliance: A Comparative Perspective," in Weiss and Jacobson, eds., *Engaging Countries,* 39–62, at 40.

20. Kyoto Protocol annex B.

21. *See* David Kestenbaum, "Japan Wrestles with Kyoto Accord Promises," *National Public Radio,* October 1, 2007, www.npr.org (accessed 2/6/09).

22. Rome Statute of the International Criminal Court art. 8(2)(b)(iv) (defining as a war crime, *inter alia,* "[i]ntentionally launching an attack in the knowledge that such attack will cause . . . widespread, long-term and severe damage to the natural environment which would be clearly excessive in relation to the concrete and direct overall military advantage anticipated.").

23. *See generally* Organisation for Economic Cooperation and Development (OECD), *Compensation for Pollution Damage* (Paris: OECD, 1981).

24. Examples include the 1969 Civil Liability Convention, as amended; the 1996 HNS Convention, which addresses transport of hazardous and noxious substances by sea; and the 1999 Basel Liability Protocol. As of March 2009, neither the HNS Convention nor the Basel Protocol had entered into force. By raising the costs of accidents, liability regimes such as these also serve to deter future damage, so they do not have a solely compensatory function.

25. Pelly Amendment to the United States Fishermen's Protective Act, 22 USC § 1978.

26. Although the president's failure to impose sanctions under the Pelly Amendment suggests that NGO influence is limited and that perceptions of national interest remain important.

27. As noted in Chapter 10, debt-for-nature swaps, in which developing countries commit to nature conservation in exchange for foreign debt forgiveness, also often assign implementation responsibilities to local NGOs. Michael S. Sher, "Can Lawyers Save the Rainforest? Enforcing the Second Generation

of Debt-for-Nature Swaps," *Harvard Environmental Law Review* 17 (1993), pp. 151–224.

28. John H. Knox, "A New Approach to Compliance with International Environmental Law: The Submissions Procedure of the NAFTA Environmental Commission," *Ecology Law Quarterly* 28 (2001), pp. 1–122.

29. Kal Raustiala, "Police Patrols and Fire Alarms in the NAAEC," *Loyola of Los Angeles International and Comparative Law Review* 26 (2004), pp. 389–413, at 399–402.

30. For a discussion of the CITES compliance regime, see Rosalind Reeve, "The CITES Treaty and Compliance: Progress or Jeopardy?," Royal Institute of International Affairs Briefing Paper BP 04/01 (London: Chatham House, 2004).

31. Daniel Bodansky, "What's So Bad about Unilateral Action to Protect the Environment," *European Journal of International Law* 11 (2000), pp. 339–347.

32. The seminal work articulating the managerial approach is Abram Chayes and Antonia Handler Chayes, *The New Sovereignty: Compliance with International Regulatory Agreements* (Cambridge, MA: Harvard University Press, 1995).

33. Ibid, 3–10.

34. A recent empirical study concluded that the management approach is dominant in almost 95 percent of the cases studied and that "those who create and administer international regimes exhibit an overwhelming preference for procedures featuring management in contrast to enforcement." Helmut Breitmeier, Oran R. Young, and Michael Zürn, *Analyzing International Environmental Regimes: From Case Study to Database* (Cambridge, MA: MIT Press, 2006), pp. 182, 186.

35. O. Yoshida, "Soft Enforcement of Treaties: The Montreal Protocol's Noncompliance Procedure and the Functions of Internal International Institutions," *Colorado Journal of International Environmental Law and Policy* 10 (1999), pp. 95–141, at 135–139.

36. *See, e.g.*, Chayes and Chayes, *New Sovereignty,* 2 ("The effort to devise and incorporate . . . sanctions in treaties is largely a waste of time.").

37. *See generally* Kamen Sachariew, "Promoting Compliance with International Environmental Standards: Reflections on Monitoring and Reporting Mechanisms," *Yearbook of International Environmental Law* 2 (1991), pp. 31–52. This section draws from Daniel Bodansky, "The Role of Reporting in International Environmental Treaties: Lessons for Human Rights Supervision," in Philip Alston and James Crawford, eds., *The Future of UN Human Rights Treaty Monitoring* (Cambridge: Cambridge University Press, 2000), pp. 361–380.

38. A United Nations Environmental Programme (UNEP) study of nineteen multilateral environmental agreements found that only three did not include a requirement to report on national performances, and two of these included requirements to report on more specific transactions. UNEP, *Compliance Mechanisms,* 105.

39. *E.g.*, London Convention art. VI(4); CITES art. VIII(7).

40. For example, the Vienna Ozone Convention requires that parties "take appropriate measures . . . to protect human health and the environment against adverse effects resulting or likely to result from human activities which modify or are likely to modify the ozone layer," and imposes only a general reporting requirement to transmit information "on the measures adopted . . . in implementation of this Convention." Arts. 2(1) and 5.

41. For example, the 1985 Sulphur Protocol requires states to reduce their sulfur emissions by 30 percent and to report on their "levels of national annual sulphur emissions and the basis upon which they have been calculated." Art. 4.

42. Raustiala, "Police Patrols and Fire Alarms."

43. Co-operative Program for Monitoring and Evaluation of the Long-Range Transmission of Air Pollutants in Europe, www.emep.int (accessed 2/8/09).

44. TRAFFIC was jointly established in 1976 by the WWF-World Wide Fund for Nature and International Union for the Conservation of Nature (IUCN), also known as the World Conservation Union.

45. CITES art. XII(1), authorizes the secretariat to work with "suitable" NGOs "to the extent and in the manner [the secretariat] considers appropriate."

46. Raustiala, "Police Patrols & Fire Alarms," 404–406.

47. For an excellent discussion, see Raustiala, *Reporting and Review Institutions*.

48. LRTAP art. 10(2)(a).

49. For example, the statistical data in reports submitted under CITES can be used to calculate the total volume of trade in a species, which in turn can be used in assessments of the species' status and the need for additional conservation measures.

50. To date, the expert review process under the climate change regime has applied only to developed country reports.

51. Raustiala, *Reporting and Review Institutions*, 11.

52. Edmund Jan Ozmańczyk, *Encyclopedia of the United Nations and International Agreements*, vol. 1, ed. Anthony Mango (New York: Routledge, 3d ed. 2003), p. 42.

53. This figure includes official development assistance by both individual states and multilateral institutions such as the World Bank.

54. World Bank, Key Development Data and Statistics, http://web.worldbank.org.

55. Global Environmental Facility, www.gefweb.org (accessed 2/8/09).

56. *See* http://whc.unesco.org (accessed 2/8/09).

57. *See* www.multilateralfund.org (accessed 2/8/09).

58. This is true only for assistance addressing global public goods problems. Assistance to address local problems, such as adaptation to climate change or desertification, provides private benefits, like other forms of development assistance.

59. GEF, "Incremental Costs," www.gefweb.org (accessed 2/8/09).

60. By the same logic, states impose taxes to require citizens to contribute to the production of public goods such as national defense.

61. Richard Elliot Benedick, *Ozone Diplomacy: New Directions in Safeguarding the Planet* (Cambridge, MA: Harvard University Press, 1998), p. 187; *see also* Barrett, *Environment and Statecraft*, 348.

62. For example, Philippe Sands states that enforcement includes "the right to . . . obtain a ruling by an appropriate international court, tribunal or other body . . . that obligations are not being fulfilled." Philippe Sands, *Principles of International Environmental Law* (Cambridge: Cambridge University Press, 2d ed. 2003), p. 182.

63. *See generally* James Crawford, *The International Law Commission's Articles on State Responsibility: Introduction, Text and Commentaries* (Cambridge: Cambridge University Press, 2002).

64. *See generally* Cesare P. R. Romano, *The Peaceful Settlement of International Environmental Disputes: A Pragmatic Approach* (London: Kluwer Law International, 2000).

65. In the entire twentieth century, only a handful of cases were heard—the *Behring Fur Seals* arbitration, *Trail Smelter,* the *Lac Lanoux* arbitration, and the *Gabçikovo Dam* case—while the first decade of this century has already had two, the *MOX* arbitration and a case currently pending in the International Court of Justice (ICJ) between Argentina and Uruguay about pulp mills along their border; *see* www.icj-cij.org (accessed 2/8/09).

66. As of 2001, Kal Raustiala reported that the dispute settlement provisions of multilateral environmental agreements (MEAs) had never been used and had "effectively fallen into desuetude." Raustiala, *Reporting and Review Institutions,* 12. That year, Ireland became the first country to invoke the dispute settlement provision of an MEA, bringing a case against the United Kingdom under the OSPAR Convention concerning the UK's mixed oxide facility. The case was decided against Ireland by an arbitral tribunal in 2003. *See* Daniel Bodansky, "Introduction to the MOX Plant Dispute," in Belinda MacMahon, ed., *The OSPAR Arbitration (Ireland-United Kingdom) Award of 2003* (The Hague: Asser Institute, 2009), pp. 1–22.

67. The original procedure was adopted in 1990 and was revised most recently in 1998.

68. Compliance procedures have already been established for the LRTAP Convention, the Espoo Convention on Transboundary Environmental Impact Assessment, the Kyoto Protocol, the Basel Convention, the Aarhus Convention on Public Participation, the Cartagena Biosafety Protocol, and the London Protocol. Compliance procedures are also under negotiation or consideration in the Rotterdam Chemicals Convention and the Stockholm Convention on Persistent Organic Pollutants. *See generally* UNEP, *Compliance Mechanisms; see also* Jan Klabbers, "Compliance Procedures," in Daniel Bodansky, Jutta Brunnée, and Ellen Hey, eds., *The Oxford Handbook of International Environmental Law* (Oxford: Oxford University Press, 2007), pp. 995–1009.

69. Significantly, Sands includes his discussion of compliance procedures in the section of his book on "diplomatic means of dispute settlement," rather than the section on "legal means of dispute settlement." Sands, *Principles,* 205–210.

70. This assistance is sometimes referred to as "non-compliance response assistance," to distinguish it from the implementation assistance described above. *See* UNEP, *Compliance Mechanisms,* 11.

71. Ibid., 117–118.
72. Chayes and Chayes, *New Sovereignty,* 152.
73. As Oran Young notes: "[T]he prospect of being found out is often just as important, and sometimes more important, to the potential violator than the prospect of becoming the target of more or less severe sanctions of a conventional or material sort. There are, in other words, many situations in which those contemplating violations will refrain from breaking the rules if they expect their non-compliant behavior to be exposed, even if they know that the probability that their violations will be met with sanctions is low." Oran R. Young, "The Effectiveness of International Institutions: Hard Cases and Critical Variables," in James N. Rosenau and Ernst-Otto Czempiel, eds., *Governance Without Government: Order and Change in World Politics* (New York: Cambridge University Press, 1992), pp. 160–194, at 176–177, *quoted in* Chayes and Chayes, *New Sovereignty,* 152.
74. In its first finding of non-compliance with the Kyoto Protocol, the Protocol's Compliance Committee found in April 2008 that Greece was not in compliance with the requirements for a national system to account for emissions and suspended Greece's eligibility to participate in the market mechanisms, including emission trading. Since then, Greece has demonstrated compliance with the Protocol's requirements and is once more eligible to engage in emissions trading.
75. To the extent that states have an interest in trade in wildlife or emission credits, trade suspensions not only prevent problems from spreading, but they also serve a deterrent function by giving states an incentive to comply in order to regain their trading status.
76. Ronald B. Mitchell, *Intentional Oil Pollution at Sea: Environmental Policy and Treaty Compliance* (Cambridge, MA: MIT Press, 1994).
77. Klabbers, "Compliance Procedures," 996–997.
78. Martti Koskenniemi, "Breach of Treaty or Non-Compliance? Reflections on the Enforcement of the Montreal Protocol," *Yearbook of International Environmental Law* 3 (1992), pp. 123–162.
79. Raustiala and Victor, "Conclusions," 684.
80. Chayes and Chayes, *New Sovereignty,* 17–22. As the Chayes sum up: "[T]he choice of whether to intensify (or slacken) the international enforcement effort is a political decision. It implicates all the same interests, pro and con, that were involved in the initial formulation of the treaty norm. . . . What is acceptable in terms of compliance will reflect the perspectives and interests of the participants in an ongoing political process, rather than some external, scientifically or market-validated standard." Ibid., 20.

12. Is International Environmental Law Effective?

1. Mark Simmonds, "New International Agreements or Empty Pledges?" (on file with author).
2. *Compare* Oona A. Hathaway, "Do Human Rights Treaties Make a Difference?" *Yale Law Journal* 111 (2002), pp. 1935–2042.

3. *See, e.g.,* Edward L. Miles et al., *Environmental Regime Effectiveness: Confronting Theory with Evidence* (Cambridge, MA: MIT Press, 2002); David G. Victor, Kal Raustiala, and Eugene B. Skolnikoff, eds., *The Implementation and Effectiveness of International Environmental Commitments: Theory and Practice* (Cambridge, MA: MIT Press, 1998).

4. Evan J. Ringquist and Tatiana Kostadinova, "Assessing the Effectiveness of International Environmental Agreements: The Case of the 1985 Helsinki Protocol," *American Journal of Political Science* 49 (2005), pp. 86–102, at 86 (asserting that the Helsinki Protocol "had no discernible effect on emissions").

5. This section draws from Daniel Bodansky, *What Makes International Agreements Effective? Some Pointers for the WHO Framework Convention on Tobacco Control,* Doc. No. WHO/NCD/TFI/99.4 (Geneva: WHO, 1999).

6. *See generally* Oran R. Young, *International Governance: Protecting the Environment in a Stateless Society* (Ithaca, NY: Cornell University Press, 1994), pp. 140–160 (discussing various meanings of "effectiveness").

7. Miles et al., *Environmental Regime Effectiveness,* 6. The caveat that behavioral change must be in the "right direction"—that is, in furtherance of a regime's goals—is important because international regimes can have unintended, perverse effects, exacerbating rather than ameliorating problems. For example, the success of the first round of the Strategic Arms Limitation Talks (SALT I) in limiting nuclear weapon launchers had the unintended effect of increasing rather than reducing instability, by leading to the development of multiple warhead systems (MIRVs), which are more difficult to deter.

8. Kyoto Protocol annex B.

9. UNFCCC art. 4.1.

10. The point is illustrated by the perhaps apocryphal ordinance enacted by the French village, Chateauneuf-de-Pape, in response to UFO sightings, which prohibited flying saucers from landing within the village. Robert V. Percival et al., *Environmental Regulation: Law, Science, and Policy* (Boston: Little, Brown, 1992), p. 141. Although the ordinance has achieved an enviable record of compliance—to the best of my knowledge, a flying saucer has never landed in the village—its causal effectiveness is open to question.

11. Interestingly, a U.S. law aimed at promoting wildlife conservation—the Pelly Amendment—allows the United States to impose trade sanctions against other countries for "diminishing the effectiveness" of an international conservation agreement, even if no violation has occurred. *See* Pelly Amendment to the United States Fishermen's Protective Act 22 U.S.C. § 1978.

12. Louis Henkin, *How Nations Behave: Law and Foreign Policy* (New York: Columbia University Press, 2d ed. 1979), p. 47 (italics deleted).

13. *See* George W. Downs, David M. Rocke, and Peter N. Barsoom, "Is the Good News about Compliance Good News about Cooperation?" *International Organization* 50 (1996), pp. 379–406. As Kal Raustiala explains: "Governments initiate treaty negotiations, determine their scope, and fix the content

of their international commitments collectively. By doing so, governments also largely—though not totally—determine compliance levels with the resulting international obligations. . . . Because compliance levels are often an artifact of the legal standard employed, the significance of high or low compliance levels in any given MEA is not self-evident." Kal Raustiala, *Reporting and Review Institutions in 10 Multilateral Environmental Agreements* (Nairobi: UNEP, 2001), p. 7.

14. A. Myrick Freeman III, "Water Pollution Policy," in Paul R. Portney and Robert N. Stavins, eds., *Public Policies for Environmental Protection* (Washington, DC: Resources for the Future, 2d ed. 2000), pp. 169–213, at 180.

15. *See* James C. Murdoch and Todd Sandler, "The Voluntary Provision of a Pure Public Good: The Case of Reduced CFC Emissions and the Montreal Protocol," *Journal of Public Economics* 63 (1997), pp. 331–349, at 332 (asserting that the Montreal Protocol may be "more symbolic than a true instance of a cooperative equilibrium"). Similarly, some attribute the decline in ocean dumping in the North Sea to technological innovations in land-based incineration rather than to the Oslo Convention. George W. Downs, Kyle W. Danish, and Peter N. Barsoom, "The Transformational Model of International Regime Design: Triumph of Hope or Experience?" *Columbia Journal of Transnational Law* 38 (2000), pp. 465-514, at 499.

16. Whaling Convention preamble, para. 2.

17. To distinguish between immediate and ultimate effects, policy scientists use different terms: outcomes and impacts. *See* Ronald B. Mitchell, "Compliance Theory: Compliance, Effectiveness, and Behavior Change in International Environmental Law," in Daniel Bodansky, Jutta Brunnée, and Ellen Hey, eds., *The Oxford Handbook of International Environmental Law* (Oxford: Oxford University Press, 2007), pp. 893–921, at 896.

18. Arild Underdal, "The Concept of Regime 'Effectiveness,'" *Cooperation and Conflict* 27 (1992), pp. 227–240; *see also* Arild Underdal, "One Question, Two Answers," in Miles et al., *Environmental Regime Effectiveness*, 3–45, at 8–9.

19. *E.g.,* E.-S. Yang et al., "Attribution of Recovery in Lower-Stratospheric Ozone," *Journal of Geophysical Research Atmospheres* 111, D17309 (2006); Elizabeth C. Weatherhead and Signe Bech Andersen, "The Search for Signs of Recovery of the Ozone Layer," *Nature* 441 (2006), pp. 39–45.

20. Underdal, "One Question, Two Answers," 8.

21. *See* Jon Hovi, Detlef F. Sprinz, and Arild Underdal, "The Oslo-Potsdam Solution to Measuring Regime Effectiveness: Critique, Response, and the Road Ahead," *Global Environmental Politics* 3(3) (August 2003), pp. 74–96.

22. For a critique, see Oran R. Young, "Determining Regime Effectiveness: A Commentary on the Oslo-Potsdam Solution," *Global Environmental Politics* 3(3) (August 2003), pp. 97–104, at 99–100.

23. Beth Simmons's forthcoming study on human rights regimes takes this approach. Beth A. Simmons, *Mobilizing for Human Rights: International Law in Domestic Politics* (Cambridge: Cambridge University Press, forthcoming 2009).

24. *E.g.,* Helmut Breitmeier, Oran R. Young, and Michael Zürn, *Analyzing International Environmental Regimes: From Case Study to Database* (Cambridge, MA: MIT Press, 2006). The study compiles a database on twenty-three environmental regimes examining more than 150 variables.

25. For example, compare the differing assessments of the effectiveness of the oil pollution regime in Miles et al., *Environmental Regime Effectiveness,* 331–356, with Ronald B. Mitchell, *Intentional Oil Pollution at Sea: Environmental Policy and Treaty Compliance* (Cambridge, MA: MIT Press, 1994).

26. Harold K. Jacobson and Edith Brown Weiss, "A Framework for Analysis," in Edith Brown Weiss and Harold K. Jacobson, eds., *Engaging Countries: Strengthening Compliance with International Environmental Accords* (Cambridge, MA: MIT Press, 1998), pp. 1–18, at 15–17.

27. David G. Victor, Kal Raustiala, and Eugene B. Skolnikoff, "Introduction and Overview," in Victor et al., eds., *Implementation and Effectiveness,* 1–30, at 26–28.

28. Jon Birger Skjærseth, "Toward the End of Dumping in the North Sea: The Case of the Oslo Commission," in Miles et al., *Environmental Regime Effectiveness,* 65–85, at 65.

29. National Research Council, *Oil in the Sea III: Inputs, Fates and Effects* (Washington, DC: National Academies Press, 2003), p. 76.

30. Ronald Mitchell, "Intentional Oil Pollution of the Oceans," in Peter M. Haas, Robert O. Keohane, and Marc A. Levy, eds., *Institutions for the Earth: Sources of Effective International Environmental Protection* (Cambridge, MA: MIT Press, 1993), pp. 183–247.

31. Jørgen Wettestad, "The Vienna Convention and Montreal Protocol on Ozone-Layer Depletion," in Miles et al., *Environmental Regime Effectiveness,* 149–170, at 151.

32. World Meteorological Organization, *Scientific Assessment of Ozone Depletion: 2006* (Geneva: WMO, 2006), p. xxiv. The ozone layer will recover earlier over mid-latitudes than over the Antarctic, where the ozone "hole" is not projected to disappear until about 2070.

33. Scott Barrett, *Environment and Statecraft: The Strategy of Environmental Treaty-Making* (Oxford: Oxford University Press, 2003), pp. 31–32.

34. United Nations Development Programme, "Biodiversity for Development CD-ROM," www.undp.org (accessed 1/22/09).

35. *E.g.,* Millennium Ecosystem Assessment, *Ecosystems and Human Well-Being: Biodiversity Synthesis* (Washington, DC: World Resources Institute, 2005), p. 36 (estimating the rate of species extinctions and threatened extinctions over the next century); International Union for the Conservation of Nature (IUCN), "Red List of Threatened Species," www.iucnredlist.org (accessed 1/22/09) (estimating that almost 17,000 known species are threatened with extinction).

36. Energy Information Administration, *International Energy Outlook 2004,* p. 13, www.eia.doe (accessed 1/22/09) (estimating that the rate of increase in emissions will be higher from 2000 to 2025 than in the 1990s).

37. Global Environment Facility (GEF)-International Fund for Agricultural Development (IFAD) Partnership, *Tackling Land Degradation and Desertification,* www.ifad.org (accessed 1/24/09). A hectare equals about 2.5 acres, and 12 million hectares is about 46,000 square miles. Assessments on the rate of desertification vary widely, however, and are not considered very reliable. Millennium Ecosystem Assessment, *Ecosystems and Human Well-Being: Desertification Synthesis* (Washington, DC: World Resources Institute, 2005), p. 7.

38. Harold K. Jacobson and Edith Brown Weiss, "Assessing the Record and Designing Strategies to Engage Countries," in Weiss and Jacobson, eds., *Engaging Countries,* 511–554, at 512.

39. Ibid., 512-513. Two other comparative studies reached similar conclusions about the effectiveness of international environmental law. Miles et al., *Environmental Regime Effectiveness;* Victor et al., eds., *Implementation and Effectiveness.*

40. Edward L. Miles and Arild Underdal, with Steinar Andresen, Elaine Carlin, Jon Birger Skjærseth, and Jørgen Wettestad, "Epilogue," in Miles et al., *Environmental Regime Effectiveness,* 467–474, at 467.

41. For example, in trying to understand why the legal restrictions on trade barriers set forth in the General Agreement on Tariffs and Trade (GATT) have been more effective than the UN Charter's prohibition on the use of force, the explanation presumably has less to do with differences between the agreements themselves than with the fact that trade issues are intrinsically more susceptible to legal regulation than warfare.

42. *See generally, e.g.,* Breitmeier et al., *Analyzing International Environmental Regimes;* Jacobson and Weiss, "Framework for Analysis," 6–8.

43. *See* Underdal, "One Question, Two Answers," 15–23.

44. Determining which side of the road to drive on is an example of a coordination game. Once a traffic rule has been agreed upon, there is no incentive to cheat by driving on the wrong side of the road. Compliance with international agreements relating to civil aviation and postal communication has been unproblematic for this reason. In contrast, the prisoner's dilemma is an example of a cooperation game. In a cooperation game, a player achieves the highest payoff when others comply but it defects. In environmental regimes addressing cooperation problems, states have an incentive to cheat if they think they can get away with it while others continue to cooperate. *See generally* Arthur A. Stein, *Why Nations Cooperate: Circumstance and Choice in International Relations* (Ithaca, NY: Cornell University Press, 1990).

45. *See, e.g.,* Arild Underdal, "International Cooperation: Transforming 'Needs' into 'Deeds,'" *Journal of Peace Research* 24 (1987), pp. 167–183.

46. *E.g.,* Anne-Marie Slaughter, "International Law in a World of Liberal States," *European Journal of International Law* 6 (1995), pp. 503–538.

47. *See, e.g.,* Barbara Koremenos, Charles Lipson, and Duncan Snidal, eds., *The Rational Design of International Institutions* (Cambridge: Cambridge University Press, 2004); Mitchell, *Intentional Oil Pollution at Sea;* Victor et al., eds., *Implementation and Effectiveness.*

48. Kal Raustiala and David G. Victor, "Conclusions," in Victor et al., eds., *Implementation and Effectiveness*, 659–707, at 685–688.

49. *See generally* Rüdiger Wolfrum and Volker Röben, eds., *Legitimacy in International Law* (New York: Springer, 2008).

50. Mitchell, *Intentional Oil Pollution at Sea.*

51. Proposals under the UN climate change regime to make buyers of emissions allowances liable for violations of a country's emissions target have an analogous rationale. *See* Robert O. Keohane and Kal Raustiala, "Towards a Post-Kyoto Climate Change Architecture: A Political Analysis," ssrn.com (accessed 5/24/09). Since buyers of emissions allowances are likely to be from Western countries, which will have strong domestic enforcement, imposing liability on buyers would give them a strong incentive to be prudent, by purchasing allowances only from countries that are likely to meet their emissions target.

52. One recent study concluded that treaty secretariats, by contrast, had little effect on compliance and effectiveness. Breitmeier et al., *Analyzing International Environmental Regimes*, 86.

53. Miles and Underdal, "Epilogue," 467.

Conclusion: Taking Stock

1. James Gustave Speth, *Red Sky at Morning: America and the Crisis of the Global Environment* (New Haven, CT: Yale University Press, 2004), p. xi.

2. The EU proposal in 2005 to create a new UN Environmental Organization was along these lines. *See* Nils Meyer-Ohlendorf and Markus Knigge, "A United Nations Environment Organization," in Lydia Swart and Estelle Perry, eds., *Global Environmental Governance: Perspectives on the Current Debate* (New York: Center for UN Reform Education, 2007), pp. 124–141.

3. Adil Najam, Mihaela Papa, and Nadaa Taiyab, *Global Environmental Governance: A Reform Agenda* (Winnipeg, Canada: International Institute for Sustainable Development, 2006), p. 14.

4. *See, e.g.,* Frank Biermann and Steffen Bauer, eds., *A World Environment Organization: Solution or Threat for Effective Environmental Governance?* (Aldershot, United Kingdom: Ashgate, 2005).

5. *See* Najam, Papa and Taiyab, *Global Environmental Governance*, 22–23 (describing twelve UN reform initiatives over the past decade, none of which has yielded results thus far).

6. Daniel C. Esty, "The Case for a Global Environmental Organization," in Peter B. Kenen, ed., *Managing the World Economy; Fifty Years after Bretton Woods* (Washington, DC: Institute for International Economics, 1994), pp. 287–310.

7. Daniel Bodansky, "The Legitimacy of International Governance: A Coming Challenge for International Law?" *American Journal of International Law* 93 (1999), pp. 596–624.

8. Philip Allott, *Eunomia: New Order for a New World* (Oxford: Oxford University Press, 2001).

9. Speth, *Red Sky*, 197.

10. Daniel Bodansky, "Does One Need to Be an International Lawyer to Be an International Environmental Lawyer?" *Proceedings of the American Society of International Law* 100 (2006), pp. 303–307.

11. *See, e.g.,* Scott Barrett, *Environment and Statecraft: The Strategy of Environmental Treaty-Making* (Oxford: Oxford University Press, 2003); Barbara Koremenos, Charles Lipson, and Duncan Snidal, eds., *The Rational Design of International Institutions* (Cambridge: Cambridge University Press, 2004); Kal Raustiala, "Form and Substance in International Agreements," *American Journal of International Law* 99 (2005), 581–614.

12. Lawrence R. Helfer, "Exiting Treaties," *Virginia Law Review* 91 (2005), pp. 1579–1648, at 1591.

13. Raustiala, "Form and Substance," 614.

14. As Helfer observes, "Treaty restrictions that are too easy to satisfy will encourage self-serving denunciations and lead to a breakdown in cooperation. Restrictions that are too onerous will discourage such behavior, but may prevent parties from reaching agreement in the first instance or, if agreement is reached, may lead to widespread treaty violations if the costs of compliance rise unexpectedly." Helfer, "Exiting Treaties," 1600.

15. George W. Downs, Kyle W. Danish, and Peter N. Barsoom, "The Transformational Model of International Regime Design: Triumph of Hope or Experience?" *Columbia Journal of Transnational Law* 38 (2000), pp. 465–514, at 468.

Treaties and Other Instruments

Aarhus Convention — Convention on Access to Information, Public Participation in Decision-Making and Access to Justice in Environmental Matters, *adopted* June 25, 1998, 38 I.L.M. 517

African Wildlife Convention — Convention for the Preservation of Wild Animals, Birds, and Fish in Africa, *adopted* May 19, 1900, 94 B.F.S.P. 715

Antarctic Environment Liability Annex — Protocol on Environmental Protection to the Antarctic Treaty annex VI, *adopted* June 17, 2005, 45 I.L.M. 5

Antarctic Environment Protocol — Protocol on Environmental Protection to the Antarctic Treaty, *adopted* October 4, 1991, 30 I.L.M. 1455

Antarctic Treaty — Antarctic Treaty, *adopted* December 1, 1959, 12 U.S.T. 794, 402 U.N.T.S. 71

Basel Convention — Basel Convention on the Control of Transboundary Movements of Hazardous Wastes and Their Disposal, *adopted* March 22, 1989, 1673 U.N.T.S. 126

Basel Liability Protocol — Basel Protocol on Liability and Compensation for Damage Resulting from Transboundary Movements of Hazardous Wastes and Their Disposal, *adopted* December 10, 1999, www.basel.int (accessed 1/23/09)

Biological Diversity Convention — Convention on Biological Diversity, *adopted* June 5, 1992, 1760 U.N.T.S. 79

Biosafety Protocol
Cartagena Protocol on Biosafety to the Convention on Biological Diversity, *adopted* January 29, 2000, 39 I.L.M. 1027

Cartagena Convention
Cartagena Convention for the Protection and Development of the Marine Environment of the Wider Caribbean Region, *adopted* March 24, 1983, 22 I.L.M. 227

CITES
Convention on International Trade in Endangered Species of Wild Fauna and Flora, *adopted* March 2, 1973, 27 U.S.T. 1087, 993 U.N.T.S. 243

Civil Liability Convention
International Convention on Civil Liability for Oil Pollution, *adopted* November 29, 1969, 973 U.N.T.S. 3, *amended by* Protocol of 1976, *adopted* November 19, 1976, 1225 U.N.T.S. 355, *amended by* Protocol of 1992, *adopted* November 27, 1992, 1956 U.N.T.S. 255

Desertification Convention
UN Convention to Combat Desertification in Those Counties Experiencing Drought and/or Desertification, Particularly in Africa, *adopted* June 17, 1994, 1954 U.N.T.S. 3, 33 I.L.M. 1328

Driftnet Fishing Resolution
UN General Assembly Res. 46/215, U.N. Doc. A/RES/46/215 (December 20, 1991)

ENMOD Convention
Convention on the Prohibition of Military or Any Other Hostile Use of Environmental Modification Techniques, *adopted* December 10, 1976, 31 U.S.T. 333, 1108 U.N.T.S. 151

Espoo (EIA) Convention
Convention on Environmental Impact Assessment in a Transboundary Context, *adopted* February 25, 1991, 1989 U.N.T.S. 309

Fish Stocks Agreement
Agreement for the Implementation of the Provisions of the UN Convention on the Law of the Sea of 10 December 1982 Relating to the Conservation and Management of Straddling Fish Stocks and Highly Migratory Fish Stocks, *adopted* August 4, 1995, 2167 U.N.T.S. 3, 4 I.L.M. 1542

Helsinki Accords
Helsinki Accords, Conference on Security and Co-operation in Europe: Final Act, *adopted* August 1, 1975, 14 I.L.M. 1292

HNS Convention
International Convention on Liability and Compensation for Damage in Connection with the Carriage of Hazardous and Noxious Substances by Sea, *adopted* May 3, 1996, 35 I.L.M. 1415

Kyoto Protocol	Kyoto Protocol to the United Nations Framework Convention on Climate Change, *adopted* December 10, 1997, 2303 U.N.T.S. 148, 37 I.L.M. 22
London Convention	Convention on the Prevention of Marine Pollution by Dumping of Wastes and Other Matter, *adopted* December 29, 1972, 26 U.S.T. 2403, 1046 U.N.T.S. 138
London Guidelines	London Guidelines for the Exchange of Information on Chemicals in International Trade, UNEP Governing Council Decision 14/27 (June 17, 1987), *amended* by UNEP Governing Council Decision 15/30 (May 25, 1989)
London Protocol	1996 Protocol to the Convention on the Prevention of Marine Pollution by Dumping of Wastes and Other Matter, *adopted* November 7, 1996, 36 I.L.M. 7
LRTAP	Long-Range Transboundary Air Pollution Convention, *adopted* November 13, 1979, 1302 U.N.T.S. 217, 18 I.L.M. 1442
MARPOL	International Convention for the Prevention of Pollution from Ships, *adopted* November 2, 1973, 34 U.S.T. 3407, 12 I.L.M. 1319, *amended by* Protocol of 1978 Relating to the International Convention for the Prevention of Pollution from Ships, *adopted* February 17, 1978, 1340 U.N.T.S. 61, 17 I.L.M. 3
Montreal Protocol	Montreal Protocol on Substances that Deplete the Ozone Layer, *adopted* September 16, 1987, 1522 U.N.T.S. 3
NAAEC	North American Agreement on Environmental Cooperation, Canada-Mexico-U.S., *adopted* September 14, 1993, 32 I.L.M. 1480
North Pacific Fur Seals Convention	Convention Respecting Measures for the Preservation and Protection of Fur Seals in the North Pacific Ocean, July 7, 1911, 37 Stat. 1542, TS 564
NOx Protocol	Protocol to the 1979 Convention on Long-Range Transboundary Air Pollution Concerning the Control of Emissions of Nitrogen Oxides or Their Transboundary Fluxes, *adopted* October 31, 1988, 28 I.L.M. 212
Nuclear Damages Liability Convention	Vienna Convention on Civil Liability for Nuclear Damage, *adopted* May 21, 1963, 1063 U.N.T.S. 265

OILPOL   International Convention for the Prevention of Pollution
                        of the Sea by Oil, *adopted* May 12, 1954, 12 U.S.T. 2989,
                        327 U.N.T.S. 3

OSPAR   Convention for the Protection of the Marine Envi-
Convention   ronment of the North-East Atlantic, September 22, 1992,
                        32 I.L.M. 1069

POPs Convention   Stockholm Convention on Persistent Organic Pollutants,
                        adopted May 22, 2001, 40 I.L.M. 532

Ramsar   Convention on Wetlands of International Importance
Convention   Especially as Waterfowl Habitat, Ramsar, Iran, *adopted*
                        February 2, 1971, 996 U.N.T.S. 245, 11 I.L.M. 969

Rhine Convention   Agreement for the Protection of the Rhine Against
                        Chemical Pollution, *adopted* December 3, 1976, 1124
                        U.N.T.S. 405, 16 I.L.M. 242

Rio Declaration   Rio Declaration on Environment and Development, UN
                        Conference on Environment and Development, Rio de
                        Janeiro, Brazil, June 3-14, 1992, U.N. Doc. A/
                        CONF.151/26 (vol. 1)

Rotterdam   Convention on the Prior Informed Consent Procedure
Convention   for Certain Hazardous Chemicals and Pesticides in
                        International Trade, *adopted* September 10, 1998, 2244
                        U.N.T.S. 337, 38 I.L.M. 1

SPREP   Convention for the Protection of the Natural Resources
                        and Environment of the South Pacific Region, *adopted*
                        November 25, 1986, 26 I.L.M. 38

Stockholm   Stockholm Declaration on the Human Environment, UN
Declaration   Conference on the Human Environment, Stockholm,
                        Sweden., June 5–16, 1972, UN Doc.
                        A/CONF. 48/14 and Corr. 1, *reprinted in* 11 I.L.M. 1416

Sulfur Protocol   Protocol to the Convention on Long-Range Transboundary
1985   Air Pollution on the Reduction of Sulfur Emissions or Their
                        Transboundary Fluxes by at Least 30 Percent, *adopted* July
                        8, 1985, 1480 U.N.T.S. 215, 27 I.L.M. 707

Sulfur Protocol   Protocol to the Convention on Long-Range Transboundary
1994   Air Pollution on Further Reduction of Sulfur Emissions,
                        adopted June 14, 1994, 33 I.L.M. 1540

UNCLOS   United Nations Convention on the Law of the Sea,
                        December 10, 1992, 1833 U.N.T.S. 3

UNFCCC   United Nations Framework Convention on Climate
                          Change, adopted May 9, 1992, 1771 U.N.T.S. 107

U.S.-Canada Air   Agreement on Air Quality, Canada-U.S., *adopted* March
Quality Agreement   13, 1991, 30 I.L.M. 676

Vienna Convention   Vienna Convention on the Law of Treaties, *adopted* May
on the Law of   23, 1969, 1155 U.N.T.S. 331
Treaties

Vienna Ozone   Vienna Convention for the Protection of the Ozone
Convention   Layer, *adopted* March 22, 1985, 1513 U.N.T.S. 293, 26
                          I.L.M. 1516

Whaling   International Convention for the Regulation of Whaling,
Convention   *adopted* December 2, 1946, 62 Stat. 1716, 161 U.N.T.S.
                          72

World Heritage   Convention for the Protection of the World Cultural and
Convention   Natural Heritage, *adopted* November 16, 1972, 27 U.S.T.
                          37, 1037 U.N.T.S. 151

International Cases

Asylum Case · Asylum Case (Colombia v. Peru), *International Court of Justice Reports of Judgments, Advisory Opinions and Orders* (I.C.J.) 1950 (November 20), 266–389

Behring Fur Seals Arbitration · Behring Sea (Fur Seal) Arbitration (U.S. v. U.K.), *Moore's International Arbitration Awards* 1 (1893), p. 935 (Ad Hoc Arbitral Tribunal)

Corfu Channel Case · Corfu Channel Case (Merits) (U.K. v. Albania), *International Court of Justice Reports of Judgments, Advisory Opinions and Orders* (I.C.J.) 1949 (April 9), 4–169

Gabčíkovo Dam Case · Case Concerning the Gabčíkovo-Nagymaros Project (Hungary v. Slovakia), *International Court of Justice Reports of Judgments, Advisory Opinions and Orders* (I.C.J.) 1997 (September 25), 7–84

Guerra v. Italy · Guerra v. Italy, 1998-I *European Court of Human Rights, Reports of Judgments and Decisions* 210

Lac Lanoux Arbitration · Affaire du lac Lanoux (Spain vs. France), *UN Reports of International Arbitral Awards* 12 (1957), 281–317 (Ad Hoc Arbitral Tribunal)

López Ostra v. Spain · López Ostra v. Spain, 303-C *Publications of the European Court of Human Rights (ser. A)* 40 (1995)

Military and Paramilitary Activities Case · Case Concerning Military and Paramilitary Activities in and Against Nicaragua (Merits) (Nicaragua v. U.S.), *International Court of Justice Reports of Judgments, Advisory Opinions and Orders* (I.C.J.) 1986 (June 27), 14–150.

MOX Plant Case	MOX Plant Case (Ireland v. UK), Final Award of July 2, 2003, *I.L.M.* 42 (2003), 1118–1186 (Permanent Court of Arbitration)
Nuclear Weapons Advisory Opinion	Legality of the Threat or Use of Nuclear Weapons, Advisory Opinion, *International Court of Justice Reports of Judgments, Advisory Opinions and Orders* (I.C.J.) 1996 (July 8), 226–267
Öneryildiz v. Turkey	Öneryildiz v. Turkey, 2004-XII *European Court of Human Rights, Reports of Judgments and Decisions* 79
Trail Smelter Case	Trail Smelter Case (U.S. v. Canada), *UN Reports of International Arbitral Awards* 3 (1941), 1905-1982 (Ad Hoc Arbitral Tribunal)

Acknowledgments

This book has been long in the making—some might say, too long—and I have incurred many debts along the way.

My perspective on international law has been shaped by my experience working in the State Department, and by my exceptionally talented (and fun) colleagues and friends there. Although I cannot name them all, a few deserve special mention: Sue Biniaz, my muse for almost two decades, whose knowledge and skill as an international environmental lawyer are unsurpassed; Nigel Purvis and Trigg Talley, who not only planted the seeds for many of the ideas in this book, but helped them germinate; Dave Balton, who had the fortitude to read the entire manuscript and provided many helpful suggestions based on his long experience as a fisheries negotiator; and Joan Donahue, who many years ago began to teach me "how *not* to think like a lawyer."

As a largely synthetic work, this book draws heavily on the insights and research of others. Particular influences include: Jutta Brunnée and Ellen Hey, my co-editors of *The Oxford Handbook of International Environmental Law*; André Nollkaemper, with whom I began work more than a decade ago on a never-finished article that is now partly reflected in chapter 5; David Victor and Kal Raustiala, who introduced me to the world of international relations theory; Scott Barrett and Andy Keeler, who helped educate me about game theory and economics; David Freestone, with whom I co-edited Kluwer's book series on international environmental law; and Chris Stone, whose clarity of thought and willingness to challenge conventional wisdom (but never for its own sake) have long been a source of inspiration.

In understanding international environmental negotiations and institutions, I have benefited greatly from my occasional work in the 1990s for the UN Climate Change Secretariat. I am appreciative, in particular, to Michael Zammit Cutajar—the former Executive Secretary—for his generosity in allowing me to observe a negotiating process from the inside and for his always insightful analysis.

For their very helpful comments on all or portions of the manuscript, I wish to thank Kelley Barks, Scott Barrett, David Bodansky, Joel Bodansky, Jutta Brunnee, Harlan Cohen, Anne Herbert, Joe Friedman, Andy Keeler, Nigel Purvis, Chuks Okereke, Peter Sand, John Tasioulas, Kathryn Youel-Page, and the two anonymous reviewers for Harvard University Press. Thanks also to Elliot Diringer for the suggestion that led me to the title of this book.

The University of Georgia School of Law has provided me with a congenial and supportive academic home for almost eight years now, for which I am very grateful. Thanks to Dean Rebecca White, for her generous support; to my research assistant Dan Davis, for his many suggestions and his assiduous work in checking and rechecking the accuracy of the citations (although, needless to say, I alone am responsible for any remaining mistakes), and to my assistant Shawn Lanphere. Among my colleagues at Georgia, I want to thank in particular Harlan Cohen—a rising star in the international law firmament—with whom I have had many illuminating discussions about the sources of international law, the subject of Chapters 5 and 9.

Several other institutions have also provided me with assistance. Thanks to the Foundation for International Environmental Law and Development (FIELD), which hosted me in Spring 1996 when I first began working on an earlier version of this book; the European University Institute, where I spent Spring 1998 as a Jean Monnet Fellow; and Sir David Smith and his colleagues at the Smith School of Enterprise and Environment, who very generously invited me to spend six months at Oxford as a visiting fellow in spring 2009, when I completed revisions of this manuscript.

A special thanks to my editor and old friend at Harvard University Press, Elizabeth Knoll, for her astute suggestions and always gentle prodding (sometimes perhaps too gentle!).

Last—but certainly not least—thanks to my family: To my wife Anne Herbert, a fellow traveller in the world of international law, for her belief in this project, for her humor and enthusiasm, and for her willingness not only to put up with my peripatetic life, but to serve as its enabler-in-chief. To my parents, David and Beverly, for their lifelong support. And to my ten-year-old daughters, Maria and Sarah, to whom this book is dedicated, for bringing home to me the weaknesses of the rational actor model, for not sugar-coating their criticisms ("Dad, that title is soooo . . . boring!") and for their always infectious *joie de vivre*.

Index